For teaching me
all I needed to
know about marketing,
many thanks.

David

Civilizing Cities

an analysis of the major political issues of our time

David Williams has spent a lifetime working happily in planning, economic development and regeneration, first with Liverpool and Bexley councils, then with the Civic Trust Regeneration Unit. Finally, in 1997, he set up a community planning consultancy, Tellus 42, working with councils, chambers and regeneration partnerships, council estates, town centres and inner neighbourhoods, community groups and charities. In Civilizing Cities, part 1 shows how cities function and grow, and how, since about 1900, density has given way to sprawl. Part 2 discusses the loss of diversity, also since 1900, through retail sheds, globalization, road traffic and social ghettoes. Part 3 concludes by setting an agenda for city revival through a new pragmatic theory for planning, a comprehensive outline of what sustainable development actually means and, last, how to restore the balance between local and central government and involve citizens in that process. In short, restoring local democracy.

Civilizing Cities

an analysis of the
major political issues of our time

David Williams

Illustrations
Richard Just

Arena Books

First published in 2021 by Arena Books

Arena Books
6 Southgate Green
Bury St. Edmunds
IP33 2BL

www.arenabooks.co.uk

*Distributed in America by Ingram International, One Ingram
Blvd., P.O. Box 3006, La Vergne, TN 37086-1985, USA.*

David Williams
Civilizing Cities an analysis of the major political issues of our time

British Library cataloguing in Publication Data. A Catalogue record
for this book is available from the British Library.

ISBN-13   978-1-911593-79-9

BIC classifications:- JFSG, JFCD, JPP, JPB, JFSC, JKS, JPA.

Cover design
By Jason Anscomb

Typeset in
Times New Roman

Contents

List of Tables

Illustrations

**In memory of my mother, Dorothy,
and my uncle John Pemberton**

Acknowledgements

I am grateful to all the following for their comments and corrections during the drafting of this book. Richard Just not only did the illustrations but also landed us the job of writing this book in the first place. Iain Sharpe was the first to encourage me to persist, Imogene Russell showed the importance of editing and Andrew Richardson demonstrated the real meaning of community planning. Philip Spencer gave invaluable technical support and many insights, plus formatting, editing and proofreading my final version while David Spencer read chapter 8. Malachy McEldowney, John Bangs and Robin Stott read many chapters and made many helpful corrections and suggestions, as did Brian Ford for chapter 9. I must also thank all my family, including my son Sam who corrected several chapters. I am indebted to cousin Robert Pemberton for all his comments and encouragement on the whole text. Needless to say, any errors that remain are mine alone. Finally, I am indebted to Eileen for her constant support and patience.

Preface

This is not a textbook dealing with near certainties in a narrow field. It is a synopsis of all the issues that affect the quality of life in our towns and cities.

"The truth is that no man ever was or will be who understands the gods and all I speak of. If you stumble on some rocks of the whole truth you never know it. There is always speculation." (Xenophanes, trans Willis Barnstone.) The same can be said of cities. Throughout my planning career, I have been collecting rocks. This book is full of them – a rattlebag of policies and practice, home truths, half truths and a few statistics, loose analogies, bold assertions, statements of the obvious and even, possibly, some prejudices. Some may read the book as a polemic in which I am hurling rather than hoarding these rocks. In any event, whether they are rocks of truth or mere speculation only time will tell – and you, dear reader.

The book is largely confined to the UK, with some European comparisons and occasional forays into the US and elsewhere. It also contains many generalizations. "He who generalizes, generally lies" warned Bertrand Russell. Yet, for a subject as expansive as cities, the book could not have been completed if every generalization had to be justified with argument and quotes, evidence and statistics. As a guide, I rely on two broad generalizations.

The first is that civilized towns thrive on density, diversity and democracy. High density creates neighbourhoods that support a wide range of commercial and social activity around local shops, schools, workplaces, pubs, clubs and churches. This diversity creates healthy economic and social environments that are convenient and self-sustaining, while local democracy gives people control over the pace and scale of change in their town or city.

My second generalization is that, in the last century, we have reduced that density, diversity and democracy. Dense neighbourhoods have given way to spacious suburbs for family peace and quiet; mixed areas have been replaced by rigorous zoning for health and tidiness; and increasing government control has made all decisions on planning and development uniform from Cornwall to Cumbria, East Anglia to Anglesey. In my view, successful planning should be local, to foster and safeguard the practical, the personal and the precious.

Finally, for those who are pressed for time, the summary at the end of chapter 7 and the Afterword on Covid-19 indicate the political scope and key arguments of the book. Planning for public health began in cities, and Covid-19 strongly suggests that we should return to its roots, with more devolution to local government.

Figure 1: Urban form. Foggia, southern Italy

Part One
Urban Density, Change and Continuity

Chapter One: The Growth of Cities

With cities came civilization. Both words, derived from the Latin word *civitas*, define us as a social species. However, while many cities are uncivilized, civilization is impossible without them. Cities are theatres in which our social nature can blossom. Civilization only emerges when many people, living and working together in those theatres, somehow combine social stability and creative tension. Other social species with backbones, living in flocks, herds and shoals, have no fixed abode. Nor, though we are predators, do we live in solitary dens, lairs and eyries. Our towns and cities, permanent settlements built for communal shelter and security, are comparable only to the ant heaps, beehives and termite mounds of the social insects.

If cities are innate to the species and just as much part of our nature as mating and childcare, then we can dispense with the cliché that 'cities are one of the great inventions of mankind'. Cities do not need architects, planners and tyrants to design them, though many have tried. They are the physical expression of our social nature, within which civilization can develop. Penicillin, the bicycle, humane prisons and *Tom Jones* may be individual inventions, but they reflect our more general social customs. Caring for the old and infirm, getting around, having some system of law and order and telling stories can be considered alongside other social customs like folk music, arts and crafts, popular culture and religions, markets and fairs, festivals and funerals. Together, personal inventions and social customs reinforce our innate social nature, and are largely the fruits of civilized cities.

Over at least five thousand years, surplus wealth from agriculture, manufacturing and trade enabled cities to evolve environments of remarkably consistent form, differing only in how they have been adapted to suit local circumstances of site, geography, materials, climate and ecology. We would all recognize cities, whether in Babylon or Tenochtitlan, imperial Rome or maritime Europe, with their civic and commercial centres surrounded by dense neighbourhoods with irregular or grid street patterns and interspersed with diverse commercial and social buildings like schools and mills, chapels and workshops. Even during the explosive growth of the Industrial Revolution, cities remained compact. Growth, as much vertical as horizontal, was informal, gradual and piecemeal, all funded and managed locally.

Yet cities, unlike beehives, have also 'evolved' over those millennia. Piped water, sewers and public baths, law courts, printing presses and social medicine, carts, barges, pavements and public transport have all been crucial in the civilized progress of cities and city life. Humans evolved through sex and natural selection. Cities evolve through 'cultural transmission' and what we might call social selection.

Building cities may be instinctive, but their adaptation over time results from learned behaviour – the basic difference between nature and nurture. Cities are where we have nurtured the concept of civilization. Hence the book's title. This means that we can study cities as ethologists study animal behaviour such as bird courtship, mammal grooming, family life cycles and mimicry. The ethologist Niko Tinbergen posed four basic questions: what is the function of any animal behaviour, how has it evolved, what causes it, and how does it develop? (with apologies to Manning and Dawkins 1998, for this crude adaptation). I address these questions in three parts:

1. Chapters 1-3 outline the function of cities and how they have evolved over the centuries. This review is largely confined to the last thousand years in Britain. After about eight centuries, the twentieth century saw too much low density suburban sprawl and destructive urban redevelopment, too little conservation of the built fabric and continuity.
2. Chapters 4-7 look at the social and economic causes of this urban decline in terms of town centre decline, globalization, road traffic and neighbourhood ghettoes, which have weakened local economies and social cohesion.
3. Finally, chapters 8-10 suggest planning policies and government strategies that would revive our cities: first to replace normative and market-led planning with a modest problem-based rationale for planning, second to define sustainable development, and third to curb 'elective dictatorship' and restore local government and democracy.

The function of cities

The planning pioneer and natural scientist Patrick Geddes (1854-1932) thought the essence of cities were "Place, Work, Folk." This may capture the physical, economic and social aspects of cities, or as Geddes put it, environment, function, organism, but it is merely descriptive and applies almost equally to villages as to cities. The earliest planning laws defined the objectives of planning (and by inference the functions of cities) as being to secure "Proper sanitary conditions, Amenity and Convenience" which Patrick Abercrombie re-ordered and simplified as "Beauty, Health and Convenience." However laudable, these aims are prescriptive. They do not define what cities actually do.

For this, we need the great historian Fernand Braudel. In *Civilization and Capitalism* (1981), his triad of city functions are security, shelter and trade. Towns gave security against external attack by nestling under castles or within city walls. They also developed some security against miscreants within, with safe streets, social protection and prison cells. From afar, the church tower or steeple replaced the castle as the visible symbol of shelter, surrounded by houses, workshops and then schools, alms houses and hospitals. And trade centred around a market place or market hall, with high street shops, merchants' exchanges, warehouses, workshops and inns. Over time, markets had to be regulated, often through town halls, while guildhalls acted in the interests of the burgeoning crafts and skills. "Every town, wherever it may be, is first and foremost a market. If there is no market, a town is inconceivable." (Braudel)

As with other natural settlements (like rookeries and beehives), towns and cities emerge in benign environments. Harsh climates and infertile territories only support nomadic clans or villages at best; fertile river valleys can support larger populations in permanent settlements. Throughout history, there was a mutual dependence between town and country, markets and farms. Hence the first ancient cities along the valleys of the Tigris and Euphrates, the Nile, Indus and Yellow rivers.

Unlike other natural settlements, towns and cities are dynamic. There is no end state except when they are destroyed through natural disaster or human warfare, as with Pompei and Carthage. But these are exceptions. In providing security and shelter for the whole society, and markets for all their economic and social activities, towns and cities are remarkably resilient.

In general, cities with many people create a large and fairly constant demand for food, goods and services, supplied by agriculture, industry, transport and commerce. Surpluses of food and goods led to the growth of trade, improved production methods, new products and processes, more division of labour and increased wealth. It is surplus wealth that allowed cities to provide shelter and security, without which civilization is impossible. In turn, this enabled people, firms, councils and other institutions to invest in architecture as well as buildings, painting as well as pots, pure science as well as industry, literature as well as contracts, libraries as well as grain stores, and beer to drink with bread and cheese.

The distribution of this wealth reflects another characteristic of cities. As with many primate groups and social insect colonies, all human societies have developed some form of hierarchy: typically patriarchs control workers who, in turn, dominate carers. Cities, however, develop considerable divisions of labour: all rulers, whether god, emperor, king, tyrant or some regal and religious partnership, need a subservient professional elite of advisors and scribes. The *lumpen proletariat* provide soldiers and workers for all the various crafts and guilds, while women are largely restricted to home-making and childcare, though over the centuries, they have often gained some freedom, even autonomy, in such domestic industries as brewing and baking, clothing and cheese-making (and even, occasionally, in the sex industry).

We can measure personal and social wealth from household income, company profits, price indexes and public health etc, and how they have changed over time. Civilization is not so easily measured, holding to Oscar Wilde's maxim of cynics who "know the price of everything, the value of nothing." However, in *The Spirit Level*

(2010), a fascinating study into income inequality among the wealthiest nations, Wilkinson and Pickett found that in unequal societies like the USA and the UK, social problems increased, not only among the poorest 10% but throughout the population. The wealthiest cohort suffer higher rates of infant mortality, teenage births, ill health, addiction, obesity, violent crime, prison sentences, stress and lack of trust, as well as fewer qualifications and a shorter life span than the wealthiest in fairer societies like Japan and Sweden. The many graphs in *The Spirit Level* show that social species perform better when wealth differentials are lower, with more trust and social cohesion.

In summary, towns and cities function best when they are dense, diverse and democratic, with a fair distribution of the wealth generated for private consumption and for the common good. Unfortunately, in the last century, our cities have become less dense, diverse and democratic.

A brief history of cities in Britain

The history of cities would fill a whole book, even one for each city. When did they emerge? How did they evolve over centuries? Why did some prosper while others declined – by-passed by new trade routes, overtaken by new technology or destroyed by war? What were the main events and who the main actors in each town's history? Here, I focus on the three major eras of town building in our history – under the Roman empire, in medieval times and during the Industrial Revolution.

Before the Romans, perhaps only five towns - Norwich, Colchester, St Albans, Silchester and Winchester - had been established in Britain by invading groups of the Belgae tribes. Our native Celtic tribes were staunchly rural, living in small villages or dispersed hilltop settlements. Following their conquest in 47AD, the Romans built the following settlements:

- the three great legionary forts of Caerleon, Chester and York;
- fifteen regional centres at Aldborough (near Ripon), Brough, Leicester, Wroxeter, Norwich, Carmarthen, Caerwent, Cirencester, St Albans, Canterbury, Chichester, Silchester, Winchester, Dorchester, and Exeter;
- five colonial settlements at York, Lincoln, Gloucester, Colchester and London;
- just over 200 settlements, of which 43 were defended, like Carlisle and Hexham, Whitchurch and Lichfield, Peterborough, Cambridge, Towcester and Bicester, Ilchester, Marlborough, Rochester and Bitterne (Southampton); and
- the two spa towns of Bath and Buxton.

Roman towns urbanized Britain with these "centres of population and trade, and the more important of them were administrative, religious and social centres. To the Greeks and Romans, towns represented civilization and were the centres for politics and administration... laid out on a regular grid of metalled streets and provided with the buildings appropriate to their place within the Roman system. The chief administrative buildings were the forum and basilica, where administration and justice were centred. Baths were major social centres... Water had to be brought in by aqueduct... and taken away in sewers." (OS 2001)

Towns (and civilization) did not take easily in Britain, however. Having grown so quickly from nothing, towns were abandoned almost as quickly as the Roman empire collapsed. In part, this impermanence may be because, during the occupation, many wealthy and powerful Romans chose to build sumptuous villas on their large country estates rather than live in the towns. In any event, during the Anglo-Saxon period that followed – from about 450 AD to 1066 – "England became a land of villages." (Hoskins 1970)

This Dark Age is so called because it has left little more than the scanty evidence of small settlements, the place names of villages, hamlets and farmsteads to decipher, and the highways linking them. We know little about the marauding bands of Angles, Saxons, Jutes, and the various Viking hordes of Danes and Norse who successively raided and settled in Britain, pushing the native Celts to the extremities of Northumbria, Wales, Cornwall and Ireland. Here, small beacons of civilization were kept alight in monasteries like Durrow, Kells and Lindisfarne with their illustrated gospels, Jarrow for its venerable historian Bede, and Whitby abbey for its wise abbess Hilda. Most monasteries included libraries, tended their farms and developed herbal medicine. We know much less about the eighteen Christian dioceses in England:

- ten occupied former Roman towns – namely the two archbishoprics at Canterbury and York, plus Hexham, Lichfield, Leicester, Worcester, Dorchester (Oxon), London, Rochester and Winchester; while
- mystery surrounds the eight Saxon dioceses at Hereford, Sherborne, Selsey, Dunwich (Suffolk), Elmham (Norfolk), Withorn (Fife) and Lindisfarne. Syddensis Civitas (Lincs) can't even be located (Gilbert 1968).

The Dark Age also reduced most of Europe to a cultural desert, leaving local tribes to survive in much poorer rural economies after the collapse of the Roman empire. Until the medieval resurgence sometime around the new millennium, only Moorish Spain kept civilization alive. Under their enlightened caliphates, ancient Greek texts were translated, sciences and mathematics developed and towns and cities were built of stone. Cordoba, Grenada, Sevilla and Toledo among others created "a unique fusion of Arab, Jewish and Christian cultures." (Hibbert 1986) Two key features of this western outpost of the Islamic empire were the success of small city states and a tolerance of different beliefs and customs – wealth and civilization.

The second wave of town building in Britain came with the Normans. These people were descended from the rude rootless Vikings who had first invaded part of northern France in 911. Over the following century, they settled and urbanized Normandy. Before invading England in 1066, William the Conqueror had built a massive castle in Caen (one of the largest in Europe) and two very impressive churches (the *Abbaye aux Hommes, St Etienne*, and the *Abbaye aux Dames, Ste Trinité*) – all in the vigorous Romanesque style that we know as Norman architecture.

After 1066, England and Wales also gained castles to show commitment and cathedrals to suggest civilization. It is the Normans who revived so many of the Roman colonial settlements which survive to this day.

With time, however, the need for security was replaced by 'the fever of borough creation' (Hoskins). In *New Towns of the Medieval Ages* (1961), Beresford identifies about 200 new towns that were 'planted'. Most were built in the Celtic fringe and the north of England, and grew (or failed) on the strength of a royal market charter. Henry II founded Woodstock in Oxfordshire (at the gates of the royal park), Richard I founded Portsmouth in 1194 (to replace Portchester that was silting up), and King John gave the growing village of Liverpool its first charter in 1207. Lords and bishops also got involved: Launceston was set up under the castle and built by the Count de Mortain, Bideford was created by Lord Grenville, the bishops of Salisbury and Worcester set up New Sarum and Stratford-upon-Avon, and Bury-St-Edmunds and Eynsham were set up by the local abbots.

Edward I is perhaps our greatest town builder. To subjugate the Welsh, he built or rebuilt castles at Flint, Rhuddlan, Builth and Llanbadarn, and then the five great Snowdonian castles of Conway, Caernavon, Criccieth, Harlech and Beaumaris. These castles, with towns nestling under their walls, may have taken their model from Gloucester's Caerphilly in south Wales. By contrast, in Aquitaine he commissioned about 140 bastides, mostly settlements "intended not to defend the country but to develop it." (Powicke 1988) And finally, he successfully rebuilt Kingston-on-Hull and relocated the submerged Cinque port of Winchelsea (although the sea has since receded, leaving the new town high and dry).

In similar vein, the Jacobeans designed and built over 20 new towns in Ireland, intended partly to subjugate the natives 'beyond the pale'. One of the largest and most handsome was Derry, for which it is said that London produced the capital, Ireland the labour and Scotland most of the initial Presbyterian settlers. These towns were all speculative ventures that only prospered with the growth of trade and local markets, although some were protected by a castle or city walls.

Although some towns were planted with defensive or oppressive intention, most were built for trade on strategic routes, at cross roads, river fords and natural harbours. Even market towns had to import basic goods and skills to get started. Thereafter, they were supplied by local farms and villages and developed trade further afield. These links between town and hinterland were tangible in regular street markets. Today, globalization has cut most of these links, leaving little more than street names as evidence of former markets: Butcher's Row, the Shambles, Fishergate, Butter Cross, Corn Exchange, Sheep Street, Malthill, Haymarket, Flower Street and the ubiquitous Market Place. Where markets have been retained, they bring life and character even to such global cities as Seattle and Tokyo.

Historically, local markets gave each town not only protection against hunger, but also some power and independence from the state. This urban-rural spectrum was also retained in most twentieth century legislation relating to town and country planning. Unfortunately, while it focussed on protecting green belts, it signally failed to curb urban sprawl. Furthermore, protecting local trade and food markets have been quietly forgotten.

Occasionally, specialist markets evolved. By the sixteenth century, there were about 760 market towns in England and 50 in Wales, of which over 300 "tended to specialize in the marketing of some particular product." (Everitt in Clark, 1976) The most common specialist markets were for corn (133 markets), cattle (92), sheep, fish, wool or yarn (each over 30), malt, wildfowl and poultry, or cloth (20 plus), horses, swine, cheese and butter, leather and leather products (over ten), down to fruit (six), linen (eight), hemp (four) and other miscellaneous products. The growth of these specialist markets reflected better transport (by road and water) and greater skills in specific industries; such as hats at Bewdley, metal goods in Birmingham, wool in Bradford, trade through Bristol, stockings at Evesham, farming implements in Malton, shoes in Northampton, lace in Nottingham, cotton in Oldham, education in Oxford, cutlery in Sheffield, glass at St Helens, pottery in Stoke, shipbuilding on Tyneside, or wooden spoons, taps and handles in Wymondham.

These specialist manufacturing towns stimulated urban growth through increased trade with other towns, with considerable division of labour involving merchants, bankers, mercers, ostlers and transport agents as well as producers. "The guild rolls of Leicester, which date from 1196, include a remarkable variety of trades and professions such as weaver, dyer, wool-comber, shearman, tailor, hosier, tanner, leather-worker, shoe-maker, saddler, parchment-maker, soap-maker, leech, preacher, mercer, goldsmith, farrier, turner, cooper, potter, miller, baker, cook, butcher, waterman, mason, carpenter, plumber, porter, carter, and ostler." (Poole 1988)

The third great wave of urbanization came with the Industrial Revolution from the early eighteenth century. Industry was transformed by first water wheels and then steam power, which enabled cottage industry to be replaced with large-scale industrial mills and multi-storey factories. Although the first factory in this country, a multi-storey silk mill in Derby, was opened in 1718, "It was when [steam] power reached the cotton, woollen and iron industries that the face of the country really began to change on a large scale, and that was not until the 1770s." (Hoskins 1970)

This period saw greater specialization. Towns mushroomed around specific industries like cotton and fabrics, glass, steel and engineering, with pithead villages for coal, and transit towns growing at ports, alongside canals and at major railway junctions. Some of these towns were new. Both Barrow-in-Furness for shipbuilding and Middlesbrough with its iron and chemical industries (with their grid street pattern) began when the railways arrived. Generally, most of these single industry towns have suffered because they have failed to diversify, too often dependent on the fortunes of their major local employers. A few, however, became so adept at their particular industry that they became world leaders, at least well into the twentieth century.

Before the Industrial Revolution, even the largest cities were still small enough to house rich and poor close together, interspersed with the whole range of commercial, civic and cultural buildings. Only the most noxious trades and poorest hovels were banished to the outskirts. And although (since Roman times) the wealthy bought their country estates, most still kept a town house in their nearest city of fashion, if only for the winter season. So urban diversity was the rule, the contrasts between wealth and poverty, trade and leisure, field and workshop, noise and peace a part of everyday town life.

The Industrial Revolution changed this diversity in two respects. First, the sheer number and size of new industries gave rise to explosive urban growth, largely in the form of cheap housing terraces around each factory, while managers and owners fled to the western side of town and beyond, upwind of the grime, noise and smoke. Second, this rapid growth ruptured the social, physical and emotional links between town and country. For the first time, most children in larger cities grew up without any roaming in the countryside. So Victorian cities provided public parks and gardens for communal play, floral display, municipal pride and some clean air. Not a substitute but a welcome innovation.

The growth of Victorian towns was staggering. Surplus rural labour flocked to every new factory, as table 1 shows. Most cities doubled or trebled in size during the first half of the nineteenth century, then doubled or even trebled in the second half. Only the more sedate administrative capitals Dublin and Edinburgh avoided the explosive growth of their more boisterous neighbours Belfast and Glasgow.

Table 1: City populations during the Industrial Revolution (000s)

City	1750	1801	1851	1901	1951	2001
Belfast	9	37	103	349	444	277
Birmingham	24	74	233	523	1,113	976
Bradford	-	13	104	280	292	468
Bristol	45	64	137	339	443	380
Cardiff	-	2	18	164	244	305
Dublin	90	165	272	373	522	554
Edinburgh	57	83	202	394	467	449
Glasgow	24	77	357	776	1,090	579
Leeds	16	53	172	456	618	716
Liverpool	22	80	376	704	789	439
London	675	1,117	2,685	6,586	8,348	7,188
Manchester	18	90	303	645	703	393
Sheffield	12	31	135	409	513	547

Source: Mitchell

Up to about 1900, the expansion remained urban-centric, dominated by high density housing, trade and industry mixed together. Towns and cities continued to evolve through physical expansion, increased trade, more prosperous town centres and thus higher land values and increased central densities.

This intensification can be traced over the centuries in all town centres: two- and three-storey medieval buildings gave way to three- and four-storey Georgian terraces, many of which were replaced by four- and five-storey Victorian buildings. This process of incremental growth through higher densities within existing boundaries may be likened to natural ecologies like ancient hedgerows. With every century, the number of plant species, like the number of building floors, increases slowly.

From 1901, however, table 1 shows an ebb tide in population, growth first slowing down to 1951, and thereafter populations actually declining in most cities. This sharp reversal, as we shall see in chapter 2, was largely due to major slum clearance programmes and suburban sprawl beyond city boundaries. In the last century, urban evolution completely changed: towns and cities now grew out rather than up. Even tower blocks that replaced slums greatly reduced housing densities. Less visible, except from the air or on maps, was the suburban sprawl. This growth had not only to house an increasing population, but also to rehouse most of those displaced by urban renewal. Twentieth century sprawl took three basic forms: suburbia, new towns and most recently exurbia.

Suburbs

'God made the country, man made the town.' William Cowper's generalization was never true. The countryside had woods felled, marshes drained and fields enclosed to feed their nearest towns or enrich landowners. This economic relationship between dense town surrounded by a few villages and farmland gave us townscape and landscape. But the boundary between the two has always been blurred by suburbs, either for the rich or the poor. The wealthy estate provided somewhere clean and quiet away from the noise and disease of cities:

- Wealthy Romans escaped the tyranny of their Caesars by living in outlying farms,
- sixteenth century Venetian merchants escaped to their Palladian hunting villas and farms, and
- the English country house of the eighteenth century was built by city bankers and merchants while retaining a city mansion, or inherited by lords and the landed gentry who bought a town house 'for the season'.

Second homes have a long history. Lewis Mumford, in his encyclopedic *City in History*, quotes the Renaissance architect Alberti (1404-72). "The great beauties of such a [suburban] retreat are being near the city, upon an open airy road, and on a pleasant spot of ground. The greatest commendation of itself is its making a cheerful appearance to those that go a little way out of the town to take the air; as if it seemed to invite every beholder... Nor should there be any want of pleasant landscapes, flowery mead, open champains, shady groves, or limpid brooks, or streams and lakes for swimming, with all other delights of the same sort. Lastly… I would have the front and whole body of the house perfectly well lighted, and that it be open to receive a great deal of light and sun, and a sufficient quantity of wholesome air."

By contrast, the poor suburb along the routes into town provided hovels (affordable housing) for the destitute and miscreants, and cheap workshops for dirty trades like tanneries. These suburbs, removed from the injunctions of the city, were mini-versions of today's shanty towns and enterprise zones. Most medieval walled towns had them. (See, for example, The *City Maps of Europe*, published by Braun and Hogenberg between 1572 and 1617.) "Charles I blamed mob riots in Whitehall upon 'the meane and unrulie people of the suburbs' (Ackroyd 2001), while the eighteenth century London suburb was 'a nether world of dung heaps, stinking trades, blood sports, gallows, low taverns, prostitutes, foreigners, thieves, the poor and the mob'." (Inwood 1999)

From Alberti to Inwood, we see an emerging conflict between town and country, wealth and poverty, which garden cities tried to resolve (see below). This contrast was exacerbated throughout the nineteenth century by the fantastic rise in the size of our towns and cities. When the Victorians invented efficient public transport networks, however, daily commuting between the grime and smokestacks of Coketown and new, clean terraced neighbourhoods in outer suburban rings became feasible. The horse-drawn omnibus gave way to trams, buses, trains and metros. Now middle class Pooters could live well beyond walking distance of their workplace, escape the noise and bustle of towns and join the gentry. Yet these suburbs retained high densities of 150 people/acre that supported local shops, workplaces and schools etc, even when they engulfed surrounding villages. Buses and trams work well in high density areas.

The twentieth century suburb was built for the middle classes seeking the rural idyll of this green and pleasant land that receded beyond the horizon. In 1850, towns and cities were compact and one could walk across London in a day. Today, walking across any big town would take a day, but be dull, noisy and dangerous. Green belts, designed to curb urban sprawl and protect farmland, gave rise to two further problems. The stinking trades and low taverns were replaced by other fringe activities unsuitable in cities, like reservoirs and sewage plants, travellers' sites and riding stables, maggot farms and metal scrapyards, scrambler and go-cart racetracks, golf courses, 'civic amenity sites' and even an occasional dump for low-level radioactive waste. More recently, green belts have suffered a rash of exurban 'parks', discussed below.

With suburban sprawl, car dependency increased in a positive feedback loop. If two variables influence each other, an increase in one variable either reduces (negatively) or increases (positively) the other variable. Central heating systems and fox-rabbit populations operate negative feedback loops and are relatively stable. Suburbs actually create two positive feedback loops:

- as more people buy cars, they drive more and get used to longer trips, which feeds demand for more suburbs, more cars and faster roads;

- as more people use their cars, fewer passengers on buses and trains means reduced services or increased fares, which increases demand for cars.

This may oversimplify the dynamics of suburban growth, but the basics hold true. Spacious suburban houses with generous private gardens in leafy avenues are obviously popular. In 1903 Patrick Geddes justified suburbs thus: "I have to remind all concerned, first that the essential need of a house and family is room, and secondly that the essential improvement of a house and family is more room." Here is an early planning generalization with all the risks attached to 'he who generalizes'. More space may be a natural response to the overcrowded squalor of the worst slums, but also a (rather smug) endorsement of the comfortable lifestyle of the middle classes. It ignores the external costs of suburban sprawl, increased road traffic, air pollution, social alienation and loss of farmland.

A century later, the planning consultant David Lock said this of the Urban Task Force *Urban Renaissance* report. "Third, there is not much focus on the family in the city. Cappuccinos and loft living are irrelevant to the majority of households. A city without children is transient, socially exclusive, and ultimately unsustainable. A city with children needs houses with gardens, good schools, clean air and safe streets. Sounds like suburbs, Lord Rogers, of which cities are mostly made and which you have seriously neglected." (*Planning* 16/7/1999) This repeats Patrick Geddes and our peculiarly English utopian vision of garden suburbs. Forgive the London centricity, but it ignores the children who do live and go to school in Westminster and Islington, Camden and Fulham. Surely public parks and lively streets in dense cities more than compensate for the quiet ennui and garden birdsong of the suburbs with their empty pavements and speeding traffic?

Reducing the 'essential need of a house' solely to space also conflicts with Geddes' own background as a botanist. Healthy plants develop through plant density in local ecologies that support an ever-increasing diversity of plant species. Cities are social habitats which, as we shall see in chapter 3, thrive on high density and diversity. Replacing crowded slums with spacious suburbs addressed the visible symptoms of cheap housing but not the root cause of urban poverty. Slums are discussed in chapter 2, but let me revise Geddes: "The essential need of a house and family is sufficient income. Granted a living wage, the essential improvement of house and family can be safely left to the family itself."

Nevertheless, Geddes' maxim gained traction as planning policy throughout the twentieth century, from the earliest Victorian legislation to remove the worst slums, through to today's simplistic housing market of supply and demand.

- The first *Public Health Act 1848* was followed by subsequent housing and sanitation acts in 1851, '68, '75 and '90 enforcing clean water and drains;
- Building byelaws focussed on minimum distances between terraces to ensure daylight and fresh air, thereby reducing overall densities;
- Normative planning meant that suburban norms ('rules or authoritative standards', *OED*) became standard in twentieth century planning acts;

- That meant that most local plans stipulated suburban densities of no more than 12 to 15 houses an acre). This houses from 30 to 50 people an acre (72 to 120/hectare), compared with as many as 800 people an acre in the worst Victorian slums of Nottingham;
- From the 1960s, the government set internal housing space standards (from the Parker Morris report). It also set minimum parking standards for most new development, irrespective of the very different levels of car ownership in different areas. Both also reduced housing densities.

Family life has also changed. Gone are the typical Victorian bourgeois households with servants and the urban working class extended families. Both forms of large household gave way in the last century to the ubiquitous 'nuclear' family.

- Before the last war, the average household size was 3.4. It is now 2.3. This reflects smaller families, increased lifespans, younger household formation and higher divorce rates, all increasing demand for houses and flats;
- Increased disposable income has also increased pressure on the housing stock, for example through the growth of second homes and timeshare properties, particularly in tourism areas. And now we have houses being bought to let, replacing most of our social housing.

Until about 1900, suburbs played only a modest role in urban development. Yet a century later, 86% of our nation lived in suburbs according to one government advisor (*Planning* 26/11/1999). This growth of the semi reflects a number of factors: ease of supply by local builders, valuable returns for landowners, planning standards to improve family life, popular demand (with higher incomes and greater mobility) and marketing 'selling' the rural idyll, privacy, escape from city stress and 'keeping up with the Jones's'.

Table 2: Population growth in England and Wales, 1801-2001

Year	Population	Av annual increase
1801	8,893,000	na
1851	17,928,000	180,000
1901	32,528,000	192,000
1951	43,758,000	224,600
2001	52,360,000	172,000

Source: Mitchell

This explosion from compact terraces to spacious suburbs transformed our quality of life. It also greatly enlarged our urban footprints. In England and Wales, ignoring regional variation and periodic peaks and troughs, the average population growth over the past two centuries suggests that we have built an equivalent of Luton or Preston every year – but at very much lower densities.

During the nineteenth century, most Georgian and Victorian builders achieved gross residential densities of at least 100 people an acre (240/hectare). That means that the extra 23,635,000 people from 1801 to 1901 were housed on less than 236,350 acres (or almost 98,500 hectares) of green fields. Put graphically, for those familiar with Ordnance Survey Landranger maps (scale 1:50,000), nineteenth century housing covered about two thirds of one map. So by 1901, the towns and cities of England and Wales covered less than one and a half OS maps.

During the following century, there was a dramatic change.

Table 3: Land use in England and Wales, 1969

Predominant Land Use	As % of Administrative Area	As % of Developed Area
Residential	5.95	60.8
Industrial/Commercial	1.71	17.5
Community/Recreation	0.09	1.0
Transport	0.70	7.2
Urban Open Space	1.31	13.4
Total developed area	9.76 (14,850 sq km)	100

Source: DoE (1971) in Rhind and Hudson

It is notoriously difficult to define and measure urban land. In addition to the DoE figures above, Rhind and Hudson provide several other estimates from the same period:
- for 1963, Coleman thought urban land was 10.8% of the total land for England and Wales. Interestingly, the same survey for 1933 gave 7.2%. Almost all the new urban land was at the expense of agricultural land;
- for 1965, Edwards and Wibberley (see Arvill 1973) suggested 11.2% of the total was urban;
- for 1971, Fordham's urban growth figures rose from 7.9% in 1951 and 8.9% in 1961 to 10.0% (or 15,148 sq km) in 1971; and
- also for 1971, Best thought urban land was 11.0% of the total, which he suggested compared with 6.8% for the EEC. Without population densities, this comparison has little value. But in most of Europe, we can state that urban densities are generally higher than in the UK.

The south east of England has long been the most populated region with most of the best agricultural land. In 1969, the DoE estimated that the total 'developed area' in the south east was 17.4% of the 'administrative area'. Then, in the 1980s, about fears of excessive development in the region, Nicholas Ridley (as Secretary of State for the Environment) said this: "Let's put this in perspective. At the most, urban areas in the south east will only increase from 12.5% to 13.5% of the total land area." This highlights the difficulties with urban area estimates, and raises questions about the statistics used, margins of error, future projections and the tendency for political understatement. But it is surely cavalier to lose 8% of green fields (one percentage point over 12.5%) in little more than a decade in one of the most built-up regions of Europe. It also overlooks the same Secretary of State's own attempts to persuade the local council to refuse a proposed housing scheme in the field behind his own village home.

Today, suburbs surround every town, with terraced housing largely replaced by the aptly-named semi-detached villas. Take three examples. "In 1800 London, Europe's largest city, could still be crossed on foot in little more than an hour. Even at its greatest diameter, the built-up area extended only ten kilometres. As the sequence of maps shows, this area expanded so rapidly that by 1914 the diameter reached thirty-five kilometres, and today approaches seventy kilometres (despite the restriction of a Green Belt policy)." (Peter Haggett quoted by Colin Ward, 1974.) Increasing the diameter from over six to nearly 50 miles means that London covered about 30 square miles in 1800, 460 in 1914, and 1,500 square miles in 1974. In the nineteenth century that area expansion was largely matched by a six-fold increase in population (from table 1 above). In the last century, by contrast, the gain in suburban households was largely matched by the depopulation of inner areas through slum clearance and smaller households. Peter Hall (1966) put it this way: "During the period 1921-39 the population of Greater London grew by about 1.2 million or 16.6 per cent; but the built-up area grew over three times. By 1939, the zone between 5 and 12-15 miles from the centre was almost uniformly built up with housing at an average density of 12-14 to the acre."

Second, the small town of Looe in Cornwall grew from 2,550 to 4,280 residents from 1901 to 1981 – an increase of 68%. During this period, the ancient settlements of East Looe, West Looe and Shutta grew suburbs on most of the surrounding hills, building on well over three times as much land as the original settlements. A two thirds increase in population with a threefold increase in land spread is typical for most smaller towns and cities.

My third example is a settlement on the East Sussex coast of which Ian Nairn said, "What is one to say? Peacehaven has been called a rash on the countryside. It is that, and there is no worse in England. Peacehaven derives its name from the end of the First World War. Whose haven was it? Whose haven is it? Architecturally here may lie the source of the Australian or South African little man's suburb. When first built, indeed, it was called New Anzac on Sea. Small plots (or stands), yet not semi-detached, let alone in terraces. Every man his own house, even if only a few feet from the neighbours'!" (Nairn and Pevsner 1965)

Suburbia by Nairn was dubbed 'subtopia'. David Olsen was more blunt. "The suburb, as it has developed in the English-speaking world, is the antithesis of the city.

If the latter embodies diversity, concentration, excitement, movement, the clash of ideas, the former represents conformity, dispersal, boredom, serenity, loneliness. It also offers an even more appropriate environment for domestic withdrawal and personal seclusion than the single-class district of terraces and garden squares." (Olsen 1986) While suburban residents enjoyed spacious gardens and clean air, their estates suffered. Instead of daily social interactions with neighbours, passers-by, shopkeepers, family members, friends and the occasional strangers in urban neighbourhoods, the suburban resident also became semi-detached, prone to isolation and boredom, mental stress and youth disaffection. Instead of social behaviour, suburban residents engaged in what I think psychologists refer to as 'displacement behaviour': they got a dog, bought a fish tank or even started talking to their plants.

Nairn and Olsen hark back to Samuel Johnson's famous generalization of 1777 that "When a man is tired of London, he is tired of life; for there is in London all that life can afford." His biographer elaborated. "I have often amused myself with thinking how different a place London is to different people. They, whose narrow minds are contracted to the consideration of some one particular pursuit, view it only through that medium. A politician thinks of it merely as the seat of government in its different departments; a grazier, as a vast market for cattle; a mercantile man, as a place where a prodigious deal of business is done upon 'Change; a dramatick enthusiast, as the grand scene of theatrical entertainments; a man of pleasure, as an assemblage of taverns, and the great emporium for ladies of easy virtue. But the intellectual man is struck with it, as comprehending the whole of human life in all its variety, the contemplation of which is inexhaustible." (Boswell 1951)

Today, one would struggle to find the whole of human life in any British city. Few cities are magnets for politicians, farmers and merchants, most factories have closed, most popular events priced beyond most pockets and basic leisure pursuits reduced or forbidden. Even in his beloved London, Johnson would struggle in central London, most of which has become an exclusive resort (or tax haven) for the wealthy.

In summary, suburbia was an incremental speculative response supported by governments to the perceived needs and demands of families, surrounding every town and city and engulfing every village within commuting range. But suburbs also housed the overspill from inner city neighbourhoods that were needlessly redeveloped, as discussed in the next chapter. In their place, suburbs created sprawling environments of dreary inconvenience and uniformity.

Suburbs also weakened historic links between town and country by building over perhaps 20% of productive farmland. "The rate of conversion of agricultural farmland and other land to urban areas has been a matter of concern, contention, debate and high polemic for many years." (Rhind and Hudson 1980) Since 1945, they estimated that the average loss of (mostly) farm land to urban use varied from 140 to 179 sq km each year. Arvill (1973) suggested 187 sq km a year. This urban sprawl has covered about one extra OS map every decade over the past century. This is not sustainable. It raises issues of food security, green belts, town cramming and road traffic, discussed further in chapter 9. Here I would only stress how much valuable land has been developed to house people during the first century of town and country planning, simply because families need more space – apparently.

Alberti explained the difference between town and country life: "... in town you are obliged to moderate yourselves in several respects according to the privileges of your neighbour; whereas you have much more liberty in the country." (Mumford 1966) This sums up the contrast between town and suburb, or social behaviour and private seclusion. Such contrasts recur throughout this book, whether in retail sheds or street markets, in cars or buses, on computers or in libraries.

By the end of the nineteenth century, some recognized the dangers inherent in 'free range' suburbia. Something else was needed. One specific solution retained the exodus from city slum, but replaced suburbs with a peculiarly English invention – the 'garden city'.

Garden cities

Most of our towns started modestly at strategic locations on trade routes, under castles or by religious sites. Once established, they grew slowly over centuries with multiple ownerships and property law restricting development to small schemes and improvements. Large scale urban schemes (as in Bath or Edinburgh) came much later. With expansion and prosperity, towns adapted buildings to successive changes in commerce, industry, fashion and governance. The street patterns, generally adapted to existing contours, rivers and other physical features, became fixed once they were built up, with pipes and drains added.

This 'organic' growth was in marked contrast to those towns that were built to a fixed design. Empires were great new town builders, as with the Roman empire in Europe or the *conquistadors* in south America. All were designed on a regular grid layout with central agora or plaza for the main functions of state and religion.

Grids are rare in Britain. Wareham revived the Roman grid and Middlesbrough was a Victorian design. Winchelsea, in Kent, shows what happens when growth is stunted. Planted in 1283, "it never succeeds in looking like a town. The plots leased [on a grid layout] were quite large, and each original house had ample space. As the population never grew, the spaces never closed up, and so today Winchelsea with its green grass verges flanking the streets is more like a formally planned garden suburb than like a town." (Nairn and Pevsner 1965)

600 years later, one can see Winchelsea as a model for our late Victorian garden suburbs and twentieth century new towns. All display this same lack of organic growth. Two principle ideas underpin the Garden City movement: a visceral reaction against the horrors of slums and materialism of the Industrial Revolution, and a strong utopian urge for an ideal urban-rural environment. Let us deal with the reaction first.

In the early nineteenth century, there was a balance between progressives and traditionalists. Supporters of the Industrial Revolution included Richard Cobden

('The Apostle of Free Trade'), Thomas Macauley ("The history of England is emphatically the history of progress") and, later, Samuel Smiles (who thought that "the healthy spirit of self-help created among working people would, more than any other measure, serve to raise them as a class"). Against them were the rural idealists: William Cobbett and his polemic *Rural Rides*, the satanic mills of William Blake, the fixed village landscape of Gilbert White's Selborne and the small hermetically sealed world of Jane Austen's clergy and gentry.

Wiener, in *English Culture and the Decline of the Industrial Spirit* (1981), argues that nostalgia for the pastoral idyll gradually overpowered the belief in city progress, infecting most of creative Victorian life. The pre-Raphaelites painted their vacuous canvases in rural settings, poets from Southey, Wordsworth and Tennyson to Masefield and the war poets defined timeless rural sentiments (where there was usually honey still for tea), while Dickens raged against the dehumanizing factory system of industrialists in *Hard Times*, the grubby world of financiers in *Bleak House* and the destruction of neighbourhoods to make way for the railways in *Dombey and Son*. And a century after Jane Austen, would Thomas Hardy's Wessex tales of dark misery and misogyny have worked in an urban setting?

John Ruskin was perhaps the first critic of the specifically modern. "I am by nature and instinct Conservative, loving old things because they are old, and hating new ones merely because they are new." This fear of the new (and the indecent, for as executor of JMW Turner's estate, he destroyed the erotic drawings left by Turner) also infected attitudes to money and status. Thomas Carlyle wondered "whether the Secret of this Universe... does after all consist in making money." For Arnold Toynbee, the Industrial Revolution "unleashed the impulse of greed." Later, William Morris boasted of "a hatred of modern civilization", while GK Chesterton thought that "[the rich] forced [the poor] into factories and the modern wage-slavery, assuring them all the time that this was the only way to wealth and civilization." Curiously, between Morris and Chesterton, it is not easy to separate the revolutionary socialist from the reactionary tory. This nostalgia persisted among twentieth century politicians, from Stanley Baldwin and Ramsay Macdonald to gentleman farmer Jim Callaghan and John Major, the supporter of 'village cricket and warm beer.' Warm beer?

This general prejudice against cities and industry also infected our private schools and top universities. The wealth and leadership of landed aristocracy, high finance and government were set firmly above the rigours of trade and manufacturing. Wiener quotes Thomas Arnold of Rugby, who set the tone: "The fineness and capacity of a man's spirit is shown by his enjoyments. Your middle class has an enjoyment in its business, we admit, and gets on well in business, and makes money; but beyond that? Drugged with business, your middle class seems to have its sense blunted for any stimulus besides." Hence the all-abiding passion for the classics and field sports to the exclusion of science and technology until well into the twentieth century, with economics and business studies later still. This prejudice against 'trade' in favour of some fairly esoteric education was used to control access to the more powerful and remunerative trades of banking, government and law. In *Joseph Andrews* (Bk 2, Ch 17), Henry Fielding is more clear-sighted about the importance of both trade and learning.

Back to urban prejudices, these sentiments were summed up by William Morris, the arts and crafts socialist and poet.

"Forget six counties overhung with smoke,
Forget the snorting steam and piston stroke,
Forget the spreading of the hideous town;
Think rather of the pack-horse on the down,
And dream of London, white and small and clean,
The clear Thames bordered by its gardens green."
                    (*Oxford Dictionary of Quotations*)

In *News from Nowhere*, he went further.

"This is how we stand. England was once a country of clearings amongst woods and wastes, with a few towns interspersed, which were fortresses for the feudal army, markets for the folk, gathering places for the craftsmen.

"It then became a country of huge and foul gambling dens, surrounded by an ill-kept, poverty-stricken farm, pillaged by the masters of the workshops.

"It is now a garden, where nothing is wasted and nothing is spoilt, with the necessary dwellings and workshops scattered up and down the country, all neat and trim and pretty." Nowhere indeed.

As Wiener notes, Henry Ford is venerated in the US as one of their great pioneering industrialists. Here in England, the William Morris who manufactured some of our most successful cars is overshadowed by his more rowdy namesake who designed expensive wallpaper. Gladstone was one of the last to praise the city, whatever its faults. On his trip to Middlesbrough in 1862, he said "This remarkable place, THE YOUNGEST CHILD OF ENGLAND'S ENTERPRISE... It is an infant, gentlemen, but it is an infant Hercules." (Briggs 1968)

Wiener dates this loss of faith in the Industrial Revolution precisely to the Great Exhibition of 1851. Inside the Crystal Palace (one of the most extraordinary nineteenth century buildings designed by the landscape gardener Joseph Paxton) there was a precious facsimile of a gothic interior designed by AWN Pugin (1812-52). From this modest beginning, gothic trim covered the walls and wallpapers of Parliament, as well as most churches and many public schools, railway stations, hospitals and almshouses. Classical dignity was reserved for civic buildings, law courts and museums. The reactionary décor of Pugin swamped the revolutionary functionalism of Paxton, whose design was largely ignored, except in park greenhouses, train sheds and some industrial buildings.

As with buildings, so with cities. Garden Cities emerged from this collapse in urban confidence and the rise of the new 'arts and crafts' movement. The first garden suburb, in 1875, was designed by Norman Shaw in Turnham Green, north London. There followed a wave of garden suburbs built by wealthy (often Nonconformist) manufacturers, including George Cadbury's Bourneville in 1879, Joseph Hartley's estate in Liverpool in 1886, WH Lever's Port Sunlight in 1889, and Joseph Rowntree's New Earswick (by Raymond Unwin) in York in 1902.

The inspiration for these designs is unclear. Their attempt to combine town and country might refer back to the London squares of Bloomsbury and Belgravia. Or to Bath where, from the 1730s to about 1810, a fascinating sequence of spaces starting with the central Queen's Square of John Wood (the north side being "... one of the grandest Palladian compositions in England" according to Pevsner), to the Circus and Royal Crescent (probably of John Wood the Younger) and beyond to St James's Square and Landsdown Crescent by John Palmer. Finally, Robert Adam's Pulteney Street Bridge led straight to a new park. These may all derive from the transformation of western Paris from the enlarged Tuileries by the garden designer Le Nôtre in the 1660s, and its extension a century later to the green Champs Elysées and beyond.

These Arcadian schemes in cities were distinctly grandiose. Garden suburbs, by contrast, were domestic in scale: trees and wide streets, perhaps, but all the green land parcelled up as private gardens under the protection of each semi-detached villa. The first example I know, in north Liverpool from the late Georgian period, fell victim to slum clearance (see next chapter, page 58).

If garden suburbs were a prototype, my first planning guru, the engineer Ebenezer Howard (1850-1928), transformed them into cities. His *Garden Cities of Tomorrow* (1902), is at once visionary and practical. He compares three 'magnets' – town, country and his new town-country magnet – and they still make fascinating reading.

The town magnet listed these costs and benefits:
- "Closing out of nature. Social opportunity
- Isolation of crowds. Places of amusement
- Distance from work. High money wages
- High rents and prices. Chances of employment
- Excessive hours. Army of unemployed
- Fogs and droughts. Costly drainage
- Foul air and murky sky. Well-lit streets
- Slums and gin palaces. Palatial edifices."

In the country, the opposites were:
- "Lack of society. Beauty of nature
- Hands out of work. Land lying idle
- Trespassers beware. Wood, meadow, forest
- Long hours, low wages. Fresh air, low rents
- Lack of amusement. Bright sunshine
- Lack of drainage. Abundance of water
- No public spirit. Need for reform
- Crowded dwellings. Deserted villages."

By contrast, the town-country magnet was all positive, providing:
- "Beauty of nature. Social opportunity
- Fields and parks of easy access
- Low rents. High wages
- Low rates. Plenty to do
- Low prices. No sweating
- Field for enterprise. Flow of capital
- Pure air and water. Good drainage
- Bright homes and gardens. No smoke, no slums
- Freedom. Co-operation."

While the town and country magnets both contain polarities, tensions and occasional contradictions, the 'town-country' magnet is completely harmonious – what today we might call a 'win-win' situation. They tell us much about early planning values and attitudes around 1900. Unfortunately, many of his generalizations are clearly false or biased. It is false to claim that 'distance from work' and 'costly drainage' are town issues. They only became serious problems in low density suburbs and rigid zoning of the main economic and social activities. 'High rents and prices' is something of an economist's *non sequitur*. In an efficient market, high rents reflect popular locations where shops enjoy high turnover, strong competition and thus keener prices. It is only in out-of-town shopping malls, paradoxically the retailers' version of a town-country development, where prices rise.

Clear bias is displayed in the 'isolation of crowds' and in 'slums and gin palaces'. The former euphemism reflects a frequent bias among elites that crowds tend to be raucous or dangerous. It ignores their importance in our social nature. Crowds often attend 'places of amusement', but sometimes also play a vital role in democracy. Slums rightly shocked Victorian sensibilities (as we shall see in the next chapter), but they failed to see that gin palaces were also places of amusement (and warmth). Drink did cause problems and the middle classes are entitled to their prejudices, but they should not form the basis for planning policy. Samuel Johnson had a much more robust attitude to towns.

The country had complementary problems. But while 'lack of society' and 'no public spirit' contradict common perceptions of village life, then as now, 'crowded dwellings' and 'deserted villages' seem contradictory. Howard also ignored the essential market links between town and country.

Many of his generalizations have become outdated. There is now probably more wildlife in cities (including suburban gardens) than in the surrounding fields that haven't yet been built over – but for all the wrong reasons. Suburban life has increased various problems. There is now more social isolation of residents than ever before, as suggested by the growth of sedatives and anti-depressants, and our passion for gardens and pets. Commuting distances have never been greater, replacing foul air and fogs with exhaust fumes and smogs. Drains now have to address the risk of flooding because we have built over so much of the land, while both towns and villages are doing their utmost to retain not only their gin palaces but even their schools and post offices.

In *Garden Cities*, Howard attempted to fuse town and country where "Human society and the beauty of nature [could] be enjoyed together. The two magnets must be made one." The ambition is undeniable, but as a social species, we must retain cities for work, commerce and civic duties, and the countryside for food, beauty and clean air. The problem with sprawling suburbs and garden cities is that they sever town and country, and segregate residents, businesses, town centres, farms and villages. Yet Howard's magnets are a useful tool, and I have reused them to summarize chapters 3 to 7. (Of course, you should read my generalizations as critically as I have treated his.)

Howard should not be judged solely on his words. Being a practical engineer, he designed and developed the first two new towns of the twentieth century. Letchworth was begun in 1904, Welwyn Garden City was completed in the 1930s. They were followed by 27 New Towns, all built under the *New Towns Act 1946*. In that year, Stevenage was the first to be designated, while the last was Central Lancashire, designated in 1970.

Lewis Mumford considered garden cities "a consummate piece of statesmanship on a par with the founding of the Mormon communities in Utah, or the Co-operative Wholesale Society in England." This is dubious. Being self-contained and self-financing, New Towns are a valuable experiment, but as discussed in various chapters below, large-scale physical solutions usually create real problems, however they are financed. In broad terms, New Towns are little more than large suburbs with a town centre, two or three industrial estates and lots of trees. Let us now dispense with the majuscules: garden cities and new towns, however distinctive, may share a quasi-religious fervour with the Mormon communities, but they ignore the problems of sprawl and isolation. While each was designed to a unique masterplan to foster urban health, beauty and convenience, 50 to 100 years on, few have matured like similar-sized historic cities and market towns.

Furthermore, unlike the real potential of co-ops, they have added little to economic health. They may have outperformed such Victorian new towns as Barrow-in-Furness, Crewe and Middlesbrough, which suffered from an over-reliance on one or two basic industries. But garden cities have not as yet developed engines for internal economic growth, based on a healthy small firms sector and specialist clusters (as discussed in chapter 5). The famous Shredded Wheat factory in Welwyn Garden City, when bought by Nestlé, was shut down, and awaits proposals to convert it into a supermarket as part of a 'major regeneration scheme'.

This highlights another feature of garden cities. There are few shops. In old cities, there might be one shop for every 50 people (plus pubs and workshops et al to match), all set up by locals until the market was saturated (see chapters 2 and 5). By contrast, the four garden cities in Hertfordshire (the 'capital' for new towns) only provide one shop for 225 people. This reduces convenience and competition as well as choice and jobs for residents.

Table 4: Hertfordshire garden cities; population and shops, 1971

City	Population	No of Shops	People/shop
Hemel Hempstead	70,380	305	231
Stevenage	67,080	354	189
Welwyn Gdn City	40,450	133	304
Hatfield	25,360	110	231
Total	203,270	902	225

Source: Munby

In new towns, health equated to low density housing, with industry, leisure and shopping uses segregated in zones, each usually separated by green *cordons sanitaires*. Yet, despite several new towns having extensive cycle networks, none appear in the top twenty towns for cycling (Census 2011). So with greater distances for work, shopping and leisure, people use their cars more than in old towns. So most streets are congested, deterring both cyclists and walkers. This is neither healthy nor convenient.

Curiously, even at low densities with generous gardens, parking can sometimes be a problem. At a regional planning conference in Welwyn Garden City, a local planner explained the difficulty of dealing with wealthy residents who wanted to garage their three cars in front gardens originally designed for one garage – and then somewhere to overwinter the yacht. Protecting the visual appeal of a cathedral or library is vital, and any change of use should respect their aesthetic and historic importance. But modest houses? This wealthy garden city, with its own John Lewis store, contrasts nicely with Stevenage new town, the next rail station north of Welwyn. Here, the cheerful working class concrete centre is surrounded by large car parks which the council would like to increase. As argued in chapter 6, we need to reduce road traffic and car parks in both new towns and old.

While health and convenience can usually be measured with local statistics, the beauty of garden cities is necessarily in the eye of the beholder. In new towns, landscaping dominates and trees flourish. Runcorn, designed in the late 1960s, apparently invested 7% of its development budget on landscaping. Nevertheless, most new town streets are uniformly dull, partly because they are much longer than urban streets. If you are new to the town, you will have difficulty finding your way to the town centre or station (as I can vouch from bitter experience). Nor will you find a corner café or pub to stop for a drink and ask for directions. One reason why most own cars in garden cities may be that residents are bored or lonely walking those long empty streets. In short, the 'beauty of nature and social opportunity' in garden cities are an ersatz conflation – in trying to fuse town and country, they achieved neither.

With no new towns begun since 1970 (except for a handful of private new towns), the self-financing Commission for the New Towns was wound up after 44 years and its assets sold in 1998. This century, interest has revived in garden cities, now euphemistically called 'eco-towns'. However, given the modest size and rural setting of most schemes, they would be unsustainable from the outset in terms of self sufficiency and traffic generation.

With the benefit of hindsight, garden cities offered an escape from the worst of inner cities, but replaced it with a version of Nairn's subtopia, beautiful for many but incurably dull. Perhaps the true garden city has only been realized in Celesteville, the home of de Brunhoff's *Babar the Elephant*. Incurable may exaggerate but the lack of change and adaptation over time is worrying. Old towns are in a constant state of small changes, adaptations and gradual intensification. As Eric de Maré (2001) put it, "... a city is formed far less by the works of architects, planners and bureaucrats than by history as it rolls through the passing moment: by external events, by current economic pressures, by what people happen to believe, and now and then by the efforts of exceptional individuals who are the product of their period."

'The plan is the generator' according to Le Corbusier (see chapter 2). Yet for garden cities, as for other grand designs like Karlsruhe and Washington, Petersburg and Paris, the plan seems to be a straightjacket. It may be that, as with Haussmann's Paris design parameters, Howard's domestic-scale garden city designs and the new towns that followed are too inflexible, showing little change beyond the initial vision and detailed masterplan. They have yet to release the commercial, domestic, social and civic ambitions of their residents, and welcome all those small vernacular changes and local investments that give towns age, contrast and beauty as found in all old towns and cities.

The inherent contradiction in statutory local plans, between defining and controlling future change while allowing some flexibility for residents is discussed in chapter 8. Strict adherence to garden city principles has preserved historic designs and environments, but at the expense of urban diversity and social engagement. At some stage, new buildings must compromise or confront that original vision. Successful towns and cities cannot be tied down to a masterplan: small-scale change is in their nature. If, as argued in chapters 1 and 2, the scale of change in our towns and cities has been too great, in garden cities and new towns, the problem is that, from Letchworth on, our new towns have hardly changed at all. Yet, in Howard's own phrase, towns need 'freedom and co-operation' if they are to prosper.

Perhaps the most serious problem, and why they may never mature into real towns and cities, is that garden cities negate all four of Jane Jacobs' criteria (in chapter 3) for successful cities; high density, mixed uses, old buildings and short streets.

Let Howard's own words sow the seeds of doubt on his ultimately failed experiments. "The country is the symbol of God's love and care for man. All that we are and all that we have comes from it. Our bodies are formed of it, to it they return, we are fed by it, clothed by it, and by it we are warmed and sheltered. On its bosom we rest. Its beauty is the inspiration of art, of music, of poetry. Its forces propel all the wheels of industry. It is the source of all health, all wealth, all knowledge. But its fullness of joy and wisdom has not revealed itself to man. Nor can it ever, so long as this unholy, unnatural separation of society and nature endures. Town and country must be married, and out of this joyous union will spring a new hope, a new life, a new civilisation." (Howard 1898)

This is William Blake's mystic vision in words. (Howard might have benefited from an editor like mine who queried all such polemic in this text.) It reflects an ingrained fallacy that God made the country (the source of *all* health, wealth and knowledge?) and man made the town. Yet, despite its one-eyed vision, that passage reveals a real urban problem that is as true today as then; namely the 'unnatural separation of society and nature'. It's just that his solution was wrong. I believe that society evolves naturally in cities. Garden cities are a cul-de-sac, far removed from the problems of towns and cities, which need to be grappled, not ignored. The country must be reunited with the town, not built over.

Before leaving urban growth, one recent phenomenon demands attention.

Exurbs

The modern suburb was the commercial expression of domestic dreams coupled with official reaction against overcrowded slums, promoted by professionals like Patrick Geddes, medical officers of health and municipal councils, as well as builders and landowners. One reaction against this formless sprawl was given focus by Ebenezer Howard's garden cities.

Exurbia is different in kind. Like suburbs, it has moved urban functions outside towns and cities. Like garden cities, these functions are zoned, but unlike them, the zones are completely detached. The countryside is littered with a rash of business parks, executive housing, dormitory estates, distribution centres, leisure parks and retail parks, all accessed by trunk roads, bypasses and motorways slashing their way through what was once productive farmland. These have now joined the ranks of non-urban developments like airports, sea ports, oil terminals, chemical plants, race tracks and power stations. This flight of urban capital to green fields has atomized life: street life and social activities are absent in exurbia.

Recent research (by the RTPI and Belfinger GVA) found that "some 75 per cent of 165,000 planning permissions [on sites for more than 50 houses] granted from January 2012 to September 2015, were within 10 kilometres of a major employment cluster. Fewer than half (46 per cent) were within an existing built-up area, and just 13 per cent were within easy walking distance (800m) of a rail station." (*The Planner* April 2016)

There is no planning rationale for exurbia, no planning guru to lend it a patina of intellectual respectability, except perhaps the vacuous discussions about 'megalopolis' that were fashionable during the 1960s and 1970s. Exurbia is nothing more than opportunists in naked pursuit of financial gain for the benefit of landowners, developers, designers and the retail sheds and, equally clearly, dependent on private automania and the manic roads lobby in flagrant opposition to all planning principles. Should we not have examined the costs and benefits a little more closely? Perhaps the seed for exurbia and Margaret Thatcher's *laissez-faire* planning was sown by her father, a Grantham shopkeeper and alderman who impressed upon his daughter that the future of shopping was on the bypass. He saw the rise of motoring but ignored the impact on town, country and now on climate.

If Victorian bus and tram networks facilitated urban growth, and Edwardian suburban rail and telephone networks facilitated suburbs, exurbia from the 1960s on depended almost solely on good road access and large car parks. Cities can accommodate buses, trams, metros and telephones, but not large numbers of cars. Motorways, dual carriageways, ring roads and bypasses transformed people's perceptions of distance and convenience, while opening up cheap land on which to scatter these parks and sheds.

Suburban estates and exurban parks – from Bourneville to Bovis and Brent Cross to Bluewater – have replaced the familiarity and stability of terraced neighbourhoods and the way of life they supported. This reflects a society that puts retail sheds above street markets and high streets (chapter 4). Out-of-town capital investment harms local economies (chapter 5). It puts personal mobility above public transport and social interaction (chapter 6). And it promotes isolated dormitories over social neighbourhoods (chapter 7). Exurbia has replaced rational planning with the ideology of profit (chapter 8). In this flight from *civitas* and reason, the only planning standards are the number of parking spaces for each shed, the only planning justification is that they be commercially viable, and the only design guidance is that the acres of tarmac should be landscaped to conceal the sheds. One of the first exurban retail parks was built outside Detroit in 1954. It is ironic that Detroit has suffered perhaps the most dramatic urban decline in the US, even by their standards.

Exurbia has realized the concept of 'spread city', where cars are inversely proportional to pedestrians and reaches its apotheosis in Los Angeles. The architectural critic Rayner Banham, in his polemic *Los Angeles - The Architecture of Four Ecologies* (1971), defined those four ecologies thus.

1. Surfurbia. "The Beaches are what other metropolises should envy in Los Angeles, more than any other aspect of the city." Its traffic-free beachside walk "is the true artery of the beach life."
2. The Foothills defines the difference between city and exurbs. Here, "... that old [early] high density development of the hillsides belonged to a primarily pedestrian concept of cities and their workings; they were but a tiny – if likeable – segment within a city whose conception of itself was neither figuratively nor physically pedestrian."

3. The Plains of Id. "The world's image of Los Angeles... is of an endless plain endlessly gridded with endless streets, peppered endlessly with ticky-tacky houses clustered in indistinguishable neighbourhoods, slashed across by endless freeways that have destroyed any community spirit that may once have existed, and so on... endlessly. Statistically and superficially this might be a fair picture if Los Angeles consisted only of the problem areas of the City proper, the small percentage of the total metropolis that urban alarmists delight to dwell upon. But even though it is an untrue picture on any fair assessment... of the Greater Los Angeles area, there is a certain underlying psychological truth about it..."

4. Finally, Autopia. "[T]he freeway system in its totality is now a single comprehensible place, a coherent state of mind... As you acquire the special skills involved, the freeways become a special way of being alive... the extreme concentration required in Los Angeles seems to bring on a state of heightened awareness that some locals find mystical."

Early last century, Los Angeles boasted the largest streetcar network of all US cities. When this was bought by a road, oil and car manufacturing consortium (including General Motors), however, there was a shift away from electric streetcar to bus and from bus to car. And as the city expanded through suburbs and exurbs, new freeways and driving became 'a complete way of life'. Los Angeles covers about 2,000 square miles (roughly the same area as Kent and Surrey combined). It could not work without its freeways, making it one of the most polluted cities in the world, the traffic fumes also trapped by the local climate and topography.

Exurbia is a plague that contradicts urban life and civitas. And its nadir is found in those areas where almost every field with road access contains its own house or bungalow. In *News from Nowhere*, William Morris (designer of carpets, not cars) had a vision that England should once again be full of yeomen, each in their own cottage, with craft workshop and smallholding attached. This non-urban and anti-social housing can be found in some of the Celtic fringes of Europe, for example in parts of Ireland and Brittany.

Finally, exurbia has enriched our planning lexicon. To historic townscapes and idyllic landscapes, we can add theme parks, retail parks, business parks, science parks and leisure parks. But these are not ornamental gardens for public recreation. They are simply shedscapes, including retail sheds, warehouses, office blocks and leisure boxes surrounded by acres of tarmac.

In 1928, the historic *Control of Ribbon Development Act* sought to curb suburban sprawl, the first legislation to control private development solely on planning grounds. Although late in coming, it was generally effective. Exurban shedscapes have leapfrogged any such control.

Summarizing this physical review on urban growth, most of our towns and cities grew organically, intensifying through small-scale town extensions and piecemeal infill schemes, largely uninterrupted for about 800 years from before 1100. They were all largely self-regulating through negative feedback loops. Populations remained relatively stable, with occasional famines, plagues and wars followed by periods of modest growth. The settlements were stable, pedestrian in scale, much of their food supplied from local farms, their markets developing trade with other towns and beyond. Suburbs were a modest and largely unsavoury option.

Above all, towns and cities were densely populated for shelter, security and trade. The French philosopher Montesquieu (1689-1755) argued that climate affected not only landscapes but also the political form and social manners of every society. It also influenced towns. While topography largely determined where market towns, ports, castles and industries settled, it is primarily to climate that we owe the high density of towns. Throughout Europe, from the northernmost reaches to the Mediterranean basin, buildings have clustered tightly together across narrow streets. In the north this minimizes exposure to cold winds and rain and retains heat in internal party walls. In the south under the hot sun, high densities maximize cooling shadows and keep internal party walls cool.

During the Industrial Revolution, towns and cities grew exponentially in population, but not in area. From about 1900, however, urban growth suffered from a disruptive positive feedback loop in which unsustainable suburbia, zoning and private mobility fuelled each other. Towns and cities grew exponentially in area even as urban populations were falling.

After eight centuries of stable cities and small-scale changes, centripetal forces of internal growth and intensification gave way to centrifugal forces of suburbs, new towns and exurbs, designed largely around the car. In effect, we are turning towns and cities inside out: instead of towns being dense in response to climate, climate has been dangerously affected by urban sprawl and traffic. Figure 2 overleaf illustrates the scale of this problem.

Figure 2: Urban sprawl

Urbs (to c1900), suburbs and exurbs (from c1980). Loosely based on Leicester, population 320,000 (OS Landranger sheet 140).

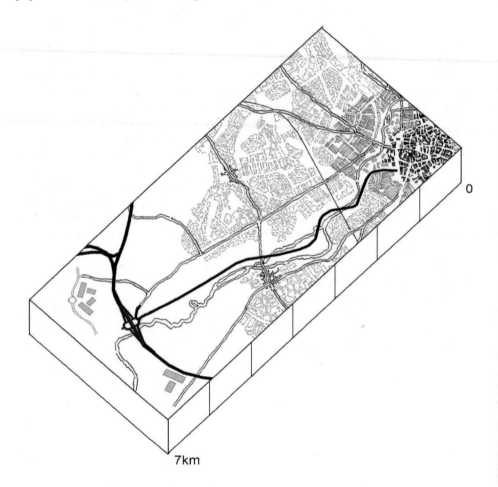

Let us now turn to the problems left behind in the cities and discuss the second form of development – urban renewal.

Chapter Two: Urban Renewal

I n cities, as in life, nothing is permanent. However successful and well-built, throughout history cities have been adapted and upgraded. Buildings wear out, fall victim to fire or fashion or fall down. Streets, however, are more inflexible, fixed by their buildings and underground services. And these street patterns give cities their continuity.

This mix of old, new and improved can be seen in the historic Market/Underbanks area of Stockport. Its buildings date back to medieval times, including a substantial medieval building with a Georgian facade, a market (dating from 1260) housed in a handsome Victorian market hall, a variety of pubs, the old parish church and large brewery to the south. There is also a Victorian cast iron bridge linking Market Place over the Underbanks west to the A6 trunk road, beyond which is the handsome railway viaduct. Such changes create a unique mix of buildings by age, function, style and materials and a very special environment.

Then in the late twentieth century, immediately north of Market/Underbanks, the large, bland Merseyway shopping centre was built with the M63 defining its long northern boundary. Like urban growth, urban renewal is grand in scale. But where new estates fled to green fields, urban redevelopments stayed in town, demolishing and replacing large areas with completely new urban environments. Such ambition was thought necessary to address three major problems. Whole neighbourhoods, deemed slums and unfit to live in, were demolished and rebuilt with houses for the future. After world war 2, run-down commercial areas, no longer deemed 'fit for purpose', were redeveloped for new shopping centres; and increased traffic congestion led to new urban freeways, like Stockport's M63, in pursuit of fast-moving urban road networks.

All these renewal schemes created problems of uniformity, impact and market distortion. Large single-purpose redevelopments might have addressed the single issues of slums and rundown shops, but they ignored the essential diversity of cities, the need for old buildings in a healthy economy and the importance of social stability. The new schemes were never satisfactorily integrated within their urban setting. Tower blocks, low shopping malls with large service yards and the physical barriers, noise and pollution of urban freeways all created problems. And the whole renewal process was top heavy with statutory plans, public inquiries and compulsory purchase orders, overriding simple market forces and challenging the very concept of local democracy. The alternatives of patch and mend and traffic restraint were not seriously considered. These are large claims, and the following text identifies the main winners and losers.

Underpinning each urban renewal scheme were government, local councils and the development industry. Governments approved the process of clearance based on normative health and housing standards, defined the statutory planning process including public inquiries, and introduced the compulsory purchase mechanism. Local council engineers, housing officers, planners and surveyors provided the technical expertise to instigate and manage each scheme, while behind politicians and council officers were the major developers, architects and contractors, major retailers, banks, funding institutions and the roads lobby. While many provided early examples of public/private partnerships, naked self-interest under the guise of 'market forces' affected them all and bribery undoubtedly corrupted several schemes.

All renewal shared three basic assumptions: that change for a better future is preferable to continuity with the past, that large scale renewal is more effective than small scale improvements, and that national standards override local needs. Unfortunately, professionals found themselves increasingly at odds with local residents, small businesses and the general public. Compulsory purchase skewed the process towards redevelopment. The people who had most to lose (with their homes, businesses and neighbourhoods) had the smallest voice and gained few benefits – if any. As we shall see in part 3, planning is primarily about people and their problems, not about city plans and development profits.

Formal planning, in its first century, focussed on managing urban growth and renewal. In other words, planning was essentially 'development-led'. By analogy with the medical profession, in creating suburbs and exurbs, planners acted as midwives to housebuilders and developers. Urban renewal promoted planners to more invasive surgeons, demolishing whole districts and grafting new transplants. This chapter considers the three major renewal programmes.

Slum clearance

"Then a man from the council decided
that all of us lived in a slum
So they pulled down our Brummagen courtyard
and we were scattered all over old Brum.

"That's summat that people call progress,
but I'd go back today if I could,
to play marlies and tip cat, and 'op, skip an' jump,
in that courtyard in old Ladywood."
(Syd Garrett, Ladywood and Bartley Green resident)

London's third airport, its motorways, the British library, Concorde, San Francisco's BART system, California's new campuses and Sydney's opera house are the subjects of Peter Hall's *Great Planning Disasters* (1980). London's motorway scheme is discussed in chapter 6. But Hall ignores slum clearance, arguably the biggest disaster of them all.

Slums and the poor have always been with us. Most people associate them with cheap Victorian housing, their perceptions based on contemporary surveys like the following:

"[In the old town, Millgate,] the streets, even the better ones, are narrow and winding... the houses dirty, old and tumble-down, and the construction of the side streets utterly horrible. [The] stroller has at once a row of old-fashioned houses at the right, of which not one has kept its original level; there are remnants of the old pre-manufacturing Manchester, whose former inhabitants have removed with their descendants into better-built districts and have left the houses, which were not good enough for them, to a population strongly mixed with Irish blood...
"This sketch should be sufficient to show the absurd planning of the whole district, particularly along the Irk... On [the south bank of this river] there are planted three rows of houses, of which the lowest rise directly out of the river... Among them are mills on the river, in short, the method of construction is as crowded and disorderly here as in the lower part of Long Millgate. Right and left a multitude of covered passages lead from the main street into numerous courts, and he who turns in thither gets into a filth and disgusting grime the equal of which is not to be found – especially in the courts which leads down to the Irk, and which contain unqualifiedly the most horrible dwellings I have yet beheld. In one of these courts, there stands directly at the entrance a privy without a door, so dirty that the inhabitants can pass into and out of that court only by passing through foul pools of urine and excrement...
"[In the] New Town... all the features of a city are lost. Single rows of houses or groups of streets stand, here and there, like little villages on the naked, not even grass-grown clay soil; the houses, or rather cottages, are in bad order, never repaired, filthy, with damp, unclean cellar dwellings; the lanes are neither paved nor supplied with sewers, but harbour numerous colonies of swine penned in small sties or yards, or wandering unrestrained through the neighbourhood. The mud in the streets is so deep that there is never a chance, except in the driest weather, of walking without sinking into it ankle deep at every step."

This extract, from Friedrich Engels' classic account of the *Condition of the Working Classes in England in 1844* (Benevolo 1967) is by no means unusual. At the same time, various government commissions and agencies were surveying urban conditions, but also discussing how they might be improved. The following, from an inspector's report from the General Board of Health in London (Morgan 1988), describes the Stoneygate area in central Preston in 1849:

"30 Turk's Head yard, on the south side of Church Street is a long irregular alley, rather narrow, paved and without efficient drains. Here are several filthy corners, and a very large cesspit, said to be the largest in town, receiving the contents of six privies. Close by is a large slaughter house in a dirty condition and giving out a most offensive smell. Mahommed's lodging-house, in a dirty crowded condition, is in this yard.

"31 Bolton's Court, in a yard, has a range of piggeries and open dung-heaps, with a large trough for the storing and mixing of manure. Near is the National School with 700 or 800 children, and on the opposite side are the gas-works, once in the suburb, but beyond which the town has rapidly spread. In Bolton's Court are also eight public slaughter houses, held from year to year under the Earl of Derby. They are in a very discreditable condition, and are stocked with pigs. The smell at the time of my visit was very bad.

"32 Between the backs of Stoney-gate and Library-street, is a narrow and very filthy passage, with an open gutter between two rows of open cesspools, clogged with accumulations of night soil. It seems to have been the plan, at one time, to build rows of cottages with this sort of narrow alley between them for the purposes of getting at their back premises. Such an alley, in Preston, is sure to be a receptacle for filth."

Both Millgate and Stoneygate were subsequently redeveloped with solid commercial warehouses and small terraced streets in the second half of the nineteenth century, most of which remain to this day. These eye-witness accounts and official inspections are probably the most reliable guide to contemporary conditions that we have. In more neutral terms, the dense housing provided a range of quality (however modest) and rent levels that accommodated even the poorest (however cramped); and in the absence of any planning, shops, houses, mills, schools and other buildings were all mixed together.

Who was responsible? First, most of the slums described by the Victorians clearly relate to housing built well before 1837. The reputation of Georgian builders, based on their handsome terraces, squares and crescents, is often belied by rear elevations of much inferior standard – which today we might call facadism. For the poor, stone frontages were out of the question. But in fairness, the Georgian builders faced acute difficulties.

Perhaps the Georgian elite was 'intensely relaxed' about their jerry-builders and conditions among the poor, as suggested by the fact that about 200 crimes carried the death penalty. Alternatively, at least Georgian slums, like today's shanty towns described in chapter 9, were built. Their shoddiness simply reflected the poverty of the residents. While table 1 showed the population growth in our towns and cities during the Industrial Revolution, between 1801 and 1831 it was extraordinary.

Table 5: Population growth in Britain, 1801 – 1831

	1801	1811	1821	1831
England	8,331,434	9,551,888	11,261,437	13,089,338
Wales	541,546	611,788	717,438	805,236
Scotland	1,599,068	1,805,688	2,093,456	2,365,807
Birmingham	73,670	85,753	106,721	142,251
Bristol	63,645	76,433	87,779	103,886
Liverpool	79,722	100,240	131,801	189,244
London	864,845	1,009,546	1,225,694	1,474,069
Manchester/Salford	94,876	115,874	161,635	237,832
Cardiff	1,870	2,457	3,521	6,137
Swansea	6,099	8,005	10,007	13,256
Edinburgh	82,560	102,987	138,235	152,403
Glasgow	77,385	100,749	147,043	202,426

Source: M Reed

Second, eye-witness accounts invariably focus on the worst slums. Our 'sink estates' may not be crumbling amid stink and filth, but our focus on statistics and anti-social behaviour still often masks the real problems, while arousing strong anti-social reactions from most media outlets. Historically, perhaps slum dwellers were worse off than the village poor who enjoyed clean air and basic sanitation in even the meanest hovel. But village life was static with few opportunities for improvement. Local poorhouses, shunned by all but the destitute, were no substitute for the social support possible in urban neighbourhoods of friends and relatives, pubs and pawnbrokers. The fact remains that the poor left rural parishes in droves because towns and cities offered work. The stench and poverty of the slums was largely due to the industrial Gradgrinds exploiting cheap labour far in excess of what was efficient or humane.

Third, the pervasive stench of damp and filth due to the absence of clean water and sewers was about to be addressed. From the late 1850s, Baron Haussmann (1809-91) transformed Paris with handsome boulevards and efficient sewers. Joseph Bazelgette (1819-91) did much the same for London following the great stench of 1858. As with shanty towns, it is clean water and sewage disposal that would enable them to improve and stabilize living conditions. And it was the Victorians who rejected Georgian indifference to poverty and tightness with the public purse. Their investment in public infrastructure not only removed squalor but also improved social conditions for all.

Fourth, perhaps slums, like shanty towns, are an inevitable consequence of rapid urban growth. Nevertheless, even in the worst slums, there was some social mixing. In Millgate, Engels noted three standards of housing: dual aspect terraces for the skilled working class, back-to-back cottages for the lower paid, and behind them, the cheapest single aspect terraces occupied by the poorest (which usually meant Irish labourers and navvies). This mixing of classes in neighbourhoods was important.

In London, the wealthy shipping magnate Charles Booth mapped every street and terrace using a colour code for his seven classes of inhabitants, from 'Upper-middle and Upper classes. Wealthy' (coloured red), to 'Middle class. Well-to-do', 'Fairly comfortable. Good ordinary earnings', 'Mixed. Some comfortable, others poor", 'Poor. 18s to 21s a week for a moderate family', 'Very poor, casual. Chronic want', down to 'Lowest class. Vicious, semi-criminal' (and painted black). These wonderful maps, from 1889, showed the vicious seldom more than 200 yards from the wealthy, the very poor often just round the corner to the well-to-do (Barker and Jackson 1990).

In Stoneygate, Preston, Morgan (1988) delved deeper into the records. "Stepping warily down Bolton's Court in 1830 we would have found (according to the Land Tax book of that year), a smithy, a wheelwright's shop, a joiner, the warehouse of a spirit merchant, and offices of the local Tory newspaper (the *Preston Pilot*); then a short side-turning, Bostock Street, where five landlords rented out eleven premises to various tenants, including a joiner, a butcher, a lawyer and leading Tory local politician (Joseph Bray), and a cotton manufacturer; and lower down, near the slaughter houses, George's Row, where three landlords shared a group of twelve cottages (eight of them built back-to-back) occupied by the families of a butcher, a chaise driver, a bailiff, a fishmonger, and four men who were employed in cotton mills... In Turks Head Yard 24 premises distributed among 13 different landlords were occupied by such people as coach drivers, shoemakers, tea dealers, cotton mill workers, painters, curriers, tailors, and a police constable."

That is an extraordinary list. How many lawyers and politicians would live in such surroundings today? However snobbish the Victorians, gated communities were not for them. Booth and Morgan show that in all ages from the Norman conquest to sometime around 1900, people from all walks of life lived cheek by jowl in towns and cities. This social mix dissolved, partly through the mobility given by buses and then cars, and partly through the insularity of the middle-class yen for suburbia, with council estates for poorer citizens.

The fifth point about slums is that jerry building was not just inevitable due to the scale of demand and the need for profits, even from the near destitute. There were also the vagaries of property law that encouraged flimsy construction.

From Engels in Millgate: "the outer walls, those of the cellar, which bear the weight of the ground floor and roof, are one whole brick thick at most... [and even some] in process of building, whose outer walls were but one half brick thick." This he blamed on "the fact that the contractors never own the land but lease it, according to the English custom, for twenty, thirty, forty, fifty or nine-nine [sic] years, at the expiration of which time it falls, with everything upon it, back into the possession of the original holder, who pays nothing in return for improvements upon it. The improvements are therefore so calculated by the lessee as to be worth as little as possible at the expiration of the stipulated term." (Benevolo 1967) We have retained this business principle, called built-in obsolescence, in retail sheds as well as our furniture and clothes etc.

In Preston, Morgan found another explanation. "The cottages behind belonged to the house at the front, and the Land Tax book of 1830 confirms that this was the normal pattern. The most likely reason for it is that the owners of the front houses were making the most of the gardens: rent-paying cottagers were more profitable than potatoes, and the investment was a permanent addition to the value of the property. Each of these courts and yards was a reflection in miniature of the effect of increasing population on the town as a whole."

Hoskins (1970) gave a third explanation. Nottingham had some of the worst slums in the country, largely because the city was surrounded by 1,100 acres of open fields along three quarters of its boundary, which the corrupt Corporation refused to enclose until 1845. This prevented the city expanding organically and created some of the highest population densities in the country, housing up to 800 people an acre. By contrast, Leicester, with a similar population and industrial history, had access to its three surrounding open fields, since the first one was enclosed in 1764. "Many large gardens were still to be seen, even in the centre of the town. The newer streets were wider than the average of manufacturing towns. The wind could blow through them and the sun shine upon them, unlike the courts of Nottingham. The working-class homes seldom rose above two storeys. Moreover, these houses had four rooms, and each room was bigger than its Nottingham counterpart, and there was rarely more than one family per house. They generally had ample yards, often little gardens, and were better built than those of most industrial towns."

Edinburgh was different again. "The purchase price for a piece of land was paid in two parts: one part was a lump sum, the other part consisted of a 'feu', or rent charge, paid in perpetuity. The feu could on occasion be extinguished by the payment of a second lump sum, usually calculated at twenty-one years' purchase. The initial feu was usually set fairly high. This meant that building land was expensive to rent, and so the answer was found in the building of high rise tenement blocks." (M Reed 1983)

The very different circumstances found in Manchester, Preston, Nottingham, Leicester and Edinburgh suggest that each city often has its own mix of solutions for its own specific problems and pressures. National solutions usually ignored and often ran counter to these local conditions throughout the past century. This is undemocratic.

Sixth, and finally, the Victorians responded fairly rapidly to the worst slum conditions, once conditions had been surveyed and problems like cholera understood. From the *Public Health Act 1848* on, legislation sought to improve urban health and housing for the working classes. There were also many wealthy philanthropists."'[T]here may be seen throughout this period, beginning as early as the seventeenth century, the gradual coming together of two powerful themes in the establishment of new communities: utopianism, millenarianism, chiliasm, communism – the idealist theme – and straightforward economic advantage – the practical (and highly traditional) theme. What happens as they grow steadily towards each other is that, to some extent, utopians become rather harder-headed, and, much more important, the practical profit-makers perceive that their profits will be, if not necessarily greater, more secure if the whole lives of the people are improved. The climax of the process may be Howard (or Sir James Reckitt) but the beginnings lie a long way back, and, as we have seen, conflicting symptoms of the process can readily be found in the course of industrialization." (From *City Fathers: The Early History of Town Planning in Britain*, C and R Bell 1972.)

This mix of legislation, philanthropy and Arcadian idealism following the Great Exhibition of 1851 may explain how we ended up with garden suburbs when most of Europe maintained their dense urban cities. Mean streets and courtyards with barely a glimpse of the sun, mixed with dirty trades that enveloped all the streets with their grit, grime, smoke and gore, gave way to suburbia and rigid zoning throughout the twentieth century. But what about the workers?

'Homes fit for heroes'

The first slums cleared by councils before 1900 left sites for builders to step in. When they didn't (and local rents rose), most councils began to build their own houses for workers, usually in the form of four and five storey walk-up blocks of flats. After the first world war, the emphasis changed. Instead of demolishing the worst housing to improve public health, now councils sought to build homes fit for heroes as well as providing them with jobs. Perhaps this was a form of collective guilt atoning for the criminal slaughter of the trenches – or an early example of successful lobbying by the building industry. In any event, by 1920 the worst slums had all been rebuilt. Few jerry-built houses would have survived a century, and from mid-century, most Victorian housing was solidly built.

Slum clearance, however, was becoming increasingly ambitious and irrational, destroying the social and economic life of whole neighbourhoods:
- main shopping streets with offices were either demolished with the housing or closed during the period of upheaval and loss of custom;
- corner shops disappeared from our planning lexicon;
- backyard workshops and garages were demolished with minimal compensation, only the more substantial relocating to industrial estates elsewhere;
- community facilities went, except for pubs and churches that were then too expensive; and
- the mixed tenure of slum residents, with owner occupiers, private tenants and some social housing, was all replaced with council tenants in council flats.

According to Briggs (1963): "Year by year we are pulling down the older parts of our cities – Victorian and pre-Victorian – with a savage and undiscriminating abandon which will not earn us the gratitude of posterity." Jon Gower Davies (1972) supplied actual figures for Newcastle. In the "housing programme covering all of the City's 87,800 dwellings, 9,400 were to be cleared between 1962 and 1967. A further 15,200 were to be cleared between 1968 and 1981, and in the meantime, they were to be modernized with 'short-term improvements and repairs'. A further 11,700 were reckoned to have a life of 30 or more years, and these were to be modernized to a standard above the 'twelve-point' discretionary grant standard... The remaining 52,500 dwellings [just under 60%] were to be preserved."

Being close to a bus stop but little else is not the same as having local shops, workplaces and social facilities round the corner and walking or cycling to work. Let me revisit Patrick Geddes' dictum. With most of our 'designated slums', the essential need was to give residents sufficient income so that landlords could fix leaking roofs, rotten timbers and window frames. The essential improvement was to install indoor plumbing, kitchens and bathrooms.

Newcastle was typical. Gower Davies vividly describes how this slum clearance programme made matters worse generally through blight, specifically in the Rye Hill area. Most major cities and towns had such corporate ambition. But now, motivation moved from public health and modern housing to aesthetics and politics. Redeveloping poor neighbourhoods would modernize a city. Such arrogance is still evident in our regeneration programmes.

The aesthetics of 'modernism' in architecture was radically new, but as so often, the new simply negated what preceded it. Ruskin wrote in 1853 that "Ornamentation [was] the principal part of architecture". Hence the Victorian (or in Europe, second empire) exuberance and eclecticism in their commercial and civic buildings. Then the great American architect Louis Sullivan in about 1890 said, quite reasonably, that architects should "refrain entirely from the use of ornament for a period of years in order that our thought might concentrate acutely upon the production of buildings comely in the nude." (Pevsner, 1960 and 62) By 1910, Adolf Loos asserted that "Ornament is crime". In any event, modernism swept aside nineteenth century folly and grandeur: traditional construction gave way to steel frames and concrete brutalism, pulsating facades with vertical emphasis were replaced by plate glass and curtain walling and, above all, buildings became monumental in scale, both horizontally and vertically.

Returning to slums, the new design ethic was first defined by my second planning guru, Le Corbusier (1887-1965). "A house is a machine for living in." He then put 340 maisonettes into his magnificent *Unité d' Habitation*, the 17 storey concrete block in Marseilles completed in 1952, with communal facilities, internal shopping street and roof garden set in landscaped grounds. This building was quite as revolutionary as Ebenezer Howard's garden city. But Howard's modest semis and shopfronts had as little impact on urban life as clothing fashions have on family life. With 'Corb', ambitious architects could transform whole cities and family life by the bold 'in your face' scale of their designs. None achieved the futurist megalomania of Le Corbusier's scheme for redeveloping the whole of central Paris with 60-storey superblocks punctuating long slabs of 10 to 15 floors marching across a wasteland of open space crisscrossed with urban highways, the central station and, on one roof, the airport. Impossible, perhaps, although some Chinese cities provide a glimpse of what Corb might have achieved. Only battery farms are comparable in their scale, functionalism and stunted life.

The fourth driver of slum clearance (after health, housing and aesthetics) was political. Housing became a numbers game of annual demolitions and house completions. Controlled by central government, it allowed architects, planners, housing officers and housebuilders to test new designs, layouts and construction methods. Unfortunately, they latched onto the scale of Corb's *Unité* but little else. It was simplified and repeated *ad nauseam* in almost every post-war slum clearance scheme with their urban high rise slabs and tower blocks and suburban council estates. With few exceptions (such as the LCC's Roehampton estate, Sheffield's Park Hill and Newcastle's Byker Wall), every interesting feature was simply lost in translation.

Now the slum clearance programme was driven by 'normative planning' with housing standards set by central government. These graded housing fitness in terms of structural condition, rot and dampness, internal cooking and bathroom facilities, central heating, overcrowding (judging floorspace against family size), parking space and some general external indicators. These 'objective' surveys were essentially an administrative device to facilitate and legitimize demolition 'on technical grounds' of properties that were usually sound and simply lacked a few facilities. Using those same standards, few medieval houses would have survived a slum clearance order. After the second world war (if not the first), most homes could have been improved to acceptable standards. In pre-war schemes, residents' views were simply ignored. Only from the 1960s were they heard, mostly to be overruled by professional evaluations. Even when they prevailed, less scrupulous councils simply blighted those areas with 'benign neglect'. Yet had we cherished these terraced neighbourhoods, they would still define the urban experience for generations to come.

Instead, slum clearance schemes got more ambitious, lumping fit properties with the unfit to provide sufficient land for large new estates. Mixing house improvements with selective infill redevelopment flew in the face of rational planning, for which read administrative convenience and commercial profit. Did society get value for money? In terms of costs, slum clearance was never going to be self-financing. Haussmann's transformation of Paris in the 1860s was entirely self-financing – until he came to the slums east of the old city. The asset value of a typical slum area, with its low rent housing and cheap commercial and social facilities, would not attract investors because future rents would be too low to recoup their money, unless they employed jerry builders. This confirms the economic importance of old buildings, first argued by Jane Jacobs (see next chapter).

All buildings, well-built and maintained, can accommodate rich and poor households, prestige offices, cheap workshops and other activities for centuries. Yet the economic and social value of these poor mixed neighbourhoods was ignored, as was the needless government spending on redevelopment. And in Britain, the sad truth is that few redevelopments have survived as long as the slums that they replaced. Few cities have retained their structurally sound and perfectly serviceable four and five storey blocks of flats (the 'walk-ups') that replaced slums from the 1890s to the 1930s. The great city of Liverpool had many walk-ups:

- off Scotland Road were two four-storey blocks of flats with cast iron balconies to each floor, built sometime in the early 1860s. These were the first council houses, at least in the UK, but were demolished in the 1970s;
- within 500 yards of the city centre, Liverpool built some of the most ambitious examples of early twentieth century council housing, some of national, even international, stature. North of Exchange station were Highfield and Vauxhall Gardens; south of Central station were St James, Pitt, Prince Albert and the large Kent Gardens; while east of Lime Street station were Gerard Gardens and Gerard Crescent off Scotland Road and the magnificent D-shaped St Andrews Gardens off Brownlow Hill with its dramatic archway punching through the semi-circle. Originally, all these Gardens provided drying space for clothes and playspace for children, which inevitably gave way to tarmac.

Today all have gone, even the tarmac.

Our walk-ups learned from German and Viennese examples. Their tenants were from similar backgrounds as in the UK, but they have retained their walk-ups, most with gardens and play areas, nurseries, shops, launderettes and other facilities on the ground floor. The splendid Karl Marx Hof walkup in Vienna is even on its tourist trail.

Here, it gets worse. The post-war council slabs and tower blocks were unfit for family and social life, and most have also disappeared, the turning point being the Ronan Point disaster in 1968. Even suburban council estates have struggled to survive. This government investment has been a significant drain on the national economy. And since the many local shops, small businesses and community assets were also cleared, the new estates had few economic and social assets to provide anchors and revive the local economy. This also weakened the national economy.

An alternative approach might have offered residents and firms in the slum a choice couched in the following terms.

- Option A: accept complete redevelopment at a total cost of (say) £10 million. 65% of you will be re-accommodated, the rest will be relocated elsewhere in the city. All local firms will be compensated and offered relocation. The 25 shops will be replaced by a small local centre with six units, church, school and community centre.
- Option B: accept a conservation programme costing say £5 million. No-one will have to be moved, except while homes are being renovated or rebuilt. All homes, shops and other buildings will be improved, except where demolition is

essential – all by local builders. And of the £5 million 'saved', half will return to the Treasury, half be made available to the area (whether directly or through the local council) for future maintenance and improvement.

Naive, perhaps, but this approach would have been honest, practical and democratic (see chapter 10). Against a council's legitimate concern to maintain and upgrade physical conditions throughout, people are usually happy to accept less generous homes in their own neighbourhood in return for local convenience, central location and little disruption to their family and social life. The urban slum clearance programme can only be likened to the rural depopulations that followed field enclosures and Highland clearances, but displacing millions rather than thousands. Let us now look at its personal and social impact on residents in more detail.

'Street life fell victim to redevelopment' (Chinn)

While many city histories would suit, I have chosen Carl Chinn's fascinating *Homes for People - 100 Years of Council Housing in Birmingham* (1991), because it presents both professional and resident viewpoints.

The population growth of Birmingham was no less dramatic than comparable cities.

Table 6: Birmingham's population growth, 1821-1931

Year	Population
1821	106,000
1871	343,000
1891	429,000
1911	840,000 (on larger area)
1931	1,000,000

Source: C Chinn

The highest population densities were found, aptly, in the Oxygen Street area. In eight residential acres (with a further six for business uses), there were 589 dwellings housing 2,429 people at a density of 304 people/acre (almost 730/hectare). With an average household of 4.1, residents, Oxygen Street is significantly less overcrowded than the worst slums of Manchester and Nottingham (above) or Cromac in Belfast (below).

Such densities were thought to cause ill-health and premature death. According to Dr Robertson, chief medical officer of health for Birmingham in 1906: "The herding together of large masses of people in cheerless houses, without a chance of ready access to natural beauties, affects the occupants in a profound and far-reaching manner. Thriftlessness, intemperance and a number of vices are fostered by such surroundings."

A Ladywood resident, Mrs Muckler, saw it differently. "One wonders today how we can say they were happy days, but they were, we had never known luxury so it wasn't missed or craved for, it was the small things of life, the togetherness, and love for family life."

Statistics can mislead. In 1899, an earlier chief medical officer of health (Dr Hill) compared death rates of 32.7/1,000 in the dense but depressed St Bartholomew's ward with 17.1/1,000 in the healthier low density Edgbaston. In 1904, the Edgbaston rate had fallen to 12.1/1,000. Yet in Park Street, it was still as high as 63/1,000. However, ill-health correlates more closely with household income which is strongly correlated with overcrowding. Later research in two high density wards (St Stephen's and St George's) showed that infant mortality rates were 210/1,000 where the head of household earned less than £1 a week, and 140/1,000 where earnings exceeded £1.

Rising damp, overcrowding and the absence of sunlight were mere symptoms of slums. Causes were rooted in the grinding poverty of slave labour, pollution and no education or health care – not high density. As we shall see, some of the highest density housing, in Chelsea and Marylebone for example, is also some of the most expensive property in the land with healthy wealthy residents. And in many slums, despite the absence of luxuries, local residents were not merely nostalgic but happy with 'the small things of life'. 'Street life', with its modest personal, family and social pleasures, is the basis of neighbourhoods over millennia. After slum clearance, residents seldom became richer or happier in their new homes. Health improved with proper sanitation, but in general, rents and travel costs increased and poverty persisted, often giving rise to hopelessness, isolation and a ghetto mentality. In this struggle, middle class professional judgement and technical expertise prevailed over the hopes and experience of residents. In short, platitudes trumped attitudes.

Yet Birmingham's approach, where 'municipal town planning' was first coined, was as enlightened as any. Key dates mark its progress:

- Before 1890, the corporation simply demolished the worst slum properties. But when local developers did not build new houses, overcrowding simply increased in adjacent neighbourhoods.
- The *Housing of the Working Classes Act 1890* allowed the corporation to build new houses to replace those demolished.
- In 1905, a Birmingham deputation went to Berlin and six other German cities to understand their town planning and powers to control new building. It didn't like the preponderance of flats in walk-ups.
- In 1909, Birmingham was enlarged by incorporating Quintin, and another 3,000 acres in Aston, Erdington, Handsworth, Kings Norton, and Northfield and Yardley in 1911.

- In 1913, the corporation developed 1,443 acres in Saltley, Washwood Heath, Little Bromwich and Small Heath, and in 1921, a new suburb at Pineapple Farm.

These suburban estates took Bourneville as their model with wide streets, 12 to 18 houses/acre (30 to 45/hectare), and separate factories and allotments. Yet these spacious new suburbs created new problems. For the residents, rents, food and transport all became more expensive, with far fewer facilities on the estates. For example, in 1951, the Sheldon suburb had one shop/228 residents. The city average was one/56 people, and higher in the slums. For the council, peripheral estates with few shops, resident shopkeepers and tenant mix raised problems of boredom and isolation. Urban depopulation also stretched public transport services.

Between the wars, Birmingham began building four-storey walk-ups that were already common in Leeds, Liverpool, London and Glasgow. Thus, in the inner area, the Emily Street and St Martins flats of the Ashcroft estate achieved densities of 150 to 180 flats an acre. Yet the inner city population continued to decline. Between 1924 and 1939, Birmingham built 50,000 houses in the suburbs, for both council tenants and private owners – see table 7 below.

This planned sprawl was typical. Replacing slums with medium density inner estates and low density outer suburbs was the norm. It involved all political parties, national and local, major developers and housebuilders, the national, local and professional media, and all relevant housing, planning and architectural professions in central and local government – all in fact except the residents themselves, those displaced and rehoused.

Table 7: Changes in Birmingham's urban population, 1921-31

Population	1921	1931	% change
Central wards	242,000	188,000	-22.5
Middle ring wards	380,000	288,000	-24.1
Outer ring wards	c300,000	571,000	+91.0

Source: C Chinn

From my experience, I believe that all post-war slum clearance could and should have been avoided. As a student, a small team of us surveyed residents in the Cromac area of central Belfast. This mixed (Catholic and Protestant) neighbourhood, with a large slaughterhouse in its midst, comprised small terraced houses, typically of 500 square feet in four rooms, two up, two down, with a backyard and lavatory. Such cramped quarters enforced some reliance on the extended family, providing beds for the children of larger families (two families I met had eight and ten children). Today, such cramped conditions would be deemed unfit. Yet few residents complained, the terraces were in fair condition, and could have been conserved, providing suitable homes for single people, students, couples young and old, and even families by knocking two houses into one. Although improvement grants were available at the time, they were set very low at up to ten times the rateable value of each house (then about £40). When the 'troubles' began, the mixed community evaporated and, eventually, the area was cleared and replaced with a gated suburban housing association scheme.

Another slum clearance area (in north Liverpool in the late 1970s) included an unusually handsome square of late Georgian semi-detached villas with large south-facing front gardens on the north side of the square and large back gardens on the south side. Some of the eighteen properties had minor structural faults and damp in the spacious basements, but all were solidly built, requiring only modest improvements. Nevertheless, the square was included within the larger clearance area. Re-opening the CPO (compulsory purchase order) inquiry would create too many problems with council colleagues, a senior colleague justifying its clearance 'because that's where the new school playground will be'.

Slum clearance often targeted lively night life districts as another way of tackling problems associated with lodging houses, rowdy pubs and red light activities. Preston's Stoneygate is just one example. A century after the Victorians had cleared away the piggeries, the local council and owners demolished some notorious terraces and rundown warehouses (that could have been refurbished), replacing them with car parks, a new road and many SLOIPs (spaces left over in planning). Plymouth's Stonehouse district near the naval dockyards suffered a similar fate.

Later, I worked in two fishing towns which offered a poignant contrast. In Hartlepool Headland, most of the seventeenth and eighteenth century core of the fishing port was demolished as a slum in the 1960s. In its place, between the twelfth century harbour wall (a Scheduled Monument) and St Hilda's church (a Listed Building), the area now sports municipal gardens, car parks, wide streets and a bit of suburban Wembley in the form of eight semi-detached houses. When the historic core of East Looe was vacated by the fishermen themselves and declared 'unfit for human habitation' in the 1950s, these unique terraces were bought by a mix of locals and incomers and used for various residential, retail, commercial and visitor uses, and remain an integral part of the town. Looe's escape from slum clearance was rare.

Once a slum had been identified, it progressed to official declaration and clearance through the sheer persistence of the local authorities and their advisors, however finely judged the decision. And as the technical justification for each scheme became less clearcut, as stated above, local authorities resorted to blight. Declare a slum clearance area and wait. Building maintenance stops, owner-occupiers start to move out, temporary migrants move in and vacant houses are left boarded up. As decay sets in, street life changes and the supposition of unfitness becomes self-fulfilling.

Two events brought the national clearance programme to an end. First was the Ronan Point disaster in May 1968, when a gas explosion in a London tower block killed (only) four people. Then, with the trial of architect/developer Poulson in 1973, the saga of bribery and corruption in the 1950s and 60s gradually unravelled, implicating, among others, T Dan Smith, the Newcastle civic leader, and Reginald Maudling, a senior government minister. How widespread such corruption was is impossible to say.

Lessons can be learned from this whole saga. First, in ignoring the commercial and social importance of local shops, offices, workshops and community facilities, the redeveloped areas lost their social stability and economic potential for growth. This seeded many 'downward spirals' of decline.

Second, replacing mixed social neighbourhoods with council estate tenants reduced diversity. The bitter irony is that, however well-intentioned, with or without corruption, whether fit or unfit, the old slums all too often gave way to new slums. The new housing slabs and blocks provided generous space inside each home, although some were not even technically sound: of shoddy construction, frequently damp, with excessive heating costs, poor sound insulation and lifts often out of order. More socially damaging was that street life gave way to parking and 'No Ball Games', creating environments that were anonymous, unsafe and prone to vandalism, particularly around lift shafts and stairwells. Conditions in many new slums were such that some called them 'sink estates', insinuating that the tenants were themselves to blame. This lie and the complex issues of community safety are discussed in chapter 7.

Third, the whole process was imposed from above, 'top down' in the jargon. From government ministers, civil servants, national contractors and professional officers, the process circumvented meaningful dialogue with local people, and was underpinned with compulsory purchase powers. Overstating the case, the social cancer of slums was replaced by a political cancer of paternalistic vandalism. This raised the issue of 'elective dictatorship' discussed in chapter 10.

Fourth, slum clearance achieved urban destruction and suburban sprawl in one fell swoop. It may have reduced infectious diseases and improved personal health, but the new estates raised more intractable social health problems as well as transport costs and pollution. This social legacy is perhaps best summed up in one last quote from the Aston slum resident Winnie Martin. "It never entered your head to move away. I think I was the first to move away when I went to Sheldon and I used to think it was horrible. I'd be crying on the bus going home. We'd never really been on our own. You'd always got somebody's house to pop into. There was our Nancy, Billy, Mayey, Lily all in the street." (Chinn 1989) Such quotes, however naive to the ignorant or intolerant, confirm the social vibrancy of neighbourhoods and the isolation of suburbs.

Eventually, as protests got louder, particularly after Ronan Point, councils and government were forced to take local opinion more seriously. This began with the Skeffington report on public participation in planning in 1969 (see chapter 8). Policy also shifted when new General Improvement Areas from 1969 at last provided an alternative to slum clearance (see next chapter).

Preston and Birmingham are fortunate to have had such insightful local historians. We can't undo history, but we should surely learn from it. Yet the strategy struts on, though the language is a little more subtle. Today we tackle deprived neighbourhoods with large regeneration schemes, promoted by the usual beneficiaries of politicians and professionals, developers and architects. Meanwhile, the poor, the young, disabled people and other minorities remain victims of the double whammy of lower wages and higher rents.

In a Market Housing Renewal area (see next chapter), the local agency identified only a couple of the worst housing terraces as unfit. But two young and fairly inexperienced consultants informed a local community meeting that, while they understood the concern of residents to retain their neighbourhood, "We have to consider the future. And most of this housing will not last much more than 30 years." This is blight based on ignorance (or a serious conflict of interest) in its refusal to consider much cheaper conservation policies. As should be clear by now, the lifespan of a solid house is determined not by its condition but by levels of investment in management as much as maintenance. Even structural faults can be repaired if dealt with promptly.

Samuel Becket, when asked why he continued writing, replied, "Try again. Fail again. Fail better." Something similar is behind this whole sorry saga: try again, fail again, fail bigger. Now we have moved on from slum clearance to regeneration schemes (see chapter 8). Different title, same impact.

Finally, almost from the beginning, Birmingham itself had an alternative to destructive renewal schemes. Its *Housing of the Working Classes Act 1890* gave the city council powers to buy existing houses as well as to build new ones. One can only speculate how twentieth century housing might have developed if councils had housed tenants in streets throughout their areas rather than in segregated housing estates.

Town centre renewal

Town centre renewal sought to replace rundown commercial areas to improve local 'amenity', the second planning objective of early legislation after health (and slum clearance). Here, amenity provides visual beauty or 'a pleasure', and 'a desirable facility' for the 'material comfort' (*OED* and *Penguin ED*) of shoppers. Town centres, the subject of chapter 4, are central to urban life.

"Constructed in the years AD 109-113, [Trajan's Forum in ancient Rome] was to remain a masterpiece. It was designed by a brilliant architect, the Syrian Greek Apollodorus of Damascus, and financed by treasure pillaged from the Dacians.

 . Apollodorus' ideas came back into fashion two thousand years later. His forum reflects the approach of modern city planners: it was the brain, heart, lungs and belly of the city, with life breathed into the whole by the ruling factor of money. Under the eye of the Imperial treasurers, who ran the equivalent of a modern finance ministry here, and separated by esplanades and colonnades, the place comprised a legal centre, with open-air law courts so that everyone would know what was going on in them, an intellectual centre with libraries and academies or scholae, and a commercial centre occupying a five-storey building with terraces which united the functions of stock exchange, big department store, galleries of specialist shops and warehousing, and which even had ponds for the sale of live fish. Imagine a modern complex in which the administrative offices of a finance ministry, a large cultural centre with museums, libraries and art galleries, a big shopping centre and a food market are all combined into a practical and harmonious whole. Trajan's Forum had everything, including restaurants." (Toussaint-Samat 1987)

Town centre renewal was triggered by the Blitz in which bombers replaced bulldozers. After the destruction of central Coventry and Plymouth, urban surgery was the only realistic option. The opportunities unleashed an enthusiastic utopianism but the results do not inspire. The new centres were heavily influenced by Letchworth and Welwyn, but in modern dress. The buildings housed shops, offices and civic uses. All other 'non-conforming' uses, including housing, were excluded. Pedestrians enjoyed traffic-free precincts within ring roads that provided access to car parks, service yards and bus stations. The buildings were low (two stories, with an occasional office tower), modern, spacious, clean and uniformly dull. As examples of mid-twentieth century planning and urban design, they contrast with comparable examples across the English Channel in two ways. The post-war centres of Brest and Le Havre provide less road-space to allow more traffic and segregate pedestrians, but all the new blocks are four or five storeys high, mostly for flats above ground floor commerce. The architecture may still be dull, but both centres have an urban scale that creates a livelier atmosphere day and night partly because of the residents.

Town centre renewal schemes, discussed more fully in chapter 4, were largely successful financially. When legislation allowed councils to declare Comprehensive Development Areas (CDAs) for rundown commercial areas, it created opportunities for ambitious or avaricious developers, national retailers, pension and insurance funds. Modern shopping malls would attract shoppers with rental growth and healthy profits to follow. CDAs were a radical change from all previous commercial development, being comprehensive – like slum clearance.

The shops demolished either ceased trading or struggled in more peripheral locations. We also lost small printers and laundries, taxi kiosks, backyard workshops, small warehouses, pubs and clubs as well as small offices and flats over the shops. This diversity brought life and spending into the town centre, however modest their input to the local economy.

When a new shopping mall opens and attracts shoppers, pedestrian footfall in the surrounding area falls. Some see this as evidence of market forces at work, but that is only to reach the first rung in any ladder of understanding. An open market works efficiently when demand and supply are roughly in equilibrium and the market forces are fair. Yet public demand for malls is modest and only evident after the event. The demand for shopping malls is almost entirely supply-led.

They satisfy large developers, national retailers and funding institutions since they generate significant profits, higher revenues and rents, and are easy to manage. They also increase the status of senior council officers managing the process. Cambridge was the last major city to build a large shopping centre, so now we have no way of testing the performance of cities with and without them. The profits (or property yields) of shopping malls may be high (or even higher than prime shops nearby), but they will have reduced property yields in the rest of the town centre. In the absence of a regular census of all retailers, it is difficult to state their impact on aggregate property yields. The point, however, is not whether malls are 'for the greater good' or not. Economic theory says that a fair market delivers 'the greater good'. Local shopkeepers who hold out against the CDAs are thought to be exploiting their position. Whether they are acting out of pure greed in holding the scheme to ransom (and remember the situation was thrust upon them) or out of genuine despair at the loss of their businesses (which might go back generations), the existing occupiers are part of that same market. Their behaviour is simply a balancing market force where, in a free and open market, both buyer and seller are willing partners in any transaction. It may even be that their ability to delay or scupper such schemes exemplifies Adam Smith's 'invisible hand' working in favour of economic diversity and social continuity. In any event, this fair and open market is undone by compulsory purchase that facilitates excessive destruction and profiteering.

Apart from their commercial impact, shopping malls also raise concerns about appearance and convenience – their amenity. Visual appeal is in the eye of the beholder. Old town centres retained their medieval street patterns of high streets, market places, side streets, narrow lanes, rear alleys and yards. On this infrastructure, street frontages were divided into varying portions of the medieval burgage plot so that the shops gave every street a welcome vertical emphasis. This 'urban grain' and brash commercial vernacular gives every town centre its distinctive character.

The monolithic shopping mall cut through this urban grain. Its commercial frontages are divided into standard six metre wide shops, the other frontages either blank or given over to vehicle access for servicing and roof parking. Paradoxically, while many slums were replaced by towers, shopping malls introduce an alien bungalow scale in most town centres. (A few even introduced a second or third floor facade with nothing behind.) With shops restricted to the ground and occasional first floor, with parking above or behind, they reduce the visual scale and diversity of their settings. More ambitious schemes, like the Arndale centre in Manchester, was also our first example of a substantial public/private sector partnership. Formerly known (before it was bombed in 1996) as the biggest urinal in Europe for its acres of tiled walls, the Arndale bore no relation to the five storey Trajan's Forum mentioned above.

Shopping malls also reduced local convenience, generally prioritizing vehicle access over pedestrian convenience. Rear access for loading bays and car parking, and blank side elevations both create 'dead frontages' with no commercial value, which traditional town centres avoid. Surrounding streets usually require traffic management, road improvements or even new inner relief roads, which also cut across the urban grain and pedestrian routes into town. And once inside, shopping malls introduced the contradiction of 'privatized public space'. Side streets and alleyways were replaced by internal malls that are shut outside shopping hours, when pedestrians have to walk round the block.

Finally, the large shopping malls rely on the same 20 or so national retailers at the expense of local shops and specialists. Hence the complaint that 'they're all the same'. The 'public demand' for these malls is questionable. The big shops inside generate high footfalls, but as stated above, the real demand is actually supply-led by the national retailers, developers and investors. This is not healthy. As with slum clearance, it raises the awkward question of who wins and who loses. This is at the heart of the planning process. And the sharpness of that dilemma increases with the scale of demolition and the resort to compulsion.

Urban freeways

Highway: 'a public road on which all have right to go' *(Chambers).*

Before the motor car, roads provided fresh air, sunlight and playspace, commercial frontage, street markets and public squares, as well as access to every property. Early public transport was both efficient and popular, until private cars took over. These impeded buses and trams, reduced passengers, and blighted every street in every town with municipal litter previously unknown. These included signposts, traffic lights, road markings, bins, bollards and barriers, street lights using energy and concealing stars, petrol stations to the same global design of tarmac, canopies and convenience stores, street parking and car parks wasting urban land and commercial frontages.

Twentieth century transport planning largely ignored public health and amenity, focussing almost exclusively on the third planning objective – convenience. In essence, this meant tackling the inconvenience of congestion with little regard to other transport modes like public transport, pedestrians and cyclists (see chapter 6). We improved convenience by relieving congestion, first with 'traffic management' and then with new freeways, our third form of urban surgery.

Perversely, some Victorian clutter was removed. From the 1950s, most cities removed tram and trolleybus gantries and overhead wires, to increase traffic capacity and street parking. Traffic management, designed to improve traffic flow (and hence road capacity), usually impeded pedestrians and made roads more dangerous:

- one-way systems increase traffic speeds, but usually reduce pedestrian numbers and commercial value of shops on those streets;
- junction improvements, with traffic lights, mini roundabouts or filter lanes, impede pedestrians and create non-commercial sites and blank gables;

- no right turns, to prevent queues at junctions, speed traffic flow, but the left-turn diversions increase traffic in side streets and trip lengths;
- at traffic lights, pedestrians usually have to walk further, with delays in central reservations waiting for the second of two-phase pedestrian lights;
- early shopping street widening schemes (lacking compulsory purchase powers) used to insist that all new buildings on one side be set back a few yards, so that when completely rebuilt ... one site at a time ... eventually .... ; and
- rear service roads, to remove lorries from high streets, often reduced back gardens and sometimes demolished whole terraces.

Nevertheless, traffic jams and bottlenecks continued to clog our arteries. So gradually, from the 1950s, ambitious engineers built new freeways. These were all designed to improve vehicle access and traffic speed. Only some sought also to reduce conflict between vehicles and pedestrians on existing roads.

The precedents for highway surgery in nineteenth century London, Paris and Vienna are examined in David Olsen's *The City as a Work of Art* (1986). The most spectacular was in Paris with a city-wide network of wide boulevards, designed by the engineer Baron Haussmann and built from 1852 to 1870. The roots for his surgery may well lie in Rome under Sixtus V and in London with Wren's designs and in the development of Regent Street by Nash. All needed compulsory purchase powers. According to Girouard, "the creative basic assumption made by Napoleon III and his ministers was that, in a city as rich and on the up as Paris, work on the enormous scale which they envisaged would pay for itself in the end. The expenditure was an investment, recoverable from rising tax revenues and increased property values... In the end the cost of public works between 1853 and 1869 was 2,554 million francs, or about £102 million. Of this about 500 million francs, or 20%, was raised by city loans – as compared to the £400,000 borrowed for the public works involved in Regent Street [which cost about £1 million]. About a quarter of the loan was taken up by the Credit Mobilier, but a high proportion was sold direct to small investors, in 500 franc bonds. These costs are exclusive of the very large, but unknown, sums spent by the contractors to develop the sites along the new roads." (Girouard 1985)

Some maintain that the surgery in Paris was for military purposes – to quell riots with cannon fire down the straight boulevards and destroy barricades. Be that as it may, the tree-lined avenues brought sunlight and fresh air above and a complete sewerage system beneath. This replaced what was still a medieval insanitary city and improved the health of all Parisians. The boulevards may also have beautified the city but they left the amenity of existing shops and street markets largely intact. And they achieved a dramatic improvement in convenience, at least for wheeled traffic. Yet this did not prevent the city investing heavily in public transport systems throughout the next century.

Despite its scale, the transformation of Paris was undertaken on commercial principles that differed little from medieval planned towns. The scheme relied on investment and speculation by individuals and institutions, and its initial success ensured further investment and development. It only faltered with the slums to the east of central Paris where, as stated above, the rents were too low to recoup the costs of rebuilding. Do we only build generous housing in the interests of equality through minimum space standards, or accept smaller cheaper housing in convenient city locations? (This dilemma for planners and politicians is addressed in chapter 8).

In any event, no UK city in the twentieth century had the resolve for such ambitious schemes. However, a superficial analysis of 85 town plans from a road atlas of Britain (AA 2013) shows how many freeways were built.

1. 38 towns and cities have built at least two thirds of an inner ring road around their central areas. These are Birmingham, Bradford, Bristol, Canterbury, Chester, Coventry, Darlington, Derby, Doncaster, Dundee, Glasgow*, Gloucester, Huddersfield, Ipswich, Kingston upon Hull, Leeds*, Leicester, Liverpool, Luton, Maidstone, Manchester*, Middlesbrough, Milton Keynes, Newcastle upon Tyne*, Northampton, Oldham, Plymouth, Preston, Reading, Salisbury, Sheffield, Southampton, Southend-on-Sea, Stockton-on-Tees, Stoke-on-Trent (Hanley), Swansea, Watford and Wolverhampton. Those marked * have significant sections of motorway in the network.

2. 21 have major roads that serve as town centre by-passes, main distributors, or less than half of a proposed inner ring road. In this group are Aberdeen, Basingstoke, Bournemouth, Cardiff, Carlisle, Colchester, Dover, Exeter, Guildford, Inverness, Lincoln, Newport, Norwich, Nottingham, Peterborough, Poole, Portsmouth, Stirling, Sunderland, Swindon and Torquay.

3. The remaining 26 towns and cities seem to have adapted the existing road network to produce informal ring roads, relying on extensive one-way systems and occasional large junctions or gyratories. This list includes Bath, Blackpool, Brighton, Cambridge, Cheltenham, Durham, Eastbourne, Edinburgh, Great Yarmouth, Harrogate, Lancaster, Llandudno, Margate/Ramsgate, Newquay, Oxford, Perth, Shrewsbury, Stratford-upon-Avon, Taunton, Tunbridge Wells, Warwick, Winchester, Worcester, York and central London.

Even from the most cautious analysis, over two thirds of our largest town centres have complete or partial inner ring roads. Only 26 have adapted existing roads and minimized urban demolition. Almost 50 years previously, only six of those towns (excluding Scotland) had significant inner ring roads. (AA *Illustrated Road Book of England and Wales* 1965.) Birmingham's aptly named Bull Ring has cocooned the life of this great city centre within a wall of traffic. Later, its designer Sir Herbert Manzoni though that the car was "... probably the most wasteful and uneconomic contrivance which has yet appeared among our personal possessions... the ratios [of vehicle to passenger] being about 10 to 1 in bulk and 20 to 1 in weight. The economic implication of this situation is ridiculous and I cannot believe it to be permanent."

What nineteenth century engineers destroyed, they replaced with boulevards lined with new civic and cultural buildings, shops, offices and housing, trees and parking. Even those dull stretches of boulevard with nothing but housing were physically 'knitted' into the urban fabric of the existing streets where shops and markets were usually near at hand. Boulevards were designed for amenity, health and convenience.

What twentieth century engineers destroyed, they replaced with freeways designed solely for the convenience of traffic. They provided town centre bypasses and ring roads, peripheral radials and arterials, their roundabout junctions expanded to gyratories with fly-overs, embankments and slip-roads.

Occasionally, the Victorians built large roads. When Sir Joseph Bazelgette developed the ring main of underground sewers and four pumping stations in London, he created the new Embankment on the underground sewer in central London – a promenade with gardens and trees by the much cleaner and sweeter-smelling river Thames. A century later, further east along the Thames is a two-level highway with no pedestrian access and no frontage onto the river. Little different, in fact, from Haussmann's and Bazelgette's sewers in its single purpose movement, except that it's an open drain for metal boxes – that pollutes rather than smells.

Back in Stockport, the Victorian 'flyover' that connects the central market and surrounding streets to the A6 is a handsome cast iron bridge that improved the social and commercial potential in the immediate neighbourhood as well as providing a better connection to Manchester, Macclesfield and beyond. The M62 north of the town centre brings no social or economic benefits to the immediate area, to set against the physical destruction, constant noise, heavy pollution and barrier to north/south movement. Unlike the splendid railway viaduct west of the town centre that sweeps over the river Mersey and M62 without impeding east/west traffic.

The theory behind urban freeways (discussed further in chapter 6) was that by separating general and local traffic, neighbourhoods could become 'environmental cells' with all traffic restricted to essential access and safe speeds. The freeways would provide a dedicated, fast-moving, safe and efficient highway network for both through traffic and general traffic between all neighbourhoods from A to Z. This approach can be seen in Los Angeles and Milton Keynes. But in all towns, freeways should not be confused with highways, on which all have the right to go. A freeway might be defined as: 'a wide fast-flowing route solely for the efficient, safe and speedy circulation of motor traffic'.

These new freeways, however, affected all other highway users, particularly pedestrians and public transport, destroyed urban fabric, charged all taxpayers, displaced people and polluted neighbourhoods. These huge capital investments had no tangible returns. Motorists had free access in perpetuity, with benefits in the cost benefit analyses seriously skewed in favour of intangible time savings on all their trips, while ignoring many real costs to everyone else. By contrast, all investments in our railways are expected to make commercial returns from passengers of at least 8%.

In their construction, freeways seriously disrupt the personal lives of all residents and businesses directly affected. In their destruction of whole swathes of solid townscape, freeways cut through neighbourhoods and blighted all nearby properties with their noise and air pollution. And freeway routes impede many pedestrian routes between station, town centre and home, as in Bristol, Canterbury East, Dartford, Doncaster, Ipswich, Nottingham, Sheffield, Wolverhampton and York. In Stowmarket, the bypass Gipping Way (ironically the same name as the long-distance riverside walk) was built between the high street and the railway sometime in the 1970s. Some 30 years later, a much larger bypass was built outside the town. Yet no-one has thought to reclaim the inner bypass for development or other uses.

All new road-space attracts new motorists (since, like nature, traffic abhors a vacuum). More traffic then inevitably congests other sections of the network that then require junction improvements, road widenings and new freeways. This becomes a vicious spiral. Increased traffic also increases demand of parking. Car parks waste valuable urban land and limit the growth potential of town centres, which in turn increases pressure for exurban parks and more car parks. These   positive   feedback loops reduce passengers on public transport. Most European cities invest far more in public transport and therefore retain more of their urban fabric.

In summary, urban renewal has destroyed far more housing than necessary, created shopping malls only with compulsory purchase and reduced urban value with freeways. Instead of minimizing disturbance, adapting the existing fabric and investing in more social forms of transport, we imposed monumental townscapes of alien scale, inflexible form and harmful impact in our towns and cities. These surgical implants have been 'top down', too many have subsequently become 'not fit for purpose' and few have created any 'sense of place' in the wake of their destruction. They reflect a worrying tendency in our political class to favour grandiose projects over cheaper small solutions that would invariably be more effective and popular.

Figure 3 opposite suggests the destructive impact of these renewal projects.

In the first century of planning, we have discussed two very different approaches to urban development. Urban growth through suburbs, new towns and exurbs reflected or refracted Ebenezer Howard's pastoral vision of garden cities. All were repetitive and profitable, led by developers, landowners and institutions. Demand was from a middle class in search of the American dream of consumerism and mobility through the comforts of spacious, leafy homes for nuclear families of 2.3 people (and reducing) and 1.2 cars (but rising). The dream is a delusion and unsustainable. The flight of people, investment and enterprise also exacerbated the problems left behind. Urban growth was based on a flawed capitalist version of supply and demand. The planner was a mere midwife to these developments.

Urban renewal has been no more successful. A drastic slash and burn response to urban problems in situ, its roots lie in Le Corbusier's *La Ville Radieuse* – a futuristic urban machine based on megalithic blocks and superhighways. It depends on a Marxist version of Big Brother in which a middle-class elite of professionals (politicians, civil servants, officers, councillors, developers and designers) 'waged class war' against the proletariat with normative planning and compulsory demolition. In practice, the new council estates, shopping malls and freeways created worse social environments than the areas that they replaced. Here the planner was performing urban surgery. Unfortunately, too often a faulty heart was replaced with a foot pump, a collapsed lung with an accordion, and an amputated leg with a bicycle wheel. Few of these transplants worked.

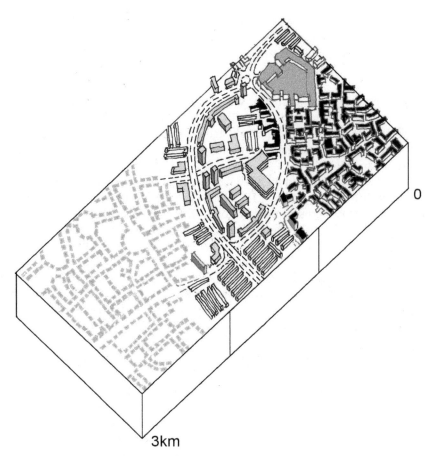

Figure 3: Urban destruction
Slum clearance, shopping mall and freeway in typical inner urban area

However exaggerated, suburban growth and urban renewal both transformed urban life for the worse. Yet all the time, there was a third way for urban development.

Chapter Three: Urban Conservation

"The world is fleeting; all things pass away;
Or is it we that pass and they that stay?"
(Lucian, Oxford Book of Greek Verse)

On the subject of mortality, we all pass away. The only constant in life is change, but the light irony of Lucian gave way to grim reality. Both the flight to suburbia and the fight against bulldozers created their own blight. Urban growth degenerated into suburban sprawl, poverty led to the disasters of urban renewal.

There is a third way, and all three can be found in the Hindu religion. Its Great God has three life forces: creation (Brahma), destruction (Shiva) and preservation (Vishnu). Let Brahma represent the creation of free-market semi-detached villas, and Shiva the tower blocks rising from the ashes of normative planning. That leaves Vishnu to preserve our cities, providing them with some stability and continuity against the winds of change.

I am always struck by how most cities in mainland Europe have retained most of their older urban fabric, and those that suffered severe war damage have been rebuilt to the same high densities and diversity as before, as noted earlier in Brest and Le Havre. Britain has invested far more in suburban growth and urban renewal. Conservation has been the Cinderella of planning. This is especially ironic, since preserving historic towns and protecting green belts are probably the two most popular policies of twentieth century planning.

One can understand why property owners and developers prefer new build and redevelopment, but conservation is also rejected by central government and local councils. New development is viewed as long-term, positive and good, a response to market forces and perhaps the key to local regeneration. Conservation is dismissed as short-term, nostalgic and hostile to growth. Conservationists are patronized as NIMBYs (not in my back yard) because they naturally oppose any scheme that affects their property or surroundings. Strident nimbies, or BANANAs, want to 'build absolutely nothing anywhere near anything'. What promoters of change ignore is that Nimbies, Bananas and others are a public voice that represents a genuine market demand for stability.

The roots of conservation

The advantages of conservation are plain. As noted earlier, medieval street patterns are essentially fixed. To demolish and create new street patterns is expensive and foolish. Apart from the cost, area redevelopment also ruins local economies and social neighbourhoods. Area conservation retains local firms, building skills and inter-generational neighbourhoods. Where feasible, it is hugely popular. And it usually is feasible. Unfortunately, few neighbourhoods, with their mix of residents, commerce and social activities, have survived apart from Conservation Areas.

Buildings with historic, social or national importance need to be preserved. The rest should be conserved. Over time, some will gain historic value simply by their age, like medieval cottages and Georgian terraces. Most buildings are flexible, making them easy to improve, adapt and extend. This provides useful cheap premises for all sections of society, an essential local economic function. Conserving buildings uses perhaps a tenth of the materials, energy, transport and capital needed to redevelop them. Longer lifespans make them efficient and sustainable. Yet too many modern buildings last less than 50 years, a few in Docklands less than a decade.

'A town without old buildings is like a man with no memory'. Luis Buñuel clarified this cryptic remark: "You have to begin to lose your memory, if only in bits and pieces, to realize that memory is what makes our lives; without memory is no life at all... Our memory is our coherence, our reason, even our action; without it we are nothing... " Throughout the first era of planning, our towns and cities have been losing their coherence. Few have understood the danger.

Edmund Burke (1729-97) provides the rationale for conservation. In *Reflections on the Revolution in France*, he wrote that 'society is indeed a contract' and 'a partnership not only between those who are living, but between those who are living, those who are dead, and those who are to be born'. In opposing the French Revolution, many see Burke as an early Tory reactionary. This maligns a great liberal pragmatist. He supported the Americans in their fight for independence seeing that they had sufficient experience and institutions to govern themselves. He would have supported the Catholic majority in Ireland had they revolted against the injustices of the ruling Protestant minority, and he was one of the few MPs who voted against a Bill for the flogging or imprisonment of homosexuals. His opposition to the French Revolution was both pragmatic and prescient. He believed that France already had the political institutions necessary to put right the main injustices and foresaw that a total upheaval of those same institutions would inevitably result in chaos, bloodshed and dictatorship. The first victims of the guillotine did not climb the scaffold until well after his *Reflections* were published in 1790. (See Conor Cruise O'Brien's introduction to the Pelican Classic edition of Burke, 1968.)

A century later, John Stuart Mill (1806-73) clarified this rationale for cities. "The best government... is the one which tends most to give [the people] that for want of which they cannot advance, or advance only in a lame and lopsided manner. We must not, however, forget the reservation necessary in all things which have for their object improvement, or Progress; namely, that in seeking the good which is needed, no damage, or as little as possible, be done to that already possessed." (*Representative Government* 1861) Burke stressed the political and social continuity between generations. Mill stressed that progress should involve minimal damage. And in the twentieth century, another philosopher Karl Popper (1902-94) recommended only 'small-scale incrementalism' in tackling political and social problems.

Let me now be fair to William Morris, who founded the National Society for the Protection of Ancient Monuments in 1877. According to Hermione Hobhouse (1976), Morris's "often quoted dictum summarises the arguments of the preservationist right:

"It has been most truly said that these old buildings do not belong to us only: that they belonged to our forefathers and they will belong to our descendants unless we play them false. They are not in any sense our property, to do as we like with them. We are only trustees for those who come after us..."

For preserving historic buildings and ancient monuments, that could not be bettered. Preservation is inflexible. It would be vandalism to demolish Lincoln cathedral or Lincoln's Inn Fields, Kings Lynn guildhall, Kings Cross station or the Doric arch at Euston station (the first major railway terminus in the world) or ... Many cities have monuments that transcend local status: the Tyne bridges, Oxford's dreaming spires, the bottle kilns in Stoke-on-Trent and Liverpool's maritime buildings. Most towns have important railway stations, market halls and Crown post offices, banks and coaching inns, Carnegie libraries, chapels and welfare clubs.

Like our diverse countryside, these monuments form part of our national heritage. Despite legal protection, however, they are not safe. There are some 374,080 Listed Buildings in England and 19,717 Scheduled Monuments. In the early 1970s, there were only 163,029 Listed Buildings (Crosby 1973). In 2010, English Heritage estimated that 72,850 Listed Buildings (14.6% of the total) were vulnerable, with a further 36,700 (7.3%) seriously at risk. One in five historic buildings at risk of demolition is a waste of building potential and corrodes our national heritage.

Conservation works at the other end of the scale. We preserve the rare monuments, grandiose, sublime and iconic, because they have artistic, historic and social value. We conserve the modest vernacular urban fabric of homes, shops and workplaces because they have functional and personal value. Both have immense social value: monuments because they are open to all, and vernacular buildings because they create popular neighbourhoods.

After centuries of relative urban continuity, the emphasis in the first century of planning was on change. Early planning pioneers like Howard and Corbusier favoured completely new areas, echoed half a century later, by Lewis Keeble in *Principles and Practice of Town and Country Planning* (1964): "In considering the principles of Planning it is a sound maxim that the patterns of development commonly to be seen in the contemporary world are usually very different from the most satisfactory arrangements that could be devised." Here, in that last phrase, is typical professional arrogance. It recalls the mania of the Italian Futurists for anything new. "Come on! Set fire to the library shelves! Turn aside the canals to flood the museums!" (Marinetti, first *Futurist Manifesto* 1911). Great self-promoters, they became known as 'the friends of chaos', who loved speed, movement and frenetic change.

A century later, Richard Rogers echoed their confidence (or arrogance). "We must build cities for flexibility and openness, working with, and not against, the now inevitable process whereby cities are subject to constant change. The permeability of the site to the public, higher densities and multiple connections are essential part [sic] of the overall strategy to entice people back into the city." From the same booklet, (*Living in the City*), Michael Weinstock put the designer firmly in charge. "We are not bound by our familial inheritance in the same way that people were in previous times. This understanding can be extended to the reconfiguration of places and the invention of new ones. It implies that identity in a place is neither inherent nor permanent. It is something that the architect and urbanist must actively seek through the forms and materials of the buildings and spaces, and in their relations to the city as a whole." (The Architecture Foundation 2000). This could have been written by the Futurists. The great Wassily Kandinsky saw through them. "Art is a sacred thing that should not be treated with such flippancy. The Futurists merely play around with the important ideas that they come up with now and again; everything is so little thought through, so little felt."

Replace Art and Futurists with cities and architects, and we have important ideas 'little thought through' which, in their buildings of technological glamour devoid of human scale, resemble stylish battery farms 'so little felt'. And, as with Le Corbusier, they are self-serving. Constant urban change will need architects to replace historic anonymous identity with contemporary egotistic designs.

"The only constant in life is change. I'm fed up with that cliché. What we need are anchors." is how a speaker grabbed and held our attention in his evening lecture at an RTPI conference in St Andrews in the early 1990s. I reuse the idea of anchors to help explain local economies in chapter 5. Here, the point is that the existing fabric of towns and cities, representing centuries of investment, is one of our most valuable anchors. Continuity, through preservation and conservation, is vital. Change, through urban growth and renewal, should first be necessary, and then small-scale and adaptive rather than grand and destructive. The irony is that throughout the last century, we have preserved our new towns against small changes while destroying whole neighbourhoods, new estates and modern office blocks.

Conservation serves present needs while retaining continuity between past and future, in terms of buildings, infrastructure and politics. An old cliché cuts through the futurist and neo-futurist idiocies above. For any building, 'If it ain't broke, don't fix it', and 'if it is broke, mend it', to which we should add: 'Only if it's beyond repair, rebuild.' Neighbourhoods never break down beyond repair, except through earthquake, fire or war. Damascus survived and evolved over 5,000 years, enjoying religious tolerance until the recent bloody civil war. Its reconstruction, as with Beirut before it, will raise challenges much greater than the rebuilding of London after the great fire.

In post-war Britain, three conservation strategies emerged: Conservation Areas, General Improvement Areas and citizen action. In 1955, *Outrage* by Ian Nairn illustrated the visual erosion of historic centres and crushing dullness of all suburbia. The Civic Trust, formed two years later, helped to create Conservation Areas through the *Civic Amenities Act 1967*. These allowed areas of architectural and historic importance to be protected, with extra planning controls on demolition, minor development and tree protection. At much the same time (1965), the Council for British Archaeology published a list of 324 historic towns in England, Scotland and Wales that needed protection, especially against traffic intrusion.

Today there are 9,080 Conservation Areas (from 6,300 in 1988). This total may be a thousand too many or too few, depending on your point of view. English Heritage estimates that they contain about half of our Listed Buildings, and cover just 4% of the total building stock. That does not suggest a nation in hock to heritage. However, to adapt Pierre Boulez' views on music, 'There are Conservation Areas that are very attractive but not necessarily very interesting, and there are Conservation Areas that are very interesting but not necessarily very attractive'. Bath Crescent, Edinburgh New Town and many London squares are undeniably handsome, but many more lively town centres and neighbourhoods are not thought to merit Conservation Area status. This reflects a visual (and tidy) approach to planning, with little appreciation of an area's social vibrancy, however unkempt. And too often, Conservation Area status stultifies any scruffy liveliness that already exists.

The second landmark had no negative side effects. The General Improvement Area (GIA), introduced in the *Housing Act 1969*, was the first real alternative to slum clearance. Shabby neighbourhoods could be renovated and improved with modern kitchens and bathrooms. Like family planning and preventive medicine, this was genuine prophylactic planning. It followed the pioneering rehabilitation of two terraced housing areas in Macclesfield and Liverpool in the early 1960s by the housing charity Shelter. GIAs quickly spread. In the 1970s, having built 429 tower blocks following slum clearance, Birmingham city council declared 70 General Improvement Areas for the rehabilitation of 62,000 houses. Later it added 28 of the more drastic Housing Action Areas covering a further 15,000 dwellings.

Many GIAs were popular with young families and professionals who bought from existing owners and landlords. This was our experience. We bought a terraced house for £13,000 with the benefit of a £5,000 grant that covered the cost of a basic kitchen and bathroom, replacing a rotten window and lintel and a new attic window. The gradual decline of GIAs and HAAs is difficult to explain.

Few were as successful as Conservation Areas, which were in better condition with wealthier owner-occupiers able to maintain their properties. Many GIAs and most HAAs were run-down because of high levels of poverty. Perhaps government grants should have been increased to cover more of the full cost of improvements.

As we shall see (page 289 below), in the 1980s, Ipswich was offering 75% grants to convert vacant upper floors over shops into flats.

Political ideology also played its part. In successful GIAs, house prices took off, leading to a reaction from several councils (mostly Labour-controlled) who objected to this process of 'gentrification'. Instead they might have anticipated this and bought a number of the cheap homes before improvement to be used for social housing in the area. After 1979, government ideology was generally opposed to such grant aid. Yet it was a good public investment. GIAs paid their way. Given that the increased property values were largely due to public demand rather than residents' care and maintenance, inheritance tax is fully justified to return much of that social value to society. However, Conservative governments are also usually against new taxes.

Coincidentally, volume housebuilders didn't like GIAs as they greatly reduced their housing market.

GIAs demonstrated the intrinsic value of dense urban neighbourhoods with their housing terraces, local shops, pubs and schools promoting street life and social skills. Neighbourhoods can fluctuate over time in their physical and social make-up. Parts of west London, built for the wealthy of the late Georgian period, sank into poverty and slums a century later, before 'reviving' so that they now only house the wealthy or their wealth in empty investments. Most houses were built to last. As Morris said, they "do not belong to us only: ... they belonged to our forefathers and they will belong to our descendants". Unless we pull them down when they are 'down-at-heel', and start again, or we introduce a Housing Market Renewal (HMR) programme discussed below.

Third, citizen action occasionally succeeded, against formidable odds, in resisting major redevelopments. Covent Garden was saved from the bulldozer by a grass roots consortium of residents, businesses and pressure groups (with support only later from the former Greater London Council). Instead of its comprehensive redevelopment, the historic market hall was refurbished, and the whole area attracted tourists, hedge funds and private equity. This victory, which benefited from the opposition to similar proposals for Piccadilly Circus, was later repeated in Coin Street on London's south bank. Even more astonishing, citizens defeated Department of Transport schemes for 'improving' the Archway on London's North Circular road no less than three times.

Unfortunately, David rarely defeated Goliath. Outside London, bypasses, freeways and tower blocks still got built and few local groups had the resilience against Tesco and others who cynically re-applied several times until they got what they wanted. Nor has anybody found a way to stop the remorseless expansion of Heathrow airport – yet. Against the focus and power of the developers, perhaps the varied motives of the objectors weakened their case: to preserve historic areas, to retain neighbourhoods, to resist unsympathetic redevelopment, to prevent pollution, to avoid disruption or simply to be left alone. And Covent Garden may well be a victim of its own success where rising rents make it difficult for many of the original objectors to remain. It will be interesting to see if the new private equity firms adopt the same ruthless approach to their buildings as to their businesses.

Conservation Areas are settled policy, citizen action suggests how weak local democracy is, while GIAs have been replaced by the infamous Housing Market Renewal (HMR) programme from 2002. These Pathfinder areas focussed in nine urban regions: Birmingham/Sandwell, East Lancashire, Hull and East Riding, Manchester/Salford, Merseyside, Newcastle/Gateshead, North Staffordshire, Oldham/Rochdale, and South Yorkshire. In 2005, West Yorkshire, West Cumbria and the Tees Valley were added. The total number of HMR areas is unclear (there were 14 in Merseyside), but they all focussed on our remaining inner city terraced housing neighbourhoods, allowing a mix of demolition, refurbishment and new building. Whatever the intention, in practice HMR was little more than a return to urban renewal, but without slum clearance in the title.

Save Britain's Heritage (the successor to William Morris's National Society for the Protection of Ancient Monuments) gave its assessment (in the House of Commons Library report *Housing Market Renewal Pathfinders*):

"From the start, pathfinder showed an appetite for destruction... The classic English terraced house was demonised as 'obsolete'. Whole neighbourhoods were declared surplus at the keystroke of a consultant's lap-top. Bureaucratic arrogance reduced communities to inmates of a 'ZOO – Zone Of Opportunity – for house-builders. Statisticians assumed compulsory purchase and eviction for demolition were acceptable measures for householders in a property-owning democracy. Quite predictably, the cure turned out worse than the disease."

Having lived in one HMR and worked in another, I think that is fair. As a young family, we moved into a friend's house where he was born and bred, with his two aunts still living in the same Arundel Street. His home was Shelter's show house in Liverpool's first GIA, demonstrating how these modest terraces with elm trees off Granby Street could be improved. All were sturdy well-built terraces from the 1870s, with bay windows, decorative brickwork, small railed front gardens, rear extensions and yards to a back jigger and, in our terrace at least, half basements. Given long-term occupiers and proper maintenance, they should have outlived our medieval cottages. The houses were solid, and Granby Street itself, lined with three-storey commercial buildings and a Victorian primary school, served the local community with people shopping, milling on the pavements, ambling across the street and chatting with friends. 40 years on, apart from four short streets at the apex of the Granby Street triangle, the solid terraces and mature trees have gone, replaced by suburban semis with gardens and garages on new curved streets. The school is no longer a school, the commercial buildings are demolished and the once thriving Granby Street is empty.

Early this century, I worked in the Stockton-on-Tees Parkfield and Mill Lane Pathfinder area as one of the first pilots of the programme. Here the housing terraces consisted of two handsome four-storey terraces, a mix of more modest two-storey terraces and many commercial properties and workshops. The neighbourhood was rundown, largely because much of the housing was converted into small bedsits rented to transient males on housing benefit, with drug dealing plainly visible in specific streets according to a local newsagent (with 'eyes on the street'). Some streets were perceived as less friendly, even threatening, unsettling many residents, some of whom were born in the area. An exodus began, owners selling to landlords already in the area (whether local or absentee 'from Sevenoaks') increasing the number of single tenants on benefits to secure 30% to 50% annual returns for the landlords. This 'market failure' was a problem of management, not housing condition. Local drug dealing, petty crime, kerb crawling, vandalism or local gangs inevitably raise community safety issues and lead to falling house prices. It calls for effective policing (by professionals rather than the often-ineffective Community Safety Officers), decriminalizing drugs or more effective health, drug, youth and training services in the area.

In Stockton-on-Tees, as in other pathfinder areas, the programme focussed on irrelevances. One manager mentioned the lack of family houses locally. Yet while all towns are surrounded by family housing with three or four bedrooms, gardens and garages, there is increasing demand for smaller homes for single people, couples young and old, small families, empty nesters, divorcees and most vulnerable groups, whether as first-time buyers, downsizers or tenants. This is the value of compact terraces, together with their location near town centres. In fact, it is the suburbs that lack a choice of house types. And the lack of specific house types should never justify demolition. Most terraces can be adapted to provide larger homes or smaller flats as required.

Also, the focus on low house prices in HMRs should have been seen as an opportunity rather than a market failure. Councils, housing associations and local co-ops might have bought some of the houses for those on their waiting lists, sell them to young people, single or couples or even offer them, unimproved, as opportunities for young 'homesteaders' with perhaps a loan or council mortgage to get them started. (We even had a council mortgage for our Shelter home in Liverpool.)

HMR brought us back perilously close to slum clearance. What brought us full circle was yet another failure of conservation, when most of those handsome walk-ups that replaced slums were themselves demolished within 80 years (see page 53). And today, even some post-war redevelopments are being destroyed, this time in the name of 'regeneration', which vexed subject is discussed in chapter 8.

In short, the major fault with twentieth century planning was its reliance on new construction and redevelopment. Rather than conserving and adapting the existing built fabric, we focussed only on Listed Buildings and Conservation Areas. Planning not only ignored underlying social and economic problems in those areas demolished; it also seriously reduced public and private investment in more useful and necessary services. The wanton destruction of priceless terraced streets and social neighbourhoods, often over the fierce objections from those millions displaced, is an uncomfortable heritage to pass onto future generations.

Social cities

At the outset, I stated that civilization is impossible without cities. According to *The Penguin English Dictionary* (1965), civilization is the "social, moral, and intellectual attainments of a particular society, cultural development; state of not being primitive or savage." I discuss key aspects of civilization – liberty, equality and fraternity, written records, the rule of law and care of the young – in chapter 7.

I am not suggesting that civilized cities develop from primitive societies, nor that they are superior. The main differences between primitive and civilized societies are that one is rural, tribal and nomadic, the other urban, communal and settled. The pastoral lifestyle of primitive societies reflects the harsh conditions of their habitats and the real difficulties of winning enough food and basic materials to survive. The Bedouin caravans of the Arabian and Saharan deserts, the first residents of Australia and North America, the Inuit from the Arctic, the tribes of equatorial rainforests and, in Europe, the Romanies all live under traditions that are known to work and handed down orally over generations. New ideas are less likely to emerge from small groups, and more likely to be rejected because the risks of failure and group extinction are so high in such unforgiving environments. This restates Montesquieu's view that climate and geography largely determine a nation's *esprit general*.

The urban cradles of civilization, in which cities provided the physical theatre, emerged in the neolithic age: in fertile river valleys of China about 9,000 BC, India and Mesopotamia about 8,000 BC, South America perhaps 7,000 BC and in parts of Europe from about 5,000 BC. The major breakthrough is thought to be the 'discovery' of agriculture. While men were out hunting for flesh, the women, left behind to bear and rear children, also gathered seeds, roots, berries, fruit and firewood. The act of grace came when some planted a few seeds and fruits and started gardening. Then animals were tethered and reared, and gardening and husbandry became agriculture. Many men, now relieved of food duty, could build permanent homes in larger villages as the fertile valleys could now support much larger populations than hunter-gatherer tribes. With permanent settlements came division of labour. New skills included not only farming but also industry and technology, commerce and storage, defence and administration. Progress within civilized cities occurred when writing was invented to manage these activities, writing contracts, codifying laws, recording events and developing ideas.

Essentially, rural culture is traditional, urban culture is progressive. This contrast is recorded in the first chapter of *The Epic of Gilgamesh* written some 2,000 years BC. Gilgamesh, the king of Uruk, has grown too powerful in his own city:

"His lust leaves no virgin to her lover, neither the warrior's daughter nor the wife of the noble." So the goddess Aruru created "noble Enkidu... His body was rough, he had long hair... He was innocent of mankind; he knew nothing of the cultivated land. Enkidu ate grass in the hills with the gazelle and jostled with wild beasts at the water-holes." Then Gilgamesh was persuaded to send him "a harlot, a child of pleasure... At the drinking hole, [s]he was not ashamed to take him, she made herself naked and welcomed his eagerness… For six days and seven nights they lay together [but] when he went back to the wild beasts… they fled. Enkidu would have followed, but his body was bound as though with a cord, his knees gave way when he started to run, his swiftness was gone… Enkidu was grown weak, for wisdom was in him, and the thoughts of a man were in his heart. So he returned and sat down at her feet, and listened intently to what she said: 'You are wise, Enkidu… Why do you want to run wild with the beasts in the hills. Come with me. I will take you to strong-walled Uruk, to the blessed temple of Ishtar and of Anu, of love and of heaven: there Gilgamesh lives'… When she had spoken Enkidu was pleased; he longed for a comrade, for one who would understand his heart. 'Come, woman, and take me to that holy temple…' "

This short extract (Sandars 1964) contrasts the rustic life, tough, swift and solitary, living on grain and water, with the walled city, division of labour (with kingship, defence, cultivation, religion and prostitution), and the ideas of friendship, love and heaven. The *Epic* may reflect the pride and prejudices of the city scribe who wrote it, but the key point is that it was written, incised on clay tablets over 4,000 years ago. Cities gave people a glimmer of self awareness, a dawn of light on the human condition.

This doesn't mean that cities are superior. Many cities in ancient Greece and Renaissance Italy were spectacularly uncivilized, at least by our standards. And during the last century, cities were no protection against the dark murderous insanity of tyrants, whether under Hitler's slaughter of innocents, Stalin's slaughter of opponents, or the widely unremarked slaughter of natives under 'mad' King Leopold in the Belgian Congo.

Cities and citizens, however, are our best safeguard against dictators and centralized ideology. The meaning of the Roman *civitas* is, first and foremost, the rights and ambitions of 'citizenship', involving all our social, economic, religious, civic, military and family affairs. This is why towns and cities need much greater autonomy to manage their own affairs in terms of planning, development and politics, which is the general subject of Part 3.

The second meaning of *civitas* means a town, city or *urbs*, in which the streets and buildings provide shelter, security and markets. Conservation is not just about protecting monuments and vernacular streets – we must also maintain and adapt the whole urban fabric through what we might call 'intensification'. So, to conclude Part 1, we need to ask what are the physical features of cities that provide the theatre for our social behaviour, where civilization can flourish.

To answer that question, we had to wait until 1961 when our third planning guru emerged. Jane Jacobs (1916-2006) was anything but visionary, being a mum, a local activist against urban renewal schemes and, most importantly, an intelligent hard-nosed journalist who closely observed, not how cities should work, but how they *actually* work. In her seminal *Death and Life of Great American Cities*, Jacobs identified four essentials for successful cities: short streets, high densities, mixed uses and old buildings. Combined, these four features create successful cities. They owe nothing to design principles like garden suburbs and Radburn layouts, nor market principles or computer models. She observed people going about their daily lives and saw street theatre as the basis for local security and markets. Consider each in turn.

i)   Short streets – walk or drive
Look at any old map of London, Edinburgh or Dublin, of English cathedral cities, Cornish fishing ports, Welsh market towns, Scottish burghs and Irish planted towns. Before 1900, short streets are the rule. Whether they grew organically or were planned, town centres developed around a central market place and high street, with specialist shops and offices above and in side streets, repair services and workshops in back alleys and rear yards, surrounded with tightly-packed housing, local church, school and community hall, sometimes with small market gardens and orchards tucked away.

The Victorians retained short streets between the main roads into town. As these radials got further apart, the infilling terraces got longer, so they split these side streets into two or three blocks, with cross streets, or minor radials, linking them together. People still supported shops and pubs along the main roads, but the cross streets introduced a Victorian innovation – the ubiquitous corner shop. For example, midway in our street (about 250 yards long), there is a short road link to the next street. On one corner of that link, the landowner/developer built a pub, as it had greater commercial value than four house plots that were lost to the link road. It has survived since the 1860s because it attracts locals from two streets rather than one, plus some commuters nearby who use our streets as a cut on their way home from the railway station. Even in grid layouts like Middlesbrough, the wide terraced streets are generally less than 150 yards long.

Short streets are convenient. They reduce the distance between home and destination as one doglegs almost 'as the crow flies'. With long streets, one has to walk two sides of a triangle – there is no hypotenuse. In this respect, the organic street pattern of radials and cross streets is slightly better than the regular grid of so many empire cities. Hence, some American cities (like Philadelphia and Washington) imposed a few diagonals across the grid to provide more direct avenues.

Short streets reduce trip lengths and support local commerce – two vital features of neighbourhoods. In suburbia, as terraced housing gave way to semi-detached villas, multi-storey factories and mills moved out to single-storey industrial estates and shops went out of town or out of business, so trip lengths increased and walking has largely disappeared. Street lengths increase exponentially as one passes from central areas to suburbs and beyond. Suburban streets, where the medieval street pattern would be anachronistic, average three to five times the length of Victorian streets. And instead of short cuts and corner shops, the suburbs invented the cul-de-sac. This takes pedestrian inconvenience one stage further, there being only one way out.

ii)   High densities – proximity or privacy?

Short streets also increase urban density. There is a seeming paradox here, since the dense network of streets in inner urban areas occupy far more land/acre than long suburban avenues. However, increasing the cost of roads in terraced neighbourhoods encouraged higher densities – both to recoup those costs, and to maximize the social benefits of convenience and local commerce. This is the city as a natural social habitat. By contrast, suburbs were a simple form of 'market-led planning' that reduced infrastructure costs to increase profits while ignoring social costs. After eight centuries of high density urban life, we fled to the privacy of suburban family life with remote facilities and few pedestrians. The suburb may provide high quality shelter, but security has become a personal responsibility rather than a natural feature of urban streets and local economies are negligible.

The general justification for suburbs was that high densities created slums, so low densities were healthy. Jane Jacobs saw through this. Slums were a consequence of the extreme poverty imposed on families by the industrial Gradgrinds, leading to low rents, cheap housing and thence to chronic overcrowding of large families in buildings that were pokey, damp and insanitary. Robert Owen (see page 169) showed a much fairer alternative that was still profitable. And then councils installed clean water supplies and sewers for immediate social benefit before building homes themselves.

According to Jane Jacobs, successful cities require densities of at least 100 people/acre (240/hectare). History offers confirmation. For example, in the 1550s, the ancient walled city of Exeter covered 93 acres and housed 9,000 to 10,000 people (W G Hoskins, from P Clerk 1976). That density compares with central and inner London today. The major differences are that in Exeter the average household size was six. Today it is 2.3, but the housing density has increased to maintain a similar population density. This is due to 'intensification' as buildings have gradually extended back and risen higher over the centuries.

Density is crucial to the structure of cities. It is density that fosters our social behaviour beyond our personal circles of family, friends and the more formal settings of school and work. Every greeting on the street, every smile in the park, every chat in the cafe and pub and every smile and thank you in our local shops and street markets is what makes us human. Density also underpins the importance of diversity which, as discussed in part 2, creates social wealth through clusters of local shops, small businesses and friendly neighbourhoods. And in dense cities, it is democracy that attempts to balance the often competing needs for private and social wealth.

Unfortunately, few British cities have retained high densities. Gross densities (including parks, cemeteries, high streets, offices and industrial estates) for our 66 largest towns and cities (with over 100,000 people or covering more than 3,000 hectares) only averages 40.3 people/hectare, or 17/acre.

Table 8: UK urban population densities, 2001

Town/City	Population (000s)	Area (has)	People/ha
Brighton and Hove	206.6	3,170	65.2
Luton	185.5	3,715	49.9
Southampton	234.2	5,056	46.3
Blackpool	142.3	3,092	46.0
Sunderland	177.7	3,874	45.9
London	7,172.0	157,208	45.6
Bradford	293,7	6,437	45.6
Southend	160.3	3,528	45.4
Oxford	143.0	3,163	45.3
Coventry	303.5	6,754	44.9
Ipswich	138.7	3,905	35.5
Norwich	174.0	4,975	35.0
Rotherham	117.3	3,393	34.6
Peterborough	136.3	4,047	33.7
Poole	144.8	4,329	33.5
Telford	138.2	4,180	33.1
Crawley	100.5	3,035	33.1
Milton Keynes	184.5	5,730	32.2
Bolton	139.4	4,446	31.4
Sutton Coldfield	105.5	4,343	24.3

Source: ONS *Urban Areas*

(These figures are estimates for the English built-up or 'primary urban areas' only, not the generally larger and fixed council boundary areas.)

While Chelsea, Islington and Westminster have some of the highest densities, they also have some of the most expensive housing in the country and by far the most expensive per square foot. Outside inner London (averaging 85.9 people/ha), Brighton and Hove is the most compact by a significant margin. At the other extreme are new towns, expanded towns like Peterborough, traditional industrial towns with extensive slum clearance and suburban towns built in the last century, like Sutton Coldfield and suburban London, with just under ten people/acre. Finally, let us return to Ebenezer Howard's Letchworth and the spectacular city of Liverpool:

- Letchworth's 33,000 citizens occupy 7.8 sq miles at less than seven/acre. Over a century, it has hardly changed, quietly efficient for car traffic but with few pedestrians, economic activity or social bustle outside the town centre;

- the *City of Liverpool Development Plan* of 1958 estimated that the "population of the city (June 1951) is 802,500, and the plan is based on the assumption that this will be reduced to 707,500 by 1971." By 2001 it had fallen to 439,000. Dense urban terraces and walk-up flats have been replaced by suburban semis 'all neat and trim and pretty'. Even the Town and Country Planning Association (founded by Howard in 1899) might find it hard to justify this depopulation.

European cities have retained their densities.

- Foggia, a regional capital in south east Italy with a population of about 155,000, occupies perhaps eight square kilometres (from a 1:200,000 scale map of the region). This gross density of about 195 people/ha (or 80/acre) – three times denser than Brighton and Hove – is clear in figure 4 below (page 93).
- Rome, up to 90 people/ha, is comparable to our inner London boroughs, while
- Paris retains about 200 people/ha (85/acre). After Haussmann had transformed central Paris with wide boulevards and modern sewers, a problem emerged. In avoiding the commercial free-for-all of most modern cities (except at Montparnasse), the rigid height restrictions on all new building have prevented central Paris from growing organically over time. Perhaps these restrictions should be relaxed, every 100 years raising height limits by one or two floors. This would retain the urban form and allow some modest intensification, as noted earlier in our cities as they increased in height almost imperceptibly from medieval times to about 1900.

Yet here, many remain prejudiced against high density neighbourhoods and what they call 'town cramming'. This persists despite the fact that in most inner areas, local shops, pubs, schools and churches are closing for want of sufficient residents. Perhaps our officials, professionals and politicians should visit European cities more often, where such densities are the norm.

Low density settlements have high social costs. First, they make less efficient use of land. As towns grew, so they expanded both out into new high density streets and up slowly in taller buildings. Over the centuries (see chapter 1) two- and three-storey medieval buildings became four- and five-storey Victorian buildings. This reflected slow but steady commercial growth, improved building technology and higher land values.

During the Industrial Revolution, factories, mills, breweries and warehouses all went multi-storey, enveloped by dense housing terraces. From the mid-nineteenth century, blocks of flats for working class families appeared, first by the Peabody and Guinness trusts and Liverpool council, and from the 1890s, the walk-ups in most cities. This dense urban tapestry remains fairly typical throughout Europe. The compact jumble, very gradually intensifying, kept central areas and local facilities convenient for all. As noted earlier, in 1800 you could comfortably walk across London, then the largest city in Europe, in one day. Throughout the last century, suburban sprawl and low density shopping malls have unpicked this urban tapestry and reversed the process of intensification.

We also lost rich farmland. In pursuit of spacious housing to improve family life, we lost perhaps 15,000 sq. kms of countryside. In 1901, I suggested that 32 million people occupied about 1.5% of the total land mass of England and Wales. A century later, to house 52 million people, we had built over 10% of the land (see page 28). A six-fold increase in land-take to house only 60% more people is not sustainable. However crude these figures, the drastic loss of green fields means that arable farming now relies heavily on artificial fertilizers, pesticides and prairie farming, livestock farming on drugs, battery farms and super dairies.

And third, suburban household privacy has severely curtailed social life. Fewer local shops, pubs and other facilities meant fewer chats between shopkeepers, customers and strangers, longer trips meant fewer pedestrians, buses and bikes, and more cars, pollution and danger. And it is the random nature of these meetings, in pubs and markets, on buses and pavements, that underpins social tolerance and urban civilization. As a footnote, some believe that the density provided by tower blocks is supported by Jacobs. This is false. Most tower blocks seldom achieve the density of terraces. They also create anti-social environments. Lifts are not streets; they actually discourage conversation. I return to sustainable housing and tower blocks in chapter 9.

iii)   Mixed uses – viability and vitality

The convenience of short streets and high density are undone if your nearest newsagent, school and workplace are over a mile away. Mixed uses are essential. The separate zoning of housing, industry, commerce, town centre and civic functions is inconvenient, inefficient and dull. Jacobs argued that mixing some work, leisure, community and civic facilities with housing generates pedestrian traffic throughout the day. This enlivens neighbourhoods and supports a range of 'secondary uses' such as newsagents, florists, betting shops, cafés, restaurants and pubs. A café that is busy throughout the day makes more efficient use of that building, generates a higher turnover, increases rental value and strengthens the local economy. Healthy local economies underpin social neighbourhoods.

Unfortunately, as with high density, mixed uses (including that abattoir in Cromac, Belfast and those piggeries in Preston) became indelibly linked with slums. While the Victorians did much to curb child labour and improve working conditions, largely through the emerging trade unions and legislation, they were largely indifferent to the external costs of noise and pollution. Rather than compel industry to clean up its operations, the difficult but sustainable choice, early planning sought to relocate 'dirty' industry outside urban areas. Sadly, zoning became entrenched just as the worst by-products of the Industrial Revolution were being eradicated. Electricity was much quieter and cleaner while legislation gradually reduced the dumping of toxic wastes on land and in rivers. By the 1950s, most industry could be classed as 'light industry', being that which is acceptable in residential areas – just when neighbourhoods had no factories left. Zoning, an early planning principle, was the easy choice that suited factory owner, developer and landowner, but it was the wrong choice.

Today there is little need to separate jobs and housing. Yet now most of our remaining manufacturing jobs, and many office services are being exported to China and India etc, with working conditions and pollution levels that would not be tolerated here. We return to the economics of empire in chapter 5. The first century of planning has largely eradicated mixed-use neighbourhoods through urban renewal and zoning. The suburbs never had them. And with the rise of 'customer choice', it is possible that zoning has become self-fulfilling. There is a noticeable trend that newcomers to a neighbourhood object not only to any new schemes there but also to existing businesses that have history there.

Sutton harbour in Plymouth has been the city's fishing port for centuries. Home to the substantial fishing fleet and fresh fish market (plus two marinas), with their associated on-shore buildings and activities, it is managed by the Sutton harbour company with its own Victorian Act of Parliament.

In the 1980s two large redundant warehouses by the harbour were sold and converted into flats, which merged into the general setting of harbour, commercial buildings and council housing blocks nearby. Some years later, another single-storey warehouse was redeveloped for a new block of maritime apartments. Thereafter, the harbour company started to receive complaints. Some incomers objected to the activities of the workshops, the oil on the quayside, the smell associated with the fishing fleet and, on one occasion, being woken up in the night by the distress siren of a vessel towing another ship that had got into difficulties.

In the 1990s, the harbour company had a choice: either sell its business and landholdings, or invest in the harbour. Had the company been part of a large corporation pushed by financial gain or debt obligations, it would have sold it as a 'major regeneration opportunity' for a maritime Cote de Plymouth with new apartments and offices overlooking the marinas – but no fishing fleet. Instead, the harbour company decided to remain, building a new harbour lock, a new fish market and other on-shore facilities. This secured existing jobs and created new ones, perhaps totalling 1,500, retained the economic and social character of the area and benefited the whole city. Conserving the fishing industry and improving harbour facilities was how this company balanced the forces of change and continuity. Incomers should welcome this heritage or move to the suburbs.

By contrast, the late-Victorian Hither Green hospital had a dozen two-storey isolation wards, various administration buildings, maintenance workshops, boiler room, central hall and other ancillary buildings, all set in landscaped grounds with mature trees and an imposing central water tower. It had served as the area's major employer and social 'anchor' for 100 years. In 1997, the hospital trust needed to raise money to invest in its other two hospitals. So Hither Green hospital was sold for redevelopment. Instead of converting the bulk of the solid historic buildings (with some new infill buildings where needed) to create a mix of flats and studios, local surgery, small workshops and modest community facilities, the site was redeveloped with typical Beazer homes in a gated community and a Tesco supermarket.

This comparison of hospital and harbour suggests a general planning principle – that in residential neighbourhoods, non-residential buildings should be retained for non-residential use, whether through conversion or redevelopment. Had Sutton harbour suffered the fate of Hither Green, it would have replaced an historic fishing industry and associated activities with yet more waterfront private flats and a few prestige office suites, overlooking the ubiquitous marina. Such 'regeneration schemes' put the short-term market force for profit over any long-term market forces for continuity – the difference between hoovers and anchors as discussed in chapter 5. It also highlights Jacobs' fourth essential for towns and cities – old buildings.

iv)   Old Buildings – and New Uses

Old buildings are essential. Oxford's colleges and Stoke's bottle kilns are rightly regarded as part of our national heritage, but this meaning of heritage is relatively recent. Although the roots of conservation might date back to *The Ancient Monuments Act 1882*, only from the late 1950s has heritage been defined as "a nation's historic buildings, monuments, countryside etc, especially when regarded as worthy of preservation." (*OED*) And English Heritage was only set up as an independent agency in 1983. Preserving the most precious buildings and monuments is now a part of the tourism (or heritage) industry. This industry either exploits our nostalgia for things past for commercial profit, or celebrates those same things that exemplify the best characteristics of our island nation, according to taste.

The root (*OED)* meaning of heritage, however, is "that which has been or may be inherited." This is much broader. Solid old buildings, with little architectural or historic interest, are valuable because, as Jane Jacobs saw, they are adaptable and cheap. Replacing old buildings with new may increase profits for owners and landlords, but cities lose opportunities to provide affordable premises for small businesses and start-ups, young couples and community venues. These all strengthen local economies, generate local pride and a sense of social continuity that may be as precious as a few priceless buildings.

As with area conservation, upgrading old buildings is cheaper and more sustainable than redevelopment. Granted sound foundations and structure, construction work is simpler, uses far less building materials, improves energy efficiency and extends the lifespan over centuries rather than decades. This makes economic sense, both for Listed Buildings or monuments of national importance (which usually command a premium over new buildings reflecting their intrinsic quality) and for local buildings of modest distinction but solid construction.

For Listed Buildings, it is important to find sympathetic uses.

- One of Europe's finest twentieth century civic buildings is the former GLC (Greater London Council) County Hall. After the GLC was abolished, the London School of Economics sought to move into the complex. Unfortunately it was outbid by a bank-led consortium that converted it into a hotel, private flats and some fish tanks in the basement. Privatizing an important public monument elevates private gain over social wealth, and benefits those who 'know the price of everything and the value of nothing'.

- By happy contrast, the Greenwich naval college, perhaps the grandest Baroque pile in this country, now houses Greenwich university.
- The Tate shows how monuments can increase social wealth, with Tate of the North occupying Liverpool's Albert Docks, the largest nineteenth century complex in Europe. It might have shared this complex with more public uses like a university wing or research centre instead of commercial offices, private flats, a maritime museum and some rather forlorn tourist shops, but that is secondary.
- Back in London, Tate Modern shows the potential in its reuse of Bankside power station. Unfortunately, the sublime and much larger Battersea power station, a landmark for the whole city, will be dwarfed among tower blocks of flats, many of which, on current trends, will be kept empty as 'investment vehicles'.

Unlisted buildings are much more robust. In a typical market town, the best old buildings beside the town centre usually house local solicitors and accountants. Larger towns with an industrial past will usually offer cheap workspace in old industrial estates and multi-storey mills and factories, plus occasional awkward sites for timber merchants and scaffolders' yards. Similarly, redundant schools and station buildings have potential (largely untapped) as business centres for incubating start-ups and small businesses.

Cornwall offers two modest examples. East Looe has a handsome Victorian chapel-of-ease between the seafront and the harbour. When this church was declared redundant, local community meetings came up with 78 suggestions for its re-use. These included a community centre, council office, library, museum (of fishing or bicycles), art gallery, small workshops, craft centre, sailing club, sports centre, indoor bowling alley, sheltered accommodation, a nursery playground, a walled garden – even a multi-storey car park within those same walls. Everyone wanted the building kept, including a local architect who, 'for a client in Birmingham', had shown how it could be converted into 14 time-share holiday flats. Subsequently the town council, with assistance from a housing association, converted it into 12 flats for local young people at affordable rent. Historic conservation and community benefit are not mutually exclusive.

Sometimes conservation and social objectives are in opposition. In another small town, the Conservation Area had retained most of its handsome original shopfronts, except for one shop. The shopkeeper committed most textbook mistakes in fitting out his shop, with pebble dash render and large plastic windows upstairs, Delabole slate veneer and out-of-scale fascia downstairs. Yet the (aptly named) Jolly Bodger was a helpful local retailer, offering friendly service and professional advice to customers, with cheaper prices than the DIY sheds outside town. Retaining quality in Conservation Areas is important, but superficial blemishes can be tolerated when supporting small businesses. Heritage purists should relax. The bodger's foibles are reversible and they are tiny compared to the visual and environmental blight of the retail sheds dumped in the nearby countryside.

Successive governments, however, have set one major obstacle to re-using old buildings. For many years now, VAT (at the full 20%) is charged on all building conversion and maintenance work – except interestingly on Listed Buildings. On the other hand, all new construction is VAT exempt. This disparity between maintaining the old and building the new is absurd. Until it is reversed, or at least equalized, the situation will only get worse. All our vital old buildings – both the historic and the useful – are at risk. This issue is ignored in the disgraceful *National Planning Policy Framework* (*NPPF*) which purports to support sustainable development. The main beneficiaries of this VAT largesse are developers, major housebuilders and architects, joining landlords of whom the economist David Ricardo said that "the interests of the landlord are opposed to the interests of every other section of society."

Collectively, old buildings are part of our heritage, recording centuries of architectural design and taste, building form and function, local materials and structural techniques, visual appeal and economic activity. Their loss also has a social impact. Destroying evidence of each town's unique history reduces the sense of place and local pride in each neighbourhood, sweeps away the comfort of familiar streets and buildings, leaving many people with a sense of loss, some even 'crying on the bus on their way home'.

When combined, Jane Jacob's four essentials of short streets, high density, old buildings and mixed uses create neighbourhoods that are convenient, efficient, interesting and friendly. She called this 'street theatre', in which everyone plays out their various roles in their social environment. And it is not simply a matter of size, number or scale. Ian Nairn called Llanidloes (in mid Wales with about 2,500 citizens) a pocket metropolis. Most commuter villages and dormitories, though twice as big, are not social, and Milton Keynes, the largest new town with a population of 184,500, is more like Los Angeles ('seventeen suburbs in search of a city') than Brighton.

Finally, twentieth century suburbs, garden cities and exurbs negate all four of her urban essentials and the 'natural' process of intensification:

1. long streets increase road traffic and inconvenience,
2. low densities promote privacy over proximity, social behaviour and farmland,
3. zoning increases road traffic and weakens local economies, and
4. the needless loss of old buildings is incomprehensible, enriching landowners and developers at the expense of local economies and social stability.

Cities and beehives

If cities are innate to the species, our human behaviour can be compared to that of social insects with their heaps and hives. Analogies can be useful but treacherous. They may help us to understand the structure and nature of cities, but there are risks. We might strain similarities between subject and analogue, ignore differences that undermine the analogy and draw conclusions that are dubious or false. Using analogies to guide policy is positively dangerous. The city may indeed resemble a body with its heart in the city centre, or a hospital with freeways linking neighbourhoods as corridors link wards (from chapters 4 and 6) but using them prescriptively to redesign cities can lead us wildly astray. My analogy is purely descriptive, to clarify the nature of our social behaviour. Even the differences are instructive.

Among the social insects, I have selected bees for their diversity (within the order *Hymenoptera)*. Various bees are solitary, living like hermits, while several bumble bees live in nests of about 200, rather like our tribal villagers perhaps. But it is honey bees (*Apis mellifera*) that most closely resemble humans in their behaviour, with physical, economic and social similarities between hive and city.

Physically, both serve Braudel's functions of shelter, security and trade. Both build permanent settlements for large populations, built to a common pattern with distinct types of accommodation for their residents, stores for their produce and channels for moving throughout the settlement. Both are continuously maintained and, in the event of severe damage, quickly rebuilt to the existing pattern. After the Great Fire, for example, central London was rebuilt to the existing medieval street pattern (unlike post-was Coventry and Plymouth centres).

Hives accommodate up to 50,000 bees, but there seems to be no limit on cities. Both provide shelter and security against external threat, in which residents collectively protect and maintain their society. Whether cities (like termite mounds that occasionally collapse under their own weight) may yet collapse is a moot point. Some American cities are close to breaking point. (Forgive my use of Detroit, but it shows that their urban failures are due largely to non-physical factors.)

Both exploit their rural hinterland; hives within four miles, market towns historically from 12 to 20 miles. Bees simply forage and store the necessary nectar and pollen within that radius. With agriculture, cities are also self-sufficient. What is unusual is that both species store any surplus for the whole community, not just for individuals like squirrels. This greatly enhances long-term survival prospects for both settlement and species. However, while hives are absolutely self-sufficient and need their surpluses to survive winter, cities can also use surpluses to trade with others, increasing local wealth and chances of survival.

Other similarities might loosely be called **economic**. In both hive and city there is considerable division of labour. This is rare. In other social species like rookeries and warrens, families group together but there is no division of labour or storage of surplus food. Each family looks after its own nest or den. Honey bees and humans are different. Every worker bee performs the full range of jobs throughout her six-week life span: general cleaning duties, nursery care, serving the queen, ventilating passages, building and repairing the hive, setting honey, capping cells, maintaining stores and disposing the dead, before venturing outside, first on guard duty against intruders and, in the last half of her life, foraging for nectar and pollen. Human workers only differ in that each tends to train and spend most of their working lives in specific trades.

Only cities, however, develop beyond their natural boundaries through trade, acting as regional centres, city states, national capitals and the occasional hub of empire.

Socially, too, there are similarities. Perhaps division of labour has created a similar class structure in hives and cities, but this is superficial. The queen bee is not a ruler, the many workers are all female, and the few drones may resemble those pampered members of the Drones' Club (founded by P G Wodehouse), but then sacrifice their lives when, on their Spring mating flights, they find a queen, have sex and die. By contrast, humans have developed a command structure, from despotism and autocracy to democracy and the occasional anarchy, in all their differing varieties.

More significant is how society is managed. Hives and cities achieve a level of permanent self-containment that is based on mutual dependence. Bees seem to manage their affairs entirely communally. In late Spring, when crops, weather and (possibly?) conditions seem right for a hive to split, the queen and half the workers swarm to set up a second hive, leaving behind half the workers and a dozen or more queen eggs, from which a new queen will emerge. Building a new town today is usually decided by a ruling elite, but most old towns spawned new settlements whose founders selected locations favourable for trade.

The most interesting social feature of honey bees and humans is that both use symbolic language. This is almost certainly unique in the animal kingdom. Most animals communicate, of course, but use an inchoate range of grunts and growls, yelps and yowls, whoops and shouts to express possession, desire, hunger or danger, plus non-vocal actions to teach offspring successful behaviour by example, or reprove them with cuffs and bites. In the beehive, the honey bee tells her fellow workers exactly where a source of food is, or (in a swarm) where a new hive might be built. The waggle dance shows direction of the site in relation to the sun, its distance from the hive, and how good the site is – by the direction, length and excitement of the waggle. This is efficient. She does not have to take her fellow workers there, and the information is constantly updated as others return. It also enables older workers to forage on sites with only modest amounts of food that are closer to the hive so they can work to the end of their life span. So far as we know, only humans share this ability to communicate hard information about the external world.

Beehives (as well as the heaps, mounds and nests of other social insects) also create what biologists call supra-organisms. Each colony resembles an organism, for example, in the way it maintains a constant 'body' temperature of 38 Centigrade (the same as the human body), or when it replicates itself by swarming. Among mammals, only humans (and naked mole-rats) are comparable in their mutual inter-dependence of the individual and the community. Cities, in their social products and progress, might also be supra-organisms.

The major difference between hive and city is in their genetic diversity. Hives are relatively homogenous. The queen is mother to all the residents: her few hundred sons, the drones, are her unfertilized clones; her daughters, up to 50,000 in midsummer, may have no more that 20 fathers. This genetic puddle may explain the uniformity of each hive's hexagonal wax comb. By contrast, towns and cities are small oceans for the exchange of genes, stewpots that promote social and sexual intercourse between people from across the spectrum of ability, background and character. In civilized cities, social tolerance resembles the communal hive, but personal creativity and the clash of ideas (including anti-social greed and racism in less civilized cities) are distinctive.

This analogy suggests an hypothesis: that in contrast to the structural uniformity of beehives, the rich complexity of cities reflects three levels of genetic diversity or social technology: the personal diversity of buildings, the social wealth of public monuments, and the genetic code for cities throughout the species.

1. Personal diversity is expressed in our vernacular buildings. Cities comprise a number of dense neighbourhoods with modest houses interspersed with a mix of commercial and social buildings. The visual diversity of shopfronts and awnings, front porches and loft conversions, materials and plants, plastic and pebble dash all reflect the fashions and functions of personal needs, taste and wealth. This vernacular diversity, like the genetic differences found within families, is modest and comforting, and creates townscapes of distinctive charm.

2. Deeper social diversity is displayed in monumental buildings. Cathedrals, churches and chapels, guildhalls, market halls and city halls, schools and universities, theatres and stadiums, galleries and museums, hospitals and railway terminals, municipal parks and ceremonial avenues all perform social functions. In them, we can trace 'progress' in architecture – from the Greek post and lintel to the Roman barrel vault and dome, the Gothic pointed arch, timber, concrete and steel frames, curtain walling, cantilevers and suspended roofs etc. These public monuments reflect social rather than private wealth and genetic 'mutations' shared by all. (Private monuments that reflect excessive private wealth and corporate power are discussed in chapter 9.)

3. Underlying the diversity of vernacular and monumental buildings, however, is the basic form of cities which may be in the genetic makeup of the species. All develop around a central area where two or more trade routes cross. From that forum, all development fronts a web of highways, however modest, that provide access to every building as well as to other neighbourhoods and to farms, villages and towns beyond. Tightly developed streets provide shelter, play space, rear privacy and overall security in numbers. Underneath, the social invention of water pipes and sewers, probably dating back to c2,500 BC in Mohenjo-daro in the Indus valley, improved city life immeasurably. And following the railways came underground metros. These all required major public investment, but they made cities more efficient and improved social life

for all. Such improvements found their way into every city, whether through trade or 'cultural transmission'. But the essential point is that they retained the structural integrity of existing cities as dense collections of neighbourhoods clustered around city centres.

The glory of the city is in this mix of physical diversity and continuity. The diversity within and between the vernacular and the monumental is also found in most economic and social aspects of city life – between family life and public events, work and play, commerce and charity, politics and religion, art and science, craft and technology, private and social wealth. It is the basic genetic consistency of cities, however, that gives them their stability. This basic urban structure of neighbourhoods and streets gives everyone not just individual freedoms but also shared experiences. These occur in a relatively permanent environment, where we see the germ of liberty, equality and fraternity, and the development of social roots, a sense of belonging and ownership, of pride, tolerance and security – the true value of continuity. This urban form can still be found in most of Europe, see Figure 4 opposite.

Urban entropy 1: cities function best in a steady built state

By way of summary, from a biological analogy, let me conclude Part 1 by introducing the concept of entropy. To physicists, it is "a measure of the *un*available energy in a physical system. Since usable energy is lost in irreversible transfers, entropy increases in closed systems (the second law of thermodynamics)." (Honderich 1995) To the novelist Yevgeny Zamyatin (in *We*), there are "two forces in the world, entropy and energy. The first leads to blissful peace, to happy equilibrium; the other, to the destruction of equilibrium, to agonisingly perpetual motion." This is the difference between stasis and activity, utopia and town, garden suburb and social neighbourhood, central control and local diversity, between the Shard and a shanty.

Now (with apologies to physicists) cities are huge stores of energy. In high entropy cities, that energy is embedded and unusable, monopolized and unavailable, or withdrawn altogether. In low entropy cities, that energy is shared among the citizens, releasing their 'intellectual, social, and spiritual natures'. My five 'principles' of urban entropy deal with the following sources of energy:

1. physical energy is locked up in a city's urban fabric (from part 1 above),
2. economic energy is released by local firms or monopolized by global firms (chapters 4 and 5),
3. technological energy is more or less efficient in cars and buses (chapter 6),
4. financial energy is either stored privately or 'spread like manure' (chapter 7), and
5. political energy is released locally or controlled centrally (part 3).

My first principle of urban entropy recycles astronomer Fred Hoyle's (now discredited) Steady State theory of the universe. Cities were largely stable until about 1900. There was slow growth and evolution over centuries, with periodic setbacks

Figure 4: Urban conservation

Urban form based on density and diversity, in contrast to figures 2 and 3. Based on Foggia, (also on front cover), population c 155,000

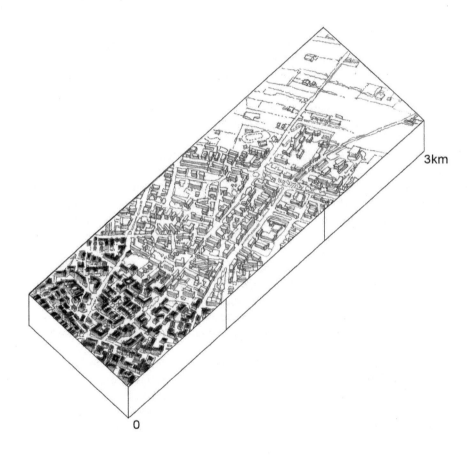

from wars and plagues. Centuries of centripetal development meant that cities were conserved, by repairing, adapting and extending existing buildings, with new buildings only to house new residents and businesses, and only rebuilding those that were beyond repair or burnt-down. If conserving an existing building consumes one unit each of labour, energy and materials, then a new building would consume at least five units of labour, ten units of energy and twenty of materials. Redevelopment would consume even more. Conserving urban fabric is low entropy, and releases construction energy for other purposes. It gives towns and cities a stability that allows other activities to develop and civilization to flourish. In other words, small is beautiful. Even when it isn't, its impact is modest as with those piggeries in central Preston.

The first century of planning disrupted this stability, first with a centrifugal force into suburbia and second with implosive redevelopment of urban neighbourhoods. The astronomers' Big Bang theory had arrived, both metaphorically and physically. The semi-detached villas and industrial crinkley sheds of suburban estates and exurban parks may embed only slightly more labour energy. But in their sprawl, they consume valuable farmland as well as building materials, and embed large amounts of drive time, fuel energy and valuable urban land for freeways and car parks.

At the same time, redeveloping whole neighbourhoods at lower densities reinforces the centrifugal sprawl. The new housing towers and slab blocks consume excessive levels of labour, energy and materials in construction, as well as subsequent energy and maintenance costs. This is a key distinction between monuments and vernacular buildings. Public monuments have high costs and entropy, but these are offset by real social benefits. Private monuments bring few social benefits for their high entropy levels.

Occasionally, cities suffer major shocks, as with Lisbon's earthquake in 1755 or the fire of London in 1666, which destroyed 436 acres of buildings. Of the many ambitious rebuilding plans, most critics regret the failure to push through Wren's Baroque plan, though I think his avenues, squares and monuments would have been overbearing and dull. But that is irrelevant. The area had to be rebuilt: it was just a question of how.

Few redevelopments since 1900 can be so justified. Most recent waterside projects display this empty rhetoric of the megalith: Belfast Lough, Cardiff Bay, Edinburgh's Louth, Salford Quays, Liverpool's Docks, urban canal sites and almost anywhere along the Thames. Of one such scheme, the developer gushed as follows: "Remastering ... Quay to introduce iconic, cohesive architecture in a beautifully landscaped environment reflects our ambitions for the wider [area] and sets the tone for the quality of development being brought forward." Landscaping usually means trees in car parks, but iconic and cohesive architecture is a new oxymoron.

Formerly, small schemes served their owners' self-interest, with little impact on their physical, economic and social setting. Today, the intrinsic value of conservation and continuity has given way to perpetual change and new icons. Suburbs have covered farmland and urban megaliths have destroyed neighbourhoods, both fuelled by developer greed, designer egos and egregious government policies enforcing a 'presumption in favour of development', VAT that actually encourages redevelopment and market-defying compulsory purchase. The self-interest of the fat cats behind these schemes is apparent, but the social benefits are as fleeting as the Cheshire cat's grin.

Unlike most European cities, London is beginning to resemble those new Arabian cities between desert and sea, where the wealthy stopover (they surely don't live there), flitting between airport, penthouse suite, restaurant and marina along eight-lane superhighways under dramatic skylines, all dependent on foreign workers and other slaves. When PG Wodehouse created the world of Bertie Wooster and the Drones club, he could hardly have foreseen that, a century later, the drones would have taken over so dramatically, creating disastrous environments in so many places.

Newton's first law of motion states that "A body continues in a state of rest or uniform motion in a straight line unless it is acted upon by external forces." Cities might be considered 'in a state of rest' when they are in their steady state, their 'motion in a straight line' merely describing the activities of citizens engaged in the daily routines of urban life. Apply a major external force, whether slum clearance, urban freeway or exurban retail park, and a city's 'state of rest' is seriously disturbed.

Consider Damascus. If we could travel back to any time in its 5,000-year history, we would need translators to decipher the coded messages and designs of the buildings, we would quickly appreciate the lack of those inventions that we take for granted, and perhaps find other innovations to marvel at. But we would instantly recognize and fairly quickly become familiar with the dense city with all its facilities within walking distance. There might be no plastic shopfronts and only river water to drink, but for most of its history, Damascus was a beacon of religious tolerance and quiet industry into which time travellers would soon assimilate.

During the twentieth century, we have lost that shared sense of urban diversity and physical continuity. Change is the mantra and cranes the measure of progress. Major forces for change, as we shall see in Part 2, are that large retailers have largely forsaken town centres, global firms have hollowed out local economies which are no longer hives of independent industry and services, and road traffic has facilitated urban sprawl at the expense of public transport, walking and cycling.

More specific to this review of physical development, our urban vernacular has completely changed. The vibrant vernacular of the high street has given way to the plastic veneers of shopping malls while our dense vernacular of terraced housing with shops and factories interspersed has been replaced by low density suburbs. These are resistant to small adaptations that over time create vernacular interest. Conservation through personal idiosyncrasy seems to have ceded to the stasis of preservation. This may reflect over-zealous planning control or the suburban homogeneity that makes homeowners reluctant to 'step out of line'. Social conformity may create these self-perpetuating enclaves (or ghettoes) where residents are much more likely to meet (and mate with) people from similar backgrounds, reinforcing social divisions of class, income and race.

We have also changed the concept of monumental development. Traditional domestic-scale terraced areas have been replaced with megalithic blocks and towers, often with alien circulation patterns and public buildings have been increasingly 'penny pinched' since 1979 – replaced with private monuments that confirm corporate status rather than social wealth. Libraries, schools and hospitals all too often have had to fight for sufficient funds as part of a much larger commercial regeneration project in which the bankers, developers, consultants and owners seek cost savings. Not only are most of London's rash of towers owned by global corporations and billionaires, but the properties, however physical their presence, are owned offshore to evade all property taxes.

As a final generalization, we have followed the American experience of urban growth through suburbs, freeways and superstores, while also bulldozing whole areas to regenerate inner cities. As we shall see in chapter 8, we have also centralized most planning functions and overloaded them with bureaucracy and statutory procedures. Thus, we achieved the worst of both worlds – the neo-con American nightmare managed by a bureaucratic Big Brother.

Before leaving urban morphology, let me pay belated tribute to Ebenezer Howard and encapsulate the preceding three chapters by revising his three magnets for the twentieth century. Needless to say, they are generalizations.

The three forces of modern urbanism

New towns and suburbs (created by Brahma – the American dream)
1. large scale low density garden cities or amorphous suburban sprawl
2. loss of about 6,000 square miles of countryside in a century
3. private motoring at expense of public transport and walking
4. small buildings with garages in leafy avenues
5. no diversity – monocultural areas for housing, commerce and employment
6. private property and privacy rather than neighbourhoods and local facilities
7. no relation to existing urban form – shapeless, repetitive, verdant, dull
8. suburbs supply-led by developers and landowners, unpopular with NIMBYs
9. unsustainable, excessive use of fuel, energy, building materials and farmland
10. do not trust volume housebuilders
11. planner as midwife
12. *The Truman Show*

Slums and renewal areas (destroyed by Shiva – and Big Brother)
1. large scale medium density monumental projects, 'concrete jungles'
2. urban destruction and uprooted communities – perhaps half to overspill estates
3. convenient for walking and local public transport services
4. large structures with communal gardens and parking
5. no diversity – monocultural housing estates, shopping malls or freeways
6. emphasis on affordable housing and shared space
7. no relation to surrounding urban form, 'the shock of the new', anomie
8. supply-led by normative planning, upheaval unpopular with those affected

9. unsustainable, excessive use of energy, materials and social upheaval
10. do not trust regenerators
11. planner as surgeon
12. *Blade Runner*

Existing neighbourhoods (preserved by Vishnu)
1. existing high density buildings adapted and re-used over time, plus small infills
2. historic townscapes retained with stable population and urban footprint
3. convenient for walking and local public transport services
4. no change on existing mix of buildings, gardens and parking
5. diversity to create a rich visual tapestry of functions and activities
6. settled communities, multi-cultural areas and wealthy enclaves close together
7. 800 years of townscape, continuity of scale, density and street pattern
8. demand-led by occupiers, very popular but too often over-ruled
9. sustainable – reusing buildings, reducing waste and retaining communities
10. trust conservators
11. planner as general practitioner
12. *Gone With the Wind ?*

Part Two
Urban Diversity, Forces for Change

Chapter Four: Town Centres

P art 1 outlined the function of cities and how they developed and evolved. We now pass onto Tinbergen's third question (page 16) and look for the causes underpinning the physical changes of the last century. We focus on perhaps the most important social and economic activities – shopping, work and transport – largely because of the visible hegemony of retail sheds, global firms and road traffic. Together, these have made our cities less efficient, sociable and resilient.

We start with town centres, priceless in their compressed diversity, because they are the most visible and popular aspect of our urban heritage. Commercial, civic and cultural buildings include department stores, shops, market stalls and kiosks, Crown post office, central library, banks, professional offices, insurance brokers and estate agents, town hall or civic centre, cafés, restaurants and hotels, pubs, clubs and inns, small workshops, printers, repair shops and perhaps a local bakery or brewery in side streets, with bus and rail stations, police and fire stations, church and chapel, cinema, theatre, snooker and concert halls, museum and art gallery, schools and college or university nearby and, above all the shops, commercial offices and private flats.

All town centres perform the same roles, but each is unique, offering a shop window into the health and wealth of the whole town. Each has its landmark buildings and brash shopfronts, dignified monuments and noisy markets, busy pavements and quiet gardens. Before Jane Jacobs' *Death and Life*, few understood that congestion was an inevitable consequence of this dense mix of commerce, civics and culture that stretched back over centuries. That was their success and fascination.

Throughout the twentieth century, there has been an exodus.

- First factories and mills relocated from edge of town centre sites to edge of town industrial estates. From multi-storey buildings to single-storey sheds, plus a few substantial Art Deco plants, each was pushed from high value sites, or pulled to cheap green fields.

- New county halls and civic centres also found their own peripheral sites in the thirties and fifties, followed by many district councils after local government reorganization in 1974.
- In the late sixties, new universities such as East Anglia, Kent, Keele and Sussex all developed green field campuses. And from the 1980s, many new secondary schools, colleges and hospitals followed suit – again exchanging valuable urban sites for green fields under Private Finance Initiatives.
- And throughout the twentieth century, there has been a silent exodus of residents from flats over the shops, leaving valuable floorspace vacant and town centres less sociable at night time.

Now even the shops are leaving. The first wave, from the 1930s but quickening after the war as industry continued to decline, left to convert vacant warehouses and factories into large shops selling furniture, electrical goods, DIY, auto parts and other bulk items. This was cheap and suited both landlords and motorists. After the war, it became cheaper to demolish the vacant buildings and replace them with the ubiquitous retail sheds.

War instigated a second option for new shops: comprehensive town centre redevelopment following the examples of Coventry and Plymouth. Lewis Keeble (1964) set the tone for dissatisfaction with old towns, which "applies with special force to the town centre, which has generally grown in so haphazard and unsatisfactory a fashion that existing forms provide little guide to satisfactory Planning ... [I]nvariably the town centre, which should be the area of greatest accessibility in the town, remains the least accessible part of it, around and within which movement is most difficult and parking space for vehicles hardest to find." Few saw that congestion meant success and that it could be managed.

Like others before and since, Keeble did not like conservation, confusion or congestion. So he simply rebuilt whole town centres. The following text shows his *Principles*. "A typical ENGLISH TOWN CENTRE [showing] the disadvantages which inevitably attach to such an arrangement at the present time can be removed simply, without undue expense and without disrupting the building pattern." New shops and car parks within new ring roads reflected the sublime arrogance of Le Corbusier and others, with all the subtlety of the bulldozer. "The brain, heart, lungs and belly of the city," as in Apollodorus' Rome (page 59), were simply wrong. This mania for rebuilding suited developers and large retailers, motorists and the roads lobby. But it is a plague, and ignores most European practice of investing in public transport so that town centres were left relatively undisturbed.

Few cities could follow Coventry and Plymouth. Most simply redeveloped rundown central areas with shopping malls and inner ring roads (as described in chapter 2). This kept shops in town, but sucked much of the pedestrian footfall out of the high street.

With CDAs (comprehensive development areas) came our first public/private partnerships. The local council would seek planning approval through public inquiry and compulsorily buy the land and businesses affected. The developers would then build the mall, find tenants and sell the investment onto pension funds and insurance companies. However, the process was expensive (with no economies of scale through repetition) and very time-consuming, It was also divisive, with compulsory purchase favouring developers, large retailers and pension funds against the interests of those shops directly affected and the town centre generally.

The exurban 'shopping mall' was invented by another modern architect and city planner. Victor Gruen (1903-80) designed Northland Mall outside Detroit in 1954, and followed it with his 800,000 sq. ft. Southdale Mall in Edina, Minnesota. Since then, the US has built 43,000 shopping centres, of which about 1,500 are larger regional malls. "A wartime émigré from Europe, Gruen... saw the shopping centre as a place for modern community life "like that of the ancient Greek Agora, the Medieval marketplace and our own Town Square." A stage director in his youth, Gruen was also the first to realize the potential for dramatizing the mall with lighting, colour, and art, as if it were a stage set. In the 1980s, disillusioned by the loss of civic values that accompanied commercial real estate development, Gruen returned to his native Vienna." (Washburn and Thornton 1997)

In this country, our first 'retail parks' were built in the countryside from the mid-1970s. These were followed by science and leisure parks, corporate headquarters, hotels and distribution centres. All relied on easy access by car. Brent Cross in north London opened in 1976, to be followed by the Metrocentre near Newcastle, Meadowhall outside Sheffield, the White Rose centre in Leeds, Merry Hill in Greater Birmingham, Cribbs Causeway outside Bristol, Trafford in Greater Manchester, two centres serving Glasgow, four centres in Wales (near Bridgend, Llanelli, Newport and Swansea) and off the M25, Lakeside in Essex and, less than 10 miles away, Bluewater Park in Kent. Regional parks affect nearby centres. When Merry Hill opened, nearby Dudley lost 70% of its trade and Birmingham 10% (Roger Tym and Partners 1993).

Town centres might have survived all this new competition from retail sheds, shopping malls and retail parks so long as the convenience sector, including food, remained. It was not to be. During the 1980s in England, some 900 large supermarkets were built, most of them out of town. This increased "the proportion of all retail sales in out-of-town stores... from under 5% to 17%". This trend has continued. By 2000, town and district shops only accounted for 53.9% of total retail floorspace, with 16.9% in town centre malls. Outside town centres, superstores had 14.3%, retail parks, regional malls and factory outlets had a combined 15.8% of floorspace (*Planning* 20/10/1999). Over a third of trade is now in exurban sheds and parks. Unfortunately, without a national Census of Distribution, it is impossible for ordinary mortals to gauge the precise impact of these sheds on existing town and district centres. And while no regional parks have been built this century, today's e-commerce has probably reduced turnover in shops and sheds by a further 10%.

After over 800 years of continuity with town centres anchored by their shops, the disruption largely since 1979 has produced great uncertainty for both shopkeepers and landlords. All stable doors were thrown open, allowing major retailers and developers to decide what and where to build, unfettered by any planning concerns for town centres and green fields. Unsurprisingly, most retailers bolted, preferring cheap land with good road access for their sheds. This left most town centres on an ebb tide – cast adrift as increased motoring encouraged all large retailers to slip anchor. Slowly drained of pedestrians and unable to attract new investment, many town centres are becoming quiet one-stop shops during the day, rowdy drinking dens in the evenings.

Yet in this march to exurbia, the market has actually reduced the overall quality of shopping in terms of experience, access, choice, value and external costs.

Shopping experience

"A bicycle shed is a building. Lincoln Cathedral is a piece of architecture." (Pevsner)

The compressed diversity of town centres has three important aspects.
- Centuries of investment in civic buildings, shopfronts, street markets, leisure facilities, parks and other landmarks fix those all-important first impressions, before one has stepped inside any building.
- This functional mix of commerce, civics and culture animates town centres socially, supporting a whole range of secondary functions like eating and drinking, various services and small workshops.
- This interdependence, noted in chapter 3, means that all buildings are used more efficiently, rents and capital value rise, and the local economy is strengthened.

Even modest market towns retain this historic, social and economic diversity. In Knighton, on the Welsh border, the weekly cattle market dates back centuries. Farmers 'invade' the town on market day selling their cattle and sheep, doing some weekly shopping, meeting neighbours and bank managers and using local hotels, pubs and cafés. This market also supported some 15 businesses in the town, including the auctioneer, a feed supplier, seed merchants, a tractor garage, land agent, NFU office and several other specialists. Late last century, there was a scheme to relocate the cattle market and redevelop the auction site for a supermarket and housing. This would have made commercial sense for the developer and supermarket, but not for the town. The relocated market and ancillary services might have survived on some green field, but it would have left commercial premises vacant, closed many local food shops and reduced social town life by ending the weekly congestion and social theatre that is market day. (Unusually, Knighton also has a successful specialist factory that makes and refurbishes heavy-duty tractors for work in marine environments.)

At its heart, there is a contradiction in the word. Supermarkets are not markets where you can move through the high street and market square, comparing the range, quality and price of foods as well as their service. Supermarkets are simply foodsheds with till queues. The quality of what they sell is discussed later.

On the shopping experience, despite the idealism of Victor Gruen, foodsheds, shopping malls and retail parks are widely perceived to be dull, even by children. This relates to their appearance and lack of diversity. Most malls and parks have a charmless bulk, often cloaked with a pretentious veneer of plastic Tudorbethan, mock Georgian or fashionable black glass. Foodsheds are cheap bulky air-conditioned sheds surrounded by acres of tarmac on cheap land. There is nothing inherently wrong with sheds. Many of our train sheds are sublime marvels of Victorian engineering. But only rarely do foodsheds show an occasional flash of incongruity. My particular favourites include brutal concrete blocks in Gravesend and Redruth from the 1960s and, about 30 years later, cheap black glass frontages in Cork and Prague – all Tesco foodsheds. Rather than investing in their shops and factories, as the wealthy Victorians did, today's retailers reflect the business trend to release capital for running the business and easing cash flow, replacing architecture with sheds (see chapter 5).

Retail parks also reflect a more serious planning attitude for tidiness and zoning. Large cities have other functional ghettoes. The City of London, one of the world's major business centres, is almost lifeless in the evenings and at weekends. London's two cultural ghettoes; the splendid 'Albertopolis' around the Albert Hall and national museums in south Kensington, and the South Bank concrete jungle with Royal Festival Hall, National Theatre and Haywood Gallery, are both largely lifeless. In Liverpool, the Walker Art Gallery, Picton Library, City Museum and St George's Hall opposite Lime Street station are all magnificent buildings but exist in a sterile environment partly ruined by heavy traffic. Retail parks have this same drearyness but without the splendid architecture.

As retail parks and sheds reduce customers in existing town centres, these are increasingly polarized, serving either the haves or the have-nots. Thriving cities and historic towns like Leeds, Bristol, York and Oxford are successfully competing with out-of-town sheds, reflecting the low yields retained in their central areas. Cities in decline, even as noble as Liverpool, and too many industrial and market towns show signs of stress. Budget shops outnumber national chains, vacancy levels reach 15%, Monday morning queues form outside local foodsheds (selling off the fruit and veg left over from Saturday), and sales even in charity shops are frequent. These signs deter further investment.

Galbraith's private wealth and public squalor have become segregated. The manicured privately-policed setting of retail parks attract the comfortable classes indulging in 'retail therapy', even if the trip involves an hour's drive. Some even complain of time poverty. This problem of wealth sits uncomfortably with real time poverty among the poor, many of whom struggle to rear a family by commuting between cheap suburban lodgings and two very low-paid part-time jobs curtesy of night buses. That is poverty exacerbated by time poverty.

The social profile of public squalor – yob culture, rowdy behaviour, street begging and binge drinking etc – is usually associated with poor town centres. Yet it is precisely in those vulnerable centres where one sometimes finds a social mix, low prices and a lively street atmosphere animated by a street market.

However, the loss of convenience and comparison shops to retail sheds means that town and district centres have shifted towards service outlets. This national trend can be seen in a study of two east London suburban centres.

Table 9: Retail shift in a suburban centre, 1937-2001

Shops – Number (%)	1937	1969	1998	2001
Convenience shops:	26 (45)	39 (37)	26 (24)	23 (22)
Comparison shops:	14 (24)	41 (39)	38 (36)	29 (27)
Service outlets:	6 (10)	25 (24)	36 (34)	40 (38)
Vacant units:	12 (21)	1 (1)	7 (7)	14 (13)
Total:	58	106	107	106

Source: LB Havering and Tellus 42

In more detail, from 1969, here are the changes in each sector. Convenience shops declined from 39 to 23, including bakers (5 to 3), butchers (5-3), chemists (no change at 3), cobblers (0-1), fishmongers (3-1), greengrocers (5-2), national chains (2-3), newsagents and confectioners (7-3), off licences (1-1), and grocers (6-3).

Comparison shops, also down from 41 to 29, included bike shops (only 1), car parts (1), charity shops (0-4), childrenswear (2-1), electrical goods (4-2), fashion and menswear (8-2), florists and garden shops (2-3, furniture/carpets (5-3), giftware/cards (1-3), haberdashers (5-0), hardware and household (2), jewellers (1), mobile phones (0-1), pet shops (2-1), shoe shops (5-1), soft furnishings (1-0), sportswear (1-2), video hire (0-1),

Service outlets, by contrast, increased from 25 to 40. These include banks and building societies (3-5), betting shops (2), dry cleaners (4), estate agents (2-5), beauty salons and hairdressers (4-7), photographers (2-1), printers and stationery (0-1), opticians (0-1), pubs (1), restaurants and takeaways (5-12), and travel agents (2-1).

This range of services is inadequate compensation for the loss of regular trips to your local butchers and newsagents and those comparison shops whose traders can offer specialist advice on what they stock. In both, shopping can be as much a social occasion as a commercial transaction.

During that study, I asked a school class of ten-year olds to compare the borough's main town centre with the nearest retail park. For the town centre, all comments were positive – lots of shops, pedestrian areas, shelters, parking, the railway station, the new shopping scheme, the cinemas, Sainsbury's, McDonald's, the arcades, sweet machines (for candy floss and ice cream), local events and the large street market. For the retail park, the children mentioned three things – lots of parking, sheltered pedestrian areas and the popular bear factory.

We have not yet reached the nadir that is the American retail experience. "If you do not know U.S. 41, then you do not live in the United States of America, and you are unfamiliar with any redline highway that crisscrosses the nation and spreads blight upon the countryside. The *Tamiami Trail* may once have been just that, a dirt track hacked out through the palmettos and palms, but them days is gone for ever, Gertie. Today, U.S. 41 is a four- (and sometimes six-) lane concrete thoroughfare lined for miles and miles with fast-food emporiums, gift shops, car washes, gasoline stations, pizzerias, furniture stores, nurseries, carpet salesrooms, automobile dealers, shopping malls, movie theatre complexes, and a variety of one-storey cinderblock shops selling plaster figurines, citrus fruit, discount clothing, rattan pool and garden furniture, cigarettes and beer (free ice if you buy a case), stereo equipment, lamps, vacuum cleaners, typewriters, burglar alarms, swimming pools, and (the only such shop in all Calusa), adult marital aids, games, and reading material. In short, U.S. 41 is your typical American highway bazaar, ugly and blaring and tasteless." (McBain 1984)

Convenience and access

In any city, simple geometry shows that the centre is the most efficient location for all important civic, cultural and commercial activities. Average trip lengths are little more than half the city radius (or less than half with dense inner neighbourhoods). Today, however, more than a third of all shopping trips to exurban sites are at least double those trip lengths. That means longer drive times, or two bus trips each way, or longer bus trips that now detour to new foodsheds before or after their town centre stops.

Diverse town centres allow people to combine two or three activities on each trip, like shopping, meeting friends or swimming after a hospital visit. Disperse these functions round the perimeter and trips become both longer and more frequent. This increases road congestion on all main roads, dangerous levels of pollution and rat running in side streets while, with new freeways, reducing town centre access for buses, pedestrians and cyclists (see chapter 6). Too little has been invested in public transport or traffic calming to make cycling and walking safer.

Once in these retail parks, however, access to the shops is far superior to that found in most town centres. Internal streets with smooth surfaces, wide entrances and no kerbs or steps allow easy access for wheelchairs, pushchairs and shopping trolleys.

Apart from their location, the other inconvenience has been caused, at least since 1971, by the sharp reduction in the number of shops as the sheds got bigger.

Table 10: Retail sector trends in Great Britain, 1971-2001

	1971*	1991	2001
Single retailers			
• business/outlet no	403,876	205,641	173,113
• no employed (000s)	1,608	759	708
• retail turnover (£bn)	6.3	34.2	35.3
Small chains**			
• business no	-	25,510	22,212
• no of outlets	-	65,574	51,575
• no employed (000s)	-	305	270
• retail turnover (£bn)	-	15.5	15.4
Large multiples			
• business no	-	894	1,237
• no of outlets	82,822	71,107	65,306
• no employed (000s)	953	1,303	1,401
• retail turnover (£bn)	7.2	82.9	105.9
Total retail trade			
• business no	-	232,045	196,563
• no of outlets	485,346	342,321	289,996
• no employed (000s)	2,562	2,367	2,379
• retail turnover (£bn)	16.2	132.5	156.6

Source: ONS *Annual Abstract of Statistics*

* Since 1971 (the date of the last complete census of distribution), annual statistics have been based on 5% or 10% surveys for its 'intermediate' inquiries.
** Up to 1971, figures for single retailers and small chains were combined.

In 30 years, the near tenfold increase in total turnover was spent in less than 60% of the shops, and these fell from 8.77 shops/1,000 people to 5.1. In Victorian Birmingham (chapter 2), it was 17.9 shops/1,000. This may suggest efficiency. Tesco had 771 branches in 1974 but only 377 stores in 1987, while its turnover rose from £1bn to over £2bn between 1979 and '82. Yet fewer shops increase car mileage, journey times and aggregate travel costs. And as we shall see in chapter 9, there are fewer shops in lower density neighbourhoods.

Choice – market or supermarket

As the major retailers have increased their market share, so customer choice has reduced. For some decades now, the 20 largest UK retailers have controlled about half of all retail spending. In 2018 (with major acquisitions since 1991), these were Tesco (UK turnover £40.2bn), Sainsbury's (including Argos, £28.5bn), Asda (£21.7bn), Morrisons (plus Safeway, £17.3bn), Marks and Spencer (£10.7bn), Dixons (merged with Carphone Warehouse, £10.5bn), John Lewis Partnership (£10.2bn), The Co-op (£9.5bn), Next (£4.1bn), B&Q (£3.8bn), Sports Direct (£3.4bn), J D Sports (£3.2bn), Primark (UK turnover perhaps £3bn), Debenhams (from the Burton group, £2.3bn), Wilco (£1.5bn), W H Smith (£1.3bn), Superdrug (£1.2bn), Halfords (£1.1bn) and Greggs (£1.0bn), plus privately-owned Arcadia (from the former Burtons clothes shops) and Boots (£3.7bn turnover in 1991), for which figures are not available. Restricting half of all food and goods sold to 20 buyers is unhealthy.

What makes town centres special are the local independents. These include the specialist or 'destination' retailers who attract customers from much greater distances because the shopkeeper has developed a niche market and offers expertise, customer care and after-sales service, whether in clothes, kitchen equipment, exotic pets, motorcycle spares, model railways, furnishings, ceramic tiles or galleries, etc. There are also the recyclers who work best when clustered in groups to create a destination market. These include antiques and junk shops, charity shops, old and nearly new clothes, second hand books and furniture, ephemera, records, stamps and other collectables. Bermondsey enjoyed a national reputation for its antiques market, around which antique shops, furniture restorers and antiques manufacturers (!) settled. Hay-on-Wye, once a pleasant market town, was transformed almost single-handedly into a vast secondhand bookshop. While Hay has retained its local shops, perhaps helped by this influx of booksellers and visitors, Bermondsey, alas, has suffered an influx of developers transforming the area into an enclave for the wealthy. And finally, all the small independent food shops formed a cluster.

This diversity is at risk as the relationship between national retailers and local independents breaks down. Large chains and department stores pulled in the crowds, the lifeblood of any centre, while local shops offered specialist goods and more personal service. Chains went for volume, shops provided value. This symbiosis between popular and specialist, national and local, is threatened as the chains leave town, leaving centres struggling with lower footfalls.

In this mix, comparison shops, convenience stores, specialists and various services are all important, but food has always been the anchor for all town centres. The dominance of the foodsheds (from table 11 opposite) poses a serious threat, and it is not typical for Europe.

Table 11: Market share of food retailers in Europe, 2002

Country	Large retailers %age (outlets)	Small retailers %age (shops)	Total food shops	Shops/1,000 population
Austria	91.3 (7,890)	8.7 (12,631)	20,521	2.5
Belgium	91.7 (3,229)	7.8 (18,610)	21,839	2.1
Denmark	85.8 (3,680)	14.1 (7,216)	10,896	2.0
Finland	82.7 (3,494)	17.4 (3,469)	6,963	1.3
France	79.5 (9,523)	20.5 (129,650)	139,173	2.5
Germany	63.6 (26,755)	36.4 (168,814)	185,569	2.3
Greece	53.7 (6,908)	46.2 (168,814)	55,450	5.3
Ireland	37.3 (233)	62.7 (11,025)	11,258	2.9
Italy	73.0 (14,983)	27.0 (226,064)	241,047	4.2
Netherlands	81.5 (9,249)	18.4 (17,154)	26,403	1.6
Norway	76.1 (4,892)	23.8 (7,014)	11,906	2.6
Portugal	90.4 (2,773)	9.6 (30,740)	33,513	3.3
Spain	74.0 (14,616)	26.1 (255,363)	269,979	6.8
Sweden	74.3 (3,746)	25.6 (6,933)	10,679	1.2
Switzerland	75.9 (2,699)	24.1 (11,547)	14,246	2.0
UK	83.3 (10,277)	16.8 (78,235)	88,512	1.5

Source: Euromonitor

Only Finland and Sweden have fewer shops/1,000 people. Only in the smaller nations of Austria, Belgium, Denmark and Portugal do the large food retailers (supermarkets, hypermarkets, co-ops and discounters) have bigger market shares than in the UK. The inverse holds for the market share of small retailers, comprising convenience stores, butchers, bakers, fishmongers, greengrocers and other food specialists. In countries of similar size to the UK:

- German large retailers only achieve a 63.6% market share despite having over two and a half times as many stores as the UK;
- France achieves a comparable market share for its large stores, largely through its 1,200 hypermarkets that control 41% of the market. Despite this, it retained a significant number of small shops, suggesting that local shopping is still important; and
- most graphically, there are only 1.3 small food shops per 1,000 people in the UK, compared with 2.1/1,000 in Germany, 2.2 in France, 3.9 in Italy and a healthy 6.5 shops/1,000 in Spain. As one Yorkshire shop window put it: "Your local butcher is for life, not just for Christmas."

It may be that we are in the shopping vanguard and our European neighbours are becoming more 'efficient' more slowly. On the other hand, only the former communist countries achieved such a centralized industry. Like them, we have little control in the matter since local councils are effectively denied the power of veto (see below).

In many areas, this dominance becomes a quasi-monopoly with over 50% of the grocery market; Tesco in Milton Keynes and Salisbury for example, Sainsbury's in south west London, and Morrisons (Safeway as was) in Dumfries (*The Observer*, 1/10/2000). Only after a third Groceries Market Investigation (July 2009) by the Competition Commission did it suggest a 60% limit in any local market. At the time, Tesco thought this threshold too low, Waitrose thought it should be lowered to 40%, and I would suggest 25%.

When four firms control up to 80% of their market, they form an oligopoly, from which no-one has found any lasting benefit to consumers. In fact the opposite is almost certainly true. In the US, such market dominance led to the Sherman (1890) and Clayton (1914) anti-trust Acts to break up 'monopoly capitalism' of the 'robber barons' (*Penguin Encyclopedia*). Corporate power is discussed in the next chapter.

And when four corporate buyers account for over three quarters of all food and drink sold, choice is reduced. No matter how big, no foodshed can match the range and quality of professional butchers, bakers, cheese and fishmongers, and specialist delicatessens. Near me, for example, are a Turkish supermarket with eight types of fresh olive and a whole range of feta, haloumi and hummus, an Indian 'cash and carry' with at least 30 different pulses and more than 60 herbs and spices available in three different sizes, a Chinese supermarket with a wide range of noodles and rice, an Italian deli with fresh parmesan and pesto sauces, an African shop with its exotic range of fruit and vegetables – and all offering their own packets and tins of mystery.

Every foodshed has a bland uniformity, distinguished solely by its colour branding. Economists call this the 'principle of minimum differentiation' (eg Lipsey 1975). The four foodsheds attract most of their customers from the middle 70% of the population. (M&S and Waitrose attract most of their customers from the wealthier half of the population, Aldi, Lidl, Iceland and street markets from the poorer half.) Each shed jostles around the market leader that positions its offer as close to the midpoint of this 15% to 85% income range in order to attract customers throughout the range. The other three then focus a little above or below that midpoint, but if one strays too far, setting its own plimsoll line at say 65%, what they gain from the upper 50% to 85%, will be counter-balanced by losses from the lower half of the range. They are thus in a perpetual dance in step with each others' purchases, their collective focus fixed firmly on the bottom line. Diversity from thousands of buyers supplying for all tastes and castes gives way to four buyers providing a uniform offer aimed at the mid-range of everything.

When these leviathans expand, they either buy smaller chains or they diversify. Wal-Mart, that owns Asda, is the largest retailer (and one of the largest companies) in the world. Yet to its critics, Wal-Mart is simply a huge American distribution chain for products from the cheapest suppliers around the world, irrespective of any external costs in their supply chains. And as the large out-of-town foodsheds are gradually deflating, they are now opening local stores, usually by buying local chains. They have also diversified, not competing with the specialist food shops, but with newsagents, chemists, florists, off-licences, clothes, kitchenware, electrical goods, petrol stations, post offices and banks.

Value and economies of scale

Like all oligopolies, foodsheds defend their size on the well-established principle of economies of scale. A greengrocer needs a van to drive to market most mornings before opening the shop, a grocer with five shops needs a larger van and driver, at least four shopkeepers and perhaps a bookkeeper, while a chain of twenty shops might need three vans and drivers, an accountant and central computer system. Scaling up leads to more efficient use of plant (vans and computers) and division of labour. Yet the fruit and veg from local greengrocers and market stalls is often less than half the price of the food sheds.

With every expansion, from sole trader to local chain, regional group, national brand and international corporation, economies of scale are offset by what we might call 'management drag'. Serving the food sheds are a distribution infrastructure of warehouses, fleets of HGVs and computerized stock control, teams of specialist buyers, contract lawyers, estate agents and property specialists, financiers raising capital for expansion and handling foreign exchange, tax accountants and others. This all requires an HQ where management tiers increase, salaries inflate and costs rise. With expansion, bureaucracy also rises, diluting or diverting management focus with paperwork, personal ambition and internal politics. "In 2003, Tesco's chief executive, Sir Terry Leahy received a pay package of £2,838,000 – some 255 times higher than the average income of the British farmer (about £11,000) on whom the supermarkets rely." (*Observer Food Magazine,* January 2004) I suspect that economies of scale peak somewhere in the mid-range of retail chain as with a 'bell curve', rather than increasing with company size in an open-ended 'J curve'.

Value generally refers to price and quality. Concerning price, the idea that 'Customer is king' is a lie. Lower farm gate prices are seldom passed onto customers, except through the dubious marketing ploy of loss leaders (see below). Even when the lower prices are passed on by foodsheds, "Consumers may gain from lower costs, but the motives of the companies are largely to gain increased market power – something of dubious benefit to consumers." (Sloman 2006)

Customers are also subjected to various tricks of the trade. Some are harmless, like blowing the smell of fresh bread through the sheds when no bread is being baked. Some are dishonest.

- Where they have a local monopoly, foodsheds 'flex the prices' by charging more than in their other sheds,
- Many offers and promotions ('Buy One, Get One Free' etc) merely bring the unit price down to that found in local grocers and newsagents.

- The expiry date on these offers have to be checked, however small the print. A website in 2008 claimed that Tesco was making £7.8 million profit a week charging the full price for items bought after the expiry date, even though the offer was still on display. Tesco refused to refund customers who noticed and sought a refund.
- This behaviour affects all retail sheds. When I bought a digital TV and black box some years ago from a wonderful local electrical (and repair) shop and asked, "Do I need a new aerial?" the shopkeeper said "No. All the TVs you see here are running off our ordinary aerial. Wait until the digital changeover happens and see." What shed would be so honest and lose an extra (and, as it turned out, unnecessary) sale?

The quality of food has also declined over the last 50 years. This is not nostalgia. When one foodshed trumpeted a new range of tomatoes for their taste, that might be thought a step in the right direction, had they not been responsible for removing flavour in the first place. Today, flavour is a secondary concern. Most tomatoes, on the vine or off, are grown hydroponically in water troughs without soil but with various fertilizers and chemicals added. They crop quickly, heavily and reliably to the required size and colour specification, mostly without blemish or flavour.

Global sourcing means that most crops have to be picked before they are ripe, then waxed, gassed, chilled or frozen before being sent to this country. Increasingly, fresh food means chilled or frozen. Even with British foods, freshness isn't guaranteed. In 2010, Tesco 'guaranteed' that its English strawberries and lettuces were in store within 48 hours of picking. With an efficient wholesale market system, food harvested one afternoon can be in shops the next morning. And when the wholesaler reduces the price of items held for more than a week, then local markets sell those items in bulk to shift them. Five pineapples or mangoes for £1 (in a local market) might have one or two bruised, and have lost some of their vitamins, but for many, they are welcome bargains, and it all reduces food waste.

Finally, quality and choice have usually been subservient to uniformity. The Brogdale research establishment in Kent has 2,000 different varieties of apple, plus 800 pears, 300 plums and gages, and many other fruits. The food sheds stock just three apple varieties from a range of about a dozen – usually a Cox, a Red Delicious (replacing the wet tasteless Golden variety), and a Granny Smith. All of them are large (Grade I), firm, heavy, uniformly coloured, without bruise or blemish. Gone are the first apples of summer like Beauty of Bath (considered too small and pink-fleshed), the James Grieve for either eating or cooking (easily bruised and soften quickly on the shelf), Russets (too small, with brown blotches in the flesh), and genuine small Cox Pippins (that would store for eating until the first early apples next summer – why bother?). Large apples are more profitable, since people still tend to buy apples by number rather than weight. Apples bred for size and unit weight have much higher water content. This reduces flavour, which may be inversely proportional to profit. (One can only speculate how measuring quality by size would affect galleries, libraries and theatres, stocking nothing but Monet's water lilies, wading through Richardson's *Clarissa* and endless loops of Wagner's *Ring*, perhaps.) The value of food is not measured by the size of fruit and profit yields but by their flavour and nutritional content, which brings us to the hidden costs of our foodshed industry.

Diseconomies of scale

So far, we have seen that fewer shops are less convenient, offer less choice and (probably) less value for money. These are internal costs or savings. However, foodsheds also impose external costs on society at large. These 'externalities' affect existing markets, suppliers and competitors, transport, waste, food quality, the environment, property yields and government influence.

i) Food markets
Foodsheds 'cut out the middle man', bypassing wholesale markets and buying direct from their suppliers. With their purchasing power, foodsheds can reduce the price they pay to all their small suppliers, without passing these savings onto customers. This is what purchasing power and shareholder value means. Their prices reflect more what the market will bear than increasing customer savings. In economists' jargon, foodsheds are 'price makers', small shops are 'price takers'.

Wholesale markets are a vital part of our economic and social heritage, where the law of supply and demand applies: in livestock markets, buyers bid against each other, pushing prices up for the farmers and fishers; in fruit and veg markets, the wholesalers compete with each other. Crucially, the market is an open system. Anyone can check prices in their local wholesale market and high street before deciding to set up their own shop. In effect, wholesale markets act as a balance, ensuring a fair price between producer and retailer. If their market share drops much lower, from about 25% to 20% or less, would they survive, where would local shops and street markets get their supplies, and how would independent farms and producers sell their produce?

ii) Suppliers
By contrast, the direct contract between foodshed and producer is closed to outside scrutiny. The immense purchasing power of these leviathans over all but the largest and equally powerful food manufacturers means that they can usually state their own terms: 'If you can't supply at this price, we know others that can, at home or abroad'. They are not interested in where the food comes from – except to charge a premium on local or fair trade produce. Their focus is on low costs, high prices and maximum profits. It is difficult for new competitors to enter this closed market.

Power tends to corrupt, and foodsheds are not immune. According to Simms (2007) and the Groceries code adjudicator (*The Observer* 31/3/13), they regularly:
- delay payments, a common curse for all small firms dealing with large companies, or underpay 'by mistake' and frequently don't make good,

- change agreed contract terms and conditions retrospectively, even reducing the price just before delivery, letting the farmer accept the loss or destroy the crop,
- demand payment, also retrospectively, for the foodshed promoting that product as 'locally grown' or on 'premium shelf space',
- fine suppliers if customers complain about their product, or fine them if they can't supply more of their popular products above the agreed amount,
- stipulate that suppliers use specific third parties like hauliers or abattoirs, from whom the food sheds demand a fee, and
- make contracts exclusive, not allowing the suppliers to diversify their clients.

Perhaps the worst abuse is forcing farmers to subsidize the cost of the foodsheds' own loss leaders. For example, milk pricing is largely determined by four foodsheds and three milk processors. Few farmers are large enough to negotiate an equitable price. One estimate (on *Rip-Off Food*, BBC 29/10/2012) gave the profit per litre of milk as about 20 pence for the foodshed, tuppence for the processor and a loss of tuppence for the farmer. In 1999, there were 34,000 dairy farmers; in 2019, according to the NFU website, just 7,800.

This market was unregulated until it was 'self-regulated' under a voluntary code. (As we shall see, self-regulation is an oxymoron.) The abuses continue. Fear of losing their livelihoods silences most farmers, commercial confidentiality protects the foodsheds and the closed market lacks independent regulation.

iii) Competitors

Loss leaders are not how foodsheds compete against each other. They are anti-competitive against all smaller retailers. Pricing staple items like bread, eggs, baked beans, bananas, wines and beer at well below their cost price threatens all bakers, butchers, grocers, off-licences, wine merchants and pubs. Foodsheds make up for loss leaders in other ways, for example, charging 75 pence for a popular tube of mints, or two for £1. Local newsagent sell them for 50 pence each. Who is being honest? (Predatory pricing reappears in chapter 6 with private bus companies, where the Competition Commission does intervene, however weakly.)

iv) Food miles

Over the last century, food miles increased tenfold, from about 100 to 1,000 miles. For every food calorie bought, about ten calories of energy are burnt. Transport costs are included in the price of all the food we buy, but not the environmental costs. As long as foodsheds can sell the stuff, they will import it. By one of life's ironies, Tesco loyalty cards can be converted into free air miles. We fly the fruit in, we fly the punters out.

Excessive food miles can be mitigated slightly when we use energy to produce early crops under glass, and by the often healthy foods from Africa where natural manure replaces dangerous fertilizers and pesticides. Global food chains are not only less fresh, waste energy and pollute the air. Food sheds have also replaced seasonal variety, ensuring an all-year-round supply not only of oranges and bananas, but also

French beans from Kenya, plums from California, bottled water from Turkey, strawberries airfreighted from anywhere and in summer parsnips from Australia.

These transport costs far exceed those of traditional markets and local shops. Once sucked into their distribution networks, the food sheds use the national trunk road network at little cost with their ever-larger HGVs, as discussed in chapter 6. And completing their distribution chains are the motorists' car boots and home. Moving five kgs of flesh 60,000 miles by HGV (as part of a 40-tonne load) burns the same amount of fuel as moving it 30 miles by car. In 2003, the department for transport estimated that "we drive 209 miles per year to buy food" (Simms 20009). Every little congests and pollutes.

v) Local economies
Global sourcing also raises the issue of fair trade, which accounts for less than 1% of all food sales in this country. This suggests that most food trade with poor countries is unfair. Trade between strong and weak economies may provide healthy profits for the food sheds, freight firms, importers and the local barons in undemocratic states. Without fair trade, however, there is no guarantee of fair working conditions in the field, nor of local wealth distribution to pay for fresh water supplies, local schools, new housing and healthcare etc. The unification of Italy and the US both show how difficult it is for agricultural economies to progress when dominated by stronger economies, even within the same nation. Most international trade agreements simply exploit the relative weakness of the food exporters and reinforce the status quo.

Global food chains also compete unfairly with local producers. Importing most of our apples from California, South Africa and New Zealand means that English apple orchards are being grubbed up. In 1981, our 60,000 hectares of orchards produced 405,000 tonnes of apples, pears, plums and soft fruit. By 2004, acreage was down to 33,000 hectares and produced 283,000 tonnes. During the same period, our import of fruit and vegetables rose from £1,718.5 million in 1983 to £4,918 million in 2004 (ONS). This is well over 40% of our total spend on fruit and vegetables.

Foodsheds also change the nature of local jobs and retail economies. From table 10 above, the total number of retail jobs has remained fairly constant. Contrary to their assertions, foodsheds do not create extra jobs. What they do is replace half a million full time independent shopkeepers, market traders and their staff with largely unskilled drivers, tillers and fillers, mostly part time, on minimum wage with few employment rights. This is all part of a more general deskilling of our employment base. And, lest we forget, all their profits are extracted from local economies to head office.

vi) Food waste
Apart from the nuclear industry, it is hard to find another sector where waste is such a problem. In a healthy economy, waste is a contradiction in terms – it being a raw material for new ventures. Food waste occurs at every stage of the chain; in field and packaging, in foodshed and at home. In the field, estimates vary, but I have walked

across fields in Hertfordshire and Kent where perhaps a quarter of the crops – beetroots, cabbages and spring onions – with no obvious bruises or blemishes, were left to rot in the field, being the wrong size or length. This couldn't be gathered separately and sold through local markets due (probably) to exclusive contracts. Other crops, like cauliflowers, celery and leeks, have up to half their goodness chopped away, leaving only the heart to be washed and plastic-wrapped.

We are dealing here with cosmetics and convenience. Apparently foodshed customers only buy good-looking vegetables that require minimal preparation. However, as in the cosmetics industry, this conceals an uglier truth. Foodsheds are rigging the market to maximize profits on each crop. Mixing the blemished and outsized with the pristine would increase the volume by perhaps 30%, but reduce its scarcity value and hence selling price. Or they could sell the discarded crop separately as part of their basic range (packaged in those garish white or yellow bags to depress demand), but profit margins on these is minimal, and they would reduce sales of the premium crop.

The wrapping of fresh fruit and veg in trays and cellophane is also largely cosmetic, far exceeding that found in most shops and market stalls. And, despite distribution networks, their 44 tonne lorries return to each centre empty, resisting calls to reuse more glass and recycle more paper and plastic.

Waste is also rampant in livestock farming. Intensively reared cattle and pigs require seven to ten tonnes of cattle feed to produce one tonne of meat, whereas naturally pastured animals require little or none. Cattle rearing has destroyed much virgin forest, while cattle feed is produced on land that could produce crops for human feed. These are serious social costs.

Within each foodshed, perhaps 10% of all fresh fruit and veg is thrown away, either looking tired or approaching its sell-by dates. This has created fregans, urban groups who live partially and healthily on what they find in those foodshed waste bins that aren't locked up.

And at the end of this chain, in restaurants and at home, there is more needless waste. Every year, about 900,000 tons of waste food is thrown out from London's restaurants. This used to be fed to local pigs and chickens. Not anymore. At home, fridges and freezers in lofts or garages may be mini warehouses. Paradoxically, while foodsheds minimize the stock they hold on the 'just in time' principle, many households now overstock 'just in case' they need anything – and then throw perhaps a third of it away. Too many people rely on sell-by dates. So, for example, eggs beyond that date are thrown out rather than tested for freshness with the simple water test. Food producers and foodsheds like sell-by dates as they increase turnover. Waste 'is not our problem'.

Estimates for waste are notoriously variable, but anything higher than 20% reveals a serious market inefficiency. Reducing such waste would reduce prices as well as the need for intensive farming and GM crops.

vii) Food quality

Corn Flakes were invented in 1894 to reduce dyspepsia, masturbation and excessive sexual intercourse, apparently. After removing the husk (or fibre) and the germ (with most of the protein), the flake was rolled and roasted with added salt and sugar for flavour. Early tests on rats by a sceptical scientist suggested that there was more nutrition in the packaging than the cereal. The irony is that, many years later, most governments forced food manufacturers to restore those vitamins and nutrients that their manufacturing processes destroyed – to avert serious public diet deficiencies.

Yet food manufacturers continue to 'add value' to their products with a battery of colourings, flavourings, sweeteners and stabilizers to mask the lack of flavour, prolong shelf-life, add visual appeal and increase turnover, at the expense of nutritional value and seasonal variety. For many years, manufacturers and foodsheds both resisted giving clear unambiguous information about the content and source of their products, and the national traffic light guide to salt, sugar and fat contents of all prepared foods. All companies must be more transparent (see next chapter). Allowing customers to make more informed choices about what we eat would improve both food quality and market efficiency.

But food quality remains largely judged by speed of growth to satisfy producers, long shelf-life to satisfy the foodsheds and cosmetic appearance to satisfy alleged customer preferences. In response to this distorted market, most arable farmers now depend on an alarming range of fertilizers, herbicides, fungicides, insecticides, antibiotics and hormones. These can create unusual choices. Organic bread is too expensive for half the population, yet commercial white bread is almost nutrition-less and commercial brown bread retains some pesticide residues. More seriously, agrochemicals and prairie farming have created wildlife deserts, denuded of mammals, birds, insects and even earthworms. This cannot be sustained.

Livestock farming is not exempt. The pig was a wonderful source of good wholesome food (except for vegetarians). In 1990, a meat packaging plant director explained the process. Six weeks before slaughter, they were injected with polyphosphates which made them very thirsty and, in those last weeks, they were given only water, no food. Immediately after slaughter, the carcass was chilled, dressed, packaged and frozen. So most pork is up to 12% water by weight, which explains why most bacon no longer fries in its own clear fat, but broils in a yellowish liquid gunge. (When I queried this phenomenon, the director said that "we're trying to do something about the colour." Gunge may represent pure profit, but Dewhurst has since gone bust.)

There are inadequate controls on the use of pesticides, but we know the problems. More insidious is the reduction in food quality. Since the war, the nutritional value of our fresh crops has declined by about two thirds, and is still reducing. (Compare, for example, McCance and Widdowson's *The Composition of Foods* 1991 with post-war ministry of agriculture food analyses.) Today's crops developed for their speed of growth absorb all the nitrogen, phosphates and water needed to develop their starch, sugars and fibre, but are seriously deficient in essential vitamins, minerals and trace elements. Either the plants do not have time to absorb them or the soil is seriously deficient. Hence we are all advised to eat five portions of fresh fruit and vegetables a day (which some nutritionists think should be doubled). 50 years ago, two or three daily portions were sufficient.

viii) Property values
The flight of retail sheds to green fields also disadvantages town centre stores in more expensive buildings on valuable urban sites. This affects secondary shops in particular. As more become vacant, rents fall (though not business rates, exacerbating the problem). Lower rents mean less maintenance, so reducing the lifespan of these solid buildings, thereby increasing pressure for more renewal.

This positive feedback loop is not sustainable. As rents fall, commercial yields rise. Briefly, the yield on any property is the annual rent expressed as a percentage of its capital value. It is also a measure of risk: the higher the yield, the greater the risk to the commercial investment and hence the higher the rent as a percentage of property value. In prime locations, high rents reflect very high capital values with low risk and therefore low yields. In marginal shopping streets and industrial estates, lower rents and higher yields reflect low capital values and more frequent vacancies.

Table 12: Commercial property yields (illustrative only)

Location:	Prime shop	Secondary	Industrial
Capital Value (£/sq ft)	4,000	400	40
Rent (£/sq ft)	100	20	5
Yield	2.5%	5.0%	12.5%

Retail sheds have escaped this gravity field. Though the properties are very cheap, with a 20 to 30-year lifespan, the returns on those investments are very high. Before market saturation, a £25 million investment in a new foodshed was recouped from trading profits within about five years. This 20% yield exceeds that for most industrial sheds but with minimal risk. In fact, the foodsheds traded as well as prime retail space, where a typical yield of 2.5% would require a payback period of 40 years or more. It is this gold rush that is turning our towns and cities inside out.

According to Adam Smith (1723-90), "The rate of profit [or yield] does not, like rent and wages, rise with prosperity and fall with the declension of the society. On the contrary, it is naturally low in rich and high in poor countries, and it is always highest in the countries which are going fastest to ruin." High yields, though profitable in the short term, seldom work in the long term.

Today, the gold rush is over. The large foodsheds are struggling, from a mix of saturation, customer dissatisfaction and the emerging e-commerce. Their business model, however unsustainable, is also becoming uneconomic. Hence the foodshed scramble back to high streets and district centres with their locals and metros. Unfortunately, this simply increases their market share.

The future of exurban foodsheds is important. When they close, they will want to sell the sites as 'brown fields' for redevelopment, rather than restore them as green fields. This would reinforce both their balance sheets and unsustainable exurban development. We return to 'windfall' gains and sustainable planning in chapter 9.

ix) Influence on governments

As a generalization, effective access to government is largely restricted to the rich and powerful. The foodshed oligopoly represents one such group, and enjoys a benign trading environment:

- their business rates are low, despite trading as well as prime town centre stores which pay much higher rates/sq. ft,
- as members of the powerful British Transport Federation, they lobby for new roads and larger vehicles while resisting road access charges, stricter lorry inspections and safer road speeds etc (see chapter 6),
- there has been no regular Census of Distribution since 1971, so clouding the negative impact of their sheds,
- despite clear evidence of monopolistic behaviour, no government agency has regulated them for any anti-competitive behaviour, restrictive covenants and their substantial land banks, and
- they persist with planning applications despite, occasionally, repeated refusals. In Sheringham
- for example, the local battle to keep a Tesco out finally lost after a 14 year struggle and consistent local opposition. Only large shameless companies have the resources to persist and overturn local planning decisions.
- This contrasts with government intolerance of those councils who persistently refuse inappropriate housing applications.

And, unsurprisingly, there is tax evasion, which is relatively modest when compared with the multinationals (discussed more fully in chapter 5). Selling CDs through one of the Channel Islands to avoid VAT gave them an anti-competitive 20% discount over independent competitors. One foodshed also set up off-the-peg companies for some of their new sheds, again in the Channel Islands, simply to evade Stamp Duty. Let me be clear about tax evasion. Tax schemes to avoid paying tax through tax havens have three very precise interpretations:

- the companies and their accountants refer to tax efficiency,
- tax inspectors and courts of law refer to tax avoidance, which means legal however shifty, while

- to the rest of us, it is tax evasion which, in plain English, is the "action of evading or escaping, by artifice or contrivance; dodging, prevarication. Means of evading; shuffling excuse, subterfuge' (*OED*). Hereafter, in order to avoid legal obfuscation, all references to tax evasion (ipE) are *in plain English*.

In summary, 20 retail chains operate a closed market, with foodsheds in the vanguard, in which choice, convenience and value are all reduced. We are replacing diverse town centres with themed retail parks, architecture with sheds, seasonal variation with year-round uniformity, local with global, and knowledgeable shopkeepers with 'Customer Care' posters in back offices telling staff to 'Make eye contact, Smile. Say "How can I help you?" But staff should not chat among themselves. That, according to Wal-Mart (Asda), is time theft from the company.

The human social theatre of shopping is giving way to a sanitized anti-social trip to car park, trolley bank, shopping aisle, checkout queue, back to the car and home.

"Always remember that, if we continue down our present road, we are likely to end up exactly where we seemed to be heading." (ancient Chinese proverb) In their drive to exurbia, retail sheds are leaving in their wake empty town centres where 'there's no there there', no street markets, few people, fewer shops and even fewer activities. Let me just repeat that, in terms of value, despite all their economies of scale, purchasing power and anti-competitive advantages, foodsheds still charge twice the price that local greengrocers and street markets charge for comparable fruit and veg.

If we are to turn the tide, we will need a) government regulation, b) effective local management, and c) more transparency to inform customer choice.

A national retail framework

A skeleton of national retail policy might read as follow.
- Before 1945, policy was led by those retailers, such as Burtons, M&S and Woolworths, building national chains with their distinctive stores in most towns.
- The *Planning Act 1947* introduced comprehensive development areas for new shopping precincts, which were development-led in partnership with local councils.
- From 1979, with the rise of food sheds, we adopted a market-led or *laissez-faire* approach, in which 'competitive innovation' overrode planning objectives. This unregulated market was extremely disruptive, and soon controlled by a few powerful retailers, developers and landowners, acting against the interests of suppliers, competitors and customers, town centres, farming, the environment and society at large.

In 1996, the department of the environment recognized the danger. *Planning Policy Guidance: Town Centres and Retail Development* (PPG 6 1996) replaced market forces and political inertia with planning protection, at least in theory.

"Town centres are part of our national and civic heritage and securing their health helps to foster civic pride and local identity...

"The three key tests for assessing [new] retail developments [are]: impact on vitality and viability of town centres; accessibility by a choice of means of transport; and impact on overall travel and car use."

There was even "a general presumption against allowing new out-of-town superstores".

The later *Planning Policy Statement 6: Planning for Town Centres* (*PPS 6* 2005) repeats the key objective to promote town centre vitality and viability. After some well-meaning waffle about existing centres, accessibility, social inclusion, economic growth, high quality design, tackling deprived areas, better transport choices and more sustainable patterns of development, paragraph 1.7 then adds the get-out clause. "It is not the role of the planning system to restrict competition, preserve existing commercial interests or to prevent innovation." It is no coincidence, perhaps, that since 1979 the government has employed various foodshed executives as special advisers on national policy.

Current government policy is contained in the 2nd edition of the *National Planning Policy Framework* (2018, hereafter *NPPF2*), and replaces all previous guidance. Section 7, "Ensuring the vitality of town centres", takes "a positive approach to their growth, management and adaptation." However, without an up-to-date plan, schemes are likely to be approved over the heads of the local planning authority. Even with one, only "Where an application fails to satisfy the sequential test or is likely to have significant adverse impact on one or more of the considerations in paragraph 89, it should be refused." The vagaries of the sequential test and impact assessment become a licence to print money for barristers and consultants when applicants go to appeal.

NPPF2 also requires local authorities to "allocate a range of suitable sites in town centres to meet... anticipated needs for retail, leisure, office and other main town centre uses over [at least the next ten years]". This retains the idea of large-scale redevelopment. Sustainable development is the stated basis of the *NPPF*. Yet

- it seems to prefer town centre redevelopment schemes over conservation and adaptation;
- while it supports street markets (existing and new), it is silent on the threat posed by foodsheds. It is naive to support both;
- it is silent on the need to reduce shopping trips by car and parking spaces; and
- it retains coy ambiguity about large exurban sheds. By now, there is sufficient evidence to make an informed policy decision: either these sheds seriously reduce town centre viability and generate excessive traffic, making them 'unsustainable', or their impact is manageable and 'sustainable'. The *NPPF* refuses to say which. This allows developers and retailers to slip anchor and build yet more cheap sheds, against all reasonable planning grounds for refusal. Such ambiguity infects the whole *NPPF*, as we shall see in later chapters.

Rather than dancing around policies for sustainable retail development, *NPPF2* should define national priorities to underpin local policies. These priorities might be to:

- conserve existing hierarchies of town centre, district centres and local shops,
- impose VAT on all new retail development and withdraw compulsory purchase powers,
- source more local food (and other goods) through local markets and supply chains, and
- protect all farming and green belts with a presumption against exurban sheds.

The government should also revive the Census of Distribution, strengthen the Monopolies Commission, reduce car dependency and introduce realistic trunk road access charges for HGVs (both discussed in chapter 6), rationalize the Uniform Business Rate and tax Amazon fairly.

Until 1971, we had accurate information on floor space, jobs and sales for every shop, updated every three years. Had we kept this Census, the impact of every exurban shed would have been accurately monitored, giving those councils that wanted to refuse new schemes robust arguments. Alternatively, some might have used the Census to negotiate profit-sharing or 'clawback' clauses for any new retail park that exceeded figures used at any inquiry.

Stopping this Census was an act of self-harm. All retail planning decisions were less well-informed and put the commercial interests of the sheds above those of councils and local shops. All we know is that every retail park and exurban foodshed reduced pedestrians and turnover in all shops in the nearest centres – not just those shops in competition. Today, few local shopkeepers have a business to sell on to relatives or new entrants when they retire.

Scrapping the Census is an early example of government outsourcing, which has cost taxpayers more in the long run. Private retail research is not cheap. In 2010, for example, the British Retail Consortium, through Verdict Research, offered me its *Out of Town Retailing*, dated 2005 for $3,170. And to refuse a major scheme, councils had to engage commercial agents and expensive barristers to argue their case for them, even while their agents' access to commercial data is restricted and time-consuming. By comparison, agents not only have inside information from client retailers and developers, but there may also be substantial follow-up fees if the schemes are approved. The Census levelled this playing field. Its absence put private information above public knowledge, commercial confidentiality and a more closed society above transparency and freedom of information. Most economists agree that an efficient market relies on accurate data. In Germany, Census information is still collected every year on the floor space, turnover and employment of every shop.

The government should also clarify the issue of fair and unfair competition by the retail oligopolies. The two currently relevant agencies, the Competition Commission and the Office of Fair Trading, are either reluctant to act or lack the necessary powers. So, five foodsheds became four when Morrisons bought Safeway in 2004, with control of about 75% of the food market. And in the drive from superstore to locals, Asda (Wal-Mart) bought Netto in 2010 and Tesco bought the Booker group (including the Budgens and Londis chains) in 2018.

Ralph Nadar (1973) suggested that when four companies control over 50% of their market, they should be broken up. I would suggest that no company should have more than 10% of any market. Without such action, town centres will continue to decline and local shops continue to close.

The Uniform Business Rates (UBR) needs to be reformed. There are at least two problems as they apply to shops. At present, the UBR is related to some notional rental value of the property at some fixed date in the past, rather than to current trading conditions. For marginal and secondary shops, business rates were formerly about a third of the rents. Today, they often equal or exceed those rents. This forces many retailers to stop trading, forcing landlords to reduce rents to attract new tenants, often to levels that preclude proper maintenance of the buildings. By contrast, the UBR on foodsheds are too low. In 2000, the UBR for five foodsheds in Nottinghamshire and Wiltshire were lower per square foot than for small secondary shops in the nearest town centres (and would be lower still if the service areas and car parks were included). If this small sample is typical, the UBR is anything but uniform. With their high turnover and profitability, the rate for the sheds should equal or exceed the UBRs for prime shops in the nearest town centres.

The UBR should be fixed as a percentage of a tangible current measure, preferably on annual turnover. This would reflect changes in local trading conditions and equalize the tax more fairly between town centre shops and exurban sheds.

Finally, there is one 'monopoly' that governments seem powerless to control. Within five years, Amazon has become the world's second largest retailer, after Wal-Mart. While its distribution costs would be high and comparable with the retail sheds, it has avoided most of the capital and running costs of all shops and sheds, except their huge warehouses. This saving is courtesy of the world-wide-web which is free to all users. Two possible approaches to this tax loophole (as well as ensuring that Amazon pays its corporate taxes) are first, to impose a tax on every commercial transaction on the web, in much the same way that governments collect a tax on mobile phone networks. Alternatively, we might impose the UBR on its distribution warehouses as if they were shops, with the rate set on the spectacular turnover of each warehouse.

With such a national strategy and regulatory framework, towns and cities could then develop their own retail strategies.

Town centre management

Town centres need to be managed. The success of shopping malls and retail parks is in part because they are managed as a unit. The Meadowhall retail park, for example, with 270 shops on 2,000 acres, employs 360 staff responsible for securing tenants, negotiating leases, estate maintenance and security, promotions and marketing. What makes management relatively simple is that the whole estate is fixed, highway access is fixed, parking is either free or controlled by a rapacious parking firm, public transport is largely irrelevant, tensions between landlord and tenants are passed onto lawyers, and a security firm manages the estate with few risks when shut.

Town centres are far more complex – and interesting:

- strategic planning prepares town centre action plans, development control processes all planning applications;
- county highways are responsible for main roads (sometimes as agents for the department of transport) and traffic management, local councils deal with local roads and maintenance;
- traffic-free zones involve most public and private agencies;
- managing public car parks, owned by a mix of councils and private owners, national, county and local, is challenging. Co-ordinating parking fees is rare;
- few transport authorities co-ordinate public transport services. Bus, tram and train companies compete to maximize profits rather than increase revenues; and
- police and community safety officers are responsible for general public safety, while most shopping malls are protected by private security firms.

Effective partnerships are rare, too frequently with tardy or non-committed key officers, stuttering over petty boundary disputes and endless meetings for even the simplest action. For example, in return for a new inner relief road (built to accommodate two retail sheds), the high street of a small east midlands market town was to be traffic-calmed, resurfaced and the no-waiting restrictions lifted for the benefit of local traders. Two years later, the double yellow lines, painted on the new road surface by mistake, were still there.

More seriously, also in the 1990s, one of the safest towns in Hampshire, itself one of the safest counties in England, installed town centre CCTV cameras. Yet cheaper and perhaps more effective solutions are available, including:

- better lighting and securing back alleys and service yards,
- removing graffiti quickly. If left, more appears,
- encouraging chippies and takeaways near pubs. Boisterous drunks are less likely to throw bricks or punches when their hands are full, and
- attracting evening activities as people on the streets reduce the fear of crime.

Historically, town centres have been venues for regular social events: street markets, pub tournaments, whist evenings, annual carnivals, local parades, Christmas festivities, annual fairs, Charter weeks, Lord Mayor shows, fun runs, open days for gardens, studios and buildings – even festivals for buskers. Traffic-free streets enhanced the social atmosphere, with people spilling out of shops, pubs and cafes.

In tourist areas, tensions rise between resident and visitor when gift shops and cafes, paying higher rents, displace local butchers, chemists and greengrocers. In one Cornish town, where gift shops are at saturation point, a local bookie saw an opportunity: whenever a new pasty shop opened, he took bets on which pasty shop would close first and when. Promoting and protecting local trade is difficult and requires effective management and determination. Suggestions include the following.

- An annual directory of town centre goods and services might encourage more residents to visit the centre more often, perhaps with regular promotions and special events out of season as rewards.
- Deterring yet another 'inappropriate' shop runs against the principle of an open market. Totnes town council, however, refused permission for a global chain cafe, partly because there were sufficient local cafes, and partly to protect them from what it considered unfair competition.
- Some might even negotiate with shop owners and landlords to ensure that sufficient shops are retained specifically for local year-round shopping, restoring a balance between residents' needs and tourists' fun.
- Shop opening hours should be co-ordinated. Few centres can compete with 24 hour opening of the large foodsheds, but early evening opening when most workplaces close could be profitable and recapture some revenue.
- Dress vacant shops as temporary exhibition space for local schools, artists and photographic clubs. Too many To Let and For Sale signs, with whitewashed windows, posters and junk mail strewn inside, merely advertises the fact that a town centre is struggling. Until 2009, dressing shop windows made the owners liable to full business rates even while they sought tenants for the vacant shops. Such petty government reinforces the need for more local control of local taxes.
- Revive more local fairs and markets in town centres. Boot fairs and specialist markets are usually sited out of town, on private land. Located in town centres would revive them and encourage some shops to open even for Sunday events.
- Farmers' markets should also be relocated. I have yet to find one alongside an existing street market. It is as if fussy shoppers and real farmers do not want to mix with *hoi polloi* and stroppy market stallholders. Yet surely combining the two would encourage at least some crossover between the foodie and the vulgar.
- More ambitiously, we need to develop local trade. For example, local food chains should be developed between local farmers, street markets, shops and restaurants. Local chains should also involve intermediaries like abattoirs and local firms processing or manufacturing that local food.
- It could also involve setting up a local distribution service between the farms, outlets and customers, either developed by a local van hire firm or as a joint venture by the retailers themselves.

Which brings us to the need for some local agency to manage town centres and oversee strategy. While councils are largely responsible for public services (street cleaning and lighting, refuse, public services and most car parking), no-one speaks for the traders, large and small. The various government-imposed local partnerships (like local strategic partnerships (LSPs) and local economic partnerships (LEPs)) are too remote, unfocussed and dependent on Treasury funding to be effective (see chapter 5).

Town centres need a local partnership between councils and chambers, preferably led by revived local chambers of trade and industry. In France, chamber membership is compulsory, with annual fees reflecting size of company. Properly-funded, local chambers here could employ staff to undertake local research, promote inter-trading, develop relevant strategies and speak for the local business community.

The chamber of trade wing could assume the role of town centre management and, in partnership with the local council, develop strategy. In an era of ever-increasing specialization, one might query the need for yet another generalist function. Given a strong chamber, however, managers would ensure that the needs of all central businesses and traders were fully reflected in strategies and management. It is those businesses and traders, after all, on whom overall success largely depends, and it is they who have the most to lose. As to funding, with newly-enriched chambers and properly-funded local councils (see chapter 10), the new partnerships would be more independent of government control, able to fund key functions and initiatives outlined above, and negotiate match funding in the event of shortfalls.

Customer or consumer

"I shop, therefore I am" was a cynic's amendment to Descartes' 'proof' of personal existence. However, "I shop, therefore I am" could also be read, in former times, as evidence of our social nature. Shopping was never solely an economic activity between buyer and seller, but developed as a social custom, mixing banter with barter. Regulars of local shops and street markets graduated from mere consumers to qualified customers, to be rewarded with friendly service and even the occasional discount. Within ten minutes of my home:

- the fishmonger shouting "Come on Gran. Get your purse out. The fish is all fresh today"; while
- a granny stallholder, explaining how to prepare her fresh olives for eating, said 'We tried it once, but it's too much bother.' (She was right.);
- the Chinese shopkeeper sometimes reducing my bill by ten pence because I brought my own bags: "You save me money. I save you money"; or the scoop stallholder who complained: "What, no bags this week? You'll have to go";
- the greengrocer ("what's in the allotment this week?"), now shutting on Thursdays. "I'm at the market 5am six mornings a week and at 62 I need to take it a bit easier";
- the 'Gentlemen's Outfitter' who, fitting me up with a proper suit, explained the differences between English and German tailoring. So, I also bought a flash shirt and tie; and
- I can be confused. "Yes, young man, what can I get you?" Or "Good morning sir. What would you like today?" "Sir?" "OK, mush. What d'ya want? Is that any better?"

Competent traders offer advice, gossip and jokes not simply to pass the time but to generate custom and loyalty. This improves customers' social skills, even elevating mundane purchases from shy and lonely people with a greeting and a smile.

In foodsheds, gossip, banter and 'overhears' are rare. Shopping has become almost 'friction-less'. The only human interaction on the round trip from front door to foodshed is at the till, and with self-service check-out tills, shopping can be done with no human contact at all. The comments of artist Ozenfant (who worked with Le Corbusier) apply equally to consumers and society in general: "The individualism of today is the spirit of liberty made subservient to SELF: the universe and mankind are at the feet of the individual. The one consideration is that the self be satisfied..." (from Rothenstein 1957). Though he was talking about artists, this also defines today's shopping, which has largely replaced the social custom with private consumerism and 'retail therapy'.

Reduced social behaviour is not restricted to shopping. It is a theme running through this book, from how suburbs reduce social interaction and chance meetings, to work being de-personalized, public transport replaced by cars, pubs converted to restaurants and neighbourhoods becoming ghettoes etc. All have inevitably reduced our social skills.

In little more than 50 years, supported by suburban growth and personal mobility, the corporate greed of 20 retailers has seriously damaged centuries of gradual change and social continuity. Large firms are usually justified on the principle of 'the survival of the fittest' or, in their terms, the most efficient. This comes from Charles Darwin's (1809-1882) theory of evolution, where species evolve over long periods in local habitats through natural selection. Every different habitat involves complex relationships, both predatory and symbiotic, in which all are engaged in the struggle for space, food and mates. Generally, only the fittest survive.

Adapting this analogy to our natural urban habitats, while citizens jostle for space, food and mates, in every town centre and street market, shopkeepers and traders jostle for space, supplies and custom. Adam Smith's market theory is that many small shops and stalls are sufficient to cater for all tastes and pockets by competing for their individual share, and that when any trader fails or retires, there are always new entrants to take their place. Smith suggested that it was 'an invisible hand' that kept these market healthy through perpetual small-scale competition, collaboration and replacement. In fact, his concept might prefigure Darwin's 'natural selection', except that, being in a city, our markets depend on 'social selection'.

Now visit your nearest foodshed. It is the antithesis of a real market: its offer meets a limited range of taste and pocket, choice is determined by head office, social selection is limited to four leviathans that smother the competition and control the market, making it increasingly difficult for new entrants, and social behaviour is almost completely absent. And, under the ideology of 'free market capitalism', successive governments, through indolence, ignorance or corruption, have supported the growth of these gross retailers. There are no leviathans in natural habitats.

Globalization, to which subject we now turn, has had an even more damaging social and economic impact on local economies. Before that, however, let me again re-use Howard's magnets to summarize this chapter. Only two magnets are required to illustrate the tension between local shops and national sheds, between local and global and, if my social reflections have any weight, between customer loyalty and consumer individualism.

Retail park   or   Town centre

Shedscape uniform, clean, brightly-lit, tidy, car parked or
                    Townscape brash, full of variety, contrast and character
A closed market controlled by oligopolies or
                    An open market for all local entrepreneurs
Choice limited to a few buyers – uniform quality or
                    Choice of product, quality and price diverse
Impersonal service, Customer Care information posters or
                    Personal service varied, banter among traders and shoppers
Many staff untrained and ignorant of products or
                    Knowledgeable traders and staff
Global sourcing – cheap goods, high transport costs or
                    More local sourcing, lower transport costs
Excessive waste due to cosmetic criteria or
                    Minimal waste
Price makers – they set or limit the competition or
                    Price takers, traders accepting prices in competitive market
More convenient for cars and the disabled or
                    Less convenient for cars and the disabled
Branding, bland or
                    Local, distinctive
Cheap buildings, low overheads or
                    Historic buildings, high overheads
Often excessive power over suppliers or
                    Wholesalers offer balance between retailers and suppliers
Retail parks 50 years old – innovation or aberration or
                    Towns centres have survived nine centuries in UK
Personal retail therapy or
                    Enjoyable social custom

Chapter Five: Urban Wealth

From the retail industry, we now look at whole economies, local to global. And as this is the longest chapter, a few generalizations at the outset might help clarify the key arguments. While the Industrial Revolution saw jobs move from the production of raw materials (food and minerals) to manufacturing to the service sector, every firm is as much a social as an economic enterprise.

Second, healthy local economies are anchored by SMEs (small and medium sized enterprises) that focus on improving products and services to produce clusters. The focus of global MNEs (multi-national enterprises) is on increasing profits, but their size breeds inefficiencies, hoovers wealth out of local economies and corrupts national governments. Small is beautiful. Big is bad.

And third, the key lesson from post-1979 ideology of small government, privatization and minimum regulation is that 'market forces' are no longer checked by Adam Smith's 'invisible hand' but by the mailed fist of powerful oligopolies.

Wealth generation

Cities and beehives are the only natural habitats that thrive on division of Labour, the main wealth creator according to Adam Smith. Wealth from Land and Capital is more circumscribed by supply and demand: the occasional spectacular fortunes either temporary, following gold rushes, or illusory, like the bankers' bubble based on CDOs. Division of labour creates jobs within and between each industry, develops personal and social skills, tests ideas and inventions, improves products and processes and provides personal income and local wealth.

Jobs divide into three sectors. The *primary sector* produces food, fuel, raw materials, energy and water through farming, fishing and forestry, mining, quarrying, generating and supply. In *manufacturing*, workers cast, found, cut and finish new materials, forge, craft, assemble and package products, and maintain and repair them. The *service sector* includes accountants, bankers and solicitors, architects and developers, insurance and estate agents, civil servants and council officers, voluntary and community workers, the police, security firms and armed services, transport, hospital and school staff, shopkeepers, hairdressers, hoteliers and workers in the arts, sport and recreation.

Now, while Land is obviously crucial in the primary sector, and Capital underpins financial services, all three sectors depend on Labour. By their very nature, firms are as much social as economic enterprises. Work is part of the human condition.

It even creeps into our language. It's not only farmers who 'plough their own furrows' or 'sow their wild oats' before 'reaping their rewards'. Nor are spinsters the only ones to 'spin a yarn', 'unravel a mystery' or 'tease' a 'thread of discourse' from a 'homespun' 'web of life'. Some vocabularies do not migrate into everyday use. Only in the Potteries (producing hollow-ware and flatware, earthenware, statuary porcelain and ceramic tiles etc) is the potters' clay and saggars' marl levigated with paddles, mixed in mechanical blungers and kneaded in pugmills, then shaped by throwing, fly pressing or slip casting. The jollies and jiggers are fired in bottle ovens and muffle kilns (electricity now replacing coke), then fettled and decorated by sliptrailing, sprigging, bat pointing or ground laying before final glazing.

During the Industrial Revolution, jobs shifted. Before 1800, the land employed up to 80% of the working population throughout Europe. During the nineteenth century, jobs shifted to factories. In 1841, in Europe about half tilled the soil, while in Great Britain, it was only 26% (Cipolla 1973). During the twentieth century, the shift was to services.

Division of labour, the multiplier effect and specialist clusters underpin all healthy economies. The multiplier effect arises not only from the labour involved in the many manufacturing processes from raw materials, components, sub- and final assembly, finishing and packaging, but also in negotiations with suppliers and various financial and marketing services. Back in Stoke-on-Trent, only about 2,000 firms remain from perhaps 7,000 a century ago. Although many household names have either closed or been sold, the remaining few hundred pottery, porcelain, clay and china manufacturers still support a range of specialist merchants of materials and ceramic products, suppliers of ceramic slips, glazes, colours and transfers, millers, engineers, equipment manufacturers, design consultants and others. There is also research into, for example, the use of ceramics in engines, and support for the local school of art and design, the city art museum and the Gladstone pottery museum. This is a cluster, discussed more fully below. Neither farming nor banking develop such complex networks.

Table 13 opposite shows the continuing shift to services even during the late twentieth century. Less than two jobs/100 are in the primary sector, one in seven jobs remain in manufacturing (one in ten if construction is excluded), leaving five in every six jobs in the service sector. Yet within services, jobs in public administration and other public services declined by up to 40% from 1989 to 2009, largely outsourced to 'other business services'. Put simply, the nineteenth century saw increased demand for manufactured goods. The twentieth century saw demand grow for services in public health, education, leisure and recreation.

Table 13: Employees by sector in the UK, 1979-2009 (thousands)

Employment sector (SIC)	1979	1989	1999	2009
Primary Sector - subtotal	829	765	523	433
1 Agriculture forestry fishing	-	300	318	255
2 Mining and ore extraction*	-	-	74	56
3 Energy and water supply*	-	465	131	122
Manufacturers – subtotal	6,161	6,232	5,158	3,919
4 Food products	-	549	499	403
5 Textiles	-	226	294	85
6 Leather goods	-	311	30	8
7 Wood products	-	246	84	70
8 Paper and publishing	-	494	469	326
9 Petrol and nuclear*	-	-	26	24
10 Chemicals and fibres	-	333	249	171
11 Rubber and plastics	-	215	244	162
12 Other non-metallic	-	202	140	88
13 Metal products	-	510	534	343
14 Machinery	-	771	368	251
15 Electrical equipment	-	643	497	272
16 Transport equipment	-	503	403	285
17 Other manufacturing	-	171	211	154
18 Construction	-	1,058	1,110	1,277
Services - subtotal	14,594	15,474	19,362	22,140
19 Vehicle sale and repair**	-	217	576	524
20 Wholesale trade	-	944	1,167	1,102
21 Retail trade	-	2,289	2,582	2,808
22 Hotels and restaurants	-	1,140	1,649	1,787
23 Transport and post	-	1,377	1,459	1,530
24 Financial services	-	888	1,074	1,002
25 Other business services***	-	2,230	3,572	4,504
26 Public administration***	-	1,556	1,400	1,465
27 Education	-	1,778	2,044	2,460
28 Health and social work	-	1,465	2,600	3,527
29 Other services***	-	1,630	1,240	1,430
Total all sectors	21,584	22,661	25,045	26,493

Source: ONS, *Annual Abstract*

(Some caution is needed reading this table. The SIC (Standard Industrial Classification) of 1980 was revised in 1992. Briefly: * row 3 for 1989 combines rows 2, 3 and 9 for 1999 and 2009, and shows the job losses in mining and the privatized energy and water suppliers; ** the 1989 figure on row 19 excluded car sales; and *** it is difficult to reconcile rows 25, 26 and 29 between the two SICs.)

In 30 years, of the total workforce, primary sector jobs declined from 3.8 to 1.6%, manufacturing from 28.5 to 14.8% while service jobs rose from 67.6 to 83.6%. And while all three sectors are crucial, the importance of manufacturing can be seen in our balance of payments.

Table 14: UK exports and imports, 1983-2008 (£millions)

Sector	Food/drink	Mfd goods	Services	Total
1983:				
• Exports	4,240.7	41,754.1	18,710	64,704.8
• Imports	7,869.2	46,380.8	15,351	69,600.0
Trade balance	-3,628.5	-4,626.7	3,359	-4,895.2
Balance of payments*				1,258
2008:				
• Exports	13,708	237,935	170,758	422,401
• Imports	31,118	313,906	115,616	460,640
Trade balance	-17,410	-75,971	55,142	-38,329
Balance of payments				-21,975

Source: ONS, *Annual Abstract*

(* The balance of payments is the difference between imports and exports, plus 'invisible' earnings of salaries, capital transfers and investment dividends.)

In 25 years, food exports fell from 53.9% to 44.1% of food imports, manufactured goods fell from 90.0% to 75.8% of imports, while service exports rose from 121.9% to 147.7%. 1983 was the last year since 1945 when our balance of payments was in credit. Since then, "A record balance of payments deficit of £96.2bn (5.2% of GDP) [occurred] for 2015, and £32.7bn (7% of GDP) for the fourth quarter alone – both higher in percentage terms than in any year since the second world war..." (William Keegan, *The Observer* 3/4/16). As we export less, so we import more.

The damage can be seen in table 15 opposite. No manufacturing sector, apart from printing and publishing, is secure against foreign competition. This reduces the social wealth created through its multiplier effect and specialist clusters.

Table 15: Import penetration as %age of home demand, 1977-2007

Manufacturing sector	1977	1987	1998	2007
All manufacturing	25	35	47	62
food and drink	17	18	22	28
tobacco	"	"	9	15
textiles	27	47	56	79
clothing	25	39	73	110
leather goods and footwear	32	49	83	112
timber and wood products	28	31	36	36
pulp and paper products	21	22	38	44
printing and publishing	"	"	6	7
chemicals and fibres	27	43	62	97
rubber and plastics	17	28	28	39
other mineral products	12	18	20	26
basic metals	32	na	66	98
metal goods	9	18	20	27
misc machinery, equipment	30	38	59	74
office machinery, computers	84	93	84	151
electrical machinery	30	49	55	76
radio/TV equipment	51	58	89	104
precision instruments	"	"	71	86
motor vehicles	35	48	60	74
other transport equipment	45	42	64	99
other manufacturing	34	46	52	74

Source: ONS, *Annual Abstract*

(As with table 14, the revised SIC of 1992 alters some sectors.)

During the 1980's, total output under Thatcher actually fell by some 25%. Labour wasn't *able* to work. From 1989 to 2009, manufacturing lost over 2.3 million jobs (37%). Sectors hardest hit were textiles, clothes and leather goods, with jobs falling 83% from 550,000 to 93,000. Jobs in wood products fell by 176,000 (72%), in machinery by 520,000 (67%), in electrical equipment by 371,000 (58%), other non-metallic products by 114,000 (56%) and transport equipment, including car assembly, by 218,000 (45%).

The major causes of this decline were the high exchange rate of the £ making exports dear and imports cheap, the high costs of borrowing which reduced industrial investment as banks and investors could get well above the perfectly solid 6% to 8% returns in the global market, and large firms exporting their manufacturing to low wage economies, forcing smaller competitors to follow suit, diversify or go bust.

Today, most of Britain's major centres of production have vanished: not just the 'dark Satanic mills', but factories, engineering workshops, shipyards, steelworks, coal mines, dockside warehouses and railfreight depots, taking their jobs, skills and supply chains with them. Today, the Industrial Revolution is largely a matter of scrap metal, archaeology and the heritage industry celebrating what's lost.

According to economists like Evan Davis (*Made in Britain*, BBC2 2013), jobs lost in manufacturing are replaced in other sectors. But these are usually lower skilled and lower paid jobs in warehousing, transport, security, tourism, high street and domestic service. 16 years after the Raleigh cycle factory closed in Nottingham, former workers were interviewed on "the 50th anniversary of the archetypal post-war English working man's novel, *Saturday Night and Sunday Morning*. The Raleigh bicycle factory where Alan Sillitoe's hero Arthur Seaton worked had long since closed down, frame-making had been outsourced to Vietnam, and all the job-for-life certainties that came with it had been outsourced too. The men I spoke to mostly did piecemeal bits of things: former miners were making sandwiches for supermarkets; precision toolmakers were running tanning salons. Several of the men at the Radford working men's club, where Seaton sank pints, had never worked a day in their life." (Tim Adams, *The Observer* 5/4/15)

The haemorrhage of so many factories, skilled jobs, industrial clusters and capital investment in the past 40 years is unparalleled among our industrial neighbours. While we deregulated the banks and maintained an exchange rate that made our manufacturing less competitive, Germany maintained its stronger manufacturing sector and has run a continuous trade surplus (*Euromonitor* 2003). Globally, trade surpluses and deficits equal out. But a nation that runs deficits over decades finds it increasingly difficult to reverse long-term industrial decline, even with devaluation.

This decline reflects that distaste for industry that Wiener found among our private-schooled ruling elite (see page 32 above), who still prefer the greater rewards and certainties of land, finance and government. Nor is the contra flow of capital into the UK compensating, it being heavily skewed towards office and housing development in London. We need more manufacturers making things, and less investors making money. In his epic survey of *The Mediterranean and the Mediterranean World in the Age of Philip II* (1975), Fernand Braudel wonders whether "... banking increases in importance when commerce and industry are in difficulty; that one type of activity can only develop to the detriment of others and not necessarily in harmony with them?" Either banking is there largely to support industry, or manufacturing is simply another investment vehicle for banks. For most of the Industrial Revolution, industry was in the ascendant. In the last century, and especially since 1979, finance has been firmly in control, led by bankers, brokers, accountants, insurers and investors. Of Adam Smith's three wealth creators, Labour has ceded to Capital and private equity, aided by Land and property development.

Local economies – a) size matters

Adam Smith saw that in local economies many small firms ensured healthy competition and customer choice. Forgive the smirking advertisers' innuendo, but in business, size really does matter. In discussing the microeconomics of each firm, let us replace the 'four Ms' of business management (materials, men, money and marketing) with four Ps:

- production includes the process and all the plant, equipment and materials used,
- people covers staff, training and motivation,
- profit involves income and costs, pricing and investment, while
- promotion includes advertising and public relations.

The first three roughly equate to Adam Smith's three creators of wealth – Land, Labour and Capital. Promotion, like planning, is largely a twentieth century phenomenon.

Generally, small firms focus on production and people. Start-ups concentrate on product or service quality to win new custom, and finding competent assistants and colleagues. Prices are set by the market and success is largely hand-to-mouth, veering between feast and famine. SMEs (small and medium-sized enterprises) focus on production, people and profit. In clusters, there is collective interest in innovation and staff skills. Larger contracts of greater complexity generate higher prices and more secure cash flows, to be invested in long-term growth developing new products and niche markets. Promotion is still largely restricted to word-of-mouth within their clusters.

Large firms focus on profit and promotion, as discussed below. Once local family firms outgrew their towns, they developed national brands, like Baxters foods, Boroughs Wellcome pharmaceuticals, Bulmers cider, Clarks shoes, Clay press printers, Colmans mustard, De La Rue printers, Eastern Coach Works, English China Clay, EverReady batteries, Fry's chocolate, JCB diggers, London Brick, Merryweather fire engines, the Norwich Union, Patak foods, Penguin books, Pilkington glass, Redland building materials, Rowntrees sweets, Shepherd Neame brewery, Tetley tea, Tri-ang toys, Turner and Newall asbestos products, Wedgwood ceramics, the Woolwich building society and the Ulster and Yorkshire banks. Of these, eight went bust, 15 are part of larger conglomerates and only five remain independent.

Historically, from table 16 overleaf, workshops gradually increased in size. Braudel (1982) identified four types:

- small family workshops around a master craftsman,
- cottage industries based on home workshops supplied by a local merchant,
- the early factories in brewing, tanning and glassmaking etc, and
- large steam- or electric-powered factories bringing cottage industries under one roof.
- The last century added large assembly plants.

Table 16: Distribution of manufacturing units by employment size, 2008

Manufacturing Sector	% Micro (1 – 4)	% Small (5 – 49)	% Medium (50 – 249)	% Large (250+)	Total number
Metal products	58.9	36.8	4.0	0.3	29,575
Publishing	69.7	26.8	3.0	0.5	28,800
Misc mfg	66.8	30.3	2.6	0.3	19,100
Machinery	52.4	39.8	6.7	1.2	13.525
Food mfg	39.4	45.8	10.6	4.2	9,880
Wood products	62.9	34.3	2.6	0.2	8,720
Rubber products	40.4	47.3	11.1	1.1	7,460
Other non-metal	56.1	36.0	7.1	0.8	6,265
Precision instr'ts	52.7	39.0	7.1	1.3	5,570
Electrical mach'y	53.9	36.9	8.0	1.3	5,345
Textiles	57.4	31.6	6.0	0.5	4,980
Chemicals	44.5	37.9	13.7	3.9	4,235
Clothes	63.4	33.7	2.7	0.1	3,870
Vehicles	51.1	35.0	10.1	3.9	3,475
Transport equip't	59.2	29.4	7.8	3.6	2,955
Radio, TV	60.0	31.3	6.9	1.8	2,825
Pulp paper	43.6	39.4	15.1	1.9	2,155
Basic metals	40.5	40.8	13.3	2.5	1,840
Office machinery	67.0	25.4	4.8	1.8	1,140
Leather products	57.0	32.5	5.3	0.0	755
Coke, nuc' fuels	50.8	30.2	11.1	7.9	315
Total mfg units	58.1	35.1	5.7	1.1	162,785

Source: ONS, *Annual Abstract*

Despite this trend, small firms remain the norm. Thousands of micros, hundreds of SMEs and tens of large firms give a normal J curve. Plotting the number of jobs against size band, however, gives a typical bell curve as follows:
- 94,578 micros (allowing two jobs/firm) employ 189,156,
- 57,137 small firms (with 20/firm) employ 1,142,750,
- 9,277 medium firms (with 100 staff) employ 927,745, and
- 1,796 large firms (with 300 staff) employ 537,180 staff.

2,796,831 manufacturing jobs roughly agrees with 2,642,000 (excluding construction from table 13) one year later. Though guestimates, these figures confirm that most jobs (75%) are provided by SMEs. Micros and macros employ 6% and 19% respectively. This bell curve peaks somewhere between 40 and 50 staff/firm. The size of firms in local economies, like height in populations, conform to this Gaussian distribution. The primary and service sectors will have similar distributions: from shepherd and smallholding to battery farm and super dairy; local newsagent and surgery to national retailer and teaching hospital. Generally, small firms give value and diversity, SMEs innovate and specialize and large firms provide volume and consistency.

Three other points emerge from table 16. The bell curves vary between industries. We might expect chemicals and vehicles to be skewed towards large firms at the bottom of the J curve. Yet the food sector is even more skewed. Food, like furniture, joinery, clothes and publishing, should be the easiest to develop from home – unlike nuclear fuels. The lower level of micro and small food firms may reflect market domination by foodsheds and manufacturers like Unilever, Nestlé, Kraft Heinz and Mars.

Second, in the ten years since 1998, when ONS first collected this data, the number of manufacturing sites fell by 10%, the medium and large sites falling from about 15,020 (8.33%) to 11,050 (6.77% of the total). The bulk of lost jobs in manufacturing were from large sites.

And third, losing a large local firm can be devastating.

"I had a terrible shock. I drove to Tri-ang's majestic nineteenth century mill which, with its modern extension, was the home of Tri-ang's business, but I couldn't find the mill. I decided I wasn't in the right place because I was staring at a cleared building site. But I soon discovered that the area was scheduled for housing development, and the mill... had been demolished. I couldn't believe it.

"I picked my way across the site with a heavy heart and I saw pathetic signs of the past. The plastic wheel of a Tri-ang toy lay forgotten in the rubble, vividly illustrating what I think has gone wrong in the UK over the last few years: the people who eventually occupy the houses on this site will need work and income in order to live in the houses, but the mill and the Tri-ang business which provided that work and income have gone. How can the people who come to live here support themselves if the businesses don't exist? And how can the UK create wealth and healthy export markets when an empty building site is valued more than a business which contributes to that wealth?" (John Harvey-Jones 1992)

"Labour isn't working" was a political slogan that helped Margaret Thatcher win the 1979 election, when over one million people were unemployed. Since then, Capital has not worked either. Since 1979, the number unemployed has averaged about two million, and for some years was over three million. (Regrettably, official statistics became unreliable as many unemployed were reclassified by government and put on long-term sickness or incapacity benefits. Later, in one of those circles from Dante's *Inferno*, many on sickness benefits became scroungers on the state, because they 'were not really sick'.)

High unemployment and a deskilled labour force reduces local wealth and devastates urban communities. More people are ill, depressed, isolated and suicidal, and more turn to drink, drugs and domestic abuse, theft and petty crime. Even boys in primary schools are affected, many under-achieving compared with girls and earlier times. Perhaps they realize what's in store for them after school: the casualization of work with more part-time jobs, short-term or zero hour contracts (only paid when required), self-employment (to reduce overheads), fewer employment benefits, lower pensions and, the final insult, internships to gain work experience but no money. One might compare this with the depression of the 1930s, but then there was more social cohesion. New business parks largely ignore this structural problem.

"It is not possible to build a strong economy on the ruins of society." (Jean-Claude Paye, OECD secretary general, 1995) High unemployment diminishes us all.

Local economies – b) anchors and hoovers

"The only constant in life is change. I'm fed up with that cliché. What we need are anchors" is at the heart of conservation (see page 71). Anchors are essential in local economies as on ships, providing "support, stability and security, a mainstay" (*Penguin ED*). I would suggest five main business anchors:
- old buildings that supply cheap business premises (from chapter 3),
- town centres (chapter 4),
- many small firms and start-ups, the seedbed for all local economies,
- a well-established family firm with local suppliers and subcontractors, and
- local clusters of small and medium-sized firms (SMEs) specializing in specific sectors like ceramics.

Clusters are vital for their specialist prowess and resilience. "Large symbiotic collections of little enterprises" are the basis for *Cities and the Wealth of Nations* (Jacobs 1984). Between Bologna and Venice, there are a number of industrial clusters. "Sabel [a social scientist at MIT] was amazed at the small size of these innovative and highly successful firms, most of which "employ from 5 to 50 workers, a few as many as 100, and a very few 250 or more... specializing in virtually every phase of the production of textiles, automatic machines, machine tools, automobiles, buses and agricultural equipment," and was impressed by the sophistication and quality of the work being done in production of ceramics, shoes, plastic furniture, motorcycles, woodcutting machinery, metal-cutting machinery, ceramics machinery. He reports the ease with which new enterprises have formed through break-away of workers from older enterprises, and the amazing economies of scale that are obtained not, as has been conventionally assumed, within the framework of huge organizations but rather through large symbiotic collections of little enterprises."

Most of our industrial clusters in textiles, clothing, shoes, shipbuilding, engineering, machinery and electrical engineering disappeared during the twentieth century. The chemical, pottery and vehicle industries are hanging on.

A century ago, there were about 2,000 car manufacturers worldwide, of which we had our share. Today the 15 major producers are based in Japan, Germany, South Korea, the United States, France, Italy and China. Since Rolls Royce was sold to Volkswagen in 1998, and the Reliant Robin ceased production in 2002, Britain no longer has an independent mass car producer.

In the niche sector of motor racing, however, the UK is apparently pre-eminent. In Oxfordshire, there are specialist garages, body workshops and research labs engaged in most aspects of vehicle technology. It is likely that general car performance has improved because of this noisy little cluster, although governments had to impose social objectives to improve vehicle safety and reduce petrol consumption, noise levels and engine emissions. Had we retained 200 car makers, these technical and safety improvements, as well as alternatives to the internal combustion engine, might have emerged more quickly. Major car firms, like food sheds, conform to the principle of minimum differentiation. Most new models are largely cosmetic redesigns to raise demand and sell more cars. Innovations from clusters are more likely to be motivated by curiosity about real improvements than simple desire to increase turnover and profits.

From noisy workshops in Oxfordshire, the Cambridge science park was only founded by Trinity College in 1970. By 1997, it had attracted 72 assorted firms employing 3,500 people (averaging 48.6 staff/firm) with an estimated aggregate turnover of £260 million. This cluster, working in high-tech instruments, computer software, biotechnology and pharmaceuticals, co-operate with university research groups and with each other. The science park "now boasts that it has the largest concentration of high-technology enterprises in Europe." (*The Observer* 26/10/97) By November 2014, according to its website, the science park has over 100 companies employing "roughly 5,000 people in total". So, 17 years of expansion has brought more SMEs (still averaging 50 staff) rather than bigger firms.

This modest size gives SMEs independence and flexibility, with very different working methods to the large firms. Within clusters, small firms develop networks and specialist markets, share ideas and complementary skills, set up supply chains, joint ventures and strategic links with universities and research institutes. These networks are more open and creative than one large research department. This 'connectivity with the outside world' reinforces their social as well as economic behaviour. While the profit motive remains essential for survival, the driving force in clusters, as in social enterprises, is personal motivation and creative collaboration within these 'symbiotic collections of little enterprises'. If personal reward were the prime motivator, then most of these innovators would have quickly sold out to large corporations, killing any cluster before it took root.

Clusters, being owned, managed and staffed locally, enrich local economies. They are also more resilient. When a large firm like Tri-ang goes bust, it takes everything with it. One failure in a cluster has little impact, and sometimes networking can help it survive. If a whole sector is at risk, then given time, decline can be managed or even reversed from within.

Anchors strengthen local economies, hoovers weaken them. Unlike Hoovers that remove dust and detritus, business hoovers extract money and skills from local economies. Foodsheds only put about 7% of their turnover in local economies through staff wages. The rest pays for the goods, buildings, transport, management, finance, marketing and up to 25% for profits. Like cattle, these firms suffer from hoove, 'a disease characterized by an inflation of the stomach, usually due to eating too much grass fodder' (*OED*). Like cattle, hoovers are bloated by their greed, growing fat on their fodder and smothering competitors, before infecting adjacent economies. (Some retailers take this further: Amazon resembles Hoover (J Edgar) in Jeff Bezos' surveillance of all staff in his warehouses.)

The focus of all hoovers is profit: 'sweating the assets', increasing profit margins and maximizing returns for shareholders and directors. An early example is the Hanson conglomerate, active for 30 years from the mid 1960s. It achieved unprecedented growth by buying ever-bigger companies rather than by internal expansion. Its business model was to buy what it thought was an underpriced poorly-managed company and sell those assets with little potential for profit. This 'asset stripping' recouped much of the purchase price, thereby providing windfall profits for a year or two to pay shareholders generous dividends, so maintaining a high share price for future purchases. The companies retained as 'cash cows' had to produce a minimum 7% return (the annual profit on the capital invested) for head office.

The record of those companies is not inspiring.

- In 1981, the British Ever Ready battery maker employed 3,500 people with 80% of the domestic market. After 11 years in the Hanson group, it employed just 1,800 and its share of the market had shrunk to 35%. Sold back to the American Ever Ready parent company in 1992, the last UK factory was closed in 1996.
- In 1983, Hanson bought the Allders chain of department stores and floated it on the Stock Exchange ten years later. Allders closed down in 2005, except for the founding store in Croydon which survived until 2013.
- In 1986, Hanson bought Imperial Tobacco for £2.5 billion, selling off subsidiary companies like the Courage Brewery, Golden Wonder, Finlays and Imperial Hotels. This gave rise to disputes over company pension schemes, an issue with many major takeovers. Ten years later, it de-merged Imperial Tobacco.
- In 1991 Hanson failed to buy ICI, then the largest UK company. (In defence, ICI split itself into two companies; Zeneca drugs and ICI paints.)
- Thereafter, Hanson began selling its assets. The last company, Hanson Bricks (London Bricks as was), was sold to the German company HeidelbergCement in 2007 for £8bn. (Main sources, Wikipedia.)

Key points stand out. To maintain shareholder loyalty, Hanson had to buy ever-larger companies to increase the windfall gains so they could maintain or increase dividends. This resembled a Ponzi scheme, and eventually the whole bubble burst. By contrast, the large corporations that bought Hanson firms were focussed on profit growth through market share. Hanson Brick (formerly London Brick) followed the sale to foreign firms of our other main building materials suppliers: Lafarge (French) bought Redland and Tarmac, CRH (Ireland) bought Ibstock, Cemex of Mexico bought RMC and Holcim (Swiss) bought Aggregate Industries. Here, the danger is not asset stripping but anti-competitive price fixing. Finally, once sold, the separate firms were found to be worth more in total than when in the group. This was confirmed when the two ICI offshoots were worth more than the parent company.

The Hanson model survives with private equity groups. Buy big firms, sell assets to reclaim much of the purchase price, extract generous 'dividends' for the managers and hope to sell the leaner rationalized firm at a significant profit. They confirm one important point. Most large firms are inefficient. Any economies of scale are exceeded by inefficiencies inherent in their size (discussed below). But private equity has inflated the profit motive. While Hanson was satisfied with 7% returns, in the 1990s, expected returns (or annual profits) were 8% for the public sector, 13% for the private sector and 30% for venture capitalists (Davis 1998). 20% was not uncommon in local newspapers, train companies and new foodsheds among others. Extracting inflated profits from stable industries like prime shops and public utilities usually means cutting all costs in staff, research and investment, rather than improved efficiency. And like Hanson, it is always short-term.

Consider a typical private equity firm buying a public limited company (plc) with a small amount of capital and large loans from banks and investors. In converting a public capital asset into private debt, former profits become debt repayments. The target is to repay this debt within say five years, sell the private company back to the public as a leaner, fitter plc and reap what can be very large capital gains. This process redistributes wealth with distinct winners, including:

- plc shareholders who receive a windfall capital gain when selling their shares,
- banks and consultants who earn large fees for concluding the deal, and
- banks earning high interest rates on the substantial loans to cover the risks attached to the buyout,
- the new private owners who, for a modest stake, award themselves large dividends and bonuses which are taxed at lower rates than income tax, and again
- when they sell the company back to shareholders, if the short-term results show improvement, the temporary owners receive a substantial capital gain on their investment. This may reflect 'added value' but the leaner company with fewer assets and demotivated staff will struggle to survive.

There are also real losers. For staff, an initial redundancy package is the default mode once private equity firms take control. Those not sacked may then have increased workloads or reduced wages. When a local chain of care homes was bought by one of the largest care providers, the new owners 'discovered' that the wage bill of the company just bought was too high and that salary cuts were needed if the company was to survive.

Customers lose. When *Radio Times* was sold to a private equity group, within five years the price doubled from £1.40, well in excess of the housing bubble, let alone the retail price index. This profiteering reduces the number of customers, but while total revenue increases (plus savings on the smaller print runs) no-one is hurt. There are other media listings on offer. However, profiteering raises real problems when applied, for example, to bus and rail fares. The private companies don't mind losing some passengers so long as revenues rise. However, the poor make even fewer trips, and we all suffer extra pollution, congestion and roadkill as more passengers transfer to car or plane.

Saving money reduces quality. Older citizens have their own anecdotes. After my vain attempts to conserve our 40 year old gas cooker, the fitter agreed that it was probably past it. "Never mind" I said. "This new one will see us out." He looked puzzled: "Will you be dead in seven years?" Built-in obsolescence increases turnover and GDP while wasting materials, energy and labour – and costing us money.

Taxpayers. Converting equity into debt means that all corporate taxes paid on former profits now become tax relief on the private company's borrowings. In effect, banks replace HMRC. Lower wages mean lower taxes, and redundancies require unemployment benefits. This means higher taxes or less government spending.

The market itself suffers. In privatizing a plc, new owners hide most company data. Privatized service providers can even be shielded by government ministers under the guise of commercial confidentiality. Secrecy is the enemy of a healthy market. Private equity groups do not create wealth. They siphon it. Paying themselves at the expense of their staff is a zero-sum game. Private equity may have identified substantial inefficiencies inside large firms. But to make plc's more efficient and profitable, we only need to break them up into smaller companies, when everyone gains through a non-zero sum game.

In short, anchors stabilize local economies and add social value, hoovers disrupt and devalue. Consider one local economy.

Cornwall has a fascinating economic history. It began with farming, fishing and mining, with market towns like Truro, Bodmin and Launceston for farmers, fishing ports like Padstow, Newlyn, Mevagissey and Looe, hard rock mines around Camborne and Redruth (now closed except for tourism trails), and the moonscape of china clay pits surrounding St Austell, the home of English China Clays that supplies the pottery and paper industries. In the 1990s, the chief executive moved the head office to Reading to be near the City and possible financial deals. In 1999, ECC was sold to a French firm, and the old HQ in St Austell is now NHS offices.

The county (or nation) was also in the forefront of the Industrial Revolution. Its rich heritage developed from its global reputation for a range of metal products and mining machinery. These included Newcomen's steam-driven pumps, Davy's miners' lamps, Murdoch's town gas in Redruth, Holman's (then CompAir) mining machinery in Cambourne from 1801 till 2001, Trevithick's first steam-driven vehicle tested between Redruth and Cambourne, and Harveys foundry in Hayle. This foundry made the large beam engines that were used to 'reclaim' much of the Netherlands from the North Sea. When the foundry closed, the site was bought by a speculative developer whose neglect resulted in most of the foundry buildings being demolished. The county archaeologist was once stopped by a group of German tourists asking where they would find these buildings – a photo of which was on the front cover of their guidebook on the industrial archaeology *of Europe*. Such is our regard for heritage and speculators.

Phoenix-like, a small specialist foundry in an industrial estate in Hayle supplies the food and pharmaceutical industries, employs over 40 skilled and semi-skilled staff, and has invested in training and equipment to clean its emissions. It is a valuable anchor. When new housing was built nearby, the council started to receive complaints about the (harmless) foundry smell on warm, calm days leading to visits from council officers. Fortunately, the company remains. As in Plymouth's Sutton harbour (pages 85-6 above), anchors should not be put at risk by new residents with minor concerns.

Today, manufacturing has largely given way to tourism. Here again, local anchors are at risk from hoovers. Despite a major 'Food from Cornwall' initiative, a national chain hotel overlooking a small fishing port on the north coast has all its fish delivered frozen from Grimsby. On the south coast, a major holiday camp (part of another chain), catering for up to 1,000 people, has its beer supplied by one of the two national brewers instead of the local brewery. Central purchasing might reduce costs and increase profit margins, but in both cases the product is inferior, transport costs are higher, the holiday experience is homogenized and local managers and producers are both marginalized.

The ancient fishing port of Looe offers an alternative. With up to 100,000 visitors a year, about 2,500 coaches used to park on Buller Quay beside the Guildhall and new fish market in the heart of the town. The harbour commissioners wanted to build some small fish handling units beside the fish market. Many objected that coaches would boycott the town, losing more than £500,000 a year from visitors buying postcards, ice cream and cups of tea. However, the fish handling units were built, and Looe now employs over 20 local people full-time, adding value grading, filleting, chilling and packaging much of the £4million worth of fish sold in the market. Meanwhile, the coaches simply park further out and visitors have to walk a little further.

Mega-corps – and microeconomics

In 1998, half of the world's biggest economies were corporations (rather than nations), with 500 controlling 25% of the world's economic output (*The Observer* 6/2/98). And in 2015, "69 of the world's wealthiest 100 economic entities were corporations... When looking at the top 200 economic entities... 153 [are] corporations." (Global Justice Now, from *Ethical Consumer* no 163.)

These corporations, with ever larger mergers and takeovers, are concentrating ever more output from fewer outfits. Between 1997 and 2004, deals exceeding $1million ranged from just under 30,000 to 43,000, while the total value of all deals reached $4.2 trillion in 2000 (Sloman 2006). He also noted "an acceleration in the process of 'globalization'. With the dismantling of trade barriers around the world and increasing financial deregulation, international competition increased. Companies felt the need to become bigger in order to compete more effectively."

The management guru Pete Drucker had another explanation. "I will tell you a secret: deal making beats working. Deal making is exciting and fun, and working is grubby. Running anything is primarily an enormous amount of grubby detail work... deal making is romantic, sexy. That's why you have deals that make no sense." According to Warren Buffett: "The sad fact is that most major acquisitions display an egregious imbalance. They are a bonanza for the shareholders of the acquiree; they increase the income and status of the acquirer's management; and they are a honey pot for the investment bankers and other professionals on both sides. But, alas, they usually reduce the wealth of the acquirer's shareholders, often to a substantial extent. That happens because the acquirer typically gives up more intrinsic value than it receives." (Connors 2010)

After the bankers' crash in 2008, "With confidence rising, mergers are returning. A Wall Street lawyer thought "that mega-mergers had a psychological component: once transactions start happening, chief executives do not want to be left behind. Deals breed more deals." A central reason for the return of big transactions is the big amount of cash on corporate balance sheets. After the financial crisis, companies hunkered down, laying off employees and cutting costs. Today corporations in the S & P 500 are sitting on more than $1 trillion in cash. With interest rates near zero, that money is earning very little in bank accounts, so executives are looking to put it to work by acquiring businesses." (*The New York Times* 24/2/13)

The desire to grow – because executives find it exciting, feel it essential to compete, or not be left behind – is irrational. The economist Ronald Coase (1910-2013) justified large corporations. They buy firms in their supply chain in order to reduce 'transactional' costs, a dry economist's term for all social aspects of trade of barter, negotiation and collaboration. Later, Oliver Williamson suggested two economic models: Adam Smith's 'classical markets' of symbiotic clusters or SMEs; and Coase's economic 'hierarchies' based on vertical integration and 'command management'.

"Power tends to corrupt, and absolute power corrupts absolutely" (Lord Acton 1887) foreshadowed the worst twentieth century tyrannies. It may explain why right wing economists and neo-conservatives (neo-conomists?) reject large government. Yet while power affects all walks of life – religion, the media, sport, even the home – neo-conomists seem relaxed about multinational corporations. "For an economist and business school professor such as myself, globalization can be defined as 'the activities of multinational enterprises engaged in [about 90 per cent of the world's] foreign direct investment and the development of business networks to create value across national borders'. Sociologists... argue that such an economic definition of globalization is too narrow. They believe that it is multi-dimensional, best 'understood in terms of simultaneous, complex related processes in the realms of economy, politics, culture, technology and so forth..." (Rugman 2000).

Let us call multinational enterprises (MNEs) and transnational corporations (TNCs) 'mega-corps'. And let us discuss them: first as micro-economic corporations (if that's not an oxymoron), looking at how they create 'value across national borders' under the four P's of production, people, profit and promotion; and second, as macro-social entities with impacts 'in the realms of economy, politics, culture, technology and so forth'.

i) Production

As firms get bigger, so potential economies of scale increase. But, as Coase recognized and as we saw with foodsheds, those savings have to be set against increasing overheads. The idea that one production plant can supply a nation or whole continent ('region' to mega-corp) is undone when we include all internal and external costs.

Risk is inherent in any business but it increases exponentially with size. Remote control can lead to humanitarian catastrophe. Union Carbide (UC) had 54 subsidiaries plus 23 majority-owned companies in 39 countries with plants in at least 175 cities (APPEN 1985). When its pesticide plant in Bhopal "released a large volume of toxic gases" on December 2nd 1984, highest estimates were 8,000 killed within two weeks and 8,000 more dying later from gas-related diseases. Cost estimates also ranged widely: UC offered $350 million, while the Indian government sued in the US (unsuccessfully) for $3.3 billion. Eventually, UC paid $470 million, plus $17 million for a hospital specifically for Bhopal. The catastrophe raised key issues:

- Economies of scale. Doubling the number of UC pesticide plants to 32, with smaller tanks, would have reduced transport (and possibly construction) costs, the release of toxic gas and scale of harm.
- Safety. The tank that ruptured held 42 tons of the toxic methyl isocyanate, more than safety rules allowed. Small independent firms would be safer, if only because managers themselves would be on site.
- Justice. Had Bhopal been in Tennessee or Indiana, UC would have incurred large fines, compensation for victims and prison for those found culpable. Instead, having benefitted from cheap production costs, UC suffered modest corporate fines.
- The market. 'Classical' markets let successful firms prosper and weed out failures. A Bhopal plant owned locally would have gone out of business, lessons would have been learned and implemented across the whole sector, even 'adding value across national borders'. Instead, a poorly-managed mega-corp with large financial resources survived, simply because it was big.

Risk affects every business. "The most devastating human-caused environmental disaster" occurred on March 24th 1989, when the *Exxon Valdez* tanker ran aground, spilling up to 38 million gallons of crude oil into Alaska's Prince William Sound. Then, on 20th April 2010, after "BP officials [had gathered] on the platform to celebrate seven years without an injury on the rig", the Deepwater Horizon drilling rig exploded, spilling oil into the Gulf of Mexico. By July 15th, when BP finally capped the leak, between 72 and 144 million gallons of crude oil had spewed into the gulf.

Oil also destabilizes political regions, not just in the middle east. "In the 1990s, the Nigerian government carried out a horrific crackdown on protesters against pollution caused by oil giant Shell in the Ogoniland region [culminating in the execution of the Ogoni nine. Last year, Amnesty research] pointed to the Anglo-Dutch company's complicity in murder, rape and torture committed by the Nigerian government." (Amnesty International Ltd: *Annual Review* 2017) Yet Shell remains in the area and leaks continue. International pressure, national sovereignty, habitat destruction and local livelihoods are all subservient to shareholder interests. And now Gazprom (with Shell) has started exploratory drilling in the Arctic shelf. Is there a bookmaker taking bets on the next catastrophe?

From our 'heritage' of hundreds of Victorian high street banks, just seven remain: Barclays, HSBC, Lloyds, the Royal Bank of Scotland, Santander, Standard Chartered and the Trustee Savings Bank (demerged from Lloyds and now part of another Spanish bank), plus the Co-op and Metro banks, the Clydesdale and Yorkshire regional banks (owned by the National Australia Bank) and perhaps 20 private or retail-owned banks. This consolidation supported by all governments, culminated with the Big Bang of 1986, which deregulated the banks and led to merger mania of all financial services. Almost overnight, the cluster of brokers, jobbing firms and merchant banks that gave the City its international reputation disappeared. Fielding Newson-Smith, Kitcat and Aitken, Phillips and Drew, Wood Mackenzie, Grieveson Grant, Laing and Cruikshank, Scrimgeour Kemp Gee, Vickers da Costa, de Zoete and Bevan, Rowe and Pitman, Wedd Durlacher, County Bisgood, Pinchin Denny, Barings, SG Warburg, Kleinwort Benson, and Smith New Court were all bought out, lodged somewhere in Merrill Lynch, Citicorp, Morgan Stanley, Credit Lyonnais, Lehman Brothers (since gone bust), ING, UBS or our high-street banks.

With size and freedom, the seeds were sown for the bankers' crash of 2008. This was the result of their collective greed, lies, ignorance and incompetence, based largely on a housing bubble. It has cost us all about £1 trillion in guarantees, loans and bail-outs (and $5 trillion in the US), plus a following (ill-judged) decade of austerity. Yet it is impossible to embarrass the bankers, who continue to act unlawfully. HSBC was fined almost $2bn in the US for 'laundering' $7bn from Mexican drug cartels to HSBC's US operations. The US Senate committee report (July 2012) also found other 'irregularities' involving Iran, Saudi Arabia and Russia (*HSBC money laundering report: Key findings*, BBC 11/12/12). The bank put its failures down to a 'restructuring' that cut costs, including cuts to the internal compliance departments.

Nor do the high street banks give better service, often treating their own customers with breath-taking dishonesty over insurance, mortgages and pensions etc. Meanwhile, Germany has 20 main banks, nearly 1,200 co-operative banks, 431 savings banks (Sparkassen) and a further two dozen private or specialist banks (Wikipedia). It is this number and diversity of banks which ensures a healthy sector.

Can only meg-corps deliver jumbo jets, nuclear power stations, the Shard, Bhopal, Trident missiles, the bankers' Crash and other disasters? Joseph Bazelgette's Victorian sewers, with embankments and pumping stations, were built by a small army of engineers, builders and subcontractors. And earlier, small armies of designers and crafters, masons and carpenters, scaffolders and labourers built medieval cathedrals, one of the wonders of the world. Mega-corps are not the only solution: there are always smaller, safer, more reliable, less polluting and usually cheaper options.

ii) People

When Adam Smith identified the division of Labour as the mainspring for wealth, he did not distinguish between manager and machinist. Coase's command management, however, has effectively divorced mega-corp boardrooms from their many shopfloors – memorably summed up by Michael O'Leary of Ryanair. "MBA students come out with: 'My staff is my most important asset.' Bullshit. Staff is usually your biggest cost. We all employ some lazy bastard who needs a kick up the backside, but no-one can bring themselves to admit it." (www.telegraph.co.uk.) No handwringing regret in O'Leary's blunt honesty, though surely in private, he would argue that most staff are lazy. Wasting management time on one lazy bastard doesn't make sense. Equally revealing is his 'them and us' attitude, with 'my staff' being 'your biggest cost'. Few see business as a social enterprise involving staff and managers equally.

Most executives crave status. 'What's good for General Motors is good for America', (or ICI for Britain) fuels any boardroom sense of omnipotence before hubris sets in. Some managers seek gurus. For Bernie Ecclestone, Hitler "was – in the way that he could command a lot of people – able to get things done." Far more capable, he thought, than in democracies (*The Times* 4/7/2009). Ecclestone had to clarify this provocative statement. Perhaps Hitler was efficient in building autobahns as well as slaughterhouses for Jews, Gypsies and dissidents. The wise J K Galbraith (in a footnote somewhere) broke this illusion. Throughout his period in power, Hitler was surrounded by the same coterie of ministers, solely for their commitment to his 'vision'. So while Britain greatly increased production, Germany never introduced two- let alone three-shift working, nor allowed women into factories where they had never been. There are similarities between 'command management' and tyranny.

Do not expect insight from business leaders, whose acumen is usually corrupted by greed and ego wrapped in glitter. Kevin Dutton suggests that "a number of psychopathic attributes are arguably more common in the boardroom than the padded cell... Psychopaths and Chief Executives both display superficial charm, egocentricity, independence and restricted focus." (*The Wisdom of Psychopaths*, as reviewed in *The Observer* 7/10/12.) Lord Acton should be quoted more fully. "Power tends to corrupt, and absolute power corrupts absolutely. Great men are almost always bad men. There is no worse heresy than that the office sanctifies the holder of it." Earlier, Henry Fielding distinguished between the great and the good. "That while it is so easy and safe, and truly honourable, to be good... greatness consists in power, pride, insolence and doing mischief to mankind – to speak out – while a great man and a great rogue are synonymous terms." (*Jonathan Wild* 1754) All, perhaps, originate with Machiavelli's *The Prince* (1513). *The Corporation* documentary (2004) thought that even mega-corps are psychopathic. They lie, show no concern for others, develop no long-term relationships, have a disregard for safety, have no feelings of guilt and do not conform to social norms.

Staff alienation, from apathy to sabotage, reflects the yawning pay gap between boardroom and shopfloor. "Real wages [fell] by more than 8% between 2007 and 2014. Yet CEO pay has been steadily rising… despite losses and job cuts… Analysis by the independent High Pay Centre shows FTSE 100 CEOs are paid an average of almost £5m a year, 183 times the average UK employee, up from 160 times just six years ago. Thirty years ago, these multiples were a fraction of what they are now." (*The Observer*, 24/4/16)

This inevitably sours relations between directors and staff. The social historian Studs Terkel (1975) summarized it thus. "There are, of course, the happy few who find a savor [sic] in their daily job… For the many, there is a hardly concealed discontent. The blue-collar blues is no more bitterly sung than the white-collar moan. "I'm a machine," says the spot-welder. "I'm caged," says the bank teller, and echoes the hotel clerk. "I'm a mule," says the steelworker. "A monkey can do what I do," says the receptionist. "I'm less than a farm implement," says the migrant worker. "I'm an object," says the high-fashion model. Blue collar and white call upon the identical phrase: "I'm a robot.""

Martin Sprouse captured this 'hardly concealed discontent' in *Sabotage in the American Workplace: Anecdotes of Dissatisfaction, Mischief and Revenge* (1992). The following quotes capture the resentment of the 137 workers interviewed from small companies, government departments and large corporations in all sectors, such as Bank of America, Bechtel, General Motors, Kodak, Kmart, Pacific Gas and Electric, and Toys R Us.

- "Sabotage is different than revenge because it's a means by which you can express yourself and free yourself from oppression and dehumanization. You aren't attacking a person, you're dealing with an issue… I saw other people like me who were drudging through life, making pretty good money and benefits, but whose lives were shit. Being human is so wonderful. If we're pushed apart from that, we tend to struggle because you can't be human in America and work in industry. When you work for the auto industry, profit is number one… They're trying to compete with Japan, but… They don't treat you like a human being, they treat you like a robot, and your function is to produce the profit. You're dehumanized. The carburetors [sic] were our way of equalizing the situation."
- For a pickling plant engineer, working with children in a sweatshop without unions or rights, "the foreman told [us all] not to socialize. When he told me to be a robot, I was a robot. But I was a thinking robot." He would slow down the belt for the packers and sometimes break it completely.

- "The work [in air freight] was insanely boring, but it was hard... There was one asshole who... was constantly on our backs. We'd be working our asses off, drenched in sweat and he'd come over and yell at us, "Alright, put your shirts on and shut up. I'm tired of this shit!"... Whenever he started acting like that, everyone thought, fuck it, and slowed way down. There wasn't much he could do about it."

- Unfair pay also led to problems. Typesetters are paid "anywhere from $10 to $15 an hour... [but] billed to the client at $75 to $150 an hour... I've never met a typesetter who didn't steal his or her own services from an employer."

- Indifference to staff was also resented. At a discount chain store, what "was really depressing was seeing people who had families work there, making the same amount as a teenager. The day after Christmas, 1979, the store laid off a lot of people, even people who had been working there longer than I had. To get even with the company, I started stealing... In 1981, the store had $500,000 in invisible waste [the worst yearly inventory of any store in the country]. That year... The same people who were stealing were doing the inventory, so we were able to cover our asses real good... In reality, the store probably had lost between $750,000 and $1,000,000 to invisible waste."

- On promotion: "I worked really hard... for the first three years but was never promoted beyond that because there weren't any women in top management positions. That really pissed me off... [I published a magazine for three years on their photocopier, and] stole anything I could get my hands on... I never felt any remorse. I think good mischief is well worth the personal effort."

- Some raise ethical issues. "A couple of weeks after we got the job [mapping shops on streets], we realized it was really stupid to be working for a large real-estate company... there's a lot of really shitty stuff that goes on with [them], like kicking people out of homes and demolishing affordable housing... At the same time, we worked out that no one at the company was about to go around verifying the information on the maps we drew, so we figured it wouldn't be a problem to start faking them."

- And stifling creativity is fiercely resented. Working on a large bank's payroll programme, "with a clumsy old in-house system... I was supposed to make the system work better, but I wasn't allowed to make any fundamental changes. I could only patch things up... [The bank] was getting pushy because I wasn't getting the work done as fast as they wanted me to... [My supervisors] said that I was incapable of doing the job because they didn't want the bosses to know how shitty their computer system really was. They made me look really bad, then went a step further and stopped paying me. I got so pissed off at them that I planted a logic bomb in the system, a kind of electronic "Fuck you!"" [This trick recurs in *Flash Boys* by Michael Lewis.]

I also learned from a soft-drinks plant manager that bottles were only filled and capped so quickly "to prevent bored workers inserting dead flies." Does this behaviour originate on the shopfloor or in the boardroom? Social history gives a voice to those seldom heard, showing that companies aren't simple profit machines. They rely on social intercourse among all staff.

Sprouse includes reactions to these interviews, ranging from soft liberal to neo-conomist. For the liberal, "A wave of mergers and closings has lowered employee morale, which often leads to increases in shrinkage figures. Says Walter J Salmon, professor of retailing at the Harvard Business School. "If people think they're likely to be fired, they may not be enormously protective of their company's assets." New York Times Magazine." For neo-conomists, "People who purposely abuse their paid working time are stealing from their employers, just as they would be if they stole money or products," says Robert Half, the employment expert who first identified time theft."

Sabotage is big business. "Employee theft is a $40-billion-per-year disease eating away at the health of American companies." (American Journal of Political and Social Science). But its impact is very different in big firms and small. "A female secretary employed by the [retail] chain in Kansas was stealing at a rate of $1600 in four days. She said she stole a total of $10,000, but the total was probably more. Her boss says, "If we were a single-store operation, we would have been out of business." (Sprouse). Sabotage ruins small firms. Large can absorb the costs of bad management, contradicting the business mantra of 'the survival of the fittest'.

Rewriting George Bernard Shaw's jibe about teachers: "Those who can, do. Those who can't, become managers, or even more highly-paid management consultants who don't manage but are called in to help managers who can manage, apparently." Of course this offends most managers who, like teachers, are decent, hardworking, honest and aware that they are only part of the workforce with essential but complementary skills in any firm. Mega-corps, however, have created a separate world for their directors, as remote and powerful as any central government in any empire. They can survive catastrophic explosions, pollution, faulty products, sabotage, incompetence, even corruption and other 'acts of God' that would bankrupt small firms instantly. Large banks are even protected from bankruptcy by government 'corporate welfare'. And, without irony, some boardrooms then blame local saboteurs rather than themselves, as with UC in Bhopal and Shell in Nigeria.

iii) Profits
If SMEs focus on product or service quality, mega-corp boardrooms focus on profit, their measure of success. The 'grubby detail work of management' usually means cutting costs in production and people, increasing market share through mergers and acquisitions, and raising prices through PR.

Cutting costs brings its own costs. Ring-fencing rewards for directors, advisors, banks and shareholders while employing fewer staff with lower pay, fewer benefits and bigger workloads means the gains are strictly short-term windfalls. Stressed and demoralized staff become disloyal lazy bastards or angry saboteurs. The difference between naked boardroom self interest and healthy 'enlightened self interest' affects long-term prospects.

The relentless short-term pressure on costs also raises ethical problems in dealing with customers, suppliers and competitors, as found with foodsheds (pages 107 and 109-10). General Electric (GE), employing about 300,000, is one of the most profitable mega-corps, engaged in aviation, computing, energy, finance, healthcare, oil and gas, power and water, television and transport. Inevitably, the drive for profit often raises controversial issues, like the design of their reactors in the Fukushima nuclear power plant and various citations for tax evasion despite earning $billions in worldwide profits. According to the Multinational Monitor, between 1990 and 2001, GE "was fined or ordered to pay damages by a court 42 times, amounting to at least $934,026,215" (Wikipedia). Almost $1 billion in fines hardly figures in their annual accounts, and may even be exceeded by the profits made from those activities.

An infamous example emerged in 1973, when Ford decided not to recall its Ford Pinto cars and fix their faulty tanks. An internal memo showed that the cost of likely fatal and serious crashes was less than half the cost of recalling and fixing all the cars. Putting profit above human life would be worthy of any mafia family.

Mergers and acquisitions, while raising company rankings and boardroom egos, seldom increase capital value. As mentioned earlier, ICI paints and Zeneca drugs were worth at least 50% more than the former ICI firm. (Both were later bought out by larger competitors.) Similarly in Germany, after the war, the chemical giant IG Farben was split up into four constituent firms – Agfa, BASF, Bayer and Hoechst. All have prospered since and remain independent except for Hoechst (now a subsidiary of Sanofi-Aventis).

By contrast, Glaxo (GSK) is one of the top six pharma mega-corps, largely by buying independent laboratories. Glaxo (or to give it its full name Glaxo-Affymax-Allen&Hanburys-Allergan-BeckmanInc-BeechamGroup-BlockDrug-BoroughsWellcome-CellZome-CNS-FrenchLaboratories-GlycoVaxyn-InternationalClinicalLaboratories-HumanGenomeSciences-JosephNathan-Kline&Co-LaboratoriosPhoenix-Maxinutrition-MeyerLaboratories-NordenLaboratories-PrestigeBrandsHoldings-RechercheetIndustrieTherapeutiques-Smith-StiefelLaboratories) has replaced at least 24 research departments with one mega-corp. This has reduced the diversity of its research output and, while enjoying a good reputation among its competitors, it also engages in malpractice:

- In 2012, it paid $3 billion for mis-selling two of its antidepressants and making false statements on the safety of another drug. It also signed "a five-year Corporate Integrity Agreement with the U.S. [authorities, obliging] GSK to make major changes to the way it did business, including changing the way its sales force is compensated ... and to implement and maintain transparency in its research practices and publication policies."
- A year later, "Chinese authorities announced that since 2007 more than 700 travel agencies and consulting firms had been used by GSK to funnel nearly three billion yuan in kickbacks to GSK managers, doctors, hospitals and others who prescribed their drugs." (Wikipedia.)

All drug firms face ethical dilemmas. For example, we know that regularly eating junk food makes people fat, affecting at least 30% of our population, and that clinical obesity and diabetes account for about 25% of the annual NHS budget. Now, should drug firms fund research to establish the links between diabetes and junk food, or should they focus on developing and marketing their own diabetes drugs to profit from this growing market? In boardrooms, the arguments would boil down to social health versus company profits. Unlike research institutes, public services and social enterprises, mega-corps should not be trusted with such dilemmas. 'Free' markets favour profit over prevention. Even governments seem to put the interests of mega-corps above social health and stressed hospitals. Perhaps drug firms should be nationalized, or at least socialized.

iv) Promotion
Like its competitors, Glaxo spends more on marketing than research. It spent $4.5 billion on lobbying EU and US institutions in 2013, and a year later, £2.954 billion on research from a total revenue of £23 billion (www.statista.com). As Glaxo bought out 24 drug firms, it seems that its spending on marketing grew more than its spending on research.

Marketing is largely a twentieth century phenomenon, through advertising and public relations. Advertisers try to persuade us, through suggestion, that buying whatever they are peddling will make you sexy, revered or popular. Behind the mask is the auto-suggestion that if you don't buy it, you are impotent, lack self-esteem, or haunted by pester power or peer pressure. Some advertisers argue that a successful advert reduces the unit price of the item being sold, but those marginal savings are swamped by the costs of adverts, promotions and 'brand management'.

The success of McDonald's is largely due to effective advertising, though with creative accounting, it is difficult to tell whether 20%, 30% or even 40% of that £5 burger meal is spent on adverts. Whatever the figure, it is effective. The McLibel trial (lasting three years from 1994) did not seriously affect its business. Although the trial judge found the two folk heroes guilty, Helen Steel and Dave Morris did convince him on some serious allegations. McDonald's did "exploit children through its advertising," "endanger the health of customers who eat there several times a week," "pay its workers unreasonably low wages," and "bear responsibility for the cruelty inflicted on animals by many of its suppliers" (Schlosser 2002).

(The unfairness of our libel laws, in which freedom of speech and fair comment offer little protection, means that defendants have to prove their allegations, reversing criminal law where prosecutors have to prove the defendant guilty. This is against the interest of free enquiry, healthy scepticism and open debate – the foundation of truth and democracy.)

Schlosser describes how just six US fast food chains (McDonald's, Burger King, Subway, Wendy's, Pizza Hut and Taco Bells), with four meatpackers and two food chemical plants, control the market between two million farmers and 245 million customers. He contrasts them with the In-N-Out chain of about

150 restaurants. Its staff are among the highest paid in the industry, while prices remain competitive. "There are no microwaves, heat lamps, or freezers in the kitchens at In-N-Out restaurants. The ground beef is fresh, potatoes are peeled every day to make the fries, and the milk shakes are made from ice cream, not syrup." In-N-Out wins national surveys on "food quality, value, service, atmosphere, and cleanliness", and is one of the most profitable fast food chains in the country, but spends little on marketing. Personal approval ('word of mouth' in the jargon) keeps In-N-Out in business but would not keep McDonald's afloat for more than a month. Junk food chains are addicted to advertising – and PR.

> "You cannot hope to bribe or twist,
> Thank God, the British journalist.
> But seeing what the man will do
> Unbribed, there's no occasion to." (Anon)

If adverts fool most of the people most of the time, PR is anything but public. It only needs to 'persuade' those in the know, aimed solely at policy makers and opinion formers, politicians and the media. Instead of (or as well as) bribes, PR arranges press releases for stressed journalists, hospitality lunches, events and holidays dressed as conferences, secondments to government departments and party political donations. Advertisers use PR when they want to avoid advertising bans on cigarettes, alcohol, gambling, junk food or anything aimed at children.

In *The End of Globalization* (2000), Rugman profiled 20 mega-corps. In one, he found "a new core competence (firm-specific advantage) in organizational learning and managing political risk... It has been one of the first firms in a stable and traditional energy-related sector to develop a knowledge-based business, staffed by skilled and well-trained people who are managers rather than engineers. This gives Enron a competitive advantage compared to the average energy business. Even commodity-type utilities can become effective international businesses by developing such dynamic organizational capabilities."

In December 2001, the firm went bust due to spectacular levels of fraud and corruption. The annual accounts could 'mark to market' likely future revenues, give them HFV (hypothetical future value), and bring them forward as income. These same accounts also concealed real debts in a web of offshore companies (paying Enron director Fastow fees to manage them). Some revenues were real. When it bought PGE (Portland and General Electricity) and California had deregulated its energy market, Enron would shut down some of its power stations ('for maintenance') thereby raising the spot price for electricity and their revenues. Despite annual audits, these accounts gave a completely false picture of the company. It is unfair to single out Rugman. Enron fooled most academics, management gurus, independent analysts, ratings agencies, investment houses, banks and the financial press. Cruver (2003), who joined Enron shortly before it collapsed, was given a term for this collective failure: 'intellectual inertia'. All were fooled by ever-increasing profits and dividends, it seems, except one young journalist, Bethany McLean, who as late as March 2001 dared to write an article for *Fortune* entitled "Is Enron Overpriced?"

We now learn that Ms McLean was not alone. Enron's auditors Arthur Anderson went bust rather than face criminal charges. Some banks and lawyers also knew. After its collapse, "Enron's new directors sued 11 financial institutions for helping Lay, Fastow, Skilling and others hide Enron's true financial condition [including Royal Bank of Scotland, Deutsche Bank and Citigroup]... As of 2008, Enron has settled with all of the institutions [and] was able to obtain nearly $20 billion to distribute to its creditors." (Wikipedia)

Two uncomfortable truths emerge from this web of deceit. First, Enron succeeded for so long because of its PR strategy. It "even had a computer programme to calculate the political cash flows: it was called the Matrix. As part of an operation based in Washington, the software was used to calculate business costs based on the quantitative elements of deregulation, such as lobbying costs, inflation, and growth factors. It was simply a cost-benefit analysis relating campaign contributions to pro-Enron legislation. Enron was playing the political money game as it related to the future of the energy industry, in the hopes it would pave the way to free-market bliss." (Cruver 2003) Beware all deregulation.

Second, none of this fooled Enron's advisors. Their bankers, accountants and lawyers were not stupid. They too were crooked. With inside information, they could lead the bull market while Enron share prices rose (thriving on hints, deceptions, inaccuracies and simple lies), then 'short the stock' and leave the herd to take the losses when the bubble burst. Let us hope that Ofgen and Ofwat have greater control over our energy and water companies.

The global economy

From the four P's of internal management, let us now turn to the external impact of mega-corps and delve "in the realms of economy, politics, culture, technology and so forth" (Rugman, page 140) with the PEST analysis covering politics, economics, social issues and technology.

i) Politics

"The greater the power, the more dangerous the abuse" (Edmund Burke). The East India Company was "A British trading monopoly, established in India in 1600, which later became involved in politics, eventually wielding supreme power through a Board of Control responsible to the British parliament... " (*Penguin Concise Encyclopedia* 2005).

Despite evident corruption flowing from the company (which Burke sought to curb), successive twentieth century governments encouraged the 'rationalization' of industry, in banks and builders, cars, chemists and defence. The UK textile industry eventually merged into either Coats Viyella or Courtaulds, which are now owned by four private companies. By contrast, Prato in Italy, with 180,000 residents, retains about 7,000 SMEs producing and developing the full range of fabrics, natural and synthetic.

Here, typically, four to six mega-corps control 50% to 80% of their market, smothering local competition, innovation, choice and diversity. Yet governments continue to ignore these market-distorting oligopolies. Where anchors strengthen local economies by retaining local control, skills, innovation and profits, hoovers weaken local economies with their dangerous positive feedback loops (or treadmills) in pursuit of ever-lower costs and ever-higher profits. These often conceal staggering levels of inefficiency and risk, and their size and power allows mega-corps to transcend market discipline and become too big to fail. Mega-corps are not the fittest firms in a healthy economy, but resemble natural disasters like viral plagues, human cancers, algal blooms, Japanese knotweed or the Dutch elm fungus (which the Dutch blame on the Italians).

Fast Food Nation provides a rare example of anti-competitive behaviour. Schlosser quotes the president of one US mega-corp at a secretly recorded meeting with executives of a Japanese competitor. He "preached the virtues of collaboration. "We have a saying at this company [Archer Daniels Midland, producing food additives]," he said. "Our competitors are our friends, and our customers are our enemies"." Collusion "may seem like a paranoid fantasy", but is an inevitable temptation that comes with size and market force. Mega-corps prevail because of their unfair leverage over suppliers, customers and markets, coupled with their excessive influence over governments and international trade.

Winston Churchill foresaw the danger of bad management. In 1909, he set up wage councils to agree minimum wages for various industries where, in his words, "the good employer is undercut by the bad, and the bad employer is undercut by the worst." Even when foreign workers clearly benefit, there are social consequences here, not only in lost jobs and skills but also in lower wages. Private equity firms that now manage one seventh of UK businesses, with mega-corps, see their firms not as investment vehicles for innovation and motivation, but vehicles for financial engineering with ruthless cost cutting for private gain. Healthy clusters and social enterprises are undercut by large firms that are undercut by the worst Gradgrinds in mega-corps and private equity groups. The last wage council, the Agricultural Workers Wages Board, was disbanded in 2013.

The baleful mindset of mega-corps against any government regulation can be seen in the big six agrochemicals; BASF, Bayer, Dow, Dupont, Monsanto and Syngenta. In five weeks, SumOfUs subjected Monsanto to the following web-based campaigns to stop it:

- suing the US state of Vermont to block a law requiring the labelling of foods containing GM ingredients;
- contesting Guatemala's highest court, which struck down the 'Monsanto Law' that had prevented farmers saving seeds from one year to the next. This law was included under the free trade deals to develop the market for their 'suicide

seeds'. These seeds produce crops that are infertile, surely an unsustainable and infamous restructuring of nature;

- suing the Hawaiian island of Maui, which had passed a moratorium on genetically engineered crops; and
- to stop Starbucks and others supporting Monsanto in its legal threats against Vermont re GM crops. (SumOfUs: 11/10/14, 20/10/14, 11/11/14 and 15/11/14)

Mega-corps now pervade almost every market in the primary, manufacturing and service sectors. This includes accountants, the very people who should be exposing any abuse of power through their annual audits. In 30 years, Britain's ten big accountancy firms have merged into just four mega-corps:

- Deloitte was created in 1989 after Deloitte Haskins & Sells merged with Touche Ross and Nobuzo Tohmatsu, plus Drivers Jonas estate agents. Deloitte's global fees in 2014 were $34.2 billion;
- PwC, with income of $34 billion, was formed in 1998 from Price Waterhouse and Coopers & Lybrand, plus the insolvency firm Cork Gully;
- EY, $27.4 billion, was formed in 1989 from Ernst with Whinney, Smith and Whinney, Young with Broads Paterson & Co, and the remnants of Arthur Anderson in 2002 post Enron; and
- KPMG, $24.8 billion in fees, was formed in 1987 when Peat Marwick International merged with Klynveld Main Goerdeler.

This global dominance is mirrored in the UK, where they audit 99 out of the FTSE 100 largest firms. In 2014, the fourth largest (EY) had an income of £1.721 billion. This was matched only by combining the income of the next eight UK accountancy firms. Perhaps size gives them the resources, skills and weight to audit other mega-corps competently. Or perhaps they are no different and simply collaborate.

- Arthur E Anderson (1885-1947), the Chicago founder of the firm was "a stickler for honesty, [arguing] that accountants' responsibility was to investors, not their clients' management." Today, the big four too often act as both auditor and consultant for the same mega-corp, developing unhealthy relations with managers and clear conflicts of interest, as frequently reported in *Private Eye*. Large management fees put at risk the integrity of any audit.
- Following the collapse of Arthur Anderson, rather than tackle this conflict between audit and management fees, our government was persuaded to introduce limited liability partnerships (LLPs) similar to public liability companies (PLCs). This protected senior partners from personal liability for such corporate disasters as Enron, the banks and Carillion. Britain is now the business address for a large number of 'off the peg' and offshore LLPs, engaged in any mix of arms dealing, drug trafficking, money laundering and other activities that are completely unregulated, the owners unknown and Companies House grossly under-resourced.
- Insolvency work is also corrupted when auditors work more closely with the banks than with client firms in financial difficulty. In this grey area of being viable and cutting further losses, too many firms are shut down or sold on at

prices that grossly underestimate their true value. Owners are made bankrupt, auditors extract large 'administration' fees and banks recover their loans and overdrafts, leaving other creditors, staff and shareholders with pennies in the pound.

- This problem is compounded by the appeal process. As with solicitors, all disputes involving accountants and receivers are dealt with by their own professional body rather than an independent authority. Self-regulation is an oxymoron. Rarely does the 'regulator' find in favour of the aggrieved party and strike off the accountants involved.

- Conflicts of interest also infect the public sector. "PwC [is] not only auditor and adviser to the Macquarie Group [part owners of Thames Water], but also acting as adviser/delivery partner to Ofwat (the water regulator) and re-valuing Thames Water's pension schemes." Since 2007, when the group bought Thames Water from RWE, it halved the rate of water leakage (as it was supposed to, leaks having been ignored by the previous owners). In the same period, however, the company (controlled from Luxembourg) paid its shareholders "nearly £3bn in dividends, [raised long-term debt] from £1.6bn in 2005 to more than £10bn in 2014... [while] the pension fund deficit is also up from £36m in 2005 to £249m in 2014." (Private Eye no 1419, 27/5/16) Ofwat should appoint an independent 'adviser\delivery partner' from the next tier of accountants who would probably be cheaper and possibly help Ofwat curb this profiteering.

- The big four, with banks and lawyers, promote and sell what is known in the trade as efficient tax management schemes. This is viewed as aggressive tax avoidance by HMRC and, to the rest of us, as rampant tax evasion (ipE, defined on page 115 above).

- More insidiously, the oligopolies are prominent government advisers. They approved all those PFI contracts for new hospitals, prisons and schools, based on clearly false comparisons with traditional public-funded capital projects. They earned generous fees simply by repeating what successive governments wanted them to say (on the lie that it keeps public spending down). Things have moved on. The big four are now advising many NHS trusts on how to buy themselves out of these ruinously expensive PFI contracts, for a second fee that extracts yet more money from the health service. An honest politician might call this a double whammy.

We have revived the East India Company in all but name.

ii) Macro-economics (or mega-nomics)

"Globalization, based on the free play of comparative advantage, economies of scale and innovation, has produced a genuinely radical force, in the true sense of the word. It essentially amplifies and reinforces the strengths, but also the weaknesses, of market capitalism: its efficiency, its instability, and its inequality. If we want globalization not only to be efficiency-boosting but also fair, we need more international rules and stronger multilateral institutions." Pascal Lamy, a former EU trade commissioner (from Sloman 2006) is more balanced than Rugman.

David Ricardo (1772-1823), second by reputation only to Adam Smith, was the economist who proposed the law of comparative advantage. Briefly, if nation A produces say cheaper cloth while nation B produces cheaper shoes, then both nations gain if they export their best product and import the other. Comparative advantages accrue from the economies of scale and innovation arising in each nation, one in cloth, the other in shoes.

Mega-nomics, whether between nations, within empires, between cities or within mega-corps, can't be understood without this law. Between nations, the law of comparative advantage is hypothetical, or it doesn't work. Would the US and Japan ever agree to cease production, one in cars, the other in computers? Jane Jacobs (1984) described how the post-war industrial growth of Japan in cameras, electronics, cars, heavy plant and trains etc, was achieved through import substitution – the antithesis of Ricardo's comparative advantage. It is also more sustainable. Local production retains local jobs, skills and diversity, and reduces transport costs and pollution. Importing evermore goods (see table 15 above) reduces diversity and increases unemployment, transport costs and trading deficits. (We may be the only nation that consciously ceded volume industrial production under Thatcher and Lawson, with no comparable trade advantages elsewhere. This left us more dependent on our arms industry and financial services.)

In trade between rich and poor nations, too often comparative disadvantages are reinforced. Trading finite low value products like food, minerals and tourism (with little scope for adding value) for high value manufactured goods, arms and financial services usually reinforces the status quo of local despots and extends the market of mega-corps. In *Hegemony or Survival*, Chomsky explains how US foreign policy in Central and South America has supported brutal dictatorships in the interests of leading US mega-corps, often with military interventions, rather than support those attempting social democratic reform. (When Grenada was invaded in 1983, President Reagan announced it as a 'pre-dawn vertical incursion', which quickly became slang for early morning sex.) Jacobs thought that the wealth of nations was best served when rich nations trade with rich, poor with poor. Trade between poor nations would develop each economy and gradually replace unfair trade with rich nations. Only in this scenario of collective import replacement might the law of comparative advantage be tried to best advantage.

Empires are based on the comparative disadvantages between conqueror and conquered nations. From imperial Rome and Spain to the British empire and Russia, subject nations provided raw materials, cheap labour and a larger export market for the imperial nation's more profitable manufactured goods and financial services, which all helped to fund the necessary management 'overheads' of soldiers and officials. This internal trade is always unequal and usually unfair. According to Chomsky, for example, when we colonized India, we closed their more advanced clothing factories and imported the processes to our Lancashire mills. Inevitably, this creates resentment and insurrection.

If the history of cities largely records the tension between manufacturing and finance (from Braudel, page 130 above), this might explain the essential difference between city and empire, as those who make things or those who make money, in open or closed markets, with independent city states or subservient nations, local diversity or central conformity.

In city states (as in ancient Greece, Renaissance Italy, the Hanseatic League and during the Industrial Revolution in Europe and the United States), manufacturers were dominant, prospering through their innovations, efficiencies and expanding trade. The many banks competed to supply the necessary financial services. In simple terms, city states were, like bee hives, self-governing centres of production and management.

- The main weakness was that, as in ancient Greece and Renaissance Italy, the nation was insufficiently developed to protect its city states from neighbouring nations and aggressive empires.
- The strength was that, in cities, the law of comparative advantage worked to everyone's advantage, through their manufacturing clusters of excellence and wealth. If Birmingham, Manchester and Stoke-on-Trent had competed against each other in metal goods, clothes and ceramics, they would not have become 'the world's engineering workshop', the 'cotton capital of the world', and 'the Potteries'.

With empires, power shifts from manufacturing to finance. Empires centralize control in the political and financial capitals – as in Beijing, Rome, Madrid, Paris, London, Moscow and Washington. Subject nations are ruled by government servants, largely in the interest of merchants, bankers and investors, all under military protection. Eventually, all empires self-destruct. Imperial ambition, central control and unequal terms of trade reinforce imbalances of poverty and wealth, local economies are stifled, and as bureaucratic and military costs rise at home, so the forces for independence rise among the colonized. Eventually they all win, replacing colonial rule with their own versions of government.

In our present empire, global finance and the mega-corps determine levels of international trade under the umbrella of the IMF, World Bank and the 'Washington consensus'. This pursuit of eighteenth century mercantilism is supported with occasional military interventions in various parts of south east Asia, the middle east, eastern Europe and much of Africa and Latin America.

Cities develop symbiotic clusters that can compete globally, while nations mix competition with co-operation as in Europe. Mega-corps exploit their comparative advantages of cheap labour, cheap transport, ease of capital transfers and tax evasion (ipE), while empires provide the legal and military support for 'their' mega-corps. But the social costs of mega-nomics can be enormous,

iii) Social costs
"Money works best when it is spread like manure" (Persian proverb).

All economies depend on the flow of money, and work best when they flow into every pocket, however small. When boardroom pay bears no relation to average UK pay packets, at the expense of product quality, staff welfare and environmental protection, they intensify social problems throughout society. Wilkinson and Pickett (2010, see page 18 above) showed the strong correlation between excessive inequality and social problems in crime, health and education etc. Today, many mega-corps are not only too big to fail, but have become too big to be allowed to fail. So at huge cost, we all had to bail out those very banks that caused the crash of 2008. And now, as the joke has it, the banks are also too big to jail. Austerity, however, was no joke.

Lamy balanced "the strengths, but also the weaknesses, of market capitalism: its efficiency, its instability, and its inequality." Joseph Stiglitz (2002) is more critical. "It has become increasingly clear... that globalization as it has been practiced has not lived up to what its advocates promised it would accomplish – or to what it can and should do. In some cases it has not even resulted in growth, but when it has it has not brought benefits to all; the net effect of the policies set by the Washington Consensus has all too often been to benefit the few at the expense of the many, the well-off at the expense of the poor. In many cases commercial interests and values have superseded concern for the environment, democracy, human rights, and social justice." He also explained how the IMF helped the USSR government to 'liberalize' its post-communist economy and create a new class – the Russian mafia.

In exporting so many jobs, we have revived many Georgian and Victorian work practices that were outlawed here long ago. These new workers have minimal employment rights under repressive regimes that tolerate child labour and near-slave working conditions inside dangerous buildings, with safety netting to foil suicide attempts by staff, and wages as little as 2% of the final sale price. Nike employs 20,000 people directly, but over 500,000 people worldwide manufacture their shoes (Cooper 2005). Confronted with inhumane work conditions in one factory, Nike's initial response was "It's not our problem". Fairly soon, that response changed, but the reality is that improving foreign work conditions is difficult and would reduce profits. Most mega-corps, while asserting their corporate responsibility, let PR deal with such problems.

The Corporation documentary (pages 144 above) sheds some light on 'the Washington Consensus'. When the public water company of Cochabamba in Bolivia was sold to a private consortium led by Bechtel, it doubled the price of water and made collecting rainwater illegal. Three days of riots followed and the consortium pulled out. Later, it "filed suit against Bolivia for $25 million in losses. The claim was settled in 2006 for $0.30." (Wikipedia) Like sunshine on a dark winter's afternoon, 30 cents was a rare outbreak of common sense and justice.

Mega-corps resist freedom of information, manipulate local regulators and judiciaries, and dismiss cheap, sustainable and traditional practices that conflict with their commercial objectives. Who would insist on new laws to prevent farmers saving seeds or citizens collecting rainwater? How can their primary duty – to protect the interests of their shareholders – override all other responsibilities? When small firms deliver faulty products and services, mistreat staff, customers and suppliers, pollute the environment, abuse local communities and evade corporate taxes, the net social impact of their bad behaviour is modest and they either reform or go bust. Mega-corps' power corrupts by over-riding these market forces.

One can understand, or even defend, the motives of workplace saboteurs. But mega-corps commit sabotage on society at large, not just against their own whistleblowers. Their collective evasion of both taxes and justice stinks. Consider public safety.

- When four teenagers in kayaks drowned off Lyme Regis in 1993, the manager held responsible was jailed for three years, later reduced to two.
- When the aptly-named *Herald of Free Enterprise* ferry sank outside Zeebrugge harbour in March 1987, 193 people died. Only the two hapless seamen directly involved (the boatswain and assistant) were tried in court for the tragedy, and acquitted. The company (Townsend Thoresen, that had just been bought out by P&O Ferries) and five senior officers did not stand trial.

When there is a pollution spill or worker fatality (through negligence or efficiency measures etc), a mega-corp simply negotiates and pays the fine without admitting guilt. As with Enron's Matrix programme and GE's fines, mega-corps calculate the benefits of deregulation and cost savings against the price of political bribes and possible fines. Executives willingly accept the rewards of their employment or shareholdings but not the responsibilities. In small firms, the guilty party is easy to identify. In large firms, they are concealed behind a fog of bureaucracy. The defence of board directors usually relies on their not knowing what their subordinates are doing. When paper trails and emails go missing, it is impossible to prove criminal negligence, so cases rarely go to trial. In short, large firms protect their directors, leaving the workers directly involved to carry any cans. To the unscrupulous, this informal immunity from justice encourages risk-taking that no manager would endorse if held personally liable.

Even individuals can evade justice. In 2014, a German court charged Bernie Ecclestone with bribing a German banker with $44 million. It later allowed him to pay a £60 million fine (without admitting guilt) rather than face trial. Here, when HSBC facilitated tax evasion for its wealthy clients through its private Swiss bank, little action was taken. So, "Plumbers who failed to come forward [before the end of an amnesty on unpaid tax bills] were duly nailed, with five dawn raids as soon as the amnesty expired and many prosecutions (HMRC was too embarrassed to tell the Eye how many). Imprisonment followed for dodgers of around £50,000. Offshore evaders on a far larger scale, by contrast, have been left peacefully in their beds and offered further amnesties. Under the current and previous governments, those at the bottom of the pyramid of tax crime face the toughest punishment." (*Private Eye* 1386, 20/2/2015) While professional plumbers may be criminals (even those not paying the perverse VAT on building maintenance), bankers merely suffer what the Bank of England refers to as 'ethical drift'.

And while internal compliance officers and risk assessors face demotion or the sack if they stick to the principles of their jobs, and whistleblowers are sacked, become unemployable and may be taken to court, those in charge remain in charge. Yet 'market capitalism' is efficient only if the flow between supply and demand is fair and all relevant information is available on which to base social selection. Without adequate disclosure we can't choose between the good and the bad. Without transparency, corporate responsibility falls. Without responsibility, dishonesty becomes normal. And without honesty, tyranny thrives. As J M Keynes suggested, those with an insatiable desire for money are sick, like perverts and sadists. But in business, we are all their victims.

iv) Technology
The German philosopher Martin Heidegger (1889-1976), though difficult to translate, thought that every technological invention reduced social life. Bathrooms replace public baths, washing machines leave launderettes for students and the poor, and TVs reduce live events, to which we travel by car rather than bus etc. Even in the workplace, the Industrial Revolution has gradually shifted work from labour to machines. And today, mega-corps operate a global empire that allows the almost seamless transfer of their goods, finance and information, with minimal delays caused by transactional costs, customs checks and negotiations. In this, they resemble Isadora Wing, the hero of Erica Jong's *Fear of Flying* in her desire for the 'zipless fuck', wasting no time on seduction or even foreplay. Like her sexual desire, their insatiable drive for profit needs instant constant gratification. Isadora Wing grew up. If anything, mega-corps are regressing. Work conditions and unemployment, transport pollution and infrastructure costs are 'not their problem', and they resist all government attempts at regulation.

Technology has facilitated this seamless integration of mega-corps and their goods, capital and information.

- The Roman empire was sustained by an unprecedented European road network of about 50,000 miles. Mega-corps exploit a global transport network where freight terminals and computerized cranes shuffle boxes (standard containers developed in the 1950s) between ships, planes, lorries and trains. They can thus colonize new markets with ever-fewer productive plants.
- The free movement of capital, a requirement of the Washington consensus and international trade agreements, reduces the frictional costs of trade between currencies. Continental currencies like the Euro eliminate these frictional costs, largely benefiting already strong economies at the expense of weaker regions.

- And 'transactional costs' of personal service in local banks, showrooms and ticket offices are now reduced to websites and call centres – the antithesis of social behaviour.

Today's electronic titans among the mega-corps are based on a few algorithms which raise serious malfunctions:

- while Amazon, Facebook, Google and Twitter all zealously guard their privacy, they invade every user's privacy. Our lives are now preyed on by advertisers, fraudsters, trolls and snoopers, political ideologues, election manipulators and security services. No postal service or telephone company had such freedom;
- they exploit the free use of the world wide web (gifted by Tim Berners-Lee and colleagues), while engaging in tax evasion (ipE) on an industrial scale; and
- unlike all other public media outlets, they bear no responsibility for what is on their platforms. If they can get adverts to pregnant women before any of her friends or family have read her email with the glad news, then they can identify all criminal images and messages and remove them within say two hours, with serious fines for every minute they remain beyond that period of 'grace'.

Let me summarize all four PEST factors with one final example, largely sourced from Nick Davies' excellent (albeit depressing) *Flat Earth News*.

Politically, the success of Rupert Murdoch's UK newspapers owed much to his strong bond with Margaret Thatcher. Andrew Neil, editor of the *Sunday Times* two years after Murdoch had bought it in 1981, later wrote this: "On many of the biggest struggles of her decade in power, the *Sunday Times* stood shoulder to shoulder with her... Thatcher's battles were our battles." Hence the disgraceful coverage of the controversial *Death on the Rock* TV documentary, in which the *Sunday Times* manipulated the truth, even rewriting copy from its own journalists in Gibralter, all to fit with the official government version. In return, Thatcher did not hinder Murdoch's financial ambitions. The veto on 'cross media ownership' was quietly dropped, and his family business became a media empire covering newspapers, TV, radio, books and films.

Economically, some of his papers and Sky TV were very profitable, but success came at a heavy price. When Neil retired as editor in 1994, Murdoch congratulated him on "producing a paper that was three times bigger than under Harry Evans but with the same number of staff." Maximizing profits (in contrast to former owner Lord Thomson) meant "not enough staff, not enough experience, not enough time" to gather stories, attend meetings and trials, check sources, interview witnesses and report in any depth. Local newspapers are similarly afflicted.

Socially, under Lord Thomson, the *Sunday Times* had successfully campaigned for proper compensation for thalidomide children after 13 years. Its Insight team had also spent 18 months unravelling the truth about Kim Philby to the acute embarrassment of MI6 and successive governments. Investigative journalism costs serious money to unravel lies that powerful institutions want to conceal. Unearthing the truth is what serious 'broadsheet' newspapers used to do, and what scoops used to mean. One of the first things that Murdoch did with the *Sunday Times* was disband the Insight team, retaining only the 'brand'. Thence, we got the Hitler diaries (widely assumed to be a hoax hours before publication but raising circulation even six weeks later) and repeating the lie that Michael Foot was a KGB spy when he was dead, being found guilty of libel and paying damages the first time when he was alive.

In 1986, Murdoch 'broke the unions' by introducing computer technology, moving all his newspapers to Wapping and integrating journalism and printing. Lead typesetting was obsolete. However inevitable, this dramatically increased profits, but these were not used to employ more journalists and investigate real stories.

Technology also brought us the relatively simple operation of phone hacking. While illegal, Murdoch's papers were not the only guilty ones. Following several phone hacking trials, however, some journalists and junior editors were jailed, all senior managers were acquitted and Rupert Murdoch was not even charged. Inequality was now plain in courtrooms: either Murdoch and his executives knew about the phone hacking and its 'scoops', and simply lied – perverting the course of justice; or, despite all the payments to sleuths and police officers for personal information about MPs and others, Rupert Murdoch, Rebecca Brooks and others were ignorant and incurious about some serious criminal activity, which makes them incompetent. Either way, they are hardly 'fit and proper' to be in charge of a major media company.

It gets worse. NewsUK executives (while benefiting from the profits of the 'scoops' but denying any responsibility for the crimes) supplied the police with all records and emails of their more junior colleagues. (Apparently, during the internal investigations, three million emails of one senior executive were deleted, just as one ton of paper files were shredded by accountants Arthur Anderson within 24 hours of the collapse of Enron.) Nigel Rumfitt QC, defending one of those journalists on trial, said this. "The management and standards committee [chaired by another lawyer Lord Grabiner] has acted as a front for News International, plainly engaged in a wholesale cover-up for more senior people at the company at the expense of the more junior... News International is a copper's nark, and just like a copper's nark it has given a mixture of accurate and misleading information about others to the police in order to save its own skin." (*Private Eye* 1424, 5/8/16)

The coda to this whole saga was that Murdoch shut down the *News of the World* in 2011. The Monopolies Commission did not shout "Gotcha!" and order him to sell it as a going concern to another (fit and proper) company, letting them clean out the stable, retain the newspaper for its readers and diversify ownership of our media. Perhaps the Commission was on holiday at the time.

A national policy framework

A national *economic* planning policy framework is beyond the scope of this book and its author. From the *NPPF2*, however, in "Building a strong, competitive economy" (chapter 6), local councils only need to:

- have "a clear economic vision and strategy that positively and proactively encourages sustainable economic growth." *NPPF1* was more explicit, stating that councils had to meet "the twin challenges of global competition and of a low carbon future", although investors "should not be over-burdened by... planning policy expectations";
- "set criteria, or identify strategic sites, for local and inward investment", without distinguishing between the two;
- "address potential barriers to investment, [eg] infrastructure, services or housing, or a poor environment";
- "be flexible enough to accommodate needs not anticipated in the plan";
- provide "for clusters or networks of knowledge and data-driven, creative or high technology industries", ignoring other clusters and the small business sector generally; and
- "support a prosperous rural economy" in which farming, largely secondary, is to be diversified.

Economic development seems to depend largely on development. Jane Jacobs, in *Cities and the Wealth of Nations*, provides a more rational basis: "economic life develops by grace of innovating; it expands by grace of import-replacing." As stated earlier, the Japanese reduced their imports. Thus their vehicle industry developed after the second world war, as local firms started to make spare parts for their imported bicycles before making whole bicycles. Later they added motors before going on to four wheels, thence to heavy vehicles and trains. Import replacers became innovators.

In the UK plc, national economic policy for most of the last century, down to business ministers Michael Heseltine, Peter Mandelson and Vince Cable, was that "Britain is open for business." Rather than replacing imports, we imported foreign plants or allowed them to buy our own firms with little concern for their impact on local economies. A new strategy should regulate the market against known abuses and, as a minimum, treat all companies fairly, set limits on their size, retain a national currency and revise company law.

Treating firms fairly is essential. This means collecting taxes from all firms, whether micro or mega-corp. Taxing firms on turnover rather than profits, as proposed in chapter 10, would certainly reduce tax evasion by large firms. Similarly, imposing proportionate vet inspection charges on abattoirs would have avoided the catastrophic decline of small abattoirs due to vet charges (see page 312 below).

The very different treatment of banks illustrates this disconnect. When Dave Fishwick tried to set up a new bank in Burnley, (Channel 4 series, *Bank of Dave* 2012), he faced formidable barriers from the then Financial Services Authority. He could offer loans but not take deposits without a £10 million capital fund to protect against a possible run on the bank. By contrast, before the bankers' crash of 2008, the FSA and Bank of England watched while the big banks rode the bull market with grossly insufficient capital to survive when the bubble burst. All involved, bankers and regulators alike, ignored the few economists, financiers, journalists and investors who saw what sub-prime mortgages were. This disconnect shows how regulators bully small banks while themselves being bullied by those banks they should be regulating.

Concerning size, economic textbooks refer to small 'price takers' and large 'price makers'. 'Price mixers' and 'price fixers' might be more accurate. For example, in the 1980s, a highways engineer and town planner discussed a new T-junction for a town centre. He wanted a mini-roundabout to keep traffic moving. I wanted traffic-lights to keep the buildings and save money. However, he said that the cheapest traffic lights then cost upwards of £50,000 which were only produced by GEC and Marconi. (These two electrical engineering giants subsequently merged and demerged, before GEC went bankrupt and the rump of Marconi was bought by a Swedish firm.) Little known at the time, a small electrical engineering co-op in Sheffield (spun out of one of the big two) was offering traffic lights from £8,500. Our foodsheds, like those electrical giants, may yet meet their nemesis.

With few exceptions, mega-corps reduce national economies, suppress local competition, evade (ipE) taxes, manage by command, abuse suppliers and customers and export their profits of comparative advantage. As suggested by Ralph Nadar, when four firms control half their market, they should be broken up.

Despite the bankers' crash, the bailouts and subsequent austerity, within 18 months the bankers returned to their land of milk and honey, Bob Diamond having judged that 'the time for remorse is over'. To break them up into manageable units would increase shareholder value and focus management skills. First they must sell their stock brokers, building societies and insurance companies like the Cheltenham and Gloucester, Halifax, Prudential and the Woolwich. Second, they must demerge their high street (retail or utility) banks from their merchant (wholesale or casino) banks. The two cultures are fundamentally at odds, and 'internal Chinese walls', like self-regulation, is just another oxymoron.

High street banks offer interest on deposits and charge interest on personal and business loans. These are non-zero sum transactions. Dave Fishwick explains how successful business loans strengthen the local economy. With expansion, the firm employs extra staff who spend more in local shops and pubs, while Dave's bank shares its extra profits with local charities. Even when a business fails, the bank survives if it has included risk in its interest calculations. Social selection (or Smith's 'invisible hand') will continue to weed out failures while keeping the market open for others to test their own ideas and skills.

Merchant banks are usually engaged in zero-sum transactions, hence casino banking. Most deals in stocks, bonds, foreign exchange, commodities and derivatives ('those weapons of mass destruction') are simple gambles. How else describe 'sub-prime' mortgages and their 'securitization' with safe mortgages in 'collateralized debt obligations' (CDOs)? In every trade, gains match losses as in any betting shop. Even when investing in companies, as with private equity, their gains are often at the expense of staff, customers and HMRC. The often spectacular gains have created a bonus culture that bears no relation to the value of work involved, which seldom creates local wealth, unlike safe but essential high street banking.

Leave merchant banks to the rigours of the market, investors sharing the profits, and the losses when the gambles fail. Give us back our local banks and reserve 'bailouts' solely to protect local people's deposits up to £85,000 when a local bank fails. We should also break up the high street banks, reviving such names as the Clydesdale, Coutts, Girobank (which I still miss), Martins, the National Provincial, Northern, the Trustee Savings, Ulster, Westminster and Yorkshire banks. We could even demerge the National Provincial into a dozen or more regional banks. This would introduce competition with the occasional failure imposing market discipline.

A healthy national economy also needs its own currency. Retaining the £ was perhaps one of the few correct strategic decisions of our government since joining the EU. The clear advantage of the Euro is that it reduces transactional costs for businesses and tourists. The disadvantage is that it reinforces imbalances between strong and weak currencies that existed before the Euro. This danger can be seen even within nations.

- When the dollar became the common currency for the United States in 1792, the southern states never emerged from their status as poor relations.
- A century later, with the unification of Italy, the new lira from 1861 may also have condemned the south to relative poverty. (Although both these examples were clouded, in the US by slavery, in southern Italy by the mafia.)
- Two centuries later, following the collapse of the Iron Curtain and the reunification of Germany in 1990, the imposition of the Deutsche Mark on what was East Germany meant that most East German assets and industries could be bought by West Germans, condemning the eastern area to relative poverty.

Jane Jacobs suggested regional currencies. This wonderful idea would protect local economies without increasing transactional costs, by allowing goods and services to move unhindered within the nation but allowing people to buy local goods and services through local outlets with a local currency. Local 'pounds' have been created in Bristol, Brixton, Calderdale, Lewis, Stroud and Totnes as part of the wider 'transition towns' movement (Wikipedia). As with banks, however, Germany is well in advance with about 300 'Tauschringe' (local currencies) that are only valid through local outlets. These capture the 'premium' value of local goods and services within each local economy, the local money circulating more quickly than the national because it has a negative interest rate.

Finally, company law must be reformed. No firm is simply a producer or service provider acting in the sole economic interests of its owners. Every firm, dealing with staff and advisors, suppliers and contractors, customers and neighbours, local councils and government agencies as well as its owners, is by definition a social enterprise. There is no such thing as a self-made millionaire. Even sole traders have to work with suppliers, clients and customers. Since the nineteenth century, however, the primary duty of all public companies is to protect the interests of its shareholders.

This puts the short term interests of speculators, Ricardo's landlords and private equity investors against the interests of all other sections of society, including long-term investors and pension funds.

A new *Company Act* should cover ownership, governance, profit distribution, boardroom responsibilities, transparency and carbon reduction.

No company should be allowed to register with Companies House and trade in the UK until its owners have been identified and confirmed. Too many property companies and limited liability partnerships (LLPs) conceal their ownership through offshore 'brass plate' companies, many engaged in illegal activities and tax evasion. Also, UK mega-corp subsidiaries should be treated the same as UK companies in their trade, tax and legal responsibilities.

Corporate governance should also be reformed.

- Every boardroom should include one or two worker directors. In Germany, they have not impaired company performance and may have improved relations between boardroom and shopfloor.
- Boardroom salaries (and bonuses) should be set by independent remuneration committees, chaired by key shareholders (on the principle of responsibility with ownership), and
- on all outsourced public services, the contract and annual accounts should be publicly available, and a council- or government-appointed director appointed to the board to ensure compliance and probity.

Responsibility for corporate failures should now rest with named boardroom directors. At present, PR and commercial confidentiality have largely replaced investigative journalism, effective fraud police and government regulation. Now, we are ever-more reliant on the whistleblower to expose corporate corruption. These heroes need legal safeguards to protect them against corporate bullying, unfair dismissal, ruined careers and trials that all-too-often lead to penury. All company crime and negligence that could and should have been avoided, like on-site fatalities, faulty products, non-payments, pollution spills, reckless risk-taking, invasion of privacy, tax evasion and fraud etc, should be the personal responsibility of (as relevant) chief executive and/or director of production, human resources, quality control, marketing and finance. Each would be personally liable as recorded in company records safeguarded by the company secretary. Responsibility for excessive risk is a fair return for granting companies limited liability which exonerates those same directors from personal liability if the company goes bankrupt.

Regarding profits and rewards, Thatcher is widely regarded as having curbed the power of the unions. We now need to curb the greed of boardrooms which she unleashed. Annual accounts should specify all boardroom salaries (including dividends, share options and bonuses, etc), against the median or basic wages, as well as the basic wages of outsourced services. This might shame some boards to reduce extreme differentials, enable investors to compare company performance (assuming wage differentials do affect performance) and allow 'ethical consumers' to boycott the worst offenders. Good companies might merit a new version of the Fair Trade logo.

Transparency also requires that companies disclose relevant information about quality, source and contents of their products and services. Unscrupulous small print clauses, mis-selling by banks and pharmas, dishonest vehicle fuel efficiency and emission levels, and the lies within the tobacco, alcohol, junk food and betting firms all erode customer trust. It took decades before food manufacturers agreed to identify the chemical additives, preservatives and flavourings in their products. A healthy market needs more information on the price profile: not only the country of origin, but the percentage of price paid for materials, direct labour and transport costs. For example, in *The Observer* 13/3/16, a pair of 'jeans' retailing at £5.99 includes just nine pence labour costs.

Without information, how will products and production improve? Informed choice means that customers can support not only Fair Trade imports but also local goods with better-paid workers, lower emissions and less marketing. Only the indifferent and the poor would be marginally affected as products produced by slaves lose some market share. Slavery is not justified simply because it enables our poorest citizens to buy essential food and clothes. By allowing poverty we encourage slavery.

Finally, all annual reports should include a five-year strategy to reduce carbon emissions by say 25%, and repeated five years later. The energy savings would partly offset the costs involved.

While any primary school class would understand the dangers implicit in the current lack of regulation, Parliament lacks senior politicians with the grasp, intelligence and tenacity to tackle them. Can local councils and chambers curb some of the worst excesses?

Local strategies for local economies

As local planning has been subverted by successive governments throughout the twentieth century (see chapter 8), so more recent local economic strategies have suffered from excessive central control. Consider two government business agencies.

In 1993, Michael Heseltine set up Business Links (BL). In one county: "Business Link... has, using devolved funding from the South East of England Development Agency, set up projects that have piloted a co-ordinated approach for government-funded business support at a local level. With key partners, they have collaborated on a shared marketing campaign which uses one point of access for businesses (Business Link) by telephone or email. In depth training for customer-facing telephone and on-line team has allowed effective referral to relevant partners where appropriate, by sharing use of the customer relationship management system. Not only does this provide a consistent method of referral, it allows monitoring to ensure that business needs are being effectively met and partners are using the full array of government funded business support on offer" (the British Chambers of Commerce). In plain English, BL:
- is the first contact for small businesses and start-ups seeking advice,

- refers them onto specialist business trainers by phone or email, through its *customer relationship management system,*
- monitors customers to check its quality of service,
- informs them of other business support schemes, and
- promotes BL through its shared marketing campaign with its partners.

Though widely regarded as a waste of space, time and money, BL had a budget of £105 million for its last three years before being shut down in 2011.

Regional development agencies (RDAs) were set up in 1998 by the new Labour government. They produced economic and spatial strategies (RESs and RSSs) to promote "physical, sustainable and infrastructure development, economic regeneration, business competitiveness and employment and skills" – to which every local strategy had to conform. While RESs produced valuable regional profiles and performance trends, in practice, they were essentially guidelines and application forms for enterprise grants and gap funding. Local strategic partnerships and their local area agreements (inevitably LSPs and LAAs) consequently focussed on those projects that would fit RES strategy and attract RDA funding, which was largely controlled by Treasury. In their last five years, the RDAs' annual budget was about £2.25 billion. There is little to show for this spending.

After 14 years, the RDAs were abolished, the policy vacuum filled by 39 local enterprise partnerships. These LEPs are quasi-autonomous subregional partnerships and, like RDAs, still remote, undemocratic and reliant on central funding.

Let us dispense with economic strategy approved by ministers focussed on national or ideological objectives and managed by remote civil servants. Local chambers of trade and industry, in partnership with local councils, would be the most appropriate body to develop local economic strategy (as well as town centre management, from chapter 4). Currently, most chambers are modest affairs, with voluntary membership, low income and usually only a part-time director and secretarial support. Most meetings are little more than a social night out. Reconstituting chambers on French lines, with compulsory membership and fees reflecting size of company, would create an independent professional voice for all local firms, that would give weight to the BCCI (British Chamber of Commerce and Industry). Fees, together with the funding that went into BL (£35 million pa) and say 10% of the annual RDA budget (about £225 million pa) could generate annual chamber revenues averaging over £500,000.

Instead of a national economic strategy, chambers, in partnership with councils and other agencies, would develop local strategies relevant to their economies. Gradually, a range of successful policies and projects would emerge. The general failure of the *NPPF* is that no framework fits all local economies, in regions north and south, rich and poor, urban and rural.

Every local economic strategy would be different, but many would base their strategies on Jacob's import replacement and innovation while addressing current problems. Regular business surveys would provide an accurate profile of all sectors, covering for example: current sales and projections, plans for expansion, current labour and management skills, current demand for high- and low-cost workspace, any difficulties with finance, premises, skills and local transport, the strength of local SMEs and the potential to develop local clusters and supply chains etc.

Replacing imports, chambers could develop business networks that encourage local trade and new ventures. One economic development unit arranged regular business meetings hosted by a local anchor. After explaining its business and site history, subsequent discussions and lunch often revealed new opportunities for local suppliers, subcontractors and service providers. Occasionally, lateral networks would develop joint ventures and new products, as well as links with universities and research institutes to provide specialist training and project development.

Chambers might set up networks of business trainers ('Dutch uncles') among the larger firms to advise small firms on general management, cash flow and expansion, as well as specialist advice on patents and exporting. Another network of local investors might help fund company expansions. Chambers might also assist incoming firms with lists of potential local suppliers, colleges and training facilities. Some might even offer an arbitration service for local firms in dispute over payments, poaching or contracts. This might be more effective than government regulation, cheaper than going to court and quicker than both.

Local supply chains can reduce imported products and services. Food chains, for example, should link farmers and fishing ports with local shops, food processors, cafes and restaurants. In foodsheds, local food costs more because it is popular. 'Adding value' to local food, whether chilling, freezing, filleting and packaging, boiling, curing, smoking, pickling, salting, drying, canning and bottling, strengthens local economies, as does the manufacture of cheeses, yoghurt and cream, pies and sausages, chutneys, jams and jellies etc. Yet, because most small abattoirs have closed, local meat chains have become less viable. And most cod landed in our eastern fishing ports is ferried to the Netherlands where it is filleted, battered, breaded, re-chilled and packaged before being returned to the UK, all of which reduces freshness, local jobs and healthy economies.

Even sectors in decline have potential. A specialist sports clothing firm in the east Midlands closed its factory in the early 1990s, sourcing its gear from China. This import market is dominated by the two sportswear chains, leaving 'leftovers' for the small retailers. So this small firm decided to reopen its workshop and make, once again, its own high quality sportswear. Not in the 'knowledge driven, creative or high technology industries', maybe, so unlikely to receive any government assistance. But such a project would be sustainable, provide jobs, revive skills and reduce emissions.

Finally, chambers could advise on the likely impact of proposed mega-corp investments, including likely impacts on the economy, whether the scheme is self-financed, or has a history of anti-competitive behaviour, market manipulation, tax evasion, excessive pollution or undue government influence etc. Some chambers might see these as legitimate issues.

Innovation, like acorns and fish spawn, requires thousands of ideas to produce one healthy product. One estimate is that 3,000 product ideas might produce

1.7 actual products of which one becomes profitable (*The Observer* 12/4/98). Despite generous tax allowances, we spend less on R&D than our main competitors. In 1997, the R&D/sales ratio of the top 19 UK companies was 2.5% compared with 4.6% for the top 300 global R&D spenders (*The Observer* 28/6/98). In 2010, the UK was 21st in the world ranking of R&D spent per citizen, reflecting our decline in manufacturing jobs to 14% of the total, compared with 25% in Germany and 29% in Japan (Wikipedia 2015).

Research is surely related to size. 1,000 small businesses do not suffer from 'herd mentality'. What they may lack in strategic focus and funding, clusters and markets develop a diversity of skills and ideas, in accord with Darwin's theory of evolution. Clusters are innovative through being fertile and flexible in socially stable economic environments. Curiously, herd mentality is precisely the problem with a handful of mega-corps, whether in banking, chemicals, engineering or retail. In their group focus on profit, they are poor at innovation. Buying out small innovators is only to maintain or increase market share.

Well-funded local chambers, in partnership with councils and other agencies, might support their local clusters and markets with local investment banks, enterprise loan schemes and local training programmes etc.

If education enables everyone to fulfil their potential, then schools and colleges provide the springboard for all local economies, and should therefore be one of the most innovative of industries. Yet they too must focus all their skills on 'outputs' too narrowly defined by the national curriculum. This ideology is summed up by the cover blurb of Evan Davis' guide to *Public Spending* (1998). "Why is Sainsbury's so much better at selling food than most of our schools are at teaching children?"

This is meaningless. Foodsheds operate a closed, secretive system that shifts tins. All decisions on goods, pricing, marketing, returns, stock control, store layout, site security, staff pay and training ("Say hello… " etc) are made by head office managers and computers. Local managers are left to receive the goods, fill the shelves, tidy the store, bin the waste, oversee staff rotas and open and close the store. Not too difficult. When one Notts farmer offered his beef and dairy products to a newly-opened foodshed nearby (in response to its 'buying local' adverts), the store manager said he could not negotiate such a deal. Local shops can.

Pupils are not pizzas. Teaching children across the spectrum of personal, emotional, intellectual and social backgrounds (except the wealthiest) must be open and flexible. All subjects are complex, but teachers also have to gauge potential, extend abilities, encourage study, manage groups, minimize disruption, ensure application and enthuse with the power of ideas. They must offer care and support when needed, knowing that family and class dynamics can sometimes erupt alarmingly. Unlike store managers, head teachers have to work not only with staff, pupils and parents, but also with governors and local authority, while responding to ever-changing requirements from central government that are unrealistic and largely irrelevant in far too many schools. 'Command management' is counter-productive. It ignores teachers' collective experience, skills, patience, commitment and innovation.

We have replaced the ethos of developing the full potential of every pupil with the restrictive demands of 'commercial employability'. And so stressful has teaching become that few captains of industry would survive one week teaching an average class of primary or secondary pupils. (We return to education in chapter 7.)

It is local colleges of further education that provide vocational training for employment. From the medieval guilds, apprentices and masters formed the bedrock for wealth creation over the centuries, despite the occasional closed shop. Unfortunately, apprenticeships declined with manufacturing throughout the last century. So, in 1964, 26 national training boards were set up for such sectors as electrical engineering, construction and even local government. Of these government/industry partnerships, only the construction training board remains.

Training raises a political anomaly. Since 1979, while most public sector services have been privatized, training has actually been nationalized with little comment. The national Manpower Services Commission (MSC) was set up in the 1980s to train unskilled unemployed young people through work experience. It was replaced by more comprehensive regional training and enterprise councils (TECs), which then became learning and skills councils (LSCs). Increasingly, TECs and LSCs commissioned training programmes largely through local colleges and private companies. This 'hands-off' system has seldom worked well, being over-bureaucratic and remote from actual training needs in local workplaces. Vocational training is probably best provided by local firms' apprenticeship schemes working with colleges in partnership with local chambers and councils.

Social enterprises

After addressing problems and encouraging innovation and import replacement, another objective might be to develop social enterprises that Tony Blair briefly referred to as 'the third way'. Apart from voluntary sector community groups and social clubs, charities and foundations like meals on wheels and Macmillan cancer support, social enterprises and co-ops are more like private businesses in all sectors, including manufacturers, retailers, banks, publishers, housing associations and mutual societies.

A social enterprise differs from a private firm largely in how each splits its focus between social equity and economic profit. All social enterprises depend on modest profits to survive and prosper, while most private firms require some degree of social co-operation in the workplace. With growth, private firms tend to maximize profits at the expense of the workforce, social enterprises moderate this profit motive with the vocational ethos of the public sector. They are likely to be more democratic, pay everyone more fairly, avoid trade with unfair employers, treat customers honestly and distribute surplus profits fairly with staff, local neighbourhoods and charities.

Our first social enterprise, in the New Lanark Mills from 1784, developed from 1800 when Robert Owen took over from his father-in-law David Dale. Competing mill owners treated their workers (and children) as little more than slave labour. New

Lanark offered jobs with fair pay and hours, insurance, decent homes, shops and other facilities (but typically no pub), no work for children under nine and one or two days a week at school for older children, all at company expense. Productivity and profitability exceeded all competing mills, the social health improved family life, children were educated and the local economy thrived. The only other difference was that Dale and Owen, though wealthy, were poorer than other mill owners.

New Lanark was mould-breaking. Philanthropy was a viable alternative to 'free market discipline'. Adam Smith's 'fellow feeling' between capitalist and workers was more efficient and profitable than selfish capitalism that over-exploited Labour. Of course it might look paternalistic today, just as Athenian democracy was also flawed. Robert Owen and others went on to found the Co-operative and Economical Society in 1821. There followed the first co-operative store in Rochdale (1844), the Rochdale Co-operative Manufacturing Society (1854), the Co-operative Wholesale Society (1864), and a number of collieries, mills and banks (see Bury 1960). New Lanark influenced many philanthropists like Cadbury, Fry and Lever, who tended to emulate the religious, patronizing flavour of the original rather than the more democratic, egalitarian co-ops. Today, the strength of co-ops is best seen in northern Spain. Here, the Mondragon Corporation employs over 83,000 people in 256 co-ops, engaged in finance, manufacturing, retail and knowledge, with total revenues of €14,755 million in 2010 (Wikipedia).

Our social economy is relatively modest. Though estimates vary, in Europe, 6% to 6.5% of all firms are social enterprises, compared with perhaps 3.5% here. Despite housing associations and a few big names like the Co-op, John Lewis partnership and Guardian Media Trust, since 1979, the social enterprise economy has shrunk with the loss of the Trustee Savings Bank, the 'de-mutualization' of many building societies and uncertainty over the status of the Co-op Bank. During that same period, the private equity sector has risen spectacularly and now controls about 15% of UK firms. There will always be a modest role for private equity to rescue firms that are close to collapse. But our economy would be fairer and stronger if the figures for private equity and social enterprise were reversed.

What restricted the growth of social enterprises in our economy? Trade unions undoubtedly succeeded in improving wages and work conditions, taking much of the impetus out of the movement. Then boardrooms themselves realized that higher wages increased demand for their goods and services. After World War II, we introduced a third social factor, insisting that all German and Japanese firms appoint one or two workers to their boardrooms. The suggestion that these new directors were intended by the allies to curb those nations' economic recovery may be apocryphal. In any event, worker directors did not hinder their successful revival.

After 1979, we have reversed this trend. As we curbed all trade unions and reduced the power of Labour, inevitably this increased the power of Capital and our modern Gradgrinds like Richard Branson, Bob Diamond, Bernie Ecclestone, Philip Green, Rupert Murdoch, Brian Souter and those faceless executives among the banks, mega-corps and private equity firms. Their greed has realized Galbraith's maxim of 'private wealth and public squalor', their huge fortunes reaped largely at the expense of workers, tenants and those on state benefits. This is a zero sum game. The success of the John Lewis partnership is partly attributed to their positive staff relations and fair wages and bonuses. Would BHS have fared better in the Arcadia group had Philip Green's wife shared half her £1.2 billion dividend with all staff, creating a richer and happier workforce?

It is unclear how economic efficiency is correlated to social equity. What is clear is that command management in mega-corps and private equity firms all too often revive conditions found in Victorian treadmills and sweatshops. While one party is trying to protect jobs, wages, conditions and pensions, the other is partying. One sees staff as part of the firm's costs, the other treats staff as the firm's main asset.

Size affects all firms. As co-ops expanded in Mondragon, management/staff problems emerged. As a result, the movement decided on a maximum co-op size of 50 staff, confirming the 'natural' Gaussian curve of business size (from table 16, pages 132-3 above). In 2015, 257 co-ops employed 74,000 averaging over 280 per co-op.

Most social enterprises are local, and do much to capture, circulate and retain money in the poorest neighbourhoods. Drop-in centres, health clubs, playgroups, cafes, launderettes, community transport and credit unions are usually locally managed and replace external service providers. Local purchasing by councils from local firms and social enterprises, as promoted by Preston council with local health and education agencies, also replaces imports and strengthens local economies. And local councils themselves could deliver far more public services, as argued in chapter 10.

Social enterprises, large and small, take their social impact seriously. For example:

- the Scott Bader chemical manufacturer, set up in 1921 by Ernest Bader, was gifted to the workers in 1951 as a Commonwealth. It maintains Bader's principles of "Commitment, Responsibility, Team working and Fairness" and now employs 600 staff worldwide. Having no shareholders, Scott Bader is free to invest its profits in charity and community causes as well as R&D (company website). It profitably combines Adam Smith's self-interest and fellow feeling;

- the Fair Trade items sold in Co-ops are generally 30% to 50% cheaper than similar brand items, despite the premium paid to the Fair Trade producers. *Grogan's Companion to Drink* (2010) notes that: "In the UK, the Co-op has taken the lead giving double the usual forty to fifty pence per case [of wine] that typically goes to local initiatives. It may not seem much, but their quid goes a lot further in rural Chile or South Africa than it does at home." By contrast, when food sheds and cafe chains offer fair trade goods, the mark-up can put them alongside expensive brands, maximizing retail profits but reducing demand for the products; and

- while Dave's Bank in Burnley shares excess profits among local charities, the big banks are reluctant to pay even living wages to their cleaners and caretakers.

Outsourcing is rampant in regeneration programmes. Yet they usually ignored local groups, despite their potential for 'capacity building', in favour of national consultants and companies. Too many councils, health authorities and other public agencies also casually brush aside local groups and partnerships.

For example, in Derbyshire the regional health authority put two village GP surgeries (in Creswell and Langwith) out to tender. This was won by an American healthcare company (UnitedHealth Europe) which beat, among others, a realistic bid from the local GPs with local support that included rebuilding the inadequate surgery in Langwith. A resident took the case to the High Court on the grounds of inadequate public involvement and won on appeal. When the contract was re-tendered, the US company had withdrawn and the new tender was won by another healthcare company (ChilversMcCrea). According to their website "The key qualification for our team members is that we have all been round the block, are expert in what we do and are great fun to work with. There is no other team like it in the healthcare consultancy world."

Needless to say, the Langwith surgery remained inadequate and the private company had difficulty finding qualified GPs in Creswell. Complaints rose, many locals de-registered and ChilversMcCrea sold the contract on to The Practice group, another private company. Whatever the problems, the private companies probably still made profits while the NHS could book some short-term savings in providing the GP services. Entirely lost to the two villages are the social and economic benefits of local health workers running their own GP services more effectively, supported by patients, parish councils and residents, plus a slightly stronger local economy.

Urban entropy 2: cities are natural habitats for efficient markets

City economies are anchored by a wealth of small firms providing basic products and services, a few large stable firms offering economies of scale and one or two clusters creating centres of excellence, as in town centres and science parks – all supported by public services and transport systems. As argued in chapter 1, if cities are innate, we can study them as natural habitats. Let us now pursue that analogy by comparing the evolution of urban economies with natural ecologies.

According to Charles Darwin (1809-1882), species evolve over long periods in dense local habitats where all are engaged in the struggle for space, food and mates through complex relationships, both predatory and symbiotic. In each habitat, the genetic diversity of every species (plus occasional mutations) create slight variations. Those individuals with small advantages tend to survive and propagate. Hence Darwin's 'survival of the fittest' through natural selection. Similarly, firms all jostle for premises, suppliers and customers, creating healthy economies that are guided by what Adam Smith called an *invisible hand*. This insight I have translated as *social selection* by citizens and business clusters as they collectively select 'the best' firms, farms, shops, banks and pubs etc. There are similarities in the evolutionary mechanisms.

- Each habitat, woodland, estuary and heath etc, develops a distinctive mix of flora and fauna, fungi and bacteria in response to local climate and setting. Urban economies, though less distinct, still differ between market towns, ports, industrial towns, seaside resorts, financial centres, county towns and capitals.

- Every species produces more offspring than required to replace the parents. (Hence, at least for mammals perhaps, the biological joy of sex.) This maintains population density and thereby ensures constant competition for food and mates, and a healthy population. Healthy markets also contain sufficient firms to satisfy local demand, plus a few extra to compete for their share. Those firms offering slightly better quality, service or value are more likely to retain customers. As some retire and others fail, new firms enter the competition to maintain a healthy economy.

- Sex (the mixing of genes) and occasional mutations produce natural diversity. As predators develop stronger legs or keener eyesight, so their prey might develop a keener sense of smell or better camouflage. Local economies also develop diversity through large numbers of small firms and (like mutations perhaps) rare innovations. Every discovery only brings temporary success, however, as competitors respond and the improvement becomes general. We have yet to break the monopolistic power of the e-tech innovators.

- Nevertheless, healthy populations retain a mix of weak and strong. Nature does not indulge in eugenics and 'master races'. Dominant genes prevail, but recessive genes may confer advantages in specific terrains or local microclimates within their habitat, or an ability to survive major shocks. Constant diversity is the rule. Cities also provide an ideal habitat for large numbers of small firms to compete and survive. It is the density and diversity of species and firms that ensure healthy natural habitats and urban ecologies. Innovations are rare and, as in nature, most will be recessive and not survive.

- Finally, natural habitats are stable. Despite genetic diversity and constant competition, survival of the fittest only produces tiny changes over long periods. This stability arises from negative feedback loops. Too many grazers reduce food supplies or increase their predators; too many carnivores or too little grass reduce the herbivores. Negative feedback is also typical of stable economies: too many metal bashers or hairdressers, and more will fail; too few, and new firms will quickly enter the market. It seems that, as with physical entropy (chapter 3), a steady state is the general rule for both natural habitats and local economies.

As too much energy is embedded in our constant redevelopment schemes, so a few mega-corps reduce the natural urban energy that is released in a healthy local economy with its dense diverse plethora of small firms.

As there are no monocultures found in nature, so it also avoids the large-scale disruption caused by super species. Unfortunately, healthy local economies have largely succumbed to the global forces of giant corporations and their ensuing monocultures. It is as if a population of happy busy rats suddenly mutated into cannibals and, within 50 years, one million rats fought their way to a mere 500, each the size of a dinosaur. Mega-corps don't fit evolutionary theory and require a different analogy. Let me try again, fail again, fail better (than neo-conomists at least).

Jean Baptiste Lamarck (1744-1829 and predecessor of Darwin) thought species evolved by passing on skills acquired in life. Thus the giraffe, forever stretching, passes its slightly longer neck onto its children. Fortunately, life skills can't be inherited. Only genes confer slightly longer necks and advantages over the shorter necked, until limited by gravity and mobility.

Mega-corp directors resemble Lamarck's giraffes, straining for more profit and more pay. These traits are fostered in boardrooms that resemble medieval monasteries, largely cocooned from the wider community, giving the inmates power with few responsibilities. While monks monopolized the bible and local farms, mega-corp directors (misreading Adam Smith) distort the market. As with monks, they are self-selected, honing their financial skills and selecting colleagues by the shine of the brass necks among an almost hermetically sealed pool of executives, directors, bankers, accountants, lawyers, marketeers and now government ministers and senior officials. Mega-corp boardrooms are largely immune from government regulation and social selection (for which read gravity and natural selection).

Selection is all based on financial skills; market share, profit margins, cost control, price inflation, share price manipulation, competitor analysis or collusion, government influence and tax evasion (ipE), before agreeing generous remuneration contracts. Directors are not controlled by competition in a negative feedback loop, but bask in the positive feedback wake of other boardroom awards, vetted by 'remuneration committees' over which shareholders have almost no control. In this mutually reinforcing bubble of neck stretching (shameless greed), being largely immune to cultural norms and social behaviour, the executives become intolerant of all dissent. This lack of diversity through command management creates a form of tyranny that resembles the huge state monopolies of the former communist empire.

The justification for their greed is based on a misinterpretation of Adam Smith's concept of self-interest. Let me quote his relevant text: "In civilized society [man] stands at all times in need of the co-operation and assistance of great multitudes... [Like] no other living creature... man has almost constant occasion for the help of his brethren, and it is in vain for him to expect it from their benevolence only. [Every bargain] proposes to do this. Give me that which I want, and you shall have this which you want... and it is in this manner that we obtain from one another the far greater part of those good offices which we stand in need of." Smith had stumbled on the evolutionary biologists' concept of 'reciprocal altruism' two centuries before R L Trivers in 1971.

Richard Dawkins' *The Selfish Gene* (the favourite book of Jeffrey Skilling, CEO of Enron) has suffered similarly. Dawkins knows that genes are simply complex bundles of molecules that act as accurate and frequent replicators which, if successful, survive through thousands of generations. *The Successful Gene* might have been less misunderstood in some boardrooms. But in one chapter, Dawkins suggests that genes may be irrelevant to whole areas of human behaviour: 'memes' allow behaviours to evolve in society by a process that scientists call 'cultural transmission'. Thus, in sexual behaviour among species, the main options for mating are monogamy, promiscuity and harems. In some societies today, however, marriage and contraception have transformed social attitudes to pre- and extra-marital sex. Some cultures now tolerate same-sex marriage which, in granting one minority the same rights as the majority surely represents a triumph of social democracy through cultural transmission.

In their misreadings of Smith, Darwin and Dawkins, neo-conomists assert the 'dominance hierarchy' of boardrooms through aggressive behaviour rather than social selection, focus on expansion rather than territorial defence. And in moving fast and breaking things, they ignore the whole concept of an 'evolutionarily stable strategy' and the benefits of mutualism and 'reciprocal altruism'. In their behaviour, mega-corps have created high entropy economies that suck productive energy out of towns and cities, replacing Smith's *invisible hand* with the mailed fist of raw power.

If we could produce thermal images of cities and economic activity over time, the changes in both physical and economic entropy would be apparent. Up to about 1900, towns and cities would be compact warm splodges of reds and oranges with molten red cores and a few dashes of yellow suburb, set in a vast sea of deep blue with orange dashes for villages and yellow pinpricks for farms and hamlets. Today, urban thermal images would be far-flung and far cooler. Dull red centres would sit in a sprawl of pale yellow suburb with orange subcentres, surrounded by large areas of cream urban fringe dotted with blobs of orange shedscapes, yellow business parks and pale blue dormitories, the sea of deep blue hinterland receding into ever-smaller lakes and ponds, cut into irregular wedges by intersecting ribbons of blacktop. One might even spot a rare billionaire's black hole sucking energy out of the whole.

Newton's second law of motion states that "The rate of change of momentum of a moving body is proportional to and in the same direction as the force acting on it." In a healthy local economy, the skills, purchases and contracts of all its firms combine to move that economy slowly forward, benefiting everyone. By contrast, the mega-corp pursues its own interests, impoverishing local economies, often replacing local supply chains, managing by remote control, reducing local skills and competition, and extracting ever-higher profits. Rather than steady slow growth (an evolutionary stable strategy), local economies deflate.

Overleaf, again in homage to Howard, I compare the high entropy global mega-corps with low entropy local clusters.

Global mega-corps   or   Local clusters

Monopolistic, anti-competitive or
                        Pluralistic, symbiotic
Price makers, inflationary in local markets or
                        Price takers in stable open market
A closed market, buying out successful new entrants or
                        A market open for new firms, large and small
Resilient oligopolies controlling markets or
                        Resilient through number and specialist niches
Risk averse – buying market share and reducing competition or
                        Flexible, innovative, competitive and collaborative
Large externalities from scale of global operations in many sites or
                        Low costs from few small sites and local production
Global sourcing – cheap goods of high transport costs or
                        Local sourcing, lower transport costs
Mega-corp internal sourcing reduces local economies or
                        Local supply chains enrich local economies
Manipulate government policy and trade agreements or
                        Little influence on government and foreign trade
Command management, top down or
                        Management from top down to social enterprise
Averse to transparency, even with shareholders or
                        More likely to be open or inclusive
Focus on brand management and short-term financial targets or
                        Focus on quality and long-term survival
Greed at the top, Gradgrind below or
                        Less extremes from top to bottom
Design, production, admin and marketing functions dispersed or
                        Functions usually on one site
Few world brands worth emulating or
                        Few world brands
The good driven out by the bad or
                        The good set the standard
Profit driven – maximizing returns for owners and directors or
                        Quality driven – maximizing value for customers
Skills subservient to capital, deskilling most tasks or
                        Staff skills core to the business, learning with the job
Giantism driven by ego, acting as hoovers in local economies or
                        Small is beautiful, anchors for local economies
Law of diminishing social returns or
                        Law of increasing social returns

Chapter Six: Traffic Matters

Cities, dating back to about 10,000 BC, became more efficient with wheeled traffic from 3,500 BC. It improved access, developed local markets and extended trade beyond every city.

With wheeled traffic came congestion, a feature of every successful city. Circa 1900, someone predicted that within 20 years, London (or New York?) would drown under five feet of horse manure. Later, someone smugly pointed out that this Jeremiah had not foreseen the internal combustion engine. Optimists believe that problems beget solutions, pessimists that solutions beget problems, while realists know that solutions always bring 'unintended consequences'. These are sometimes worse than the problem. Twentieth century road traffic has transformed access, trade and social life.

- Suburban streets improved access for vehicles but dispersed activities beyond pedestrian reach and made public transport less viable.
- Global trade made speed and bulk critical. The infrastructure for container ships, jet engines and juggernauts transformed the scope, cost and pollution of trade. It also created mass tourism.
- Local economies declined and the social life of streets was largely destroyed.

"Locomotion – the triumph over space and time." (G Stephenson)

Speed, the physical triumph over space, transformed our urban environments as discussed in chapter 2. Let us now look at the economic and social costs of speed. Canals and then railways freed manufacturers from their raw materials and expanded their markets. When the railways were legally required to take passengers, commuting and day trips by train became part of everyday life. And in the twentieth century, cars and planes have replaced trains and transformed our lives.

Traffic and trade

"There are two reasons why we build roads. To improve people's lives and to sustain the competitiveness of the British economy." (Robert Key, transport minister, 1993 to 1994.) Let us first consider trade. If time equals money, perhaps the triumph of traffic over time does make our economy more competitive.

We build roads primarily to reduce the costs of urban congestion and regional peripherality. Consider first the nature of congestion.

Table 17: Private car traffic in Great Britain

	1982	1987	1997	2007
Bn vehicle kms	227.3	284.6	365.8	404.1
Private cars (ms)	15.3	17.4	21.7	27.0
Av car miles pa	9,232	10,164	10,621	9,300

Source: ONS, *Annual Abstract*

In 25 years, the number of cars nearly doubled while the road network only increased by 14.8%, from 343,942 to 394,879 kilometres (excluding road widening schemes). These statistics are often used to justify new roads. Every so often, the Confederation of British Industry (CBI) estimates the cost of congestion to the British economy. These range from £8 billion to £20 billion a year, based on the 'cost' of delays to motorists, to businesses with late deliveries, higher fuel consumption and pollution.

However, congestion affects business sectors differently. Assembly plants and large-scale manufacturing use the Japanese method of stock control. Stocks delivered 'just in time' replace large stores of materials, components and spares that were kept 'just in case' they were needed. This releases floor space and working capital, and reduces 'stock shrinkage'. However, for most firms, deliveries 'just in time' only means within a day or two before they are needed. Transport costs are a modest item in their annual accounts and road congestion, though irritating, seldom interrupts assembly lines.

Foodsheds, however, rely heavily on 'just in time' deliveries to keep their shelves fully stocked. Chapter 4 argued that our ever-extending trunk road network facilitated the growth of out-of-town food sheds, thereby avoiding urban congestion. Without this trunk road network (funded by taxpayers), food sheds don't work. Yet their HGVs pay very low road freight charges compared to rail freight. Keeping their shelves constantly full, largely for cosmetic purposes, makes transport and distribution costs a major item in their annual accounts.

The benefits of new roads are measured in reduced journey times. These are assumed to last 15 years, which may hold for long-distance trunk roads and by-passes, but for urban freeways the time savings last months rather than years. Furthermore, time savings are entirely speculative. The costs of disruption to residents' and workers' lives are real but impossible to value. Hence compulsory purchase. In crude Benthamite terms, small gains for the greater number justified the roads, despite the great hardship for those disrupted, displaced or left blighted by the new roads. Every cost benefit analysis carries risk, partly masked by the quasi-professional 'analysis'. In plain English, new roads put national priorities over local needs, and notional gains over real pain.

One of the most ambitious schemes to reduce urban congestion was the M25. Completed in 1986, it was designed to remove through-traffic and relieve London's roadspace. Such was the suppressed demand that it reached capacity within about six months rather than 15 years. Nor was anyone prepared for the subsequent pressure for exurban development that largely relocated jobs from outer London centres and commuter towns. Now it is criticized for being under-designed, with proposals to widen congested sections.

Nor did it relieve London's internal roads. The Victoria Deep Wharf container port on the Greenwich waterfront closed in the mid 1980s (before the M25 opened) – not because 20,000 tonne ships couldn't navigate the river and Thames Barrier, nor because the two gantry cranes couldn't handle containers, nor because of competition from Tilbury docks and beyond. It closed because road congestion made it increasingly difficult for lorries to get to and from the site via the Blackwall tunnel. An important shipping facility and jobs were lost, creating more lorry trips between London and Tilbury, Thamesport and Felixstowe. Yet, despite the M25, local congestion has worsened, with a third Blackwall tunnel under the Thames now awaiting final approval. Urban congestion is getting worse. Today, in many cities, ambulances and fire engines are sent from two or three stations to minimize the emergency response time.

The solution is not more roads but less traffic. When Oxford Street was closed to traffic except buses and taxis, many feared that central London would gridlock and force it to re-open. After the initial shock, what happened was that some traffic found alternative routes, some businesses made different arrangements, some drivers transferred to bus or tube and some trips simply evaporated. Now the scheme is to exclude buses and taxis and plant more trees to improve local air quality.

With every new freeway, congestion disappears and speeds increase for a few months. Then, new drivers emerge, average speed reduces to between 10 and 15mph (in London it is 11mph) and congestion returns here and elsewhere in the road network. Only cities like Los Angeles, defined by their urban freeways, achieve faster traffic speeds but with much longer journeys. Congestion is a feature of every successful city, and managing road space is more effective than building new roads. It is also much cheaper. New roads attract new traffic, less road space reduces traffic: that is not an assertion but an iron law of urban physics.

Concerning peripherality, a much-improved trunk road network has facilitated expansion among bulk producers like bakers and brewers. Their business model is to buy out local producers, close most of them down for significant capital gains and lay off the local workforce. They then centralize production on two or three large factory-cum-distribution sites, largely with lower skilled, lower paid workers and, despite the damage, danger and pollution caused by their lorries, pay little for the road network. In short, warehouse staff and drivers replace local brewers and bakers.

Yet, despite economies of scale and cheaper labour costs, their brands are bland and often cost more than local products. (See, for example, Richard Boston 1976.)

In peripheral areas like Cornwall, rural Wales, Northern Ireland and the Highlands and Islands, higher transport costs are offset by lower wages. New roads do not improve the competitiveness of relatively weak economies against neighbouring stronger economies. Few European peripheral regions have benefited from new motorways, and there are some nasty side effects.

The Isle of Wight has a modest but reasonable employment base. A new bridge or tunnel link would first replace all the ferries providing local jobs for local people. It would also raise house prices on the island as more workers chose to commute to Portsmouth and Southampton (or London), using the island as a dormitory settlement. Retail sheds would be easier to supply, making local shops less viable, and there would be a new rash of day trippers. All of which would damage a uniquely varied habitat and quality of life for islanders.

There are precedents. The new bridge to the Isle of Skye, in 1995, was the first private finance initiative (PFI) in the UK. It replaced two ferries that employed 34 local people and added about £2 million to the annual local economy. The new bridge tolls, paid to Scottish, German and American investors, were keenly contested. Eventually, in 2004, the investors were bought out by the Scottish government and the tolls removed. Not a happy outcome for public finances and a clear warning, largely ignored, with all subsequent PFI contracts.

New roads clearly benefit freight transport, but there is no hard evidence that they create new jobs or make the British economy more competitive. An economist once suggested that, instead of making and driving cars, it would have been cheaper to make buses and provide a ten minute service on every main road in the country. This academic exercise into opportunity costs demonstrates a simple proposition: that, as we shall see, most of Europe offers alternative, more efficient means of mass transport.

The social costs of traffic

"The present relationship between cities and automobiles represents, in short, one of those jokes that history sometimes plays on progress." (Jane Jacobs 1965)

The triumph of traffic over space, to improve lives, has had serious social consequences. Modern freeways are not like traditional highways and Parisian boulevards.

"And now we come to the Big Road... For the most part it is shaded, as here, with four lines of trees; the middle road – all hard – takes the quick traffic. In the days before rail-carriages the Sahibs travelled up and down here in hundreds. Now there are only country-carts and such-like. Left and right is the rougher road for the heavy carts – grain and cotton and timber, fodder, lime and hides. A man goes in safety here – for at every few koss is a police-station... All castes and kinds of men move here.

Look! Brahmins and chumars, bankers and tinkers, barbers and bunnias, pilgrims and potters – all the world going and coming... And truly the Grand Trunk Road is a wonderful spectacle. It runs straight, bearing without crowding India's traffic for fifteen hundred miles – such a river of life as nowhere else exists in the world. They looked at the green-arched, shade-flecked length of it, the white breadth speckled with slow-pacing folk; and the two-roomed police-station opposite." (R Kipling, *Kim*)

That may be over-romantic, but before 1900, all streets provided social space outside our buildings and between towns. With cars came Futurism and fascism. "A city built for speed is built for success" (Le Corbusier), but intrusive traffic destroys social streets. 80% of road crashes occur in towns and cities despite slower traffic being safer and average urban speeds seldom exceeding 15 mph. We can't revive our first motoring legislation – making every car should follow a man with a red flag in built-up areas – but we must relearn how to share roadspace.

In 1951, 85% of all households had no car. In 2008, the figure was 22% (ONS 2010). However popular, cars are not essential except for key workers and disabled people. In cities, where up to 40% live without them, cars (like central heating and dishwashers) are a luxury. It is cookers, running water and some form of transport that are essential. Even in rural areas, about 10% of households have no car. Rural immigrants from cities may regard their cars as essential, but that only reflects their 'lifestyle choice'. The sad fact is that their car dependency reduces further the viability of rural buses for those natives without cars.

Cars are convenient and offer status and pleasure. Few politicians would seek to reduce them: for the right, the car is a sign of freedom, for the left, it is a measure of equality. This is step one on the ladder of understanding. It puts the commercial interests of the 10 largest companies in the world (in 2005, oil companies, car manufacturers and Wal-Mart) above the wider interests of society. This road lobby wants 'car-owning democracies' even though cars are anti-social, destructive, polluting and climate changers.

In Los Angeles, "freeway-pilots [drivers] are acting out one of the most spectacular paradoxes in the great debate between private freedom and public discipline... As you acquire the special skills involved, the freeways become a special way of being alive... the extreme concentration required in Los Angeles seems to bring on a state of heightened awareness that some locals find mystical." Here Rayner Banham (1973) captures the addictive nature of driving. By contrast, most of western Europe spends far more on public transport, so even though they own more cars per household, they drive them less.

Apparently, the average Australian male spends two years watching (or avoiding) adverts on TV sport. Similarly, the average UK male spends well over two years (or about 17 days a year) driving 10,000 miles a year at about 25 mph. This time may not be completely wasted. Some relax to their favourite music, one disc jockey memorably described as 'that wriggling ponce of the spoken word' (Jimmy

Savile, as it happens). But driving requires constant vigilance to avoid crashes, injuries and road rage. Drivers share with cyclists the worst of the traffic fumes, without the exercise. Public transport allows you to relax, read, work, sleep, meet a friend or even talk to strangers.

Motorists lead different lives. Driving to parties is shared: he may drive there but she has to remain sober to drive them home (resembling early Hollywood rules where, in all bed scenes, both movie stars had to keep at least one foot on the floor). Motorists don't have larger social circles. They are simply more dispersed. At home, however, they have fewer friends as they walk less and use local school, shops and pubs less. We are becoming a nation of taxi drivers.

This traffic affects us all. On noise, the clatter of horseshoes and metal on cobbles has given way to a chorus of diesel engines, the vibrating rumble of heavy vehicles, air brakes, rapid accelerations, tyres on wet roads, sudden horns, sirens, door slams, radio blasts, broken silencers and moped whines – plus the curse of air traffic. The costs of double glazing and, in extreme, underpinning historic buildings and bridges are real. What we can't measure are the costs of personal annoyance, disturbed sleep and social intrusion.

Kerbed pavements on both sides of every street have made roads safer for pedestrians, except when crossing the roads, now seen as the domain of motorists. Pedestrians no longer have right of way as highway users. Victorian photos of people chatting and children playing in the middle of streets are folk history. Streets are dominated by cars, pedestrians often confined behind pavement barriers with too few pedestrian crossings. Inconvenient as well as anti-social.

This freedom of the highways should be set against the annual death toll that devastates families and friends of those killed.

Table 18: Road casualties: killed or seriously injured

Type of Road User	1982	%age	2007	%age
Child pedestrian	7,140	8.3	1,899	6.2
Adult pedestrian	11,725	13.7	4,900	16.0
Child cyclist	2,417	2.8	522	1.7
Adult cyclist	3,535	4.1	1,994	6.5
Mopeds and m'bikes	22,633	26.5	6,737	21.9
Cars and taxis	33,985	39.7	2,967	42.2
Buses and coaches	962	1.1	455	1.5
Goods vehicles	3,109	3.6	857	2.8
Total	85,506	100	30,720	100

Source: ONS, *Annual Abstract*

Between 1982 and 2007, road deaths have reduced from 5,934 to 2,946, with a similar reduction in serious injuries. Nevertheless, 300,000 people have been killed on the roads since the last war, and over three million seriously injured. Minor injuries, often including broken limbs and hospital visits, only fell by 12% to 217,060 in 2007. Innocent pedestrians and cyclists still account for about 30% of all serious casualties, yet 'shared road space' and 'pedestrian priority' remain largely ignored in transport policy.

And this death toll ignores the more insidious premature deaths arising from traffic fumes:

"Car pollution is now heir to the publicity throne currently occupied by aerosols and the ozone layer. It's hardly surprising. After pumping out noxious gases into the air for more than a century, we can hardly expect Mother Nature to keep mum.
"An astonishing 56% of our trees were found by the United Nations to be losing their leaves as a result of polluted air. The elements in petrol have even started to affect the elements themselves. The hydrocarbons react photochemically with sunlight to produce haze or smog. The oxides of nitrogen combine with water in the atmosphere to produce nitric acid. More infamously known as acid rain.
"Car pollution is playing havoc with our weather, our vegetation, our environment. And ourselves. The lead in petrol can attack the central nervous system. It can impair vital organs. It can affect babies even before they arrive in this less-than-spotless world. It's time for the car to try to right some wrongs... "

That unusually honest advert (for VW cars, 1989) merely promoted the use of unleaded fuel with an option for catalytic converters that were belatedly imposed by government. More recently, the government encouraged the change to diesel engines to reduce carbon emissions and climate change. Yet, "diesel fumes are significantly more damaging to health than those from petrol engines, according to research which shows that related air pollution contributes to lung disease, heart attacks, asthma and other respiratory problems." (*The Observer* 27/1/13) Today, all adverts with vehicle emissions and fuel efficiency are deeply suspect, or even faked as with VW.

Table 19: Growth in traffic pollution

Pollution from road vehicles	1968	1978	1987	1997
Lead	100	116	48	13
Carbon monoxide	100	140	160	131
Nitrogen oxides	100	135	157	120
Hydrocarbons	100	140	157	124
Carbon dioxide	na	100	127	167

Source : Department for Transport

While the reduction in lead was way overdue:

- 75% of Britain's carbon monoxide – which reduces blood's ability to carry oxygen – is produced on the roads;
- road traffic produces about half of our nitrogen emissions and acid rain;
- hydrocarbons produce smog and low level ozone, another poison;
- benzene from petrol pump fumes is highly toxic and carcinogenic; while
- roads produce about 25% of UK carbon emissions – effecting climate change.

With less public transport, discussed below, most UK cities fail current EU road pollution limits. Almost 70,000 people die of respiratory failure (7% of the annual total), and traffic is a major factor, killing 40,000 people prematurely each year. The *NPPF* is silent on this issue. Can we measure the annual costs and benefits of our road network?

Table 20: Annual highway accounts, 2004/5

Income from highway users	Total £bn
1. Vehicle excise duties from 28.7m cars, vans and taxis	4.741
2. Fuel tax (04/5) on petrol and diesel	23.048
Total	27.789

Expenditure and external costs	Total £bn
1. Government spending on new roads and maintenance	6.003
2. Casualties - deaths, serious and minor injuries	11.096
3. Congestion and physical inactivity	9.8
4. Poor air quality and impact on health and buildings	2.8
5. Cost of greenhouse gas emissions	3.7
6. Noise pollution	5.0
7. 8% return on capital value of road network	6.06
8. Opportunity costs of car parks	3.0
9. Non-productive drive time costs	45.0
Total	92.359

Sources: various, see text

The costs of the actual roads can be seen from ONS to be far less than the income raised through the vehicle road tax and fuel duties. This is often used to defend new roadbuilding. From table 20 below, the £6 billion spent on roads create jobs and the income taxes therefrom. But building new roads is little more than capital-intensive carpet-laying between tunnels and bridges. Electrifying existing railways create about twice as many jobs while building and refurbishing houses employ three times as many. If we attempt 'full cost accounting', however, the costs increase dramatically.

Expenditure costs for items 2 to 6 are from the Cabinet Office (*Planning* 13/11/09). Concerning casualties, one death costs society £1.25 million, a serious injury £140,000 and a minor injury £11,000 (Briscoe 2005). This will reflect the loss of economic output due to premature death, and the estimated costs of the emergency services and hospitals. There is no measure for the distress visited on families and friends. The comparable figure for the railways will be well under 1% of the road costs. Congestion costs are based on the physical inactivity while stuck in traffic jams. The CBI also adds the number of firms that cease trading because of congestion, increasing this cost to £13.5bn, though these two agencies may have different motives, either to minimize or to maximize this cost.

The last three items are mine and should also be treated with caution. As stated earlier, governments seek an 8% commercial return on its investments (which is far less than the profits that private bus and train companies make). If the 9,320 mile rail network is valued at £8 billion, applying this to our road network, the estimated capital value of the comparable 31,500 mile trunk road network is £23.2 billion. Including the 210,000 miles of minor roads (valued at £250,000 a mile) adds a further £52.5 billion. An 8% annual profit on this combined capital value of £75.7 equals £6.06bn.

The opportunity cost of £3 billion for car parks comes from a Friends of the Earth report (Tellus 42, see page 200). It is based on the higher rents and rates from developing workspace and homes on underused town centre car park.

Finally, the cost of commuting by car is based on the dubious assumption that time equals money. In 2002, 68% of the workforce (of 27,659,000) commuted by car, many of whom were passengers. If only 12 million commuters drive 1.5 hours a day (in free-flowing traffic), 200 days a year, and earn £12.50 an hour (the average for all industries before tax) the total cost of this 'dead time' is £45 billion. Commuting by public transport, walking and cycling are largely stress-free and relaxing, occasionally sociable or productive.

Table 20 provides an order of magnitude, suggesting an income to expenditure ratio of about 1:3.5. I have excluded some items. Roadside cafes and service stations might add £5 billion (about 5% of the UK catering and hotel market) to the credit side. Against this, we should debit the three million damage-only collisions which are costed at £5 billion. I have also excluded government estimates of 40,000 premature deaths each year from road pollution, which adds a further £2 billion or more. But even if we also exclude commuting costs, costs are still nearly double revenues. Unlike passengers, motorists do not pay their way.

In an honest accounting system, the tangible social benefits of buses and trains would include their being safer, less intrusive and polluting, more efficient and also reducing road congestion and pollution. I labour the point because, while road taxes on a simple cash basis pay all roadbuilding and maintenance costs, society pays the external costs of road deaths, pollution and opportunity costs. The figures above may only be guestimates but they are not theoretical. Roads are essential to urban life, but private motorists are clogging them up, making it difficult for businesses to survive, for emergency vehicles to arrive and for citizens to live their lives safely and socially.

Perhaps, with hindsight, five feet of horse shit would have been preferable, with cleaner air, safer streets and greener gardens. How did we get here?

1963 and all that

Twentieth century transport is largely the story of rising road traffic and reduced public transport. In government, no-one did more than Ernest Marples to set these trends in concrete – politically and literally. As minister of transport from 1959 to 1964, he commissioned two major reports: Dr Richard Beeching's *The Reshaping of British Railways*, and Sir Colin Buchanan's *Traffic in Towns*. Both, published in 1963, set policy for the rest of the century. And then, as part-owner of the Marples-Ridgway construction company, he not only represented the roads lobby in government, but also benefited directly every time his company won contracts to build new roads.

Both reports used the 'predict and provide' method. From recent trends and current levels of use, predict future demand and then provide (or reduce) the necessary networks. However, there were two fundamental differences. The remit for Beeching was to make the railways pay their way. So he closed most loss-making rural lines, reduced the 18,000 mile rail network by a third and closed more than half the stations. This drastic pruning cut some heavy losses but also reduced the viability of the remaining network.

The remit of *Traffic in Towns* was the opposite. "We accept the motor vehicle as a potentially highly beneficial invention. It is implicit in this that we reject, as an initial standpoint, a currently held view that the traffic problem in towns would take on an altogether different complexion – that it might indeed almost disappear – if motorists were obliged to pay the full economic costs of running their vehicles, including the rental of road space. We think the public can justifiably demand to be fully informed about the possibilities of adapting towns to motor traffic before there is any question of applying restrictive measures." This corrupt idiocy remains to this day.

Beeching was cost-driven to reduce subsidies and denied the potential of capital investment in, for example, electrification. Buchanan was cost-pushed to create highway networks on an unprecedented scale. The challenge was "*to contrive the efficient distribution, or accessibility, of large numbers of vehicles to large numbers of buildings, and to do it in such a way that a satisfactory standard of environment is achieved*" [their italics]. To improve road access and environmental quality would require extraordinary funding resources.

The authors were also different. Richard Beeching, from ICI, was an early example of politicians' naïve belief that business leaders with their focus on profits could re-organize complex public services better than existing managers with strategic understanding and long-term public experience. (Subsequent reports from business leaders have been no better.) Colin Buchanan, on the other hand, was a successful highways engineer and planning consultant. This raised an obvious conflict of interest. Perhaps the quote above was the professional consensus at the time, but the airy dismissal of non-highway solutions or 'restrictive measures' shamefully compromised his report.

Buchanan suggested that cities were like hospitals: roads linked local neighbourhoods, industrial estates and town centre just as corridors linked hospital wards, operating theatres and kitchens. This analogy was misconceived. Apart from staff, beds, patients and visitor traffic, hospital corridors are the setting for informal work, brief discussions, social activities and chance encounters, passing reception desks, waiting areas, kiosks, vending machines, noticeboards, stores, lavatories, cafes, pharmacies and shops. Hospital corridors are more like traditional high streets than any four or six lane freeway of non-stop free-flowing fast-moving traffic that Buchanan proposed.

Traffic in Towns included designs for Newbury market town, Norwich historic city, metropolitan Leeds and a block in central London, where the traffic difficulties were summarized thus [para 295].

i. "Bad layout, with many intersections and narrow streets.

ii. "Multi-purpose use of streets by different types of moving traffic, and for parking and for loading. This condition is particularly bad... just north of Oxford Street, where service vehicles lining both sides of streets and manoeuvring into position block the way for other vehicles.

iii. "Inadequate parking facilities and inadequate arrangements for service vehicles. These cause much inconvenience for businesses in the area.

iv. "Congestion by through traffic. We have estimated that out of a total outward peak hour flow of 3,000 vehicles, about one third is through traffic which has no need to be in the area."

"Other problems.

299. These mainly affect the considerable number of people who live in the area. There is very little open space for the 9,000 residents, and no adequate site for a primary school. Many of the living and working conditions are also sub-standard by reason of high densities, obsolete buildings, poor street layout, and the intermixture of incompatible uses."

This summary of planning concerns contradicts everything in Jane Jacobs' *Death and Life of Great American Cities* published two years earlier. Of the two, Buchanan's planning was ideological, Jacob's was practical. For Buchanan, "the awkward truth is that the motor vehicle is really demanding a radically new urban form," an assertion as dogmatic as any from Le Corbusier. For those of a nervous disposition, his redesigns still shock. Wide corridors of commercial and residential areas were to be destroyed, the disruption, costs and subsequent pollution, noise and isolation blithely ignored. Once built, visitors emerging from Newbury railway station would have found themselves between two motorway-standard carriageways, from Leeds station facing a motorway ring road and from Norwich station facing a major multi-level highway junction. In London, the five tube stations bounding the area (and not shown on the three study plans) would have disgorged their passengers from new underpasses, blinking like moles, into the environmental cell enclosed by the spaghetti of freeways, junctions, overpasses, slip roads and local distributors. (Interestingly, in both Leeds and London, these new networks mimicked the beehive's hexagonal pattern.) Complete destruction of cities and their low density redevelopment amid spaghetti motorways was the panacea.

Buchanan's dubious foundations of professional judgement and compulsory purchase underpinned most redevelopment and slum clearance schemes outlined in chapter 2. He wasn't corrupt, though it was embarrassing – to say the least – that the steering group included T Dan Smith, the Newcastle council leader and developer who was imprisoned ten years later in the wake of the Poulson scandal. The problem was that Harold Macmillan stood by such a compromised minister as Ernest Marples.

"More personal prejudice than professional judgement I fear" was an assessment of a draft report earlier in my career. After the initial shock, I confess that I then had difficulty distinguishing between the two. Condemning cramped housing, tired shopping streets, bad road layouts and inadequate parking was less professional judgement than personal prejudice, or what we might call value judgement. These invariably reflected the values and lifestyles of the professionals themselves, assisted by ideology, conceit and the occasional corruption. As we saw in Birmingham, the values that residents and firms put on their 'slums' were ignored. Even when the public had to be consulted in the 1960s, professional values still held sway in most clearance schemes, backed up with codes of practice, housing standards, retail projections and new highway standards. 'Poor street layouts' is what a cynic might call 'back engineering'.

How could so many professionals have destroyed so much on such flimsy grounds? Middle class values largely define the first century of planning. The fault lies, not with those middle-class values (suburbia and car dependency excepted), but with their imposition throughout towns and cities, from working class neighbourhoods to central London districts. Their excessive enthusiasm for extreme solutions contradicts John Stuart Mill's dictum that progress is only possible when *necessary* improvements are tempered by *minimal* damage (pages 69-70).

As with doctor and patient, empathy between professional and neighbourhood means assessing easier solutions before proposing a 'radically new urban form'. Working with the 'urban grain', better public transport, safe cycle and pedestrian networks and traffic restraint would all have been cheaper with minimum destruction and damaging after-effects.

Unfortunately, we were bent on destruction. All new road schemes would be approved if their cost benefit analysis (COBA) showed total savings greater than total costs. These professional analyses were skewed by the value judgement that cars were 'a potentially highly beneficial invention'. The costs of land, property and construction were all minimized.

- To minimize land costs, wherever possible new urban roads were built on edges of parks (including Hyde Park in London) through ancient woodland (as with the threat to Oxleas Wood) and other important green sites, alongside rivers, through allotments and over long back gardens. As these sites could not be developed, they had no development value and so, under COBA, they were given nominal values despite being priceless.
- All properties affected were valued at 'market value' rather than a fair price. Other nations add a premium to compensate owners for their unwillingness to sell and the disruption to their lives.
- Construction costs were kept to a minimum until the road scheme was approved. Then, a new road costing say £10 million with benefits of £12 million, might well rise to £15 or £18 million after CPO approval. This cynical 'cost creep' affects (perhaps) most public projects, even those in the full glare of media interest. HS2 costs do not creep, they leap and bound.

The new benefits were also skewed.

- The biggest benefits were the time savings for all motorists using the new road over 15 years. As stated above, it would be more accurate to assume that new roads reached capacity within a few years, and less in urban areas.
- Thus, many road schemes were over-designed to increase their capacity and hence the total motorists' time savings.
- New safer roads with fewer junctions and more pedestrian restrictions also reduced accident costs. COBA even added savings from side streets made safer with less traffic due to the new road, again over 15 years. Yet fewer cars in side streets usually means faster traffic and more dangerous conditions.
- Where road safety was the primary issue, better street lighting, anti-skid surfaces, speed tables and/or infra-red cameras at junctions would cost a fraction of a new junction.
- Finally, the cost of delays to pedestrians crossing the new roads and junctions, even near shopping centres and busy railway stations where they greatly outnumbered vehicles, were not included.

In practice, most new road schemes simply demonstrated the strength of suppressed demand, and created bottlenecks elsewhere in the road network. And the time savings are notional. Motorists have shown considerable reluctance to use the M6 toll road (the north Birmingham relief road). With tolls of £5.50 for cars and £11 for lorries, it only attracts half of the daily projected 76,000 vehicles.

Like Buchanan, COBA ignored alternatives. Public transport options were excluded. Comparing the capital cost of a new road with revenue costs of more buses or trains would have put public and private transport on a more equal footing. Subjecting every new public transport scheme to COBA analysis would have counted real passenger time savings, safer journeys, more local jobs, less road congestion and minimal environmental impact. However, each rail scheme simply has to show a commercial return of 8% on the investment, even during recessions. This is a healthy discipline and most reopened railway lines have exceeded projections. New roads are not subject to any market discipline, and the failure of the M6 toll road suggests that few would be viable.

1963 made concrete the priority of roads over rail. Indulging our addiction to driving fuelled suburban sprawl and the exurban cancer. Closing uneconomic railway lines simply generated more road traffic, and motorists are free to go where and when they want *at no cost at the time of travel*. This fault line between road and rail policy infected most governments throughout the last century.

Civilizing traffic in towns

Eventually, anti-road protests had some influence on government policy. In 1994, the DoE *Planning Policy Guidance 13* on transport (*PPG13*) sought "to ensure that local authorities carry out their land-use policies and transport programmes in ways which help to:
- reduce growth in the length and number of motorized journeys;
- encourage alternative means of travel which have less environmental impact;
- and hence reduce reliance on the motor car."

Typically, this policy shift was compromised by its shifty use of words: not reducing traffic but reducing *growth* in 'motorized journeys'. Later (1995/6), council transport funding bids could include public transport as well as new roads, but small schemes like 20mph speed limits to make roads safer were still excluded.

Although policy shifted from predict and provide to managing demand, privatizing bus and rail services directly increased road traffic as fares rose steeply relative to motoring costs.

Table 21: Transport costs and disposable income (Index, 1974 = 100)

Cost of	1984	1994	1998	2008
Petrol and oil	108.2	92.4	104.2	174.2
All motoring costs	100.7	98.5	99.3	113.6
Bus and coach fares	131.0	154.5	157.3	232.1
Rail fares	142.0	176.3	180.0	252.5
Disposable income	119.5	167.2	182.1	240.0

Source: ONS, *Annual Abstract*

More people bought more cars and drove them further more often. This reduced the costs of depreciation and road tax per mile but increased congestion. For the poor without a car, higher fares simply meant fewer trips or less to spend on other basics.

Also in 1994, the Royal Commission on Environmental Pollution (RCEP) published its report on *Transport and the Environment*, with eight key policies.

1. "To ensure that an effective transport policy... is integrated with land use policy... minimizing the need for transport and increasing the proportions of trips made by environmentally less damaging modes.
2. "To achieve air quality standards that will prevent damage to health and environment.
3. "To improve the quality of life, particularly in towns and cities, by reducing the dominance of cars and lorries and providing alternative means of access.
4. "To increase the proportion of personal travel and freight transport by environmentally less damaging modes and to make the best use of existing infrastructure.
5. "To halt any loss of land to transport infrastructure in areas of conservation, cultural, scenic or amenity value unless the use of the land for that purpose has been shown to be the best practicable environmental option.
6. "To reduce carbon dioxide emissions from transport.
7. "To reduce substantially the demands which transport infrastructure and the vehicle industry place on non-renewable materials.
8. "To reduce noise nuisance from transport. both daytime and night time."

This model of clarity, in contrast with *PPG13*, is the antithesis of *Traffic in Towns*. It covers all transport modes and addresses social needs rather than lifestyle choices. Unusually, the government did not respond to the report, unacceptable as it was to both road and aviation lobbies. Notably, air travel contradicts all eight objectives, yet still benefits from the simple predict and provide model. The coalition government did not revive the RCEP report to become 'the greenest government yet' (David Cameron). Instead, the RCEP itself was abolished in 2011, after 41 years of advising Parliament and the public on environmental pollution. Cameron's later remark of 'cutting the green crap' had become policy.

When the *NPPF (National Planning Policy Framework)* was redrafted in 2018, its section 9 'Promoting sustainable transport' sits unhappily between *PPG13* and Cameron's green crap. Quoting from its ten paragraphs gives its flavour.

102   "Transport issues should be considered from the earliest stages of plan-making and development proposals," including a scheme's impacts on existing transport networks, opportunities to improve existing or proposed transport infrastructure, promoting "walking, cycling and public transport use" and, in traffic schemes, aiming for "net environmental gains." This roughly agrees with RCEP 1.

103   Growth should focus "on locations which are or can be made sustainable, through limiting the need to travel and offering a genuine choice of transport modes... However, opportunities [for] sustainable transport solutions will vary between urban and rural areas." This is ambiguous. How can sustainable transport solutions for exurban shedscapes differ from urban solutions?

104   Plans should support mixed uses in larger schemes to reduce trips, be co-ordinated with highway authorities, infrastructure providers, transport operators and

neighbouring councils (again ignoring any difficulties 'aligning' rural and urban transport plans), and (again) provide walking and cycling networks.

The rest of this paragraph is dangerous. Plans should protect "sites and routes [that] widen transport choice and raise opportunities for large scale development", "provide for large scale transport facilities [for their] contribution to the wider economy." This includes "a national network of general aviation airfields… which serve business, leisure, training and emergency service needs." (I like the sly insertion of emergency services to endorse airfields.)

The fashion for large infrastructure projects contradicts RCEP sustainable policies 5 and 7 to husband resources and invest in existing transport modes. Nor does it preclude new highways. To 'widen' transport choice reads more as libertarian ideology when we should be seeking to reduce unsustainable road traffic. It also retreats from *NPPF1*, where 'large scale facilities' at least included "rail freight interchanges [and] roadside facilities for motorists (with a nice human touch) to support the safety and welfare of the road users."

105-7 concern parking. Parking standards, if required, should reflect fairly obvious criteria, like existing access, mix of uses, public transport and car ownership levels. However, "Maximum parking standards… should only be set where there is a clear and compelling justification" while town centre car parks should be improved to be "convenient, safe and secure." And "overnight lorry parking facilities" should be adequate.

These three paragraphs contradict RCEP policies 2, 3, 4, 6 and 8. Parking is tolerated, parking standards are optional but limiting parking levels must be justified.(*NPPF1* even included solicitous concern that parking fines should be 'proportionate'.) Lorry bans and freight transfer to rail are ignored. Reducing car dependency is not mentioned, nor the use of ground floors of housing blocks for parking, despite a housing shortage.

108-11 All new developments should promote "sustainable transport modes". In 110, these include priority to pedestrians and cyclists, public transport, disabled access, "safe, secure and attractive" places, deliveries and emergency vehicles, and low emission cars. However, in 109, "Development should only be... refused on highways grounds if there would be an unacceptable impact on highway safety, or the residual cumulative impacts on the road network would be severe." And in 111, "developments that will generate significant amounts of movements should provide a travel plan" and transport statement. It would seem that exurban sheds and regional shopping centres, with their safe layouts, battery chargers and disabled access, are acceptable. Carbon emissions?

If anything, *NPPF2* on transport sinks even lower than the first edition. In its brevity, it omits key issues, in its length it is often unbalanced or ambiguous.

- Nowhere does it state the need to reduce road traffic. This neutrality reads uncomfortably with its silence on chronic respiratory ill-health and road deaths.

- Cyclists and pedestrians receive two references, public transport one. It ignores buses and trains but is positive about flying. Thus, it fails to distinguish between safe cycle networks and a third runway for Heathrow, or between restoring a railway line and building a new container port without rail link. All seem possible, subject to developers and their lawyers.
- 20 years after PPG13, to "reduce reliance on the motor car", we now have this. "Significant development should be focused on locations which are or can be made sustainable, through limiting the need to travel and offering a genuine choice of transport modes. This can help to reduce congestion and emissions, and improve air quality and public health." So when car emissions are reduced, we can then build new bypasses and freeways to reduce congestion.

In seeking to offer 'a genuine choice of transport modes', the *NPPF* seems to think that, as with town centre markets and foodsheds, policy can support both road traffic and public transport. 'Having your cake and eating it', under the mantra of 'widening choice', is the triumph of ideology over rational policy.

Over the last century, governments invested in roads rather than railways, left shipping to the private sector, ignored canals, supported every expansion of London Heathrow and, until recently, ignored pedestrians and cyclists except as a road safety issue. And since 1979, no government has explained how policies on privatization, fuel taxes, rail fares, Heathrow and HS2 etc, promote sustainable transport.

Perhaps this is why the *NPPF* doesn't define sustainable transport, unlike the RCEP report which is absolutely clear. Sustainable transport means reducing the need for travel, road traffic, environmental damage, health risks, waste of non-renewable materials, and maximizing the use of existing infrastructure.

Underpinning sustainable transport is the need to reduce carbon emissions. The following estimates the carbon emissions in kgs for every 40 passenger miles:

- By plane, about 12 kgs of carbon/40miles, based on 150 kgs/hour flying at 500 mph. Private jets with few passengers would emit far more, and we might treble aircrafts' impact on climate due to their nitrous oxide emissions and vapour trails.
- By car, about 10 kgs, based on 2.5 kgs/litre of petrol, and 10 miles/litre (about 45mpg) on open roads. Commuters and lorries emit higher levels.
- By bus or train, about 4 kgs, or 0.1 kgs/mile. Emissions will be higher for high speed trains, and lower for buses, while
- walking and cycling are largely carbon-neutral.

Speed and emissions are directly proportional. The carbon footprint ratio between plane, car, bus and foot being roughly 12:10:4:0. Yet motoring is cheaper than public transport (from table 21 above) and flying is usually cheaper than the same intercity rail trip. If transport prices reflected 'full cost accounting' (including pollution, crashes and subsidies in skewed taxes and duties), then choice of transport mode would be more rational and healthy. For example, buses, trains, cars and lorries currently pay the same fuel duty. If that were halved for buses and trains or doubled for cars and lorries, it would promote cleaner, more efficient transport systems at national, regional and local level.

- For long distance passenger and freight trips, it would promote trains, ferries and ships over cars, lorries and planes, with import substitution and technology (eg video conferencing) reducing the number of trips.
- For regional traffic, trains and buses would prevail over cars, and local supply chains and transhipment depots could replace HGVs with light vans.
- For local trips, buses would increase over cars, with denser neighbourhoods and safe networks increasing walking and cycling.

The rest of this chapter discusses three broad categories of transport:

1. private transport, including freight and motoring;
2. social transport, both intercity and urban transport systems; and
3. personal mobility through walking and cycling.

Private transport – road freight

In the 1950s, UK freight tonnage was roughly shared between road and rail. Today, roads carry about 95% of the tonnes.

Table 22: UK freight traffic by mode, 1982-2007

Mode	1982	1992	2007
Billion tonne kilometres:			
by Road – total	91.1	121.3	161.5
• vehicles from 3.5 to 25 tonnes	29.0	26.3	15.7
• vehicles over 25 tonnes	62.1	95.0	145.8
by Rail	15.9	15.5	21.2
by Air	1.2	2.4	6.2
Million tonnes lifted:			
• by road	1,310	1,463	1,869
• by rail	141.9	122.4	102.4
• by air	0.3	0.5	0.9
Average trip per tonne moved (kms):			
• by road	69.5	82.9	86.4
• by rail	112	127	207
• by air	4,000	4,800	6,889

Source: ONS, *Annual Abstract*

The growth of HGVs at the expense of smaller lorries is worrying. At 60mph, a 40 tonne HGV stresses a motorway as much as 62,000 cars, while many bridges and roadside buildings are vulnerable. We could either restrict them to suitable roads as in some countries or impose road charges as with rail freight. At present we do neither.

Table 23: Road freight traffic by commodity, 1991-2007

Commodity	1991 (%)	2007 (%)	% incr
Total goods moved (bn tonne-kilometres)	124.6	149.4	19.9
• food and drink	32.7 (26.2)	45.1 (30.2)	37.9
• crude minerals	13.0 (10.4)	16.0 (8.7)	23.1
• misc manufacturers	12.4 (9.6)	16.4 (10.3)	32.3
• building materials	8.7 (7.0)	11.6 (7.8)	33.3
• chemicals	7.3 (5.9)	7.0 (4.8)	- 4.1
• iron and steel products	6.9 (5.5)	6.4 (3.8)	- 7.2
• misc transactions	20.0 (16.1)	32.3 (21.6)	61.5
Total goods lifted (million tonnes)	1,505	1,869	24.2
• food and drink	291 (19.3)	373 (20.0)	28.2
• crude minerals	298 (19.8)	390 (20.9)	30.8
• misc manufacturers	80 (5.3)	113 (6.0)	41.2
• building materials	155 (10.3)	175 (9.4)	12.9
• misc transactions	331 (22.0)	440 (23.5)	32.9
Average trip per tonne moved (kilometres)			
• food and drink	112.4	120.9	10.8
• crude minerals	43.6	41.0	- 5.9
• misc manufacturers	155.0	145.1	- 6.4
• building materials	56.1	66.3	18.2
• misc transactions	60.4	73.4	21.5

Source: ONS, *Annual Abstract*

This table only includes those goods moving over 5% of the total. Foodsheds loom large in road freight. In 16 years, food and drink tonnage increased by nearly 30%. Food miles are also increasing with more remote foodsheds, more imported foods to collect from ports, more ready-made meals from the 'food academies', and all meat from fewer abattoirs. This excludes the food miles of imports and those exporting from foodsheds to homes. Food transport generates about half of all transport emissions, which the 'efficiency' of foodsheds ignores.

5,500 years of road freight, plus navigable rivers, canals (from 1755) and railways (from 1825), we are reverting to roads to move our freight, despite the dangers and costs. It used to be said that, over long distances, the cost per mile of moving one tonne cost a penny by sea, ten pence by rail and a pound by road. Prices will have risen but the ratios roughly hold. Road freight is cheapest for short trips, and the only option for deliveries between sites without rail or port connections. For longer hauls, both rail and sea freight are viable with much lower external costs.

Yet since 1900, our rail network has shrunk more than in the rest of Europe. Up to 1950, all rail networks were expanding except in Ireland. Since then, the decline was most pronounced in both Ireland and the UK.

The reduction in our railway is only exceeded by our reduction in rail freight.

Table 24: Length of European rail networks, 1900-2003

Country (Pop	Network length in kms			2003/1950
in millions)	1900	1950	2003	% change
Austria (8.2)	6,639*	6,734	6,610	98.2
Belgium (10.2)	4,562	5,046	3,521	69.8
Denmark (5.5)	2,914	4,815	2,785	57.8
Finland (5.2)	2,650	4,726	5,851	123.6
France (59.1)	38,109	41,300	30,990	75.0
Germany (82.2)**	51,678	49,819	35,593	71.4
Greece (10.6)	1,033	2,553	2,414	94.6
Ireland (5.7)***	5,125	3,927	1,919	48.9
Italy (57.3)	16,429	21,550	15,985	74.2
N'lands (15.8)	2,771	3,204	2,807	87.6
Norway (4.5)	1,981	4,469	4,077	91.2
Portugal (9.9)	2,168	3,590	2,801	78.0
Spain (59.6)	13,214	18,098	12,298	68.0
Sweden (8.9)	11,303	16,516	11,050	66.9
Switzerland (7.4)	3,544	5,152	5,159	100.1
UK (58.8)	30,079	31,353	16,950	54.1

Source: Mitchell

In 1900, both Austria and Germany (and their networks) were larger. From 1950, German figures combine East and West Germany. Figures for Ireland are for the whole network.

Continental Europe enjoys an integrated rail network and, over the last century, increased its rail freight tonnage by 63%. In smaller nations, most rail freight is in transit between their larger neighbours which enables Switzerland, for example, to impose severe restrictions on road haulage. By contrast, rail freight tonnage in the British networks declined dramatically.

Table 25: European rail freight traffic, 1900-2003

| | Thousand tonnes (million tn kms) | | | 2003/1900 % |
	1900	1950	2003	change (tns)
Austria	25.3	35.9 (18.8)	91.3 (17.6)	361
Belgium	55.1	60.0 (5.5)	0.5 (7.1)	110
Denmark	4.2	9.3 (1.2)	7.9 (1.9)	188
Finland	2.5	16.8 (3.5)	42.7 (10.1)	1708
France	83.4	152.0 (38.9)	142 (50.0)	170
Germany	360.3	419.5 (58.2)	384 (78.5)	107
Greece	0.3	1.9 (0.2)	0.4 (0.5)	133
Ireland	5.2	3.6 (0.4)	2.1 (0.4)	40
Italy	18.0	50.5 (10.4)	83.1 (23.3)	462
N'lands	9.6	21.2 (3.0)	30.4 (4.1)	317
Norway	1.6	14.6 (1.4)	19.4 (2.6)	1213
Portugal	2.7	3.3 (0.5)	10.7 (2.5)	396
Spain	31.5	29.8 (7.3)	32.9 (11.9)	104
Sweden	21.6	44.1 (8.6)	60 (20.9)	278
Switzerland	14.5	24.0 (2.2)	62.4 (10.6)	430
UK	426.5	285.8 (36.2)	142 (18.7)	33

Source: Mitchell

Extending the 49,000 mile trunk road network merely encourages road freight. There is no comparable investment in the railways. The irony is that, in their early years, railway companies refused to carry passengers (until forced to by law) because they interfered with their profitable freight business. Railways were built for freight.

Today the position is reversed. According to the Office of Rail Regulation (ORR), freight operators pay less than 28% of the costs of wear and tear on the tracks. It suggests new charges of £1.68 per 1000 gross tonne kilometre for general freight – about 0.26 of a penny/tonne-mile (ORR website). By contrast, a 44 tonne HGV pays an annual road tax of £1,850 for free access to the road network of 240,000 miles, compared with the 10,500 miles of railway.

"It remains hard for rail and water to compete with HGVs because of market distortion. Using the latest Government figures, research carried out for Campaign for Better Transport shows that HGVs are paying less than a third of the costs they impose on society in terms of congestion, road crashes, road damage and pollution. That is why it is crucial that the Government supports rail freight which has far lower impacts on society, and is an important part of the logistics mix." (Philippa Edmunds, freightonrail.org.uk)

Restricting HGVs to the trunk road network, and at least equalizing road and rail access charges would divert more road freight to rail. Raising transport costs might raise shop prices, but largely in the foodsheds. Local shops mostly use vans. Realistic road freight charges would also threaten the business model of the bulk bakers and brewers, forcing many to demerge some of their brands back to local independence. Regional specialists and local variety might once again mean more than just local scenery, a funny accent and the odd food dish. The recent growth of local breweries demonstrates the suppressed demand for local produce.

Three other policies could reduce road freight. First, every region should upgrade their rail freight facilities and no port should be without a railhead. In 1982 there were 339 rail freight depots and marshalling yards, in 1993 there were just 61 (ONS). The rest had been compulsorily sold off for new sheds, housing and other non-transport uses. Rail policy under Thatcher was as negative as under Marples. Smithfield meat market in central London provides a poignant example. The Victorian railway sidings in the basement used to receive Scottish beef and Welsh lamb. When the market was refurbished in the mid 1990s, the basement was converted into a disco. The meat still arrives in the early morning, but is brought in by 38-tonne refrigerated lorries through the surrounding streets.

Proposals for a second bridge over the Tamar should consider a rail rather than road bridge. This could link Falmouth docks directly to the Eurotunnel and relieve shipping congestion in the English Channel.

Second, water transport is largely ignored, though coastal and river shipping are ideal for heavy high-volume, low-value goods. For more than a decade after the Thames barrier opened in 1987, six million tonnes of newsprint, grain, sugar beet, roadstone and the small container Victoria wharf mentioned above (page 179) were unloaded at river wharves upstream of the Barrier. Today, most of these wharves and factories have been redeveloped for housing under the name of regeneration.

Canals still carry about four million tonnes of cargo a year, but even that is at risk. Working barges have no priority over holiday barges, their untidy wharves and repair yards unwelcome. Canal restoration is usually driven by regeneration and the backdrop for commercial development, visitor attractions, luxury apartments, hotels and the ubiquitous marinas, with London Docklands as their model. As with Plymouth's Sutton Harbour (page 83 above), such schemes seek to remove working boatyards, wharves and freight barges. British Waterways and the Environment Agency even sought to sell off canalside lock-keepers cottages (*Private Eye*, nos 1187 and 1210), showing an ignorance or contempt of this heritage and the potential for water freight.

New canals could be dug. An east-west canal from the Mersey and Manchester ship canal to the Humber could provide a new freight route linking Ireland, northern England and the Thames to the Rhine. This great European river was itself linked by a 106-mile canal to the Danube as recently as 1992. In 2000, German waterways carried 218,000 tonnes, their railways 384,000 tonnes. In the same year, our canals and railways combined carried perhaps 145,000 tonnes.

Third, we need to civilize road freight. Most lorry drivers are professional and less likely to be involved in collisions. But when they do occur, they are more likely to cause serious damage and injury. When a lorry failed to stop at traffic lights in a Cornish town in the mid 1990s, it killed a car driver before crashing into a corner shop. A local resident told the local media: "Let those who objected at last year's bypass inquiry come here and say that now." Later it emerged that the lorry had faulty brakes, the owner had no licence and was making a local delivery so would not have used any bypass. Lorries should be subject to regular safety inspections at least as rigorous as for trains to weed out those who menace road safety.

HGVs damage roads not designed for them and cause congestion. To rid towns of this traffic, councils should investigate transhipment depots to transfer loads from HGVs to LGVs (lorries under 7.5 tonnes). Some local firms and retailers arrange, by phone, to collect some of their deliveries from out-of-town laybys or car parks. Scaling up, transhipment depots might be piloted for coastal towns like Barrow-in-Furness, Falmouth, Torbay, Great Yarmouth/Lowestoft, or Whitehaven/Workington; peninsulas like west Cornwall even Devon and Cornwall, the Gower peninsula from Carmarthen, east Kent from Canterbury, south Lakeland or Cumbria; and of course, islands like Anglesey (or north Wales), Sheerness and the Isle of Wight.

These would effectively restrict HGVs to the trunk road network designed for such traffic (perhaps with exemptions for quiet and low emission vehicles), while allowing LGVs to use bus lanes and even traffic-free zones. Costs would rise with the double handling of goods, but these would be partly offset by the time, distance and fuel savings of the HGVs, and realistic road freight charges would make transhipment more viable. Transhipment depots would replace some long distance drivers with local drivers, who could also offer local delivery services. And realistic road charges .might encourage food sheds to rationalize their HGV fleets with competitors to reduce mileage by empty lorries.

Private motoring – freeing up roads

Cars are everywhere, delaying buses, deliveries, emergency services and pedestrians. Let us now discard Buchanan and seek to reduce road traffic. Apart from improving public transport, we need to make motorists aware of, and pay for, "the full economic costs of running their vehicles, including the rental of road space." We can price car trips in five ways: road tax and fuel duty nationally, road pricing, parking tax and traffic calming locally – all ignored in the *NPPF*.

The annual road tax ('vehicle excise duty') is currently zero for electric cars, rising to £460 a year for SUVs. If the average gas guzzler is driven 10,000 miles a year, the road tax adds less than 5 pence a mile, which reduces with every extra mile. The tax is insignificant. A new £20,000 car depreciated over five years would add about 40 pence a mile. The problem is that most motorists don't include the cost of their cars. Few buses, however full, can compete with this price.

If the road tax were hypothecated, to be spent only on highway construction and maintenance, we might rebalance spending between local and central government. Revenue from cars and vans could fund all council spending on road maintenance, while a much-increased HGV road tax could fund all government spending on trunk roads and motorways.

Fuel duties, about 75% of petrol pump prices, add at least 15 pence a mile. In 1993, Chancellor Norman Lamont introduced a fuel price escalator, increasing the fuel tax annually above the rate of inflation. The policy was to shift more trips to more sustainable transport modes. Yet before motoring costs rose noticeably, fuel tax protests by a few hundred disgruntled motorists and lorry drivers blockading petrol supplies in the early 2000s (with no interference from the police) caused Chancellor Gordon Brown to abandon it. The current *laissez-faire* policy relies on exhausting oil reserves to push up petrol prices, akin to sticking one's head up one's own exhaust.

Higher pump prices would alert motorists to some of the cost whenever they switch on the ignition. Raising fuel duties as a 'pollution tax' could be made 'tax neutral' (and rational) with an equivalent income tax reduction, leaving 'the average household' unaffected. This would produce winners (poorer households) and losers (profligate drivers).

Of the local policies for reducing traffic, **traffic calming** is discussed under reclaiming the streets below.

Road pricing (or congestion charge), introduced in central London in 2003, reduced traffic volumes by 15% and congestion by 30%. However, "the impact of the scheme on business has been mixed and the jury is still out" (CBI). Road pricing raises significant tax revenue, but is expensive, intrusive and unfair.

- Fuel duties and traffic calming would be as effective but much cheaper than this technological fix.
- CCTV cameras on every street into the congestion charge area raise concerns about public surveillance and civil liberty.
- It unfairly taxes our most successful city centres. John Lewis reported a drop in sales in its Oxford Street store compared with its other London stores. If this is typical, the charge reduces profits as well as traffic, distorts local markets and reinforces the exodus of money and jobs from city centres. Imposing road pricing on all roads might be fair, but history suggests that road tolls impede trade and social life.

The cheapest, fairest and simplest way to reduce traffic would be to tax the car when it is not moving. A **parking tax** on all car parks with over say ten spaces would be easy to collect. When John Prescott (as deputy prime minister) proposed this option, it was quietly dropped, presumably through pressure from the foodshed, road, car park and motoring lobbies. *NPPF2* merely 'seeks to improve the quality of town centre parking'.

A parking tax, like a bus fare, would introduce a cost for each car trip. This would reduce demand for further exurban 'parks' and over time develop some urban car parks for more productive uses. According to Friends of the Earth research (Tellus 42 1998), urban public car parks occupy about 1,850 hectares, or 4,600 hectares including private non-residential car parks, roughly the area of Hackney and

Eastbourne borough councils respectively. (Figures based on a survey of all English local councils.) The national income from all public car parks (based on the 40% response to that survey) was about £250 million in fees plus £100 million in rates. This equates to £452 for each parking space but with wide variation between rural, urban and metropolitan car parks. Thus, four average parking spaces yield about £1,800 a year, while a two or three bedroom flat on the same site would yield at least £8,000 in rent and rates. Had they all been re-developed, annual rents and rates would have exceeded £1.5 billion. That is an opportunity cost, subsidizing parking at the expense of homes and jobs.

Is development realistic? Almost 25% of the public car parks were seldom full or half full and, being centrally located, could provide any mix of housing, hostels, shops, offices, studios and workshops, training centres, leisure and civic facilities. As an extreme example, 18% of Kings Lynn town centre is either public or private non-residential parking. But in all towns, redeveloping under-used car parks would bring people back into town, socialize streets and town centres; raise land values, revive local economies and make town centres more viable. It would also reduce traffic and local pollution.

The opportunity is that half of these under-used public car parks could provide 250,000 dwellings on three or four floors without strain, with or without ground floor commercial uses.

Urban car parks do at least pay business rates and parking fees because land is expensive. By contrast, free parking is essential to the foodsheds' business model. A parking tax would partly equalize town centres and exurban sheds, complementing fairer business rates as argued in chapter 4. It would also hit exurban sheds harder because the ratio of parking area to retail floor space is 2:1 or higher, more than double town centre ratios.

In conclusion, our roads are overloaded with HGVs and congested by cars. Both hauliers and motorists should be charged for their use of the roads, not only fairly in line with rail freight charges and passenger fares, but also sustainably to reduce their harmful emissions. Before discussing more social and sustainable alternatives, however, let us deal with the third form of private transport.

Air traffic control

Air traffic is the most explicit triumph over space and time. When vehicles took off, the world shrank and is now largely controlled by mega-corps and overrun by tourists. (Aircraft could also subject whole populations to the full horrors of war which, until 1937, had been largely confined to battlefields and combatants.)

Air traffic is almost beyond control. Forgive my choice of Heathrow, but it shows how the power of size can fly in the face of rational policy. Even its birth was corrupt. "Heathrow Airport only came into existence thanks to government sleight-of-hand at the end of the Second World War. The site, on the richest agricultural land in the country, was commandeered under Emergency Powers in 1943, purportedly for the RAF. It was never used as such. The then Under-Secretary of State for Air, Harold Balfour, revealed in his autobiography that the requisition and construction work undertaken were entirely bogus, and that the plans had always been to turn the airfield into London's principal civil airport come the end of hostilities. Playing the national emergency card simply allowed the authorities to circumvent any normal planning procedures – and so the pattern continues." (Parker 2009)

Privatizing the British Airport Authority in 1988, seven major airports (London's Gatwick, Heathrow and Stansted, Southampton, Aberdeen, Edinburgh and Glasgow) were sold for £1.225 billion as one block to maximize the price (as happened with the water monopolies). In 2006, it was sold on for £10.1 billion. This discrepancy may reflect greater efficiency under private management, but more likely it was grossly under-priced originally. In any event, in 2009, the Competition Commission ordered BAA to sell three of its seven airports – Gatwick, Stansted and Edinburgh – to introduce competition in London and Scotland. This emerged between Gatwick and Heathrow when a new runway was thought necessary to cope with foreseeable demand. In its adverts, Gatwick claimed that its second runway would be cheaper, quicker to build and less polluting than Heathrow's third runway. It also offered £1,000 towards the council tax of all households directly affected by the noise shadow. To offer about £5 million a year suggests that one busy runway generates considerable 'disposable income'.

About 30% of passengers fly into Heathrow in order to fly to other destinations in the UK or further afield. Gatwick provides a credible alternative, but regional airports like Birmingham, Edinburgh, Glasgow and Manchester could also relieve pressure on London by at least 10%.

For many, the choice for London is between Tweedledum and Tweedledee, as it ignores the jumbo in the hangar. According to a now defunct lobby group, Flying Matters, "aviation does not contribute significantly to climate change... an expansion of aviation will aid the developing world, benefit social justice, and is essential for UK tourism and for the UK economy." This is a vapour trail of hot air. Flying is the most polluting mode of transport. "[M]ost people accept the rough estimate that the global impact of air travel is about three times that which would be suggested by carbon dioxide alone. This [includes] the contrails of nitrogen oxides and other pollutants, but excludes any impact from cirrus clouds seeded by the aircraft contrails." (Goodall 2007)

Planes are also exempt from fuel duties and noise controls that apply to other modes of transport. A pilot once told my uncle that a jumbo jet weighs 200 tons on takeoff at Heathrow and 100 tons on landing at San Francisco, burning perhaps 33,000 gallons of kerosene. Jets are more fuel efficient today, but a fuel duty of 75 pence/litre as for petrol would raise nearly £25,000 on that flight – adding £82.50 to the average ticket price for 300 passengers.

Similarly, a noise tax of £2,000 for each landing and take-off would only add about £6 a ticket. This tax would be reduced for quiet planes, doubled for Sunday flights, trebled for night flights, and increased to reflect the number of residents living within the 50dB noise shadow. I have a personal interest in this subject. Four or five days a week, the quiet enjoyment of our neighbourhood is impossible, even though Heathrow is over 25 miles to the west. Garden meals, allotment visits, listening to music, picnics in the park and sleeping after 4.30 in the morning are impaired or impossible. These taxes would focus attention on engine design and airport location.

Flying gives rise to two other anomalies. 'Airmiles' give frequent flyers free flights, when instead airmiles should be rationed and progressively taxed to discourage excessive flying. And second, all major airports double as shopping centres. Unlike town centres, shopping malls and railway stations, however, airport shops, like aircraft fuel, are duty-free. Duty freedom creates a tax haven in our midst. Heathrow is not just another exurban shedscape with acres of tarmac runway and some radar kit. While it may well earn more from rents than landing fees, it is also free of most duties to the environment and society at large. Exceptionally, government airport policy is stuck in the 1963 Buchanan loop of predict and provide, where the 'national interest' trumps local democracy. 'Sleight-of-hand' above is a euphemism for government corruption and incompetence.

Let us return to solid ground and look at social modes of public transport.

National social transport – British Rail

We start with high speed trains because they directly compete with planes. From 1994, Eurostar captured about 70% of the London - Paris market, largely at the expense of planes. Now HS2 will take us north to Birmingham and beyond to Manchester and Leeds. But there are problems.

Cost estimates in the press for HS2 began at £34.5bn, £42.6bn in June 2013 (or £50bn if we include the trains), through £70bn to £85bn, and now stands at £106bn, with a five year delay to 2033. Almost certainly, final costs will be £120bn plus. (By contrast, Nasa estimates that getting people to the moon by 2024 would be £16bn-£25bn; *Private Eye* 1503, 23/8/19).

Of this total, professional fees and interest charges will account for as much as 25%. In Europe, these costs are less than 10% and in Spain, according to Wikipedia, can be as low as 3%. (Perhaps in the UK "All professions are a conspiracy against the laity" as GB Shaw suggested). Once a major public scheme is approved, cost inflation occurs. For mayor Johnson's garden bridge project, costed at £60 million rising to £200 million, £43 million of public money (plus some private investment) was "spaffed up the wall" before the garden bridge even had planning permission. (As with post-coital relaxation, the authorities seem 'intensely relaxed' about this misuse of public funds.)

Back with HS2, the department for transport (DfT) originally estimated benefits of £21bn for passengers' time savings over existing train times, as with COBA above. But then DfT added a new benefit: business passengers would be able to work while travelling on HS2. This opens a window of reason when comparing costs and benefits for any transport investment. Not only are trains quicker and safer, but all Inter-City trains and many regional services offer productive travel time. The same road trip remains dead time no matter how many minutes are saved by the new road.

Unfortunately, the HS2 cost/benefit analysis doesn't apply to rail alternatives. HS2 will relieve congestion on both east and west mainlines to Scotland and greatly increase capacity. However, upgrading these routes to remove bottlenecks would probably leave sufficient funds to electrify the whole system and improve the regional networks. These would improve reliability, greatly reduce carbon emissions and (from the RCEP) maximize use of the existing infrastructure.

Integrating HS2 with existing infrastructure also presents real problems. In major cities like Birmingham and Liverpool, new stations are needed. And where new 'parkway' stations are built, existing central stations will lose much or most of their inter-city passengers. The early proposal for Sheffield was for a new HS2 station on the line between Sheffield and Rotherham. This would see both the new 'iconic gateway' and Sheffield's handsome Victorian station functioning well below capacity. Sheffield would lose interchange passengers as most using HS2 would simply drive or taxi to and from the new station. Europe offers examples where services have not been integrated.

- In Spain, the new Burgos station (on the high-speed link between Madrid and Paris) is four miles from the town centre. The old central station was closed and the old track is now a road. Three years on, ticket staff confirm that the new station has far fewer passengers than the old.
- France, with 1,850 kms of TGV lines, has the most extensive high speed network in Europe. But the total French network has shrunk from 36,530 kms in 1970 to 29,901 kms in 2008 (International Union of Railways). Out-of-town stations on the TGV network have not been integrated with city centre stations. As a result, regional networks have suffered and lines been closed.

HS2 will also struggle to replace domestic flights. One airline advertised (in Waterloo station) that 8 out of 10 inter-city trips are cheaper by its planes than by train. HS2, probably with higher fares, will not change this. Unless and until we control air traffic with fair taxes, the railways will always be disadvantaged.

I refer to trains (with buses, trams, metros and ferries) as social transport because not only are they accessible to the public, but they form an integral part of the social infrastructure of all cities.

- Mainline stations and terminals create social and commercial hubs, an urban motorway is a bleak swathe of night light and pollution with a few service stations dumped en route in the country;
- trams in the middle of main roads have frequent stops, dual carriageways create polluting, disruptive and dangerous barriers;
- trolleybuses are quiet and clean, unlike HGVs; and
- metros are underground and efficient, Buchanan's urban freeways and spaghetti junctions destroy what they were designed to serve.

Let us now compare rail passenger traffic throughout western Europe (table 26 opposite). As with rail freight, from 1900 the number of rail passengers in Europe increased from 1,799,3 million to 4,013.4 million, or 223%. British Rail passengers fell by 65%. This decline from the 1920s was partly due to British Rail complacency but mainly tight spending controls by successive governments. This neglect merely culminated with Beeching. Mussolini showed the potential of a national rail network. Our higher average trip lengths reflects an overall decline in rail commuting, and/or the greater distances commuters travel in our suburban conurbations.

However, from 1976, the Inter-City service with High Speed Trains was an almost instant success and imitated throughout Europe. And when British Rail was split into four operational divisions – Inter-City, South East, Cross Country and Rail freight – it became much more efficient, controlling subsidies to about 20% of operating costs (confirming the efficiencies of smaller size explored in chapter 5).

Table 26: European rail passenger traffic, 1900-2003

| Nation | Million passengers (billion kms) | | | 2003 av trip length (kms) |
	1900	1950	2003	
Austria	78.7	115.2 (4.3)	188 (8.3)	44
Belgium	139.1	219.1 (7.1)	152.5 (8.0)	53
Denmark	20.1	111.0 (3.4)	162.6 (5.5)	34
Finland	7.1	46.3 (2.2)	59.8 (3.3)	56
France	430.0	545.0 (26.4)	906.0 (73.5)	81
Germany	856.0	2,426 (48.8)	1,600 (70.7)	44
Greece	6.2	- (1.0)	8.7 (1.5)	172
Ireland	27.7	11.4 (-)	34.6 (1.6)	46
Italy	59.7	527.1 (23.6)	504.3 (45.6)	90
N'lands	30.8	158.4 (6.2)	320.0 (14.3)	45
Norway	7.0	40.1 (1.5)	38.6 (2.4)	63
Portugal	11.9	57.5 (1.4)	160.1 (3.9)	25
Spain	32.0	107.5 (7.1)	401.2 (19.3)	48
Sweden	30.8	150.0 (6.6)	148 (9.1)	61
Switzerland	62.2	267.6 (6.4)	327 (14.5)	44
UK	1,114.6	704.0 (32.5)	388.4 (40.9)	105

Source: Mitchell

Since 2000, however, passenger numbers have returned to the heyday of the 1920s. 1.23 billion passengers in 2012 might suggest the success of privatization, but the numbers may be inflated. Many trips require double tickets to cover different train companies. Passengers with advanced tickets either buy another ticket or cancel their trip when they miss the specified trains. Others alighting at an earlier station than specified also have to buy another ticket. (It's in the small print apparently.) Some might buy two saver returns rather than the very expensive full fare open return, only using the flexible return portions in reverse order. And for the genuine increase in passengers, British Rail would have managed the suppressed demand better, without such high fares, irrational fare structures, compromised safety, fragmented services and, lest we forget, much higher government subsidies.

In 2011, I bought 12 singles for €53.60 for six Italian return trips covering 442 miles, or 10.5 pence/mile. Similar trips in England then cost £190.70, or 43.2 pence/mile, though cheap day returns were only three times higher. On subsequent holidays, Spanish fares were a third, German fares about half the price of our rail fares. In Germany, however, regional day tickets were much cheaper and included all public transport services. An annual pass for the whole German network was the same as an annual season ticket from Brighton to London.

In an effort to reduce subsidies, the government has applied an escalator to regulated fares by the annual rate of inflation plus 1% or 2%. Making the railways subsidy-free may be impossible, but escalating rail fares while de-escalating petrol duties indicates the 'green credentials' of recent governments.

The fare structure under British Rail was simple and fair:

- single fares were consistent for all trips at anytime, the cost/mile tapering with length of journey;
- peak hour return fares were double the single;
- outside peak hours, super saver returns and cheap day returns for local trips were usually the single fare plus £1, or half the peak return fare;
- saver returns (travelling out on Fridays or busy holiday weekends) were between peak returns and super savers; and
- season tickets offered significant discounts on peak return fares.

After privatization (1994-7), only saver returns and season tickets were protected. First went three-way saver returns. Formerly, I could travel from London via Sheffield to Cardiff and back to London on one saver return. Now I need three expensive singles, or three inflexible advance tickets committing me to three specific trains. Super saver returns were dropped, and to reduce saver returns, peak hours were extended, typically to 10.10 in the mornings, and from as early as 3.30 in the afternoons.

As with airlines, cheap advance tickets ease cash flow and serve as marketing tools for the train companies, benefiting those who can book in advance. These tickets are strictly limited, however, and unavailable on peak services. This discriminates against those making last-minute and emergency trips.

Peak-time return fares, the highest in Europe, are now about three times the cost of saver returns, instead of a third more under British Rail. So most Inter-City peak services out of London are less than half full, leading to serious overcrowding on the following non-peak trains. Business passengers are more likely to drive or fly. Some embarrassed operators quietly offer saver returns on their Inter-City peak trains to railcard holders to fill seats.

Rail safety is also a problem. British Rail had a quasi-independent safety unit that investigated every accident immediately afterwards, interviewing everybody involved. Rather than seek culprits (unless drink or drugs were involved), it sought to identify the cause(s), whether technical failure, design fault or human error, and recommend solutions, most of which were implemented by British Rail.

Privatization disbanded this unit. The following anecdotes suggest why safety then had to be regulated.

- Railtrack (the private company in charge of the tracks, signalling and most stations) saw itself as a management rather than railway company. Early on, it advertised that it was investing £3.2 billion 'to improve our railways'. Most of this was spent in the main stations to maximize retail floorspace as if they were shopping malls. Increasing rental income would enable Railtrack to increase either long-term investment or annual dividends.

- All track maintenance, repair and replacement was contracted out to major construction firms in a bid to make savings. These contractors often employed subcontractors to do much or all of the work, who themselves often employed sub sub-contractors. Throughout this chain, while extracting contract management fees, responsibilities fell between the links. On the railtracks, experienced rail workers were replaced by unskilled low paid labourers.

- To 'make the assets sweat' Railtrack lengthened the safe life of the rails. It also 'made the staff sweat', reducing 31,000 experienced way leave safety inspectors under British Rail to under 19,000. After the Hatfield train crash in 2000, when a mainline rail crumbled like a biscuit, new way leave officers had to be imported from as far afield as Romania.

- After Hatfield, the whole network suffered a 'collective nervous breakdown'. In the following three months, for example, I made two long distance and five regional round trips. 31 timetabled hours became 51 due to speed restrictions, train cancellations and bus replacements.

- More seriously, after every accident, legal advisers are on hand to avoid or shift blame. After Hatfield, it was almost six months before investigators were allowed to interview key staff. This is not the way to investigate accidents, learn from errors and put safety at the heart of railway culture.

Fragmentation is perhaps the biggest cause of inefficiency. British Rail was a separate company, independent of government except for operating subsidies and major investment projects. Safety and maintenance, track and signalling, specification and purchase of rolling stock, train timetabling and frequency, staff and station management – all were under one company, with personal skills and group experience allied to a common purpose.

With privatization, British Rail was replaced by train operating companies and rolling stock operating companies (TOCs and ROSCOs); Railtrack, replaced by Network Rail; an office of rail regulation and a strategic rail authority (ORR and SRA) until it was moved to the department for transport (DfT). A national co-ordinated network is now a mix of profiteering private companies and chronically inexperienced state agencies, in which lawyers are involved whenever two or more are joined together. This breeds inefficiency, cost inflation and dissatisfaction for all except the TOCs and ROSCOs.

TOCs bid for one of 25 area franchises lasting from seven to 30 years. (British Rail was not allowed to bid, thereby dispersing their collective expertise.) This is too short for TOCs to buy trains, so their commitment is little more than 'badging' their leased trains. On running the trains, TOCs focus on higher fares, lower costs and maximum profits. Excess profits on profitable franchises, to replace subsidies, are not paid back until the later years of each franchise. This strengthens the TOCs' position in any negotiations to alter the existing franchise, having extracted all the early profits. Franchises are inflexible. If passenger numbers rise, more trains have to be negotiated from scratch, giving the TOC considerable power over the new terms. Thus taxpayers take most of the risk, TOCs most of the profit.

On privatization, just three ROSCOs bought the 12,000 British Rail vehicles; Angel, Eversholt and Porterbrook. With only ten TOCs running the 25 franchises, this was not a healthy open market. TOCs simply covered exorbitant leasing costs with increased passengers and higher fares. In this sellers' market, the ROSCOs achieved returns of over 30%, enriching managers and shareholders rather than improving the network or reducing fares. ROSCOs were not obliged to specify and order new trains. That responsibility remains with the DfT, which is having to buy a wide range of trains for short and long haul, electric and diesel – without expertise.

ROSCO profits are excessive. Porterbrook, originally bought by a management-employee team, was bought eight months later by Souter's Stagecoach Group. Four years later, in 2000, he sold it to Abbey National for £1.4 billion, four or five times what he paid for it. In 2008, it was sold to investors for £2 billion, and again in 2014, to another consortium for about $3.2 billion (Wikipedia). ROSCOs are also powerful. The one attempt to curb their profits resulted in a voluntary code of conduct agreed by the firms themselves. Belatedly, a few small leasing firms have emerged to add some modest competition to this oligopoly. One might say that the ROSCOs are laughing all the way to the bank, except that two of them are owned by banks.

Railtrack, the third arm of our railways, bought the whole infrastructure – rail tracks, signalling, tunnels, bridges, level crossings and most of the stations – for about £2.5 billion. When it went bankrupt in 2002, the network was transferred to the current not-for-profit company Network Rail. Curiously, this company is not a co-op or social enterprise, being directly responsible to the DfT, but exempt from Freedom of Information law.

As our privatized utilities needed state regulators, so the railways needed a Rail Regulator to ensure fair play by the private firms and proper maintenance by Railtrack. He was replaced in 2004 by the ORR, although, for safety, the ORR comes under the HSE (health and safety executive). It is the HSE that insists on bus replacement services during track maintenance work, rather than the safer and quicker two-way use of single tracks as operated under British Rail. The problem with government regulators is their lack of authority in dealing with powerful adversaries.

Inevitably, fragmentation affects strategy. Initially, Railtrack inherited this role from British Rail, with strategic investment left with government. In 2001, when the industry realized that Railtrack was not going to survive Hatfield, the SRA was set up to develop strategy and manage the franchises, before being replaced, in 2006, by the DfT. Unfortunately, civil servants have no direct railway experience, so they pay large fees to transport and management consultants to advise on all aspects of strategy and investment, train services and timetabling, future rolling stock design and purchase, franchise negotiations, legal agreements and value for money.

Civil servants do, however, set targets to improve 'service delivery' on the railways. Like most government targets, these are counter-productive. TOCs are penalized for late-running trains, so they:

- add a few minutes to the timetables of vulnerable services;
- close platform barriers at least one minute before departure times;
- subject drivers to time pressure;
- don't let trains wait for delayed connecting trains, whether run by the same TOC or not, delaying those passengers twice-over;
- allow late-running trains to run through penultimate stations to arrive at the terminus on time; or
- terminate the train two or three stations before its destination so that the return train journey is on time. Such tricks force passengers to wait for later trains to complete their journeys; for which
- TOCs offer haphazard compensation for delays. In one week, I received full reimbursement from Midland Mainline for a one hour delay. For a similar delay from Virgin, I received first £5, then £10 vouchers for tickets costing £105. On a Great Western delay, an honest railway man said "only send copies of your train tickets. They have a habit of going missing"; and
- they contest the cause of any delay, usually with lawyers, to shift the blame between TOCs and Network Rail.

The ideology of privatization abuses reason and language:

- the railways are in fact nationalized, but controlled by DfT civil servants instead of British Rail professionals,
- the TOCs extract generous dividends for managers and shareholders, leasing trains from profiteering ROSCOs,
- passenger service is inferior to most European railways in terms of train fares, frequency, comfort, punctuality, reliability and connectivity,
- staff remain professional and helpful despite bearing the public brunt of a malfunctioning system,
- despite the rhetoric, no private company or consortium would deliver HS2, which remains a politician's 'vanity project' and, quietly forgotten
- John Major promised that, 'within five years', annual rail subsidies (then about

20%) would disappear. In 2015, despite the highest passenger numbers paying the highest fares in Europe, subsidy levels were about 35%, from a peak of 55% (c£8bn) in 2006. After more than 20 years, taxpayers and passengers are worse off.

Three bright spots suggest some light at the end of this tunnel of madness. First, the 25 franchises have been run by various coach firms (Arriva, FirstGroup, Govia, National Express and Stagecoach), service companies (Serco and Virgin) and foreign nationalized railways (Dutch Abellio, Deutsche Bahn, SNCF and Trenitalia). These last have been more consistent and successful because of their undoubted expertise.

Second, having excluded British Rail from all franchises, some BR professionals re-surfaced in the state-run Railway Company. In 2003 and 2007, it took over two failing franchises (run by Connex South East and GNER) that were terminated. It ran the trains more efficiently, treated the staff better and was more popular with passengers – reinforcing the benefits of social enterprise discussed in chapter 5.

The third bright spot suggests that local is, again, often better than national. Merseyrail is one of two franchises that are managed locally rather than by DfT. (A few rail services are now managed by Transport for London.) The Merseyrail franchise, operated by the Serco-Abellio consortium, is managed by the Merseyside Passenger Transport Executive (PTE). This regional network, connecting Liverpool, Southport, Ormskirk, Wigan, Warrington, Chester and the Wirral, regularly outperforms the other 24 franchises in terms of passenger growth, train reliability and passenger satisfaction. It has the cheapest fares per mile, despite the tapering cost of fares over longer distances, and the consortium still made pre-tax profits of 7.9%, 8.9% and 9.7% from 2008 to 2010 (Wikipedia). The only network that outperforms Merseyrail in low fares and passenger growth is the nationalized Northern Ireland Railways.

Nationalized rail companies and local transport authorities are better at running railways for passengers. The *NPPF* is silent on trains. Merseyrail leads us naturally to regional and urban transport, but one nice fact remains. Merseyrail used to lose money and Dr Beeching proposed closing the whole network and dismantling the tracks and stations.

Urban social transport

"Around 75% of journeys in Britain are under five miles (eight km) in length" (Ecotec 1993). The average distance of all trips is only six miles, and 25% are less than a mile (ONS, *Social Trends*, 2004). This raises two points. First, should major projects like HS2, Heathrow 3 and M25 improvements take precedence over local transport? And second, while rail networks are crucial in major cities, it is in short trips in every town where the conflict between road traffic and social transport is keenest.

From 1968, all local transport services were regulated by passenger transport authorities (PTAs), with six new metropolitan counties, London and Strathclyde PTAs created in 1974. In 1985, however, all bus services were deregulated, except in London. The re-named passenger transport executives (PTEs) were left with local ferries and metros, and could only subsidize 'unprofitable' bus routes. Despite initial investment in new buses and more competition on popular routes, deregulation led to higher fares (see table 21), fewer passengers, fewer buses and less investment.

Table 27: Bus services and passenger journeys, 1985/6-2008/9

Regions	1985/6	1992/3	2008/9
Local bus services (vehicle km millions)	2,077	2,515	na
London	273	330	
Metropolitan areas	574	678	
Shire counties	849	1,042	
Scotland	285	346	
Wales	95	118	
Local bus passenger journeys (millions)	5,641	4,483	5,233
London	1,152	1,128	2,149
Metropolitan areas	2,068	1,386	1,111
Shire counties	1,588	1,308	1,355
Scotland	671	532	515
Wales	163	129	124
Passenger receipts (£mn)	2,219	3,033	na

Source: ONS, *Annual Abstract*

Only London buses carry more passengers. Transport for London controls all social transport networks except the commuter railways. It plans all bus routes, fares, quality and frequency to provide a comprehensive service and avoid congestion on busy routes. Blocks of routes are then put out to competitive tender to ensure value, benefiting passengers, operators and London as a whole.

Elsewhere, buses travel further with fewer passengers. The initial increase in bus miles only reflected fierce competition on the profitable routes, not new routes. This led to central bus congestion, high emissions and leapfrog timetabling. 'You wait ages for a bus, then three come along' denied passengers reliable, evenly-spaced services. Many rural, off-peak and Sunday services now require subsidies which, in 2014, totalled £2.3 billion. Formerly, public bus companies cross-subsidized these loss-making services from profitable routes to provide a comprehensive network.

And the competition was short-lived. Five bus oligopolies now control 70% of the local bus market: Firstbus (over 20% of the market with almost 9,000 buses),

Stagecoach (16% and 8,100 buses), Arriva (5,900 buses), plus Go-Ahead and National Express. These have often created local monopolies. If unwilling to sell, aggressive price wars force local bus firms either to sell or go broke. In 1994, for example, the Monopolies and Mergers Commission found Stagecoach's behaviour in Darlington to be "predatory, deplorable and against the public interest." Even when guilty, the fines do not deter abuse elsewhere.

Monopolies bring higher fares and profits, but fewer passengers and social benefits. When the Go-Ahead group were losing substantial income from its strike-bound Southern Rail services in 2016, it still managed to report profits of 14.9% due to 'good performance' from its bus operations. This profiteering affects fares and wages. Fares are often raised artificially. Most large bus firms negotiate fixed prices for say 90% of their fuel over two or three years. This hedging protects both parties against volatile fuel prices and is sound business. However, some bus firms then raise fares whenever crude oil and petrol pump prices rise despite their hedging. This is legal but dishonest. Unlike train drivers, bus drivers have had their wages reduced in real terms, leading to shortages. And they are often expected to sign out of EU working directives covering safe practices in shift patterns and rigid timetabling. This can lead to driver fatigue and serious accidents. (TfL is not immune – see *Private Eye* 1503, 23/8/19.)

Bus firms also hide key statistics like mileage and income, again putting commercial confidentiality above planning statistics.

After deregulation, most cash-strapped councils found it impossible to renew their bus fleets and were forced to sell their networks to private operators. And now the five large bus fleets are also starved of investment, not because the firms are cash-strapped but because they strive perpetually to maximize profits. Re-investment is simply another cost. Only 15 bus companies (with their historic city liveries) remain with local councils, notably Blackpool, Cardiff, Edinburgh, Nottingham, Plymouth and Reading.

Few bus and train stations are integrated, even in new towns. Milton Keynes city centre, surrounded by landscaped highways and car parks, is about half a mile from the bus and rail stations that are separated by a large commuter car park and dual carriageway, giving car drivers, who need more exercise, precedence over passengers. So two station cafes, information systems, public waiting rooms and staff facilities are provided, instead of one interchange for trains, buses and taxis. With deregulation and 'privatization', integrated bus and rail services are rare. Through-ticketing, almost ubiquitous in European cities, is resisted here as our bus and train companies resist the cheaper combined fares and necessary machines that reduce short-term profits.

From Mitchell's *Historical Statistics* to *Jane's Urban Transport Systems*, we can compare our large UK city networks with those in Europe. Unfortunately, there are gaps. Passenger trips are unavailable for 18 of Europe's largest 57 cities; being Aarhus, Copenhagen, Nantes, Strasbourg, Bonn, Duisburg and Dusseldorf, Florence, Naples and Palermo, Oslo, Lisbon, Den Haag, Malaga, Gothenburg, Malmo,

Stockholm, Lausanne and Zurich. 13 of 19 British cities (68.4% compared with 32.6% in Europe) lack this data: Aberdeen, Bristol, Glasgow, Leeds/Bradford, Leicester, Liverpool, London, Manchester, Middlesbrough, Newcastle, Nottingham, Sheffield and Stoke-on-Trent. Accurate data is essential for policy and democracy.

Table 28: European urban transport systems, 1984/5 – 2008/9

City	Population (millions)	Systems (plus bus)	Control	Passenger trips 1983	2008
Graz	0.29	Tr	Mun	71.2	94.9
Vienna	1.68	Tr M LtR	Mun	552,5	803.6
Antwerp	0.472	Tr	Reg	57.1	201.7
Brussels	1.0 c	Tr M	Sta	193.9	254.8
Helsinki	0.565	Tr M	Mun	168.4	188.1
Bordeaux	0.25	Tr*	Reg	65.9	90.3
Lille	0.23	Tr M	Reg	50.4	136.0
Lyon	0.47	Tr* M Tb Fn	Mun	202.8	352.0
Marseilles	0.839	Tr M Tb	Mun	136.5	157.4
Paris	2.2	M LtR* R	Mun/Reg	1,927.5	3,037.0
Toulouse	0.435	M*	?	65.5	105.0
Berlin	3.43	Tr M Fe	Mun	1,125.9	1,044.6
Dresden	0.504	Tr Fe Fn	Mun	355 c	200 c
Leipzig	0.562	Tr	Mun	341 c	127.1
Aachen	0.258	-	Mun	43.2	62 c
Augsburg	0.269	Tr	Mun	51.3	54.0
Bochum	0.381	Tr LtR*	Mun/Reg	91.8	137.4
Bremen	0.548	Tr	Mun	97.4	97.2
Koln	0.936	Tr	Mun/Reg	170.7	260 c
Dortmund	0.586	Tr	Mun	76.8	122.7
Essen	0.518	Tr	Mun	82.9	109.5
Frankfurt	0.67	Tr* LtR*	Mun/Reg	154.2	175.5
Hamburg	1.77	Tr Fe	Mun	417.2	399.8
Hannover	0.516	Tr LtR	Mun	136.1	151.9
Karlsruhe	0.286	Tr LtR	Mun	53.1	110.7
Mannheim	0.327	Tr	Mun/Reg	50.1	162
Munchen	1.36	Tr M	Mun	453.4	614
Nurnberg	0.5	Tr M	Mun	127.5	196.3
Stuttgart	0.6	Tr	Mun	143.1	187.2
Athens	0.745	M Tb	Sta	500	645.2
Dublin	0.506	-	Sta	159	145

City	Population (millions)	Systems (plus bus)	Control	Passenger trips 1983	2008
Bologna	0.374	Tb	Reg	164	104
Genova	0.612	Tb LtR	Mun	241	170.2
Milano	1.3	M Tb	Mun	800	621.5
Roma	2.7	Tr M Tb	Mun	1,193.9	1,631
Torino	0.91	Tr	Mun	138.9	190
Venezia	0.27	Fe	Mun/Reg	110	96.1
Amsterdam	1.36	Tr M Fe	Mun/Sta	220	260
Rotterdam	0.6	Tr M	Mun/Sta	161.7	159
Utrecht	0.3	Tr	Mun	40	50.7
Bergen	0.248	Tb	Mun/Pvt	20.6	25
Barcelona	1.62	Tr M	Mun	430.7	593.7
Bilbao	0.354	Tr M* LtR*	Mun	55	132.6
Madrid	6.3	M	Reg	770	1,111
Sevilla	0.704	-	Mun	73.8	84.7
Valencia	0.807	M*	Mun	82.7	173.0
Belfast	0.276	-	Sta	29.3	134.0
Birmingham	1.0	Tr*	Mun/Pvt	471.3	313.7
Cardiff	0.325	-	Pvt	32.8	28.8
Edinburgh	0.458	-	Mun	134.1	113
Hull	0.262	-	Pvt	40.3	36.2
Southampton	0.235	-	Pvt	23.1	25.1

Source: *Jane's*

Key: under Systems: M metro, Tr tram, Tb trolleybus, LtR light rail, Fe ferry, Fn funicular. * Denotes a system that opened after 1983. Under Control: Mun municipal, Reg regional, Sta state, Pvt private. And populations are for cities. In conurbations, railways become significant.

Key points emerge.

- 58% of UK cities (11/19) rely solely on buses compared with 10% in Europe (6 of 57). All 29 Austrian, Belgian, German and Dutch cities (except Aachen) have trams as well as buses. Nine have a third system.
- All European cities retain some public control of their systems, though some may be outsourced to private firms. In the UK, only perhaps six cities have retained strategic control of social transport, though the picture is complex.
- 12 European and five UK cities built new tram, metro or light rail networks since 1983. While levels of public subsidy are not always available, our reliance on private buses means that we invest far less in our social transport systems.

Combining these statistics highlights different urban travel patterns by nation.

Table 29: Annual social transport urban trips by nation, 1983-2008

Nation	Total city populations	Total trips (mns) 1983	2008	%age increase	2008, av trips/person
Austria	1.97	623.7	898.5	44.1	456.1
Belgium	1.472	251.0	456.5	81.9	310.1
Finland	0.565	168.4	188.1	11.7	332.9
France	2.224	521.1	840.7	61.0	378.0
Germany E	4.496	1,821.9	1,371.7	(-24.7)	305.1
Germany W	10.949	2,196.4	2,840.2	29.3	259.4
Greece	0.745	500	645.2	29.0	866.0
Ireland	0.506	159	148	(-6.9)	292.5
Italy	3.092	1,289.9	1,077.8	(-16.4)	348.6
Netherlands	2.26	421.7	469.7	11.4	207.8
Spain	3.485	642.2	984.0	53.2	282.4
UK	2.556	730.8	536.3	(-26.6)	209.9

Source: *Jane's*

Three points stand out. The UK is clearly bottom of any European league for urban social transport. If we added Paris, their population of 2.2 million averaged 1,380.5 trips/person in 2008, which would have greatly increased the national average. And despite their decline, the former East German systems still carry many more passengers than West German and UK cities.

Second, despite our reliance on buses, they still lost a quarter of their passengers since deregulation. Of the three European cities that rely solely on buses, Aachen and Dublin carry more passengers. Only Sevilla carries fewer. The only efficiency of our buses is that they largely pay their way.

And third, only Dutch citizens use social transport less than the British. With their much higher densities, so many people walk and cycle. Britain's suburban densities make buses less efficient and more expensive. Transport mode is directly related to density: the highest supports walking and cycling, high density social transport, and low density private cars. Most European cities continue to cram resources and development within and in high density extensions rather than exurbs.

Bus deregulation and rail privatization have reduced investment in our social transport even while profits are being extracted, and passengers now pay far more for the privilege of becoming 'customers'. So far more passengers transfer to cars, increasing road traffic, congestion and pollution. Even our tram networks in Croydon, Manchester, Nottingham, Sheffield, the West Midlands and Edinburgh do not compare with most on the continent, while Bristol, Leeds, Liverpool and South Hants have waited many years for government approval.

Social transport can only be improved through local management – of buses and trams by local councils, and regional transport by PTEs. The comparative success of Northern Ireland Railways, Merseyrail PTE and Transport for London should be our models. Unfortunately, central government is unlikely to delegate transport strategy when these issues are ignored in its own *NPPF*. Can we change our own behaviour?

Personal mobility – reclaim the streets

Three basic attitudes affect motoring: the celestial, the dystopian and the pragmatic. Roland Barthes (1915-80) defined the celestial with his startling comparison between cathedral and motor car. Both symbolized their age, combining corporate ambition with teams of anonymous designers and crafters. One celebrated city status and the power of its religious and secular fathers, the other reflected personal status and the power of global mega-corps. The quest for the celestial life hereafter was replaced by the life of the sublime here and now.

Despite these similarities, cathedrals and cars had opposite effects on the physical fabric and social life of cities. Cathedrals, with centripetal force, drew people into the heart for communal ceremonies, sacred and profane. Cars fuelled the centrifugal forces to exurbia, replacing social wonder and cohesion with speed, comfort and isolation. Instead of sermons pointing the road to everlasting life, adverts promise you the route to personal freedoms now: freedom from the stress of the office while you relax in your exoskeleton; freedom in the manic thrill of racing through towns, powering from nought to 60 in twenty six point eight seconds; freedom of that idyllic landscape where people, vehicles, petrol stations and litter have been airbrushed out; freedom from pester power while stressing the importance of cars to your children; freedom to bask in the respect of your peers, boss and Jeremy Clarkson; and, for other alpha males, freedom to unleash your inner lech on that semi-naked half-starved young woman who happens to be draped over the bonnet.

As stated earlier, adverts actually work on your subconscious fears – of ridicule, insignificance or impotence. Not hell exactly, but uncomfortable, and once you own a car, the driving habit is difficult to break. Rayner Banham dubbed Los Angeles 'autopia', but Joan Didion (2011) captures its empty freedom. "Once she was on the freeway and had manoeuvred her way to a fast lane she turned on the radio at high volume and she drove. She drove from San Diego to the Harbor, the Harbor up to the Hollywood, the Hollywood to the Golden State, the Santa Monica, the Santo Ana, the Pasadena, the Ventura. She drove it as a riverman runs a river, every day more attuned to its currents, its deceptions, and just as a riverman feels the pull of the rapids in the lull between sleeping and waking, so Maria lay at night in the still of Beverly Hills and saw the great signs soar overhead at seventy miles an hour,

Normandie ¼ Vermont ¾ Harbor Fwy 1. Again and again she returned to an intricate stretch just south of the interchange where successful passage from the Hollywood onto the Harbor required a diagonal move across four lanes of traffic. On the afternoon she finally did it without once braking or once losing the beat on the radio she was exhilarated, and that night slept dreamlessly." Perhaps cars are the new opium of the people.

The dystopian view is captured by the inimitable Jonathan Meades. "[Vehicular correctness or pedestrianization] signally fails to acknowledge that a city modelled on some Dutch provincial town full of cycle lanes and happy, smiling, pathologically tolerant, socially responsible, new model citizens is not half so alluring as a city of entropy and chaos which you move through in a private space that adds to the degradation." (*The Times*, 11/9/1999) Take your pick: happy citizens living in Toytown, or the dysfunctional maelstrom of *Blade Runner*, living with the perpetual menace of testosterone-fuelled petrol heads.

Petrol heads also have a different attitude to vehicle crime. Stealing cars or TWOCing (taking without owner's consent, whether for joyriding or for sex somewhere warm) are criminal acts. Road crashes are accidents. TWOCing is a mortal sin, while crashes (that kill or seriously injure three to five pupils every school day) are venial. It is surely criminal negligence when society consistently resists lower speed limits, proper enforcement and tougher penalties on those who drive without due care and attention.

It also took decades before car safety was accepted as a design issue. Car makers, designing for status, fashion and obsolescence, resisted all safety legislation. Eventually, US legislators banned protruding bumpers (complementing their tail fins) that frequently ripped through pedestrian shinbones and calf muscles. Seat belts, air bags and stronger frames followed. Now, all drivers feel safer: the young hood going deaf in his music box, the mother and brood in her Chelsea tractor, the flabby executive in his exoskeleton. Unfortunately, this lulls many drivers into a false sense of security. Some drive just a little faster and take just a few more risks. Minor collisions on country lanes are now a little more serious, making roads less safe for walkers and cyclists. The safest car, a policeman once told me, was one that, in a crash, propels not an air bag but a blunt knife from the dashboard. Only then would all motorists 'drive with due care and attention for all highway users.'

Car pollution is the current issue. It took decades to phase out leaded fuel, despite strong evidence of the dangers to our health, even at extremely low levels (*The Observer* 18/3/2018). Even today, the motoring lobby remains largely relaxed to poisonous emissions and lies about fuel consumption. Corporate interests and legislative inertia continue to bypass social responsibility and even motorists' health. The Transport and Road Research Laboratory, set up in 1933, would have investigated such issues for government. Privatized in 1996, however, the website of the new Transport Research Laboratory (TRL) doesn't inspire confidence. Under Solutions, the page on 'Cities and Urban' is illustrated by a large multi-level motorway spaghetti junction in the midst of a large city. TRL is owned by the non-profit Transport Research Foundation and overseen by 80 members from the transport industry. Their identity is not available on the web (Wikipedia). Like pollution, this is insidious.

Most motorists, however, are pragmatic and the car is to get them from A to B and back, whenever they want. Few seem to care how much their habit costs beyond the cost of filling the tank and the miles per gallon. The regular and the one-off costs for tax and insurance, MOT test, new tyres, car repairs and depreciation are all accepted for the simple pleasure of spending hours in a non-productive haze, largely unaware of the outside world, secure in their soft upholstered womb, cradled in a near-foetal position, cocooned from external noise, weather and society, with instant gratifying speed at the touch of a pedal. Only traffic jams disturb this serenity. Only other dangerous drivers create sudden surges of adrenalin and rage, with rare crashes, deaths and injuries.

When price is secondary, this convenient and comfortable driving habit becomes addictive. The main household driver averages 1,230 trips and 10,300 miles each year. Non-car owners survive on 750 trips and 2,750 miles a year (ONS 2004). 25 trips a week makes motorists less sociable than non-motorists on their 15 trips.

Table 30: Trips to and from school (%), 1989-2008

| | 5 – 10 year olds | | | 11 – 16 year olds | | |
	walk	car	other	walk	car	other
1989/90	62	27	10	48	14	38
2008	48	43	9	40	21	39

Source: ONS, *Social Trends*

A defining characteristic of urban life is that most trips are short, with 25% less than a mile as noted earlier. Yet these short trips to local facilities continue to decline by all modes except by car. This may be parental choice, but it is anti-social.

Being driven to school deprives pupils of healthy exercise, street experience, risk assessment and early independence. It empties pavements and makes roads more congested and dangerous. Our roads may be among the safest in Europe, with the fourth lowest rate of accidents involving children (ONS 2004). But child deaths at 0.9 per 100,000 (down from 2.0 in the 1980s) 'was higher than many EU countries', notably Germany (0.6), France (0.5), the Netherlands (0.4) and Sweden (0.3).

It is unclear why so many crashes occur within two or three miles of home. Being more familiar with the area, perhaps drivers become more careless. Heisenberg's uncertainty principle states that "it is impossible to determine at the same time exactly where a particle is and how fast it is moving." This could partly explain the motorist's behaviour. He knows exactly where he is and sees the car pulling out, cyclist turning right or child chasing the ball, but misjudges his speed relative to the 'obstacle'. In German cities, speed limits of 30 kph (19 mph) are common in residential areas. A government road safety poster from 2005 also made the danger of speed clear:

40
KILLED – Hit at 40 mph, 17 out of 20 children are killed.
20
ALIVE – Hit at 20 mph, 19 out of 20 children survive.
Kill your speed. Not a child.

Tables 19 and 30 also raise a class issue. "Social and economic factors play a part in child road injuries. Research has shown that children from social class V are five times more likely to be killed as pedestrians than those from social class I. Children whose families have fewer resources tend to live near more dangerous road environments, have fewer provisions for safe places to play, and tend to go out as pedestrians more often than children from wealthier homes." (Child accident prevention trust, www.capt.org.uk.)

Traffic in Towns (2nd edition)

Let us rewrite Buchanan. Instead of 'adapting towns to motor traffic' through urban destruction, let us adapt towns for pedestrians' convenience and safety. These depend on three broad principles:

- within neighbourhoods (Buchanan's 'environmental cells') calm traffic to 20 or 15 mph to make all streets shared space,
- city-wide, provide safe networks for walking and cycling, which still, 60 years after Buchanan, remain the Cinderellas of transport planning, and
- throughout, reduce unnecessary road traffic to improve social transport services, access for deliveries and emergency vehicles.

If highways are 'open to all passengers' (*OED*) 'on which all have right to go' (*Chambers*), we need to calm all traffic to make urban roads safe for walkers and cyclists, grannies and wheelchairs, shoppers and trolleys, children and push chairs as well as vehicles. Throughout the twentieth century, pedestrians have been treated as second class citizens except in pedestrianized streets. Roadspace needs to be more democratic.

- General 20mph speed limits would dramatically reduce the number of crashes and dispense with the need for physical speed restrictions that annoy so many motorists (raising questions about their fitness to drive).
- Trams calm traffic, yet our tram networks rely heavily on existing railways. Putting trams back on main roads would attract more passengers, calm road traffic and complement rather than disrupt existing train services.
- We have fewer pedestrian crossings than most comparable nations (*Transport Retort* Issue 17/5). In the triangle where I live, the three busy signal-controlled

junctions have wholly-inadequate pedestrian phases. On a busy crossing in Trafalgar Square, traffic has 75 seconds in each cycle, pedestrians just 15. This is the norm.

- In Japan, most crossroads have four zebra crossings in line with the pavements, allowing pedestrians to continue their route without deviation and less delay.
- In residential streets, 15 or even 10 mph speed limits would deter through-traffic and rat running. At these speeds, drivers and pedestrians can make eye contact and agree informally who goes first on any street or crossing. Turning off a main road, the pavement should continue across the side street, thereby giving priority to pedestrians over drivers.
- In the Netherlands *Woonerven* streets provide shared space, with no separation between pavement and road, and cars reduced to walking pace. Sharing road space will take time, involving speed cameras, harsh penalties for speeding and prison for injuries through dangerous driving.

After a century of planning, in which convenience largely meant accommodating the future and cars, only now are we promoting safe routes to schools. In fact, cities should provide safe networks with more crossings and safer junctions on all routes to schools and colleges, town centres and local parades, rail and bus stations, business districts, industrial estates, health clinics and hospitals, parks and commons, allotments and sports grounds, for pedestrians and cyclists.

Cycling is healthy and popular. About a third of adults and nine tenths of schoolchildren own bikes and, like walking, it is extremely efficient, non-polluting and sociable. Yet it is dangerous when mixed with traffic and continues to decline. In 1981, 3.76% of all work trips were by bike; in 2001, that figure was 2.89% (UK National Census). This compares with 11% in Germany, 18% in Denmark and 29% in the Netherlands. Until Sustrans won £43.5 million on the lottery to develop a national cycle network, cycling was regarded as a joke. Unfortunately, as with canals, the early emphasis of the Sustrans campaign was on tourism and recreation. Even today, its webpage opens with a family cycling on an off-road track. A few British towns show the potential: in Cambridge 27% of commuters cycle to work, in Oxford 19%, and in York 20%.

Some prefer off-road cycle networks using canal towpaths, riverside walks, disused railway lines, bridleways and tracks through parks and commons, although these are primarily for walking. However, we should treat cyclists as legitimate road traffic that tame vehicles and civilize streets. All urban main roads should have combined bus and cycle lanes, with priority at junctions. Cycle networks should also access surrounding villages via designated country lanes with 15 mph speed limits, as in Jersey

Safe walking and cycling make life easier, cheaper and healthier. According to a chief medical officer report (from 2005), "about 67% of the British population take just 5,000 steps a day or less. This amount is defined as sedentary" (*The Observer* 10/1/2010). Drivers spend less time living while quietly accumulating subcutaneous layers of fat.

Living without a car in most towns is both possible and desirable, but we need a more pragmatic attitude to car ownership. In the short term we should make more efficient use of existing cars, with car sharing among commuters, neighbours and families (where the car is used by grandparents on weekdays and by parents at weekends). We should also encourage more car hiring and car-pools. Longer term, we can reduce car ownership through intensification, with higher densities, reduced parking, better social transport and more mixed neighbourhoods.

Germany and the Netherlands have gone further, building car-free neighbourhoods based on a contract between residents and city not to own a car. Here we still retain generous parking standards. The *Essex Design Guide* (1973) insisted on "one car parking space for each new dwelling in addition to a garage or a space for a garage." 20 years later, parking standards for dwellings within 400 yards of a London railway terminus was 1.1 spaces for each new dwelling. At the time, 41% of households in London did not have a car, since reduced to about 38%. Yet no city or town has made 4% or even 0.4% of their residential streets car-free. Traffic-free streets are rare but when a main street is closed one day a year for bands and entertainers, crowds throng the area, the pubs and cafes spill out onto pavements and everyone enjoys the freedom. The other 364 days and 16 hours, the streets revert to their traffic function, serving much the same purpose as an open sewer – without the stench but much more dangerous.

Before leaving transport, let me conclude on the entropy of technology.

Urban entropy 3: technology can seriously disrupt cities

The Industrial Revolution was largely driven by technological innovation. In fact, there have been many industrial revolutions (as Jane Jacobs suggested). Apart from the wheel, ovens from about 3,000 BC produced bread and pottery and introduced early manufacturing processes. Clean water pipes and sewers (c2,500 BC) transformed social health in all cities, while water- and windmills (from 200 BC) irrigated crops, drained wetlands and ground flour (Challoner 2009).

Indeed, the Industrial Revolution itself progressed in a series of stages. The agricultural revolution with crop rotation etc supported an increased population. Steam-powered machinery then powered new factories, as well as the railways, mining, farming and explosive urban growth. Factories created a new conflict between Labour and Capital (rather than manufacture and finance). Labour bore the brunt of machine efficiency with low wages and dangerous conditions, society bore the brunt of choking smogs and poisonous effluents, and the *nouveau riche* (overtaking Landed gentry) bore the brunt of the profits.

Electricity cleaned up industry, ironically just as it was being zoned out of neighbourhoods to new suburban estates. A new partnership emerged between Capital and Labour – 'consumerism'. Suburban life is inconceivable without washing machines, fridges, radios, TVs and the Sunday whine of lawn mowers, hedge clippers, leaf blowers and edge strimmers. The modest communal life of the launderette in Le Corbusier's *Unité d'Habitation* or canteen in London's Barbican estate are rare.

Throughout this period, it was cars that moved fast and broke things. And now we have computers transforming life at home, at work and in society. The philosopher Heidegger was wrong to suggest that technology reduces social intercourse. Most technology, once it has been socially accepted through 'cultural transmission', is entirely beneficial. (Only the defence industry is deeply ambiguous.) What binds cars and computers together is the mania for speed and the inability of societies to control the emerging monopolies.

Paraphrasing TS Eliot, my uncle sometimes asked: "With all this information, where's the knowledge, and with all this knowledge, where's the wisdom?" Industrial innovation illustrates this process:

- information about ideas and products, combined with experience of production, creates skills, both craft and professional;
- with skills come knowledge and rare innovations. These 'mutations', when successful, develop their markets, initially through disruption;
- wisdom, however, only percolates through the system as skills and innovations are analysed for their side effects, external costs and social impact. At present, all we can say is that we have shown little wisdom with cars – or computers..

Since 1900, wheels and electronics have seriously affected city life and their impact has largely been defined by ownership. Private cars might waste about two years of drivers' lives. But with heavy lorries, they have destroyed the social ambience of our streets and killed many innocents. The negative impact of social transport is negligible against their safety and affordable mobility for all. Car ownership is a simple market force, but the urban destruction, compulsory purchase and ensuing pollution and premature deaths, would surely give that market force a negative cost/benefit ratio or GDP. This is both unsustainable and undemocratic, to which subject we return in part 3.

Computers have taken over many skilled jobs, reduced our social skills and pose a real threat to civilized democracies. Lathes and sewing machines require skilled workers to improve efficiency and quality in production. It is a partnership. Computer-operated machines, computer-aided design and robots have replaced those operators and machinists. This again favours Capital over Labour. According to Bill Gates (in 2017): "Right now, the human worker who does, say, $50,000 worth of work in a factory, that income is taxed and you get income tax, social security tax, all those things. If a robot comes in to do the same thing, you'd think that we'd tax the robot at a similar level." Machines are tax-exempt.

Excessive use of computers might affect our mental competence; calculators, satnavs and spellchecks reduce our mental agility, constant streams of data, messages, adverts and images reduce our attention spans. Perhaps goldfish do have shorter attention spans, but excessive screen time may convert passing images into a blur (as with driving perhaps). More serious is that 'search' information and 'share' among 'friends' with 'likes' has little social meaning without direct experience. It is from personal study, library visits, meeting people and making friends that we gain knowledge, make judgements, learn from mistakes and perhaps grow wiser.

Computers have an unprecedented capacity for information, serving as booking service, encyclopedias, letter boxes, phones, shops and advertisers. Yet their impact on society has been both beneficial and destructive.

When Tim Berners-Lee and team, on their collective information and skills, developed the worldwide web, it was 'gifted' to society for everyone's benefit. Like the airwaves, it shifted society once more to an open or 'connected' society, as with printing, postal services and the telephone. On that infrastructure, such wonders as Wikipedia have been developed. This not-for-profit body converts vast amounts of information into knowledge by the (very time-consuming) process of continuous editing. It's not always correct, but it is reliable and ever-expanding.

If written records and accurate data are at the heart of civilization (chapter 7), then computers, alongside the media, are in the forefront of democracy. Yet, at present, as with the Barclays, Murdochs and Rothermeres, Amazon, Facebook, Google and other 'social' platforms, have no interest in accurate data and honesty.

The mission statements of these monopolies is to "give people the power to build community and bring the world closer together" (Facebook), "organise the world's information and make it universally accessible and useful" (Google), "empower every person and every organisation on the planet to achieve more" (Microsoft), or (for Snapchat), "contribute to human progress by empowering people to express themselves, live in the moment, learn about the world, and have fun together" (*The Observer* 8/7/2018). These are the witterings of teenagers, and they are fake. Social platforms are significantly more dangerous than the media moguls in two crucial respects: censorship and privacy.

Freedom of speech is an ideal that has to be moderated. Tyrannical censorship, as in China and Russia, is profoundly anti-democratic, merely restating the fascist principle that might is right. Unfortunately, unfettered freedom of speech, in which alternative facts, fake news and naked lies claim equal rights, is also profoundly undemocratic. In open societies, truth has to be protected, liars held to account and extreme bigots, racists and misogynists subject to the law. If the media moguls, whose mission statements are simply to make money, can abide by the law and moderate the hate of any journalists to 'acceptable' levels, then so must the social platforms. A Stanford University study of 7,800 students (from secondary schools and colleges) found that their ability to "tell fake accounts from real ones, activist groups from neutral sources or distinguish ads from articles" was, in the words of the researchers, "dismaying", "bleak" and "a threat to democracy." (John Naughton, *The Observer* 11/12/16)

Basic honesty must be upheld by all media outlets. Yet the social platforms display a 'radical indifference' to these 'rogue forces of disinformation' (Zuboff), providing them with echo chambers (or virulent ghettoes) for hate mail, violent threats, misogyny, revenge pornography, paedophilia, toxic racism, religious bigotry, electoral disinformation and phobic lies peddled as truth, which would not be tolerated in schools, pubs, newspapers and law courts. Like cars, these social platforms are creating their own ghettoes. No longer can the platforms evade editorial responsibility and set themselves above the law. If Wikipedia can edit, correct and expand its huge encyclopedia with minimal staff and a small army of volunteers, then Facebook, Twitter and Google etc must do the same, with increasing fines for repeated failures. And their 'moderators' should be employed in the US so that citizens become aware of the filth that Zuckerberg and others espouse and encourage – as it increases their profits.

Concerning privacy, a fundamental principle has been ignored, creating a serious disconnect between platform users and providers. No post office or telephone company was allowed to invade our privacy, except in emergencies. It is ironic that, after a century seeking suburban privacy, users cede it whenever we use our computers to write, search, buy or phone. The worm in this particular bud is in their 'intellectual property'. They invade our lives, yet zealously guard their strings of algorithms. When information flows one way only, we enter a closed society that Zuboff rightly calls 'surveillance capitalism'. This is even more efficient than Stalin's spying on Soviet citizens, except that the end is for economic rather than political power.

These surveillance capitalists use the huge data banks of information from every message, search, image, reading, share and purchase to create alarmingly accurate profiles of our lives, our hopes, fears, intentions and susceptibilities. From these data banks, they have developed unparalleled knowledge of our behaviour, and from this knowledge, they have created extraordinary wealth. These teenagers are clever, but their growth is stunted by greed. Wisdom eludes them.

Unregulated, technocrats are leading us to a new dark age. In this global 'community', about 100 suppliers of energy, food, clothes, household goods, leisure, entertainment, money, news and communication could keep us as house-bound consumers to be milked as passive cash cows and manipulated for as voter fodder. In this controlled market, intellectual freedom is curtailed by intellectual property, innovation quickly bought out, demand determined by suppliers, consumerism the basic measure of personality and social life replaced by the click of a mouse or having to "Please choose from the following options". Life would be little different from the last dark age; the only difference being that while goths, vandals and visigoths plundered, raped and pillaged, the new thugs are financiers plundering our markets, developers pillaging our cities and technocrats raping our privacy.

After centuries of reformation and enlightenment, discovery and social progress, the twentieth century was an era of mass manipulation through marketing, political tyranny and now technocratic tyrants. All dark ages are non-urban, whether living in villages or in battery farms, in Detroit or Dubai, and today it is largely driven by technology. Before turning to social life and civilization, below are the magnets for transport.

Private transport
- door-to-door convenience at any time
- personal status but anti-social
- comfortable inside, dangerous outside
- low trip costs, but high capital costs
- inefficient weight and energy ratios
- large impact on GDP in making and servicing cars
- roads fully subsidized, high social costs largely ignored,
- intrusive in every street, whether moving, jammed or parked
- serious pollution and a significant cause of climate change
- continuous noise, occasionally loud
- a major time waster, plus congestion
- unhealthy and addictive behaviour

Social transport
- less convenient with fixed routes and timetables
- democratic and social, mixing with strangers
- fairly comfortable inside, safe outside
- higher trip costs, shared capital costs
- efficient weight and energy ratios
- modest positive impact on GDP
- most services subsidized, high social benefits largely ignored
- little intrusion in streets
- modest polluters with much lower carbon emissions
- often noisy but sporadic and confined
- dual function, travel time can be productive
- healthier, walking to stops and stations, and not addictive

Personal mobility
- convenient for all short trips, door-to-door, anytime
- democratic, sociable but poor social status
- comfortable but usually surrounded by danger
- negligible cost
- the most efficient forms of transport
- tiny impact on GDP
- no subsidies, high social benefits largely ignored
- people enliven every street
- pollution-free with negligible carbon emissions
- quiet in noisy surroundings
- dual function, mobility and exercise
- healthy and important

Chapter Seven: Social Roots

"Civilization: social, moral, and intellectual attainments of a particular society, cultural development; state of not being primitive or savage." (*Penguin ED* 1965)

Before we discuss social roots, we need to define civilization, a concept large with lofty ideals and noble passions, cerebral invention and creature comforts. It is rooted in the idea of cities and citizenship. According to Ruskin, civilization can only be read in the story of a nation's deeds, words and art. But these are the outputs. If we are to civilize cities, we need to identify the inputs that help us avoid 'being primitive or savage'.

Our 'social, moral and intellectual attainments' largely arose through a process that we might call social evolution in cities, the human supra-organism where civilization can flourish, both civic and civil. Man's intellectual freedom, social behaviour and spiritual empathy for old, sick and disabled people emerged through the specific social behaviour that we call politics. And to civilize cities, I suggest that we must somehow balance *Liberté! Egalité! Fraternité!* supported by written records, the rule of law and care of the young.

One of history's most famous slogans is strongly associated with the French Revolution, though dictionaries differ whether it came before, during or after that heady period of rhetoric and bloodshed. In any event, stable levels of freedom, equality and fraternity underpin all civilized societies.

Liberty

According to Karl Popper (1986), "[I]f there could be such a thing as socialism combined with individual liberty, I would be a socialist still. For nothing could be better than living a modest, simple, and free life in an egalitarian society. It took some time before I recognized this as no more than a beautiful dream; that freedom is more important than equality; that the attempt to realize equality endangers freedom; and that, if freedom is lost, there will not even be equality among the unfree."

Without liberty, history would be a litany of tyrannies. Yet putting conservative liberty above socialist equality is too simplistic. The two are inextricably linked on a political spectrum. When Thomas Jefferson (1743-1826) stated our rights to "the preservation of life, and liberty, and the pursuit of happiness", these rights were to be enjoyed by all. Personal freedom based on greed has to be curbed when it threatens the lives and livelihoods of many, denying them such basic needs as shelter, warmth, clothing and food.

Some dismiss the slogan for its internal contradiction. And in disputing whether liberty and equality contradict each other, can fraternity and sisterhood endure? With total freedom, Thomas Hobbes saw that we would all live in "continual fear, and danger of violent death; and the life of man, solitary, poor, nasty, brutish, and short." At the other extreme, enforcing equality on those neither born nor raised equally is bound to fail.

Returning to the beehive, bees enjoy a degree of equality and fraternity that we could not tolerate. They do, however, also enjoy a modest degree of freedom when choosing where to forage, which eggs to fertilize, which to rear for queens, when to swarm and where to resettle. Perhaps *Liberté! Egalité! Fraternité!* applies to all social species, but in very different proportions.

In any event, finding a balance between liberty and equality is the stuff of politics, from which fraternity can emerge.

Equality

There are three basic measures of equality: human rights, national standards and equality of opportunity.

Basic rights include equality before the law and preservation of life through the welfare state. We now regard universal healthcare as a basic right, and the National Health Service is perhaps our major social achievement of the last century. All health services are funded through general taxation and made free to all citizens whenever needed. Being the largest employer in Europe, it is not without its problems. In the 1950s, a Welsh GP found an 'inverse health rule', where the best primary healthcare was provided in the wealthiest areas where they were least needed. This misfit between supply and demand has since been confirmed by several studies. (See for example The Marmot Review on *Health Equity in England*, 2010.)

Since 1979, however, the NHS has been poorly managed, seriously underfunded, with ever-increasing drug costs and 7% of its budget now privatized. Private healthcare is not better or cheaper. In the US, private healthcare accounts for nearly 20% of GDP (compared with less than 8% here). The poor are largely excluded and while the wealthiest receive good healthcare, it is inferior to that of the wealthy in more egalitarian societies like Sweden. Private healthcare, with its inefficiencies, profit focus, unnecessary treatments, demotivated staff and overpricing may lead to distrust between doctor and patient. Our NHS problems stem from size, central control and inadequate funds. In chapter 10, I suggest that all primary healthcare services like GP surgeries revert to local council control.

National standards include the minimum wage, personal allowances and graduated tax rates for higher incomes. Since 1979, taxes on wealth have been greatly reduced, tax rates on unearned income like dividends are usually lower than on earned income and yet, among the wealthy, tax evasion (ipE) is rampant. And we know that greater wealth inequality increases the social problems of crime, health and education etc (from Wilkinson and Pickett, page 18 above). This affects all strata in society, including the wealthy themselves. Reform is essential.

Slum clearance (chapter 2) relied on national standards. Standards focussed first on public health acts (from 1848), then on general housing condition, then on unsatisfactory internal facilities and finally on inadequate space standards as defined by the Parker Morris report *Homes for Today and Tomorrow* (1961). Minimum space standards for all new public housing were based on typical suburban houses. These became the norm, even though most suburban semis were smaller to protect profits. Parking standards also emerged. Unfortunately, generous housing and parking standards to satisfy future needs actually reduced our ability to meet current needs.

However necessary sunlight is, narrow streets are more sociable; however desirable, large houses push up rents; however convenient, generous parking standards waste land; however healthy, large gardens promote privacy over shared parks; however safe, junction sight lines promote traffic over pedestrians. Favouring space, privacy and speed over density, convenience, diversity, character and safety creates anomie and boredom. Instead of middle class housing for all, the only essential housing standard is that everyone should have one that is reasonable and affordable.

Equality of opportunity came first with universal education through local school boards and the *Education Act 1872* (well before public housing and the NHS). A century later, the *Education Act 1976* sought to replace selective grammar and secondary modern schools with comprehensives. First introduced under the Attlee government and promoted under Circular 10/65, their intention was social rather than socialist. Students in schools of mixed ability and background developed those social skills acquired earlier in primary schools.

'Comps' are probably more effective than schools with selective entry. In the OECD triennial studies of 65 national educational systems and the performance of 15 year olds in maths, reading and science, the UK was stuck in the middle range in all three subjects. One conclusion was that: "Stratification in school systems, which is the result of policies like grade repetition and selecting students at a young age for different 'tracks' or types of schools, is negatively related to equity; and students in highly stratified systems tend to be less motivated than those in less-stratified systems... Fairness in resource allocation is not only important for equity in education, but it is also related to the performance of the school system as a whole." (OECD 2013)

Private schools (discussed further under care of the young) may well have skewed these OECD conclusions. But even our successful comprehensives actually select pupils (see, for example, *The Observer* 28/2/10), while parental choice means that wealthier families can move to those schools' catchment areas. One online agency with over 200,000 properties on its 'books' said that '8,500 were located in areas near high performing schools'. So many comprehensives now resemble the old grammar and secondary modern schools.

The problem with these basic measures of equality is that they all become subject to government control, whether through means tests, normative standards or performance targets. Means tests mean that many people are denied access to justice, while slum clearance demonstrated the dangers of imposing national standards. Targets to improve school performance, train punctuality or hospital waiting lists etc, quickly become self-defeating. Targets not set by those actually delivering the service produce counter-productive behaviour, focussing on the easy targets and ignoring the quality of performance because it can't be measured. Thus, many schools near the bottom of the 'league tables' provide an excellent service but with poor results may be penalized and demotivated. This unfairness is compounded by the lack of targets for government performance. 'We are not all in this together.'

Fraternity

"I guess that may be as a writer I'm kind of an anachronism... because I write about places where your roots are and most people don't live that kind of life any more at all. Most writers, probably, the writers who are most in tune with our time, write about places that have no texture because this is where most of us live." (Alice Munro)

Our loss of social roots was confirmed by an English prime minister with all the sensitivity for which she was renowned. "There is no such thing as society; there are individual men and women, and there are families." This is a fair description of suburbs and gated communities but a dangerous prescription for urban policy. In replacing the social honey bee with solitary bees, it contradicts Adam Smith, JK Galbraith and Jane Jacobs et al.

Society has fragmented. Ever-smaller nuclear families (with serial monogamy and single parenthood) dispersed through suburbia experience a very different way of life to that in previous centuries. Then, social roots developed through society, communities and neighbourhoods:

- a society shares in the social institutions of the whole city, like the city council, town centre, rail links, university and football club, with common traditions around accent, cuisine and climate etc;
- a community includes all interest groups, like 'the black community', the Conservative party, the disability lobby, local sports club or civic society. Nationally, advertisers talk of the 'gay vote', the 'grey pound', 'yoof culture' and the 'tweenies'. To sociologists, these are communities of interest, while
- a neighbourhood (the sociologists' 'community of propinquity') is that area where one lives, sharing street and play area, local shops and bus stops, pubs, library and primary school.

In broad terms, society protects basic equalities, communities foster liberty and neighbourhoods develop fraternity or social tolerance. Every so often, tensions between liberty and equality erupt and, as with sectarian disputes and peasant revolts, fraternity breaks down. Burke objected to the French Revolution (page 69), not because he foresaw the murderous mayhem well before the guillotine was introduced, but because he thought the French had the legal framework and political institutions needed to resolve the tensions and curb the worst excesses of the *ancien regime*. He supported the American war of independence for the same reason; they had the necessary institutions to govern themselves.

Traditionally, Conservative governments have been libertarian (supporting personal and corporate wealth), Labour and Liberal governments have been egalitarian (redistributing wealth for social benefits). Since 1979, there has been a marked shift towards liberty and the wealth of elites at the expense of cities and social wealth. In this pursuit of wealth, (apart from the social problems identified by Wilkinson and Pickett), foodsheds close local shops and markets, factory and office jobs are exported and passengers become motorists. These trends reduce social behaviour, tolerance is strained and citizens are atomized, a process known as anomie.

Let us now agree that the "... essential improvement of a house and family is [not] more room" (Patrick Geddes). Instead, we need dense vibrant neighbourhoods, with local facilities round the corner, front doors 'left on the latch' and a sense of social security in the terraced streets (Jane Jacobs).

Neighbourhoods, however, are not 'urban villages'. While both promote social interaction, rural villages are relatively closed societies where everyone knows everyone else, with few occasions to mix with miscreants and immigrants. Women's Institutes, though usually more lively and intelligent than their parish councils, reflect that simpler life. (Yet on the national stage, the WI is an effective and one of the few positive lobby groups.)

Neighbourhoods are more complex, open to opportunists and specialists, artists and scientists, teachers and students, thinkers and performers, bureaucrats and artisans, buyers and sellers, designers and drivers, rich and poor, young and old, third generation residents and asylum seekers, the gregarious and the shy. Cities don't need WIs because the whole society with its communities and neighbourhoods cater for every interest and activity – or used to.

They have now become 'ghettoized'. The marketing firm MOSAIC has identified twelve 'lifestyle groups': High income families, Suburban semis, Blue collar workers, Low rise council, Council flats, Victorian low status, Town houses and flats, Stylish singles, Independent elders, Mortgaged families, Country dwellers and Institutional areas; to which we should add 'Retirement communities', estates reserved solely for older citizens. Which lifestyle defines you, dear reader? All deny social diversity, extended families and the mixing of generations for mutual benefit.

These ghettoes reflect local housing costs and increasing wealth inequality. They are led by housebuilders and banks simplifying their supply, and by people with less social confidence seeking those areas in their income bracket and neighbours with similar lifestyles. Broad brush planning (like painting by numbers) reinforces these trends, so that neighbourhoods increasingly reflect the sameness of shopping malls, business parks and dormitory villages. Any proposal for workshops, public house or day nursery in their street is fiercely resisted. Compare our lifestyle ghettoes with the social mix found in Booth's central London or Preston's Stoneygate (chapter 2), where an MP and a solicitor could live within a stone's throw of some prostitutes, high street shops, warehouses and piggeries.

The pursuit of suburban privacy and security reflects the rise of Victorian snobbery and sexual prudery. According to the *OED*, the peeping tom emerged in 1837, the snooper in 1864 and the nosey parker in 1907. Privacy and sociability (nosiness) are inversely related. Domestic violence may not be more likely in suburbs, but in neighbourhood terraces, cries for help can enlist prompt neighbour support more quickly than any emergency service – and help deal with the aftermath.

Yet, while many value their privacy from neighbours, they happily cede it to Facebook, Google and other 'social platforms', via the new 'communities' using their 'social platforms', discussed in pages 223-4 above. Are we content to let advertisers, governments, security services and a whole range of sinister agencies manipulate our purchases, behaviour, voting habits and our very histories? 'Social platforms' distort the meaning of fraternity, 'links' are not friends and texts are not conversation.

In social neighbourhoods, these sad misfits would be shamed or shunned by families, at school, on the street and in the pub, and denied outlets through the media. They either adjust socially or leave the area. TV soaps like '*the Street*' and *Eastenders* may not be the peak of civilization, but their enduring popularity suggests that terraced streets, extended families and social networks are ingrained in our collective folk memory. Most neighbourhoods have lost this social cohesion, some controlled by local clans, drug barons, racist gangs or religious bigots, replacing fraternity with a fortress mentality. Like all cliques, clans are exclusive communities with little empathy for those outside, resembling the freemasonry of bankers, barristers and the Bullingdonians.

In summary, liberty, equality and fraternity can be understood as three aspects of freedom: freedom to enjoy ourselves, freedom from want, and freedom from discrimination. In our pursuit of happiness, we are free to do, free to be able to do and free to be allowed to do what we want. Throughout the twentieth century, the balance has shifted:

- excessive liberty has normalized personal greed and social irresponsibility;
- excessive inequality and tax evasion has greatly increased poverty; and
- fraternity and social cohesion have suffered in suburbs and ghettoes.

Liberty, equality and fraternity are at the heart of all politics, even for the French. My other inputs for civilization, written records, the rule of law and care of the young, are less contentious.

Written records

Writing is the bedrock for all civilizations. Karl Popper (1986) suggested three worlds: the physical world out there, the internal world of each person, and the third world of stored knowledge which he described as "the world of theories, of books, of ideas, of problems." In this third world of libraries, three books helped define our civilization:

- *Domesday Book*, from 1086 in medieval Latin, was the first major bureaucratic achievement of this nation,
- *Magna Carta* of 1215 set out a national charter of rights, and
- *The Canterbury Tales* by Geoffrey Chaucer from about 1400 established the English language with their shafts of wit and wisdom.

Stored knowledge depends, crucially, on preserving hard information rather than 'fake news', reasoned knowledge rather than bigoted ideology and the occasional flashes of wit and wisdom to enlighten us all. Consider how information, knowledge and wisdom can support the wondrous complexity of cities.

Accurate information underpins every healthy market. Too often, hard information has been replaced by 'commercial confidentiality'. The triennial Census of Distribution, had it not ceased in 1971, would have enabled councils to track the impact of foodsheds, shopping malls and regional centres on their town centre shops and markets, track the growth of local monopolies and revise local business rates accordingly. And those same foodsheds (and food manufacturers) have consistently refused to state clearly the ingredients in their foods (including salt, sugar and fat levels, pesticide residues, colourings, flavourings, preservatives and other dubious ingredients). So consumers can't make informed choices and create a healthier market between supply and demand.

Similarly, large firms who export jobs and skills to low-wage economies evade responsibility for work conditions. "Not our problem" means that consumers can't choose between fair and unfair trade, again distorting markets in favour of unscrupulous producers. Private transport companies provide far less information about bus mileage and passenger numbers, making efficiency and emission comparisons impossible. Having privatized the TRRL (transport and road research laboratory), we have to rely on car manufacturers' own data on petrol consumption and exhaust emissions. And allowing 'offshore' ownership of properties and companies too often means concealed ownership, rampant tax evasion (ipE), illegal money laundering, bribes, drugs and arms dealing etc.

Hard data is essential for the knowledge (and judgements) contained in professional reports and policy statements, which are discussed in the next chapter. However, as one example of government policy that is difficult to justify from objective statistical data, the *NPPF1* contained five guiding principles of sustainable development. Number 5, "using sound science responsibly", is undermined by its own policies on transport and energy like Heathrow's 3rd runway, HS2 and wood-burning power stations.

Investigative journalism is one defence against the corruption of corporate and public life – holding those in power to account. Unfortunately, as with mega-corps, the large media companies are wedded to maximizing profits. Investigative journalism is the major loss. 1981 shook journalism as 1979 shook politics when Rupert Murdoch bought the *Sunday Times*, closed down the investigative Insight team, and appointed a new, more compliant editor who increased the size of the paper while reducing the number of journalists and costs. As stated on page 165 above, the previous owner Lord Thompson and editor Harold Evans had exposed the truth about the spy Kim Philby and the Thalidomide tragedy, each involving several journalists full-time over more than 18 months. Under Murdoch, Michael Foot was twice falsely exposed as a Russian spy while, under editor Andrew Neil, the paper supported Thatcher's government over the Gibraltar IRA killings, even contradicting its own journalists' reports from Gibraltar. Around this time, rules against cross-media ownership were 'relaxed', so Murdoch added TV and radio stations to his too many newspapers.

Sacking 'journos' and 'increasing productivity' has affected all media outlets. Today, most journalists write up to ten 'stories' a day instead of three (or less in investigating difficult stories). Interviews, checking sources and outside visits are rare. So at least 80% of their stories come direct and largely verbatim, either from press agencies (like the Press Association and Reuters) or from PR. In the 1970s, both were rare. "Britain now has more PR people (47,800) than journalists (45,000)." (Davies 2009, including Cardiff University research.)

Despite profits often exceeding 20%, cost-cutting brought its own cost. As with bus passengers, total newspaper circulation fell from nearly four million, steady since 1950 to 1980, to just over two million in 2015, one million disappearing in the last ten years. In part, free newspapers and the internet took their toll, but undoubtedly many readers could now smell the corruption of the news by PR and government spin. Merely reporting events means that only rarely do newspaper exposures themselves make the news. This failure to investigate serious abuse weakens any democracy.

- The false story about the weapons of mass destruction that underpinned our invasion of Iraq led to vicious attacks on the BBC and the subsequent Hutton Inquiry whitewashing the government. Although public support for the BBC did not weaken, there has been no serious investigation by impartial journalists.

- It took 23 years before the truth about Hillsborough emerged, from a third independent inquiry chaired by the Bishop of Liverpool (although the first inquiry, under Lord Justice Taylor, came to much the same conclusions).

- No newspaper exposed the ruinous government profligacy behind every PFI contract. Serious newspapers should be exposing false accounting, but can any newspaper seriously expose mega-corps when the Barclays, Murdochs, Rothermeres and others indulge in similar tax evasion (ipE).

Information is power, to be used to clarify issues and empower its readers, or misused to mislead readers in pursuit of owner or government ideology. This is the difference between the BBC, *The Observer* and *Private Eye*, for example, and *Fox News*, the *Daily Mail* and *Breitbart*.

Local newspapers are no different. Most of the 750 regional and local newspapers are owned by 12 mega-corps whose focus is on cutting costs, maximizing advert revenues, shutting local offices, centralizing printing, sub-editing and even journalism, in order to maintain 20% profit levels. Few journalists now attend council meetings, local trials and other events.

The expenses scandal of our MPs in 2009 illustrates the problem. Much of the early work was done by journalist and Freedom of Information campaigner Heather Brooke. Her persistence was such that the House of Commons actually sought to amend the original Act so that MPs would be exempt from Freedom of Information. At much the same time, a local newspaper (I think in Torbay) uncovered the expenses of its local MP, but could not risk publication when he threatened to sue. (Many genuine scoops are first aired in local papers. Many are spiked by the ruinous threat of libel.) Eventually, a whistle blower from the parliamentary fees office sold the full information some months before the official edited version was ready. Offered first to two other papers, it was bought by *The Daily Telegraph*. Having contributed nothing to the investigation in background research, checking sources, interviews and dogged persistence to uncover the truth and develop the narrative, the newspaper merely paid the whistleblower and gave a commentary with the facts.

For this, shamefully, it was made 'Newspaper of the Year'

Concerning wisdom, Clemenceau generalized when he suggested that "he who is not socialist when young has no heart; he who is not conservative when old has no wisdom." While the socialism associated with youth is idealistic, based on social fairness, the frequent descent into neo-conservative insular selfishness (lower taxes, xenophobic nostalgia for empire and indifference to poverty and injustice) is not the wisdom of true conservative values. Wisdom is neither socialist nor conservative but the result of hard information, reasoned knowledge and learning from mistakes. We don't learn from our mistakes when we sack investigative journalists and ruin whistleblowers.

The rule of law

One of the first legal codes (and written records), stipulating the punishment for over 280 crimes, was set down by emperor Hammurabi of Babylon over five and a half thousand years ago. Classical Greece, Rome and Constantinople developed their own codes. Most were lost during our Dark Ages, except in Moorish Spain where, along with the whole Muslim world, these texts were preserved, translated and studied to help them govern.

In his excellent book on the rule of law, Tom Bingham (2010) traced it back to the *Magna Carta*, quoting clauses 39 and 40:

"39 No man shall be seized or imprisoned or stripped of his rights or possessions [...], except by the lawful judgement of his equals or by the law of the land.

"40 To no one will we sell, to no one deny or delay right or justice."

Everyone shall be free unless they break the law, and everyone is equal in the eyes of the law. The *Magna Carta* ensured these basic rights between king and all subjects, citizens as well as nobles. Here are the seeds of liberty, equality and fraternity. Today we are backtracking.

When the rule of law breaks down, there is little protection from local disputes escalating into clan murder, urban riot, religious massacre, ethnic cleansing, civil war and genocide. The rule of law hasn't broken down yet, but we are ignoring key aspects.

- Asylum seekers are denied the right to work while their cases are being considered. They are not even allowed to play in village cricket teams. If denied asylum, they are held in detention centres during lengthy appeal processes and usually separated from their children in separate centres.

- The government's 'hostile environment' for 'illegal' immigrants was introduced by a vicar's daughter. British citizens from the Caribbean who had lived and worked here for up to 50 years (including some invited here by Enoch Powell) might find themselves detained and flown straight back to their island of birth if 'they had no papers'. Tax returns, rates bills and National Insurance number were not enough. This is government racism.

Alongside arbitrary detention, there is no longer equality before the law. Hammurabi's code contained an interesting twist to this equality: if one of Babylon's elite committed certain serious crimes, they would be punished more severely than *hoi polloi* for the same crimes (Sassoon 2005). With wealth and power, the elite had to accept greater responsibility. Not today. As highlighted in chapter 5, the wealthy have come to regard the law as another form of tax, to be bought off even while denying their guilt, or shuffling their guilt onto junior staff and any fines onto shareholders. This is power without responsibility. Meanwhile, following the bankers' reckless greed and incompetence, austerity has so reduced legal aid (another egalitarian improvement introduced by the Attlee government in 1949) that access to justice is effectively denied to over half the population.

To protect the rule of law is an essential duty of government, but it must itself abide by the same. The increasing problem with the centralized powers of Parliament was encapsulated by one of those 'Number Crunching' boxes in *Private Eye*. From memory, it read

"700 hours: time spent by Parliament to debate whether to ban fox hunting.

70 hours: time spent by Parliament to debate whether to invade Iraq."

This illustrates a general law of politics: that time spent in debate varies inversely with the importance of the issue. Tom Bingham concluded "that the invasion of Iraq violated the rule of law." Nevertheless, despite the lies, sexed-up dossiers, one leader fawning on another and the slaughter of innocents, it was a legitimate question that only Parliament could decide, even though its decision was ill-judged, illegal and inhuman. The other question (discussed further in chapter 10) is that, on matters of local democracy, surely Parliament is not the best forum to decide such a minor local nuisance as fox hunting.

Rearing the young

"It takes a village to raise a child." (African proverb)

Many vulnerable minorities have special needs, but unlike most adults, children can't seek help, demand their rights or form pressure groups. While families are held responsible for their offspring, society soon assumes various roles. And despite being our collective future, children face increasingly tough obstacles as they grow up. Safe upbringing, broad education and social integration are not assured.

For toddlers, the street was their first social experience. Meeting neighbours, making friends and talking to strangers developed self confidence and social skills. By the mid twentieth century, safe natural playgrounds outside home disappeared. The perceived threat of paedophiles and the real menace of 'rat runners' means that few children are allowed out alone. Healthy walks to school have become anti-social 'school runs'. The few who still walk meet few neighbours and fewer strangers (to be shunned). Jacob's street theatre has lost both performers and audience. Social playspace has been replaced by private gardens, remote parks or the isolation of bedroom TVs and computer games.

Without streets, formal education is now the first experience of society for most children. While colleges and adult classes develop communities and universities enrich society, nursery, primary and secondary schools enliven neighbourhoods. And here, children, through work discipline, informal play and background politics, also develop group notions of liberty, equality and fraternity. Unfortunately, these have been skewed, first by private education, and now by government funding cuts, Ofsted,   parental choice and 'free schools'.

School benefits were reduced, largely to fund tax cuts. 'Snatcher Thatcher' (as minister of education) stopped free milk in the early 1970s, followed by free school meals (except for the poor) and free school transport. With the *Education Act 1982*, school meals no longer had to provide half a child's daily nutritional needs, so private caterers and 'turkey twizzlers' dominated school canteens, to which most PFI schools and academies supply fizzy drink and junk food vending machines to maximize profits.

From the 1990s, all state schools were subjected to SATs (standard assessment tasks), with stressful Ofsted inspections and the inevitable school league tables. The government target for every primary school final year is to achieve 80% success in the SATs. This is both facile and futile. Making no allowance for the personal abilities and social backgrounds of the pupils is facile: schools either struggle with the 80% target or coast past it. Many schools have high intakes of five year olds who can't read or write, or don't speak English, have special needs or arrive hungry every morning. This will not be the norm in suburbia. These 'input' factors are necessary to assess the quality of teaching for pupils over six years, and reflect staff dedication, pastoral care, head leadership, governor support and parent involvement. SATs ignores this 'added value'.

The 80% target is futile because most primary schools now focus perhaps 70% of their lessons on English, maths and science. People unfamiliar with the current maths and English curricula would be astonished at their needless complexity and narrow focus, negating the ideal of universal education. Too many students struggle against exclusion, with little opportunity to discover and develop their own non-academic interests in sport, languages, technology, local studies, music and the arts, even history and geography, food and business studies. When my wife took a dozen inner London year five pupils on a field trip to Cornwall, the instructor of the two local gym sessions thought that three had Olympic potential if they trained regularly. Yet it was their first visit to a gym, and their last while at primary school.

As in cities, school diversity is vital in both curriculum and management. Current government ideology accepts the latter. Hence the growth of free schools, most as multi-academy trusts. These are funded directly by the department of education, and more generously than council-managed state schools. These 'trusts' (introduced by Michael Gove and Dominic Cummings) led to the business disciplines of six figure salaries for heads, six figure fees for consultants (who are often related to trustees), teaching staff reduced in favour of class assistants, cheap school buildings often unsuitable or in areas with an existing surplus of school places, advertising budgets and legal fees for threats to sue Ofsted for unfavourable inspections, unless 'resolved' by a second inspection. (State schools can't afford this 'luxury'. One state primary head complained when she found that her inspection report was near identical to an earlier report for another school except for name changes. No-one inspects the inspectors.)

And under this 'free market discipline', when an academy fails, all its assets are transferred to other schools in the trust – even that money that was raised by parents to save their failing school.

Among these free schools there is little diversity. It seems that most non-traditional education projects are turned down. Thus Benjamin's school "was to have offered pupils a learning experience that took place largely outside the classroom, from natural environments to theatres and engineers' workshops. Students would have researched and recorded their studies at five bases around the county. At the foundation's small independent school in Great Yarmouth, attended mainly by looked-after children, a similar approach has already seen impressive results [Despite support from the local council, 153 children signed up and 40 fully trained teachers committed etc, it was rejected twice]... And the most original models seemed to come from parent and community groups, who were put at a serious disadvantage compared with large academy chains and faith schools, by the crippling demands of the process on both their finances and time." (*The Guardian* 14/5/13) That free academies and faith schools are generally more traditional, with strict discipline, quiet corridors and school uniforms, is not the issue. The problem is that only the minister of education decides, rather than each local education authority.

Private schools actively pervert the meaning of liberty, equality, fraternity. Annual league tables on A level results are dominated at the top by private schools, with comprehensives holding up the bottom. According to Hobson (1999) and the media generally, these tables speak for themselves. Comparing the poorest schools in the country with some of the wealthiest schools in the world is hardly useful. It merely repeats the inverse health law – that education is lavished on those with least need. State schools receive some £5,000 pa for each pupil, private schools charge £30,000 for each boarder ('well in excess of most parental incomes') and £12,000 for day pupils (*The Observer* 29/3/15). Private schools (many with huge endowment funds) can afford the best buildings, grounds and facilities, and the best-paid teachers. What needs to be explained is how many comprehensives, on a sixth of the budget in inferior buildings, are up with the best private schools. And why many comprehensives in the bottom half of the tables are actually doing fantastic jobs, but are ignored.

The many challenges of teaching are very different, as between small classes of privileged pupils and large classes of multi-race, mixed ability, multi-lingual pupils, many with modest prospects. Private schools also offer 'generous' scholarships to about 25% of their pupils, whose parents can't afford the fees. But these are only awarded to the cleverest applicants. This bolsters their exam results while lowering that of state schools where those pupils would have gone. These scholarships also allow private schools to retain charitable status. That finishing schools for the offspring of the wealthy are charities is a perverse corruption of the English language. Even Hobson thinks it wrong.

State schools are also subject to constantly-changing ministerial 'guidance' on every subject with frequent Ofsted inspections. This puts teachers under enormous stress over and above the normal strains of teaching.

Private schools are free of this interference and represent an extreme example of unfettered liberty unaffected by principles of equal opportunity and fraternity. There are also personal and social side effects. Sending young children to any institution, whether corrective, protective, religious or scholastic, is often traumatic. Exiled from home, isolated from friends and excluded from society, pupils then had to survive rampant abuse, verbal and physical, though much reduced today. In their harsh new world, most pupils developed a carapace of self-confidence to mask their fear and isolation, and self protection through strong bonds with friends. This gave them a perverted sense of justice. Some became indifferent to injustice while others particularly damaged by the experience found no redress in later life. In state schools with larger classes and wider cross sections of society, the loner is more likely to find a few soul mates to protect against bullying and retain friends outside and family at home. There is security in numbers in which social skills develop. The fraternity of 'the old-school tie' is more like a life belt.

Plutocrats reserving the best schools exclusively for their own is divisive and damages society. 7% of our students fill half our top university places (though that is reducing), and half the seats in the National Youth Orchestra, which confirms how underfunded state schools are. Yet private students don't get better degrees than public students at Oxford and Cambridge. Perhaps many just coast, confident that their school ties and family contacts will more than compensate for any underachievement. Others simply enjoy their wealth and personal freedom to move from the insular boarding school to the Bullingdon club: 'an exclusive but unofficial all-male students' dining club at Oxford University, noted for its wealthy members, grand banquets and boisterous rituals, such as the vandalising ('trashing') of restaurants and college rooms' (Wikipedia). The baleful influence of the Bullingdon beyond Oxford contrasts with that of the Women's Institute mentioned earlier.

Private school graduates also occupy the same disproportionate number of top jobs among the ruling elite – in legal chambers and the judiciary, in parliament and the civil service, in the media, the City and the banks. Giving private students a six- to seven-fold advantage over the rest, based on privilege and self-confidence rather than merit, fitness and experience, is wrong. A self-perpetuating elite largely excluded from society in its formative years is hardly fit to govern that same society. We should not underestimate the social impact of our schools. Is apartheid too strong a word?

Had schools in Northern Ireland ('the six counties') mixed protestants and catholics, the intransigence between the two sects might gradually have melted away. For example, when a new school in Oldham replaced two smaller neighbourhood comprehensives, one predominantly Muslim, the other white working class, the students were far less racist as they worked together at school.

All cliques breed inefficiency. Powerful cliques breed injustice. There are no elites in nature, giants and geniuses are rare. Through genetic 'reversion to the mean', children from humble backgrounds sometimes rise to eminence while those from the plutocracy tend to fade in obscurity, in all walks of life. Seven out of 20 *Artists of the Renaissance* (from Vasari, Penguin edition) were either orphans or, like Giotto, sons of peasants. Many miraculous rococo churches of Bavaria were designed and built by families of plasterers while most inventors from the Industrial Revolution were skilled intelligent workers.

In summary, private schools, league tables and parental choice are actively creating social ghettoes. Each school now reflects an ever-narrower social band, bringing class into every classroom. How can state schools avoid becoming mirror versions of private schools as breeding grounds for social ignorance, group insularity and class antagonism? Parental choice, available only to the comfortable classes, contradicts our nature as social animals, and evidence suggests that 'top and bottom' pupils both do well in mixed ability comprehensives. League tables should be abolished unless they include much deeper qualitative analysis than exam results. And rather than being centrally controlled by ministers and civil servants with negligible relevant experience, it would be more innovative and democratic to allow local councils to manage their own schools, provided that they all remain non-selective. From the various systems adopted, a range of efficient school models would emerge to suit different areas and needs.

Before 1979, public education was, like the NHS, free from cradle to grave, except for modest fees for adult education. No longer. Since 1998, university students have had to pay part and now all their tuition fees and living expenses. In 2017, graduates had an average debt of £40,000. Yet the 'self-financing' student loan system hasn't benefited taxpayers when the costs of the interest-free periods, unpaid loans and private administration fees are included. If we can't agree to fund all education through taxation, at least we might recoup university costs through a graduate tax.

Universities have also changed beyond recognition. Lewis Mumford (1966) stressed their importance, where "the functions of cultural storage, dissemination and interchange, and creative addition - perhaps the three most essential functions of the city – were adequately performed." This was continuity of the past in storage, the present in interchange and the future in creativity. Like city markets for trade, universities are markets for ideas.

Unfortunately, even universities are at risk. "In 1963, the Robbins inquiry into British higher education… argued that learning was a good in itself. "The search for truth is an essential function... and the process of education is itself most vital when it partakes in the nature of discovery."" In 2009, the Labour government commissioned the Browne inquiry into university funding: "Higher education matters" it argued, "because it… helps produce economic growth, which in turn contributes to national prosperity." (K Malik, *The Observer* 18/3/2018). Browne was appointed for his business experience running BP (like Beeching from ICI before him). As Malik saw it, higher education was transformed by "the growing view of universities as businesses, of students as consumers and of knowledge as a commodity."

"No country for young men" (Deptford graffito).

Having lost their streets to cars, their schools now polarized by class and universities exploiting them as customers, what of the social life of young people? They will first be penalized with half and full fares from an early age. Anyone who travels on any bus after 3.30pm knows how sociable these school services are. Local buses and trains should be free to everyone under 25. This would reduce the number of young people who feel they have to buy mopeds and cars as soon as possible.

When I was growing up, we had to negotiate our way through the enigmas of drink and sex, but after school or university, we were all confident of finding a job with pension, training as required and a house or flat to begin our family polkas. Today, that intoxicating dance through the late teenage hazards has been spiked with drugs and Aids, just as the security of jobs, homes and pensions have receded. Jobs on offer are either highly specialized or increasingly unskilled, with terms and conditions that were unthinkable then, while for housing they are largely restricted to private flats and ever-higher rents.

On top of these pressures, the young are remorselessly targeted. Advertisers subject them to peer pressure, ostracizing those who don't buy into junk food, mobile gadgets and a cocktail of irrelevant cosmetics. Aggressive policing based on zero tolerance and curfews intimidates the several groups of older pupils I have met in various towns. Others not intimidated develop a different set of social skills. And so most of the media subject them to negative reporting. Whatever the disturbance, if they are not held directly responsible, then parents (or singe parents) are blamed, or teachers or, in extreme cases, the hapless social workers.

Yet when society itself assumes direct responsibility for the young, in care homes, youth detention centres, church institutions, private schools and football clubs etc, our record of care does not inspire confidence. The young who are abused are then ignored – making them victims twice over. (Some are thrice victimized: abused, ignored and then rebutted. From borstal "You deserved it", or from private school "You're privileged, stop whingeing.") Young people need special rather than Spartan treatment. Perhaps the UK has indeed become no country for young men.

From these general principles of civilization, we now discuss city life in terms of the general freedom to enjoy ourselves, a degree of equality that ensures at least freedom from want, and the fraternity that gives everyone freedom from exclusion.

'The pursuit of happiness'

A TV executive of Channel 5 once described her programme priorities as 'the three Fs – football, films and fucking'. Replace films with drugs and we have three representative pastimes that most cities have always provided. Sex, drugs and rock-n-roll says much the same thing.

Football (ballet for the masses) is now a global business and FIFA, its governing body, brings all the stink of corruption associated with mega-corps. Looking at the national game, our first division clubs are mostly owned by billionaires, many with unexplained wealth. In 2016, Chelsea accounts showed debts of £1.1 billion in interest-free loans with no dates for repayment. This is not a viable business and it distorts the whole game. Football has replaced horse racing as the sport of kings. These clubs employ the highest paid managers and players, and charge some of the highest ticket prices in Europe. Yet they fare no better than the best-run, community-owned football clubs in the German Bundesliga, with some of the cheapest tickets. Inevitably, many owners, managers and players indulge in tax evasion (ipE). Little trickles down to those working the pitch and turnstiles, many on minimum wage.

Outside the turnstiles, the trickle-down effect is reversed and money resounds to the noise of back siphonage. For fans who used to stand on the terraces and now fail the turnstile test, the exorbitant TV subscriptions (compared with the BBC licence fee) enrich the TV oligarchs. Yet, for all its profits, Sky UK remains a TV retailer rather than producer like the BBC. With matches now spread over the weekend and midweek (to fill up TV schedules), the traditional Saturday kick-offs at 3pm and results at 5pm have gone. It is now very difficult and expensive for fans to attend away matches midweek. It would be more sustainable to revive the two third divisions – north and south.

Since the (unnecessary?) imposition for all-seat stadiums since 1993, almost one third (29) of the four English league football clubs have relocated (*The Observer* 29/11/15). The new stadiums, usually out of town, are surrounded by car parking, a few chain stores and fast food outlets. Left behind are neighbourhoods with a residue of closed shops and pubs that used to thrive on the influx of fans most fortnights. And the FA returns most of the fabulous TV revenues to the first division clubs, devoting peanuts to develop the sport at grass roots, coaching the young in community pitches and local clubs. Football has become ballet for the elite.

Drugs are a private pleasure, except when entering your local pub. "Pub drinking remains the last of our creative social acts: for a man desperate to communicate in words, only a rising tide of alcohol in a cosy, stuffy atmosphere, the delicious prospect of the seventh veil dropping from the mind, can provide the right bardic satisfaction." (Anthony Burgess 1973) Pubs serve the weary and the lively, the wit and witless, the shy and discerning, the real ale drinker and the drunk. A good local pub is a neighbourhood asset and one of our great social inventions.

Unfortunately, like shops, there are far fewer pubs. In 1982, there were 67,800 pubs in the UK, in 2013 only 48,000. This averages out at roughly 1,200 people per pub. "In 1896 London had 393 persons per pub – a lower pub density than that of any other major English city: each Leeds pub served an average 345 people, Liverpool 279, Birmingham 215, Sheffield 176, and Manchester 168. Pubs were only scarcer in nine of the 235 boroughs outside London." (Dyos and Wolff 1973) In Liverpool, having demolished most of its Victorian neighbourhoods, each pub serves about 2,000 people. In Letchworth new town, each pub serves 3,300 people. Most Irish towns south of the border are far more sociable. Westport, Co Mayo has 45 bars serving 5,500 people – about 122 people for each bar. An evening social buzz is not exclusive to warmer Mediterranean towns.

After slum clearance and suburbia, current threats include the smoking ban, foodsheds and 'pubcos'. The smoking ban will reduce lung cancers, particularly among passive smokers, by perhaps 10-15%. This act is like the medical officer who turned off those public water taps that were surrounded by black spots on a map marking local deaths. But since lung cancer accounts for less than 6% of annual deaths in England and Wales, the health benefits are modest and less clear cut.

Drinking contributes to liver failure and circulatory problems, but the benefits of social conviviality and personal happiness may compensate. A few drinks with friends might relieve disorders related to stress, depression and isolation, as well as being safer and cheaper than prescription drugs. *In vino veritas* indeed. And for smokers, pubs now heat the open air most nights for up to eight months a year. This is wasteful, polluting and inefficient.

Had local councils been allowed to decide how best to restrict smoking in pubs, some would have imposed this total ban. Others, however, might have let pubs allow smoking where they had well-ventilated rooms, just as most used to have non-smoking family rooms. Over time, the various solutions would have provided comparative data on cancer rates among drinkers, pub viability and their carbon emissions.

For over ten millennia, alcoholic drinks have been produced, socially controlled and taxed. Now foodsheds are taking their toll, selling cheap wine and beer as loss leaders to close down pubs and wine merchants. Scotland has imposed a minimum price tax on these cheap drinks, which may reduce home drinking which can become addictive. As medical drugs are supervised by your GP, so well-run pubs informally guard against excessive drinking. We all try to avoid slurred speech and unsteady gait, and disruptive behaviour invites comment from friends ("Should we go now?") or bar staff ("Perhaps you've had enough"). Drinking at home lacks these social checks.

But pubs aren't just boozers. Three near me regularly serve a few residents of nearby hostels for those with learning or other disabilities. Neo-conomists, without having met a decent publican, would suggest that those pubs need the custom. Staff confirm that pub visits improve their residents' social skills while most customers enjoy the occasional feeling of fraternity.

Perhaps the biggest threat comes from pubcos. With no skill in running pubs but every skill in exploiting leases, the beer tie, ullage allowances and other tricks, these landlords act against the interest of tenants, staff, drinkers and neighbourhoods. When an Oldham publican sought a 'market rent only' lease so he could buy cheaper beer elsewhere, the pubco sought a rent of £72,000, more than three times the existing rent. This suggests profiteering (*Private Eye* 1443, 4/5/17). The pubcos don't care if the pubs close, because the site value for housing or commercial use protects them. (Eventually, the government set up an arbitration agency headed by a pub code adjudicator whose independence is in serious doubt, evident from his trickle of tardy decisions.) Pubs, whether free houses or tied to reputable brewers demonstrate the success of long-term commitment and investment. Financial engineers should leave pubs to professionals.

After drink, the free market for recreational drugs illustrates classic economic theory. Supply is cheap through efficient small firms (they can't be too big), overheads are minimal, storage and distribution is through human supply chains rather than warehouses and HGVs, marketing is strictly word of mouth and peer pressure, and the business is completely unregulated and tax-exempt. Demand for drugs is strong: they are cheaper than most drinks, with the added status of being illegal.

If surveys are to be believed, half of our 15-year-old students have tried at least one illegal drug. Yet ten years later, they have not all become serious drug users. Whatever the figures, it is unrealistic to regard them all as potential prisoners tying up half our police resources, or patients except for addicts who need medical help. Like drinkers, drug users include the gamut of society. But recreational drugs illustrate that trend from social behaviour towards personal consumerism, noted earlier from terrace to semi, street market to foodshed and bus to car. Your drug trip (whether alone or with friends) is different in kind to your trip to the pub.

The distinction between medical and recreational drugs is also artificial. Both carry risks and side effects. If we licensed and taxed recreational drugs as we do alcohol, then the stronger drugs with significant risk would be taxed to reduce demand and encourage 'softer' options, as beers and wine have largely replaced spirits like 'mothers' ruin' from the Georgian era.

Non-regulation creates serious problems at home and abroad. Cartels managed by drug barons are little different to mega-corps and their CEOs. The fabulous wealth of these cartels (with very modest trickle down to the gang 'foot soldiers') pose serious threats to the most sophisticated and heavily armed nations in the world. The warlords in Mexico and Columbia, for example, have been ruthless in their pursuit of power, with frequent turf wars or civil wars with their governments, civilians all too often the hapless victims caught in the crossfire or, worse, simply murdered to keep local people cowed.

In exporting drug production, the US is leaving whole farming communities that once fed themselves to rely on the drug cartels for their sustenance. Such is their power that bribery and corruption may well have infected sections of the US enforcement agencies, just as they use banks (like HSBC) to launder their money.

At home, illegal drug markets fuel the tensions in all US and many European cities between black and white, young and old, male and female, rich and poor. Celebrities and the wealthy use recreational drugs with little fear of the law. Poor, young and black citizens all have to take their chance. Prohibition is irrational, as the Americans should know from experience. It creates an underclass outside society, fosters criminal organizations, ties down stretched police resources, secret agencies and even the military, negates rational debate about freedom – and it doesn't work.

Illegal drugs are widely available because they are so much cheaper than legal drugs. Imagine if the Islamic nations sought to wage an aggressive war on the sale of alcohol worldwide. An international agreement to legalize drugs would take too long to agree too little with too many loopholes, like waiting to reduce air traffic through fuel taxes, over-fishing in international waters, or multi-national tax evasion. Better for nations to take unilateral action to control the use of these drugs, as in the Netherlands and more recently Portugal. Early indications are positive, but until we treat drugs as we do drink and tobacco, all societies will continue to suffer.

Our approach on drugs is bizarre, on sex it is shameful. Sex is a basic instinct and perhaps the most intense pleasure of life. Single people who want sex are neither sad nor bad – they're normal. Commercial sex has been available in every civilized city, with suitable locations for the barter, privacy and exchange of selfish genes. From Ayto (1990): "The first known reference to the word cunt is in an early medieval Oxford street-name: *Gropecuntlane* (it was afterwards renamed *Magpie Lane*). This was around 1230." Parker (2009) lists medieval variants like Grope Court and Grope Lane, Bird in Hand Alley, Bordhawe Lane, Cheapside, Soper Lane and Threadneedle Street. This made towns 'legible' to strangers. Even when the Victorians bowdlerized the most offensive street names, *My Secret Life* by 'Walter' identifies many streets where it was possible to hire rooms by the hour.

Criminalizing commercial sex, as with drugs, brings criminal violence. Regulated commercial sex improves life for all involved, which Cynthia Payne, a folk hero of the business, understood. Her father "... was a nice old boy at the end because he was having it off whenever he felt like it. It just goes to prove what I've always maintained – that men are much more pleasant and considerate so long as they're regularly despunked. If they're not getting their oats, they're bloody pests." (Bailey 1983) Aphra Behn (1640-89) put it more poetically.

> "That Awful Throne, that Paradice
> Where Rage is calm'd, and Anger pleas'd;
> That Fountain where Delight still flows,
> And gives the Universal World Repose."

Unfortunately, policy remains mired in Victorian hypocrisy and denies commercial sex to all except the wealthy and (according to cynics) married men. The workers involved are subjected to various occupational hazards: disease and pregnancy, bladder problems, stress, depression, alcohol or drug addiction, latex allergy and musculoskeletal injuries, plus the real dangers of violence, harassment, theft by clients and being forced to have unprotected sex (Taket et al 2014).

To Victorian hypocrisy, we have added commercial prurience. Safe sex in regulated brothels is not newsworthy. Street prostitutes in neighbourhoods often provoke vigilantism, pushing them to solicit in rundown commercial and industrial areas where streets are dark, unsupervised and dangerous.

The vulnerability of street prostitutes is ignored until such tragedies as the mass murders in Yorkshire and Ipswich. The media mercilessly exploited these terrible fusions of sex and violence with breath-taking hypocrisy, combining the laddish lechery of the tabloids with the prissy family values of the broadsheets. The insanity of the Yorkshire Ripper (finally convicted in 1981) was matched by the collective mania of the media, implicating us all in their thrill of the hunt for the killer, their frenzied chequebook journalism for any background story and their general indifference (or vicious scorn) to the fate of the victims. One of the few titles to emerge with any credit from this tragedy was *Private Eye*. When, after its partially successful appeal against the outrageous libel damages awarded to the murderer's wife, it found its libel fund had a large surplus. Rather than keep it against future trials, *Private Eye* distributed the money among the families of the victims. The Women's Institute is one of the few sane voices that has campaigned to legalize prostitution. Meanwhile, escort agencies provide for the wealthy and powerful.

We have even revived slavery two centuries after its abolition. It seems that young women are smuggled into the UK from parts of eastern Europe and the far East, sold in secret slave markets, held captive as illegal immigrants without money or passports in prison-like brothels, raped and then forced to fuck strangers in order to give their owners 'a decent return on their investment'. Wilberforce and others from the age of enlightenment would have been shocked out of their complacent Whig view about the inevitable progress of history. We don't know how many women are sex slaves, nor how many men and women are work slaves, in this country. Man's inhumanity to man, woman and child is pervasive. Today's slavery is another return to Georgian values.

Imagine sex workers plying their trade in small co-ops and licensed like any pub or betting shop. Legalizing the industry would civilize it for both parties, eliminate kerb crawling, relieve much frustration and probably reduce sexual violence and rape. Some bordellos might even offer the same service for women. Only those who frequented unlicensed premises would be criminalized as rapists, alongside the slave owners. It would also offer suitable re-uses for many vacant commercial buildings and raise significant tax revenues.

However, legalizing drugs or prostitution would raise a job protection issue, first perceived by Bernard Mandeville (1670-1733) in *The Fable of the Bees*:

> "Such were the Blessings of that State;
> Their Crimes conspired to make 'em Great;
> And Vertue, who from Politicks
> Had learn'd a Thousand cunning Tricks,
> Was, by their happy Influence,
> Made Friends with Vice: And ever since
> The Worst of all the Multitude
> Did something for the common Good."

Mandeville's original insight was that: "Private Vices by the dextrous Management of a skilful Politician may be turned into Public Benefits." Hiring police officers, lawyers, judges, prison wardens, drug and health workers all increase GDP, a rough measure of national wealth. Unfortunately, taxpayers have to fund these agents whose work is not productive. Society thought Mandeville unduly cynical and dismissed his *Fable* as a clever squib.

Yet his idea of "dextrous management by a skilful politician" is important. Legalizing these 'black economies' would convert a large drain on our taxes into an income stream for the Exchequer, making our towns and cities safer and more civilized. The police could then spend more time on white collar fraud and violent crime. Surely this is preferable to the sound and fury of the media in full pursuit of their quarry, while ignoring the hapless victims of addiction, thuggery and slavery.

The great divide

In 2013, *Forbes* magazine calculated that 1,426 billionaires had a combined net worth of $5.4 trillion. Two years later, 1,826 billionaires were worth $7.05 trillion, an increase of about 30%. Also in 2015, an Oxfam advert suggested that one bus full of the wealthiest billionaires had as much wealth as the poorest half of the world's citizens. 80 passengers are as rich as 3.5 billion passengers. A year later Oxfam's bus was only carrying 62 billionaires. The rich are getting richer.

Excessive inequality affects many nations. "On average, the wealthiest 10% of people in the UK have £770,000 each, whereas the poorest have just £877 (including pensions)." (*Private Eye* 1421, 24/6/2016) In the US, Christina Freeland found that "three decades ago the average American chief executive made 42 times as much as the average worker; today this ratio is an obscene 380." (*The Observer* 4/11/2012) In Norway, the CEO of Statoil "was paid some 27 times that national average for running one of Norway's biggest companies." When he moved to BG, after significantly reducing its original offer, BG would still pay him "90 times the average earnings of his employees, not to mention 330 times the UK national median income of £27,200" (*Private Eye* 12/12/2014).

Wilkinson and Pickett (2010) showed that wealthy nations with low differentials are relatively healthy and happy throughout. Nations with the highest differentials, the US and the UK, show significantly higher levels of social stress and discontent in all levels of society. And it's getting worse.

Since 1979, our political leaders have been 'intensely relaxed about the filthy rich.' The first tax cuts at the highest income levels did not make executives and capitalists more innovative, nor did they create more jobs. Tax cuts fuelled rather than cured their greed. They became financial engineers, increasing the wealth of their companies at the expense of the workforce, suppliers and customers, even their own shareholders, awarding themselves excessive salaries and bonuses, share options, enhanced pensions and other perks. 30 years later, chancellor George Osborne introduced ten years of austerity – with further tax cuts for the wealthy. Yet still they indulge in tax evasion (ipE).

Keynes was right. Billionaires are sick; psychopathic in their superficial charm, intelligence and ruthless pursuit of money, sociopathic in their thieving and indifference to poverty. Trump is the epitome of this mind-set. Every transaction is a struggle between two parties and, because he is the best and smartest businessman he knows, he usually wins. This is a zero sum game that reduces all trade into winners and losers, the strong only getting stronger. Back in the beehive, it is as if the few hundred drones had taken over, owning the stores of honey and pollen, charging the workers for board and lodging, renting out the woods, fields and gardens, and retaining the queen solely to confer legitimacy.

Adam Smith explained this sick behaviour, suggesting that landowners and capitalists do not know "best what is in their own self-interest." His view of fair trade was that, if you give me what I want, I will give you what you want. In his own time, the landed gentry maintained tariffs on imported grain to protect the price of their crops. Economists and historians still debate whether the landowners ultimately benefited when free trade competition replaced Corn Law tariffs. What is certain is that everyone else benefited from cheaper bread and the economy could grow on that money released.

Sociopathic greed is strongly correlated to abject poverty. In several respects, we can assert that excessive wealth causes poverty: the wealthy have lowered wages and exported rather than created jobs, they receive unjustified tax allowances and 'corporate welfare' even as they diligently refuse to pay their taxes.

Concerning jobs, income differentials are entirely natural. Skill shortages raise wages in some sectors, skilled workers earn more than trainees, bosses more than staff, bankers more than farmers, and private officers more than public servants, who have job security and better pensions. But the minimum wage is rarely sufficient to live on and absolute poverty is grinding. It creates debt, hunger, isolation and stress, with responses ranging from helplessness, depression and ill health to anger, theft and violence. It leads to homelessness, begging, dependency on welfare and charity and, according to recent research, an inability to think calmly and act rationally in one's own best interests. All this affects the children of those affected. Treating the poor with indifference or contempt is inhuman, anti-social and counter-productive. Poverty is a drain on local economies.

Cities always provided jobs for their citizens. When Oldham was the cotton capital of the world, it boasted over 200 large multi-storey mills (some only built in the 1930s), each employing up to 1,000 people. By the 1990s, less than 70 mills remained, with only a handful engaged in production. Most were used for cheap storage, small business floor space or large back offices, the rest vacant. Exporting so many skilled jobs means that cities can no longer employ all their citizens. This creates a vicious circle of unemployment, lower wages, reduced skills and the so-called gig economy.

Monetary economists since 1979 thought that the market would supply new jobs. It is true that new service sector jobs did replace many lost in manufacturing but (from page 130), most new jobs were lower paid and lower skilled in warehousing and leisure etc: "All of the executives agreed that 'zero training' was the fast food industry's ideal." One meat supplier, IBP, had the same focus. "We've tried to take the skill out of every step [in our abattoirs]." (Schlosser 2002)

With national insurance under Lloyd George and the welfare state under Clement Attlee, citizens were protected against the vicissitudes of life and poverty, including retirement, unemployment, disability, illness, widowhood, single parenthood and homelessness. Since 1979, however, poverty has increased with every welfare reduction. Citizens advice bureaux (CABs) indicate the health of a local society. In a 'collapsed mining community' in 1994, the local CAB managed over 3,100 enquiries and counselling sessions covering social security and benefit claims 24.1%, debt counselling 15.7% (with 35 debt cases totalling over £200,000), employment issues 10.2%, housing advice 10.1%, consumer rights 9.7%, family and personal matters 7.8%, and other areas 22.3%.

Structural unemployment, compounded by the bankers' crash of 2008 and subsequent austerity, now means that welfare benefits can't guarantee the basic essentials of life, affecting children particularly harshly. J K Galbraith suggested that in times of full employment, benefits could be low, but during recessions and high unemployment, benefits should be raised to keep households and local economies ticking over. That is Keynesian economics.

In 2013, half a million people had to visit their local food bank, three times more than in the previous 12 months (*The Observer* 18/8/13). Numbers continue to rise. "Despite the fact that the child population has remained largely static [at around 13 million], the number living in relative poverty has risen from two million in 1969 to 3.5 million today." (*The Observer* 25/8/13) Today, about 27% of all children are likely to be underweight at birth and overweight at 16, achieve lower GCSE results, more prone to road accident or home injury and live in poor housing conditions.

Each year, the Child Poverty Action Group (CPAG) publishes a *Welfare Benefits Handbook* covering all state benefits, working and family tax credits, disability allowances, social funds and income support et al. From the twenty third edition (CPAG 1993) we learn that: "The first edition of the *National Welfare Benefits Handbook*... was 72 pages long. Today, it is nearly six times that length... The growth in the size and distribution of the *Handbook* reflects a number of trends, most of them negative. The sheer increase in the numbers living in poverty means that more people are having to rely on means-tested benefits either as their main source of income or to top-up inadequate wages or non-means-tested benefits. In particular, the unemployment benefit scheme has proved unable to cope with the return of mass unemployment, and most seriously, long-term unemployment." In 2002/3, the Handbook had expanded to 1,193 pages with 60 pages of appendices.

The 1993 *Handbook* highlighted the following key points.

- "By the end of the 1980's, one in five of the population relied on at least one means-tested benefit."
- "Yet, in 1989, nearly £1.7 billion worth of means-tested benefits still went unclaimed."
- Despite reforms, the poverty trap still means "hundreds of thousands of low-paid workers [lose] most of a pay rise through loss of means-tested benefits and higher taxation and national insurance contributions."
- Means-tested benefits "are not the best vehicle to provide people with a secure income base" and they make it "impossible to target help on individuals within families (usually women), who need it because the 'breadwinner' income is not being shared fairly."
- "[M]any immigrants cannot claim key means-tested benefits and others may be frightened to."
- "There is no longer a [social assistance] safety net as such for most young single people and childless unemployment claimants deemed to be not actively seeking work" and most worrying
- "Social fund loan repayments are contributing to a growing phenomenon of claimants living below the income support level because of the variety of benefit deductions made at source. This would create difficulties enough if income support rates were adequate. But there is growing evidence that they are not, particularly in the case of families with children."

It is difficult to gauge the mind-set of those behind the *Handbook*'s arbitrary powers and traps. It puts huge pressure on perhaps 5,000 front-line civil servants who have to deal every day with the frustration, anger and hopelessness of so many claimants. It overloads local council welfare rights officers and volunteers in CABs, CPAGs and other agencies, and it clogs up the tribunal appeal system.

In 2013, the Universal Credit scheme was introduced to replace six means-tested benefits and reduce the complexity. Many serious problems have emerged: the six-week delay in receiving first payments cause real problems, loans to cover that gap have to be repaid, more families will lose than gain under the scheme and the costs of implementing UC rose from £2.2 billion to £15.8 billion. Most seriously, the total welfare budget was cut.

By contrast, corporate welfare is healthy in all sectors of the economy but only for large firms and the wealthy.

- 6,000 landowners (plus a few institutions like the National Trust, the Church of England and the Crown) own 70% of all farmland, while (under Pareto's Law) 80% of European farm subsidies go to the largest 20% of the farms (www.corporatewatch.org). Small efficient family farms struggle to earn a living wage and all tenant farmers, large and small, struggle as generous grants are usually 'reflected' in land rents. Young farmers have few opportunities to begin their careers.
- Private equity owners award themselves huge dividends and other disguised salary payments, mostly at the expense of company staff and taxpayers, while converting taxable profits into bank loan repayments.
- The poor struggle with debt, but still have to pay VAT on most of their essential spending. The wealthy buy expensive items like jets and yachts through tax havens to avoid VAT. Even their chauffeurs are tax deductible.
- And some firms are too big to be allowed to fail. After the bankers' crash, we bailed out the biggest banks (but not the Co-op Bank) and plunged the country into a period of futile austerity. This cost each of us about £20,000 (according to a Bank of England official) with no subsequent attempt to break them up or regulate their activities.

While millions struggle with increasing rents and the threat of homelessness, valuable offices, shops, pubs and mansions are now bought and sold offshore. In 2010, the whole of Bishops Square in central London was bought by a consortium led by JP Morgan for £559m, and registered in Luxembourg. The annual rents of £40m were then mostly paid out as interest to the investors, leaving them with total tax bills of "just £321,000 in the past two years." Now they want to sell Bishops Square for £850m, and by "selling the company rather than the property" they evade (ipE) all capital gains tax and stamp duties (*Private Eye* 1404, 30/10/2015). However shifty, this trick is deemed legal.

At the root of this discrimination between rich and poor are three policy fault lines. Tax people differentiate unfairly between earned income through Labour and unearned income from Land and Capital. Few begrudge brain surgeons and rocket scientists salaries that reflect skill and experience, risk and complexity. Few support bankers' bonuses, private equity dividends and landlords excessive rents. Second, VAT seems to be a second tax on earned income, but there is no tax on luxury goods or products that harm society through waste and pollution. And third, the conflict between manufacturing and banking has gone too far in the banks' favour, even bailing them out rather than letting them go bust.

The disparity between rich and poor infects our language. For most of us, economics is the study of scarcity, for billionaires it becomes the study of abundance. But to complain is to suffer 'the politics of envy'. Do good people really envy them their empty mansions, yachts and minds? Faced with the politics of greed, more likely reactions are anger (with our politicians and tax inspectors), hate (natural against greed but a regrettable response to illness), apathy or resignation (why complain – they always get their way), indifference (the Skinner approach to bad behaviour), perplexity at how they cope with the sycophants and survive in their hermetically sealed worlds, and genuine wonder that, despite their wealth, they are no happier than the rest of us. Their conspicuous consumption, like £143,000 on a wrist watch, usually goes unnoticed. Their conspicuous charitable donations may be appreciated but, as we love our Carnegie libraries, we remember that in life, he was a shit. Even good acts may be ambiguous. We installed solar panels to generate as much electricity as we use and ameliorate climate change, while being attracted by the original 'feed in tariffs' giving about 8% returns. Sociopaths would welcome climate change, whatever the impact on society, since it would increase their financial returns to over 10%.

Some justify excessive wealth as reward for the great entrepreneurial skill of taking *risks*. When the wealthy invest, they either gain or lose a few million. The risk is manageable. For ordinary people working on a farm, oil rig, building site or fishing boat, in an asbestos factory or nuclear plant or on duty in prison, A&E ward, school, public transport or on the copper's beat, each day brings very different risks; of accident, abuse, violence or poisoning, occasionally leading to serious injury, penury or, in extreme, widowhood.

Around their financial affairs, secrecy is the norm and language the vehicle. 'Creative accounting' is the euphemism for telling lies (rare), hiding the truth (distorting real debts and likely income etc) or muddying the waters under such flexiterms as 'due diligence' and 'best endeavours'. 'Financial engineering' promotes the wizardry of corporations into something astonishing and complex, when in plain English, the banks' 'collateralized debt obligations' were lots of unsecured mortgages; and 'tax efficiency' through 'aggressive accounting' and tax havens upholds the worst Empire habits of corporate and private secrecy to the detriment of a healthy market.

Governments also massage the truth. Since 1979, the numbers of unemployed were often reduced, not by creating more jobs but by shifting some unemployed onto other benefits. Today, the number living in poverty is also being reduced, not by reducing poverty but by lowering the income threshold of poverty. Like housing, the poor and jobless become a numbers game, but there is nothing euphemistic or neutral in how we describe the poor. Since 1979, they have been subjected to Georgian levels of contempt and harnessed to the bureaucratic skills of imperial Victorians, creating a minefield of petty regulation, simmering anger and, in extreme, suicide. Twelve million people on at least one benefit is not progress.

The tabloids often wax indignant about welfare scroungers and benefit cheats, not knowing (or bothering to mention) that total benefit fraud costs less than the unclaimed benefits or those held back in error, is usually committed by those in the know rather than those in need, and is certainly well under 5% of the yearly cost of illegal tax evasion, let alone tax avoidance.

Local councils working with local charities and credit unions would surely provide better services than ministers and senior civil servants incompetent or indifferent to the greed of private service providers and loan sharks. Both Reagan and Thatcher revived 'the trickle-down effect' that was first coined before 1900 to defend US Republican policies that favoured sociopathic greed.

It has its roots in Adam Smith: "[The rich] consume little more than the poor, and in spite of their natural selfishness and rapacity... though the sole end which they propose from the labours of all the thousands whom they employ, by the gratification of their own vain and insatiable desires, they divide with the poor the produce of all their improvements. They are led by an invisible hand to make nearly the same distribution of the necessaries of life, which would have been made, had the earth been divided into equal portions among all its inhabitants." (Smith, *Theory of Moral Sentiments*, 1759.) O'Rourke (2007) clarifies for the hard-of-hearing. "The economic benefits of wealth in a free market quickly overflow... and they do not trickle down, they pour." The worm in this bud is in the meaning of a free market. Markets can be free of regulation and therefore open to being rigged, or they can be free of manipulation, open to new entrants and guided by social selection (or 'invisible hand').

George Eliot got closer to the truth. In *Silas Marner*, the local squire at breakfast would feed his dog "enough bits of beef to make a poor man's holiday dinner." Smith's invisible hand is not working when a dog eats more meat in a week than a family in a year. My economic textbooks (Lipsey 1975, and Sloman 2006) ignore the trickle down effect, but not Galbraith. "[T]he trickle-down approach to economic policy [is] what an older and less elegant generation called the horse-and-sparrow theory: 'If you feed the horse enough oats, some will pass through to the road for the sparrows'."

All empires throw up emperors who seem to share a fondness for mass entertainment and celebrity culture. But where Roman emperors occasionally provided free bread and circuses to keep the masses happy, our little Neros make us pay for our food and entertainment. This culture is more like the bacteria cultures found in science lab test tubes rather than that cultivated in schools and universities.

Privatization has even reversed the trickle-down effect. In out-sourcing public services, especially in welfare, most private agency staff have been 'incentivized' to reduce benefits in order to maximize agency profits and reduce government spending.

This back siphonage puts all claimants at risk. For some years, *Private Eye* has reported on people with severe disabilities or illnesses being deemed fit for work, either following unfair assessments, some without any medical advisers, by the private French company Atos. In most cases, the benefits should not have been withdrawn. "[And] last week the Department for Work and Pensions (DWP) was finally forced to reveal figures showing that about 90 people a month were dying within 14 days of being declared fit to work under Atos's watch." (*Private Eye* 1400)

Some arbitrary decisions are now being brought back in-house. From *Private Eye* 1376 and 1399:

- a disabled couple who had to sleep separately had a one-bedroom fourth-floor flat. When the broken lift left them stranded for several days, they were rehoused in a two-bedroom bungalow. The wife at last had a bed to sleep in. Then George Osborne's bedroom tax reduced their benefits by £70 a week;
- a man on 15 hours a week of dialysis had his PIP withdrawn without any consultation, when an office manager within the DWP decided that "it is medically reasonable to suggest" that he only needed 10 hours of dialysis – under the 14 hour threshold that triggers the PIP; and
- a woman lost her Motobility car under PIP when, again without any medical check, it was decided that she could walk 20 metres without pain. Under the former disability living allowance, that distance was 50 metres.

In 2018, US corporation Maximus (replacing Atos) was paid £158m by the DWP to assess whether disabled people are fit for work, or eligible for ESA (employment and support allowance). That year, on profits of £26.7m profit on the contract, Maximus extracted £18.1m in dividends for directors and shareholders. Also that year, the DWP "spent £24.4m in re-examining Maximus findings in reconsiderations and appeals." (*Private Eye* 1498, 14/6/2019) Very profitable for Maximus, very costly for taxpayers and hugely stressful for every claimant. How can such wilful government incompetence be so widely ignored and unreported?

After four decades of billionaires disease, the number of children living in poverty has risen by more than 50%. This correlation between extreme wealth and poverty is a zero sum game and can only be tackled by tax reform that is discussed in chapter 10.

Let Philip Green illustrate a more common example of unearned inequality. In 2004-5, Arcadia, the private group of fashion shops which he manages but his wife owns, paid Tina a £1.2 billion dividend. At the time, Arcadia employed about 45,000 people. Assuming that that total equals 30,000 full time jobs on an average of £14,000 a year (about 10% above the minimum wage), the group annual wage bill would have been £420 million. Now, had Philip and Tina Green been full of fellow feeling and awarded their staff three bonuses of roughly half their annual wages, that would have cost Arcadia £630 million over three years. The social benefits would have been a happier workforce, richer families, more local spending on essentials and comforts, healthier local economies throughout the land and increased tax revenues.

And his wife in Monaco would still have been £570 million better off. Who knows – BHS might have survived.

In any event, Tina paid no tax on the dividend as she lives in Monaco, despite Arcadia trading almost entirely in the UK. Had the dividend been treated as income and taxed at source at 45%, £560 million in taxes could have funded about 30 new secondary schools and avoided ruinous PFI schemes. To check that this tax evasion (ipE) was legal, apparently Green phoned Dave Hartnett at HMRC and was fraternally reassured. And while Green became a billionaire, the free telephone helpline for benefit claimants was replaced by a confidential line for those who suspected their neighbours of being benefit cheats. That would have impressed Stalin.

In liberating the wealthy, the concept of equality is relegated to junk status and fraternity excludes disabled people and most minorities.

Once a year, *The Big Issue* remembers 'those we've lost over the last year'. In Edinburgh "John White died in August after losing his battle with cancer, aged 69. John was a well-known, hugely popular character in the Meadows in Edinburgh, where he had sold since 2006, and took pride in being a point-of-call for tourists and others looking for directions. After his death, tributes poured in from readers, locals, politicians and those who had met John over the years. A memorial plaque is to be fitted in the park in the New Year to celebrate the life of the cherished *Big Issue* vendor." (Issue 1134) For most billionaires, including the owner of *The Sun*, "Gotcha!" would provide a suitably succinct obituary.

Neighbourhoods and ghettoes

The first recorded ghetto, *Ghetto Nuovo* in Venice, was created in 1516 for Jews who, in exchange for some trade and curfew restrictions, received sanctuary from the various expulsions and pogroms they suffered through most of Europe. It may derive from the foundry (*getto*) already in the area, or from small boroughs (*borghetti*) found in most trading cities. Greeks, Slavs and Albanians, Luccans and Milanese lived In other Venetian boroughs, plying their trades in oil, wool, silk, founding and banking.

Some ghettoes became slums. "The cheap housing in these areas would also draw in other disadvantaged groups with low income or little capital; immigrants, single parents, the mentally ill and physically handicapped. At the same time, the gradual decline of the area pushed out those with freedom to move – with savings, skills or educational qualifications." (Harrison 1983) As described in chapter 2, the major factor was the 'jerry-built' houses with poor tenants in damp overcrowded conditions. Slum clearance destroyed ghetto workshops and skills, thereby reducing local economies. Now the redeveloped areas themselves are being 'regenerated', often with 'gated communities'. Slum clearance also led to overspill suburban estates, which often became 'no-go areas' and 'sink estates', Only a few traditional neighbourhoods were saved through 'gentrification'. Even the language of redevelopment separates the downtrodden from the comfortable.

Ryszard Kapuszinski (2008) identified three dangerous social forces: racism, bigotry and nationalism, to which we should add misogyny. Blind racism, religious bigotry and tribal xenophobia are all based on abnormal degrees of hatred that deny all aspects of liberty, equality and fraternity. Great cities as diverse and civilized as Beirut (the Paris of the middle east), Sarajavo (for 2,000 years a mixed city at the crossing of important trade routes) and Damascus (with a 5,000-year history of harmonious living between Christian, Jew and Muslim) have been destroyed, and innocents slaughtered, by a furious nationalism or religious bigotry, fuelled by the arms trade and an irrational hatred of the Other. This hatred of diversity reached a murderous apotheosis in the final throes of the Turkish empire, Hitler's Germany, Stalin's Russia and mad King Leopold's (widely unremarked) genocide in what was then the Belgian Congo. Kapuszinski quotes the Greek historian Herodotus: "Xenophobia... is a sickness of people who are scared, suffering an inferiority complex, terrified by the prospect of seeing themselves in the mirror of the culture of Others."

It is a cliché that the British are a mongrel race. From earliest times, native Celts were invaded or settled by Belgae, Romans, Norse, Jutes, Angles, Saxons, Normans, Jews, Huguenots, Italians, Russians, Poles, Chinese, Turks, Greeks and Cypriots. So our language, from Chaucer on, has roots stretching from the Sanskrit to Icelandic.

The two major social disrupters of our cities are racism and crime. Until the *Aliens Act* 1905, the poor and the oppressed of the world were welcome, provided they could get here. Victorians, both humane and rational understood that immigrants brought economic benefits to us all, exemplifying Adam Smith's enlightened self-interest. Each wave brought its own skills, traditions and vitality, enriching towns and cities. Hostility was generally partial and temporary as children, familiarity and intermarriage overcame barriers of language and custom. Some ghettoes flourished, others were absorbed, leaving behind only a trace in an isolated Slavic church or Italian bakery. Beehives also accept lost immigrants if they work and forage in their new home. Only aggressive foreigners will be repulsed.

Today's economic migrants and asylum seekers are unwelcome and denied some basic human rights. Such values display neither fellow feeling nor enlightened self-interest. Although east Europeans suffer for their language, racism remains acute for immigrants from mid Asia, Africa and the Caribbean. This is ironic. The British Empire supposedly taught the colonies our traditional values of fair play and integrity. By rights, these third and fourth generation citizens should be fully integrated, representing a rare and positive outcome of Empire – a cause for celebration even.

Yet racist harassment, ignorant, irrational and anti-social, still dogs too many British lives, persistent in all sections of society. The senseless murder of Stephen Lawrence by white youths in a south east London suburb exposed institutional racism in the Metropolitan police. The police investigation in the crucial early stages was incompetent beyond belief (and may have involved corruption between a key officer and parents of one of the murderers). Then the police officer who reinvestigated and secured prison sentences for two of the murderers almost 20 years later, was taken off before he could ensure justice for the other three. Had some black youths killed an innocent white man, the police response would have been swift, committed and ruthless. (See for example Cathcart 1999.) Meanwhile, the number of deaths of black British citizens while in custody, under restraint or in prison remains obstinately high, and Metropolitan police sergeant Gurpal Virdi received outrageous treatment from his employer.

The journalists Hammond and Mosley (1999) tested the NHS. "In 1992 Drs Sam Everington and Aneez Esmail... sent fake applications to junior hospital doctor posts, identical in all but surname. Half the names they used were Asian, half were Anglo-Saxon. The latter were twice as likely to be offered an interview. When this was published in 1993 the response of the medical establishment was swift and extraordinary. The racism was not admitted and investigated; instead, the pair were reported to the police, arrested and charged with fraud by the good folk at Hendon police station." So incensed were the two doctors at their treatment by the General Medical Council that they repeated the experiment five years later, this time for senior hospital posts and GP training schemes – with much the same result. *Private Eye* also reported on the racist treatment of health worker Younis Yukh by his NHS employer and trade union Unison.

Racism contradicts our nature as social animals. Even supposing eugenicists did discover a superior race, white supremacists confirm that it won't be Caucasian. Racism is nurtured through family upbringing and peer pressure in isolated ghettoes and insular elites.

Despite the *Aliens Act 1905*, the UK has not been overrun by immigrants. From table 31 opposite, UK population growth (reflecting in and out-migration, birth, death and marriage rates and the catastrophes of war) is one of the lowest in Europe.

- The extraordinary growth of Greece, reaching 6.2 million by 1928, reflects the massive influx of Greeks expelled from Turkey. Growth from 1951 was a more normal 38.5%.
- At the other extreme, about five million Germans emigrated or were killed during the last war. And the East German population declined over 40 years by about three million due to initial emigration and lower birth rates.
- The exceptional growth of the Netherlands seems largely to reflect a birth rate consistently twice its mortality rate. Perhaps they are 'pathologically happy'.

Yet every nationality from Empire and Europe are here. Ethnic immigrants make up about 13.5% of the population compared with 14% for the rest of Europe. It was Enoch Powell's infamous speech of 1968 about white people becoming a minority and our streets "running with blood" unless we stop immigration that gave racism a respectable gloss, he being a classical scholar and man of integrity. Alas, reputations seldom match the man. His population projections were woefully wrong and his claim that most race crime was committed by immigrants contradicted police records.

This shameless lie remained unexposed by an indolent media, and he was buried with all pomp in Westminster Abbey (Shepherd 1996).

Table 31: European populations at censuses ('000s), 1901-2014

Country	1901	1951 (% incr)	2001 (% incr)	% increase 1901-2001
Austria*	6,648	6,934 (4.3)	8,110 (17.0)	22.0
Belgium**	6,694	8,512 (27.2)	10,273 (20.7)	53.5
Denmark	2,450	4,281 (74.7)	5,350 (25.0)	118.4
Finland	2,646	4,030 (52.3)	5,187 (28.7)	96.0
France**	39,451	42,781 (11.3)	58,620 (37.0)	52.5
Germany	58,451	50,787 (22.7)	82,195 (18.8)	40.6
east***	-	18,388	16,706 (-8.2)	
Greece*	2,632	7,633(190.0)	10,575 (38.5)	301.8
Ireland*	2,972	2,961 (0.0)	3,635 (22.8)	22.3
Italy	32,475	47,159 (45.2)	57,691 (22.3)	77.6
N'lands**	5,104	19,625 (88.6)	16,032 (66.6)	214.1
Norway	2,240	3,278 (46.3)	4,519 (37.9)	101.7
Portugal	5,423	8,381 (54.5)	10,231 (22.1)	88.7
Spain	18,594	27,977 (50.5)	39,501 (41.2)	112.4
Sweden	5,137	7,041 (37.1)	8,893 (26.3)	73.1
Switzerland	2,315	4,715(103.7)	7,180 (52.3)	210.2
UK	38,120	50,225 (31.8)	58,789 (17.1)	54.2

Source: Mitchell

(* Instead of 1901 (1899 or 1900), relevant dates for Austria were 1910, Greece 1907, and 1926 for the partition of Ireland. ** Census dates 1947 for Belgium and the Netherlands, 1954 for France. *** Census dates for east Germany, 1950 and 1981.)

Looking at the wider issue of immigration (which conceals underlying racism, since emigrating Britons and immigrant Aussies and Canadians seldom feature), do they take our jobs, or are they 'scroungers'? Many among the poor, working class and young fear the loss of 'their' jobs. This is understandable but misdirected. It is governments and employers that invite 'economic migrants' to come here and work in our hospitals and surgeries (including Enoch Powell visiting the Caribbean when health minister), care homes and nurseries, schools and universities, IT and transport services, chemical plants and on our farms. Many immigrants take a long-term view, working on menial tasks for low wages in return for freedom to rear families and see their children rise in any number of professions. Skilled immigrants leave home for better resources and opportunities. We should target the policies behind immigration, like government policies to reduce taxes and training programmes, and employers to increase profits with low-paid non-union immigrant labour.

The worst tabloids often see immigrants as 'scroungers' on our benefits system, which partly contradicts the previous complaint. Economic migrants take pride in their independence. It is asylum seekers who depend on benefits while their cases are being processed. Living in limbo, not allowed to work (or play cricket) and dependent on weekly cash payments (replacing the vouchers on which Home Secretary Jack Straw didn't allow foodsheds to give any change). And if their applications are turned down, they survive on Red Cross vouchers and other charities while appealing, under constant threat of detention and deportation. The factors that cause people to seek asylum are discussed in chapter 10, lying partly in our foreign policies and arms sales. But it is in marked contrast to our shameful treatment of the various billionaire oligarchs whom we welcome, respecting their right to privacy whatever their shady backgrounds while imposing a 'punitive' £30,000 annual tax bill.

In a lecture, Lord Acton (1960) listed some rules for historians, including this: "[D]o not overlook the strength of the bad cause or the weakness of the good." I would single out one positive feature of our Empire, namely those urban ghettoes where the various ethnic, faith and language minorities have created bulwarks of urban life, diversity and tolerance in marked contrast to homogenized suburbs and most urban redevelopments. They provide shelter for their residents, a market for their distinctive shops and businesses and some collective security against racist hostility. These ghettoes have achieved, against the odds, some truly stable and independent neighbourhoods that enrich our cities with 'the culture of Others'.

Poverty and minorities can make or mar neighbourhoods. But when they are combined with crime, as in many US cities, with the worst housing, the cheapest jobs, rampant drug dealing, organized gangs and racist police forces that kill innocent young black men, hopelessness reigns:

"*Ghetto pedagogy*
Dad?
Yes?
Why do black men always kill each other?
(long pause)
Practicing."
(Walter Mosley 1994)

Every year, crime affects about 10% of the population. Nearly half of our criminals are aged between 18 and 30 and young males are the worst offenders, committing about 93% of all crimes (ONS). Young males without money are more likely to commit 'crimes of acquisition' like theft, burglary, mugging and robbery. Young males with money sometimes become rowdy and engage (or become embroiled) in pub brawls, racist abuse or domestic violence. Generalizing further, 'real' wealth tends to combine both acquisitive behaviour and 'firm' command management, many billionaires and boardrooms having links with mafia groups, that reinforce their sociopathic greed.

Even if society legalized drugs and prostitution, however, and controlled the poisonous cocktail of pills, pesticides and pollutants, genetic diversity and testosterone would always produce modest levels of crime. But today, fear of crime makes us all less confident in walking about town, reinforced by media reports on ASBOs and hoodlums, 'binge drinking', drug busts, beggars and muggers, turf wars and now knife and gun crime. How this fear of crime relates to the actual figures is unclear. In 2008, (from ONS), 2,538 were killed, 26,034 seriously injured and 202,333 received minor injuries on our roads. At the same time, 700 people were killed and some 900,000 were victims of violent assault, serious to minor.

Whatever the numerical risks, there is no meaningful comparison between a random car crash with serious injury and a brutal attack or rape in which physical violence is compounded by psychological trauma and often injustice in courtrooms. Nor should we take comfort from the fact that more than half the violent crimes are committed by young males, most frequently on other young males. Too many violent crimes occur indoors. In any event, when fewer people walk to local facilities, the street are less social and some feel less safe – unlike motorists in their 'safe' boxes.

As noted in chapter 3, mixed terraced neighbourhoods are informally policed by pedestrians and residents' eyes on the street. Today's responses to crime have generally been ineffective and sometimes counter-productive, focussing on physical solutions and technological policing. Gated communities in expensive towers, with concierge or entry-phone security, contradict the social nature of open streets.

Technology has transformed policing. Since the 1960s, Z cars replaced bobbies on the beat, the 1970s brought in closed circuit television (CCTV) followed by helicopters and now computer programmes to predict crime spots. Cars and cameras improve the speed of response to crime scenes and may help identify the criminals, but they do not *prevent* crime. There are perhaps four million CCTV cameras in the UK, though no-one knows the actual figure nor how many are regularly monitored. Cameras may deter criminals and make shoppers feel safer, but again, no-one knows. A meta-analysis of 44 studies across Europe and the US (2009) suggested that CCTV reduces crime by half in car parks, by nearly a quarter in public transport areas, but only by 7% in public places in the UK. In most other countries, reduction of crime in public places is insignificant, presumably because more people are on the streets (Wikipedia 10/15). Whatever the data, many schemes are simply a waste of public money, staff and resources., as suggested in a safe Hampshire town centre (page 124).

Town centres have always been safe because they are lively. Large numbers of people visiting shops and offices, cafes, pubs and restaurants, religious, cultural and civic venues, plus the residents living upstairs, all generated mutual safety except from pickpockets. Crowds are cheaper and more effective than any technology. Only on quiet evenings and at night time might cameras be useful, when the streets are empty. And while cameras may have been crucial in bringing justice to the Bulger family, had trained coppers regularly included that shopping centre on their beats, or the owners employed trained security guards, such tragedies might have been prevented.

Reliance on patrol cars and CCTV reduces us all to mute witnesses and reinforces Heidegger's argument about technology and alienation. At root this is a social failure. We are losing that sense of social security that Jacobs called 'street theatre' in which at least some would intervene in clearly abnormal circumstances. As with health (from pages 227 and 345), we should spend more money on public health and crime prevention. This would reduce spending on patient care and criminal conviction. And, despite the technology, conviction rates for criminals remain somewhere around one in twenty. The police officer's lot is not a happy one. CCTV has also given rise to the youthful fashion for hoodies (and burqas), a legitimate response by those who object to mass surveillance as they go about their daily lives.

With one police officer for every 400 citizens, releasing community policing from desk paperwork (caused by government targets) and co-ordinating crime reduction programmes with local agencies offer realistic alternatives to CCTV, Neighbourhood Watch schemes and poorly-trained, low paid 'community safety officers'. Two examples from the east midlands offer contrasting approaches.

In one police force, a patrol car visited each town and village once a month. In one village, we twice observed two officers parked on a Tuesday outside the community centre. Over two hours, no-one spoke to the officers while they ate their lunch. Had they ventured inside, they would have learnt that the community centre held a pensioners' lunch club every Monday. Changing their rota, they might have learnt more about the village over a cup of tea with the residents. In a nearby small town, after-school policing was left to one community safety officer who, on one occasion, was being harassed by a teenage group letting her bike tyres down while taking pictures with their phones. As part of its low tolerance policy towards young people, the force imposed evening curfews. Small groups of young women going to town were stopped by police and escorted back home. Yet young women are unlikely to feel safe on their own. Little wonder that many secondary schoolchildren found the police intimidating or aggressive.

In the second police force, an experienced community policeman and staff in the local secondary school identified those children most at risk of becoming offenders. These pupils were asked to call on one or two vulnerable residents on their way to and from school to check that they were OK or needed anything from the shops or chemist. Other children wanted to be involved but were refused. The scheme was designed for those six teenagers, it was theirs and gave them perhaps their first real responsibility.

A geneticist once suggested that crime could be eradicated if we simply aborted every male foetus. This rather extreme remedy returns us to the US and 'ghetto pedagogy'. For several decades to about 1990, US urban crime continued to rise with no end in sight. Policy options escalated from more police, zero tolerance, tougher gun controls, another war on crime, even bringing in the military. Yet from

1990, crime levels peaked and gradually fell over the decade. Economist Steven Levitt pinpointed the cause of this dramatic turnaround to the 22nd January 1973, when the US Supreme Court legalized abortion throughout the nation. For the first time, every woman had the right to have an abortion, whatever their age, income and race.

This right is now under threat from those 'fundamentalist' Christians who argue for the foetus's right to life over the mother's right to choose. Many see this argument as either/or, when there are in fact three arguments:

1. Those who oppose abortion, whatever the circumstances, base their argument on the absolute sanctity of life, even *in utero*.
2. The contrary view, from eugenicists, is that there are circumstances when the foetus must be aborted, as for example when the parents are what they used to call 'mentally defective' or involved 'miscegenation' (ie, parents of different races). Their moral compass (for want of a better word) was the health of the species rather than the sanctity of life.
3. And then there are the rights of the mothers themselves.

The first two arguments reduce women to their medieval role simply 'to carry man's seed'. Male chauvinism denies woman control of her body and it doesn't work. Abortion (like prostitution) has been a fact of life throughout history. The choice for society is whether abortion is legal, safe and humane, or whether the wealthy pay for proper treatment while the rest return to back-street abortionists or suffer press taunts from the Littlejohns for their excessive breeding. Levitt and Dubner (2006) put it fairly: "What the link between abortion and crime does say is this: when the government gives a woman the opportunity to make her own decision about abortion, she generally does a good job of figuring out if she is in a position to raise the baby well. If she decides she can't, she often chooses the abortion."

Voltaire thought that man, by nature, was "false, cozening, faithless, ungrateful, thieving, weak, inconstant, mean-spirited, envious, greedy, drunken, miserly, ambitious, bloody, slanderous, debauched, fanatic, hypocritical, and stupid." Clearly he was only referring to great leaders and statesmen rather than teachers and bus drivers. In any event, only cities can curb these personal excesses by our social behaviour developed in neighbourhoods, schools and pubs, and approved in council chambers, Parliament and the media. Cities can balance liberty, equality and fraternity to create places where people enjoy, are able to enjoy, and are allowed to enjoy their lives to the full. Yet the social health of our cities has been seriously eroded by excessive inequalities in wealth and education, by restricting the lives of at least 25% of the population, by replacing neighbourhood fraternity with suburban isolation, sink estates and gated communities, and by poor record-keeping and unfair access to justice. This is uncivilized and affects young people particularly hard.

This chapter raises serious challenges for both author and society. We have many wonderful books showing the outputs of civilizations, but very few that explain their essential prerequisites. My six essentials are clearly vital, but too often reduce to the opposition of libertarian and socialist. We are also discussing many 'low' subjects in which the strength of opinions rise with the lack of hard data. Are 'recreational' drugs more harmful than painkillers and anti-depressants? Would safe commercial sex reduce violent sexual crime? Does excessive private wealth actually cause poverty? And would street crime reduce in more mixed neighbourhoods? This lack of information almost precludes knowledge, let alone wisdom. However confident I am in the solutions above, I know that others believe the opposite equally firmly.

What we can more confidently assert is that our various responses to these problems have tended to be physical solutions. We have accepted abject poverty, street begging and homelessness. Instead, councils want to 'tidy up' rundown areas, so red light districts and 'sink' estates follow slums into oblivion, architects designing 'a better future', developers making their profits and governments supporting them. Which returns us to part 1 and urban development.

Urban entropy 4: money primarily serves a social function

Money is not just about economics. It has three functions: as a medium of exchange, a unit of account and a store of value. It thus resembles language which is also a means of exchange, with units of communication defined in dictionaries and stores of knowledge found in any library. Thus money, like language, reflects our social behaviour and therefore, following Wilkinson and Pickett, should be distributed fairly.

1. As a means of exchange, money defines the price of goods and services between buyer and seller, where both are willing parties to the deal. Compulsory purchase should only be used to curb speculators or break up mega-corps.
2. As a unit of account, money measures both private and social wealth which are inversely correlated. In societies with excessive private wealth, low taxes and tax evasion (ipE), spending on public services and social welfare is reduced.
3. As a store of value, money reflects the scarcity of an item rather than its use. Black truffles, designer trash and a bottle of Montrachet cost more than a bar of soap, pair of jeans and pint of bitter. Which are the more valuable? Philip Green's £100m yacht has no social value, its modest 'trickle down' effect outweighed by its pollution. 50 libraries, ten schools or five hospitals would be stores of infinitely more value.

This disparity between price and value is seen in company accounts. Each shows the units of income and expenditure and, in the balance sheet, the store of value, including bank deposits, building assets and 'intellectual property'. Labour costs are usually the major item of expenditure against income. Workforce skills and motivation, usually the most valuable asset, are ignored. This is the rotten core of private equity.

Since 1979, the ideology of low taxation and small government has greatly increased inequalities. At the top, the many on minimum wage. At the bottom, the few profiteers who squeeze local economies for their personal gain. Compare the different life styles.

The poor, low waged, unemployed or on reduced benefits, have doubled to 20% with perhaps another 20% surviving on a living wage. Having no disposable income, they have no store of value except perhaps a TV and an old car. Their daily grind, living from hand to mouth, is to feed the meter, fend off misery and find relief wherever they can with bitterness, violence, illness and theft never far away.

The comfortable 50%, with disposable income, can spend now and save for later. Their lifestyle dilemma is merely to balance this negative feedback loop. Spend too much and they will worry about old age and accidents, spend too little and they will lose friends. Yet they too must either accept lower standards in health, education and other public services, or go private.

The wealthy inhabit a different world based on a positive feedback loop, with money the obsession. Conspicuous consumption and charitable donations are merely ways of managing that obsession. For them, life is a tedious game of Monopoly, chasing expensive properties, lucrative deals and a higher ranking in Forbes.

John Maynard Keynes was right. 'Love of money' should be treated as a mental illness. The 'filthy rich' are like street junkies, prevented from being happy except for the occasional high. Their addiction feeds on itself and affects us all through their sociopathic ('victimless') crimes. There is no violence as they pinch pennies with every bus trip and junk meal, half-inch pounds with every TV show and sports event, nick thousands from every pubco tenant and care home, and con millions from every PFI and private equity deal. They reduce jobs, skills, pay and conditions in every sector of the economy, even as they increase corporate debt levels. And, perhaps their best trick, they reinforce Tory ideology of 'reducing the state' through rampant tax evasion (ipE).

When eighteenth century landowners resisted Corn Law reform, millions went hungry. When nineteenth century mill owners resisted all labour reform, they subjected millions to slavery, despite the higher profitability of the new co-ops. And the greed of today's bankers and private equity bosses occasionally forces austerity on the rest of us and corporate welfare for them. It is surely time that decent liberals rescued Adam Smith from the clutch of neo-conomists, right-wing ideologues and the Adam Smith Institute (named in flagrant disregard of the *Trade Descriptions Act*). Adam Smith did not promote naked self-interest and large corporations. Distributing wealth and income fairly makes everyone healthier, safer and wealthier – not just the poor. Unfortunately, distributing wealth fairly takes political will and courage. In weak democracies with media collusion, private greed trumps social need.

As the Persian proverb says, money works best when spread like manure, bringing social and economic benefits to everyone. Most societies distribute 'earned income' to a loose mix of brain and brawn, age, skill, experience and scarcity. When 'unearned income', through capital investment and rental income, becomes excessive, financiers and managers create a parallel universe of glut and glitter, with few social contacts – the danger for all elites.

Throughout history, a few landowners, industrialists and bankers have created an elite of drones that have taken control of the hives, even to the point where the workers are excluded and forced to live further afield. Fortunately, like drones, billionaires are mortal. Unfortunately, they perpetuate their greed through trusts – surely the most absurd use of that word. Private inheritance perpetuates excess wealth through generations largely by expelling their young male heirs from family hearth to private finishing schools like Eton, Harrow and Rugby (which enjoy charitable status despite their fantastic wealth). Here, the young are now groomed to rule the natives (rather than the Empire), running all key sectors of society, in government and law, in banking, industry and the media.

Inheritance tax should be applied equally. In cities, as in nature, a certain randomness ensures social mobility and a healthy society. Inherited wealth denies this principle: those with unearned fortunes and unmerited privilege are more likely to succeed over those with superior skills and character.

Newton's second law of motion (that "The rate of change of momentum of a moving body is proportional to and in the same direction as the force acting on it") applies to both economic and financial entropy. Sociopathic greed, through hoovers and havens, applies a force in the opposite direction, impoverishing local economies.

Summary of *Cities*, parts 1 and 2

Before turning to part 3 and solutions, it might help if I summarize the book so far to clarify the main issues that must be addressed. Cities affect all our lives. If the key functions of cities are to provide shelter, security and markets, the general argument of this book is that they thrive on density, diversity and local democracy. Being the theatre for most of our economic and social activities, cities are where civilization can be nurtured and thrive. Hence the book's title. You might read the following as a draft 'Ladybird' version of Civilizing Cities. It is structured on triads.

1. Part one reviewed the physical growth of cities through new building, redevelopment and conservation in which, throughout the first century of formal planning, density gave way to sprawl.
2. Part two reviewed the decline of local economies, social neighbourhoods and urban transport, and how diversity fell victim to zoning and ghettoes.
3. Part three will discuss how town planning, sustainable development and local government could revive cities.

Chapter 1: British cities were built in waves, by the Romans, the Normans and during the explosive Industrial Revolution. All were high density settlements with mixed uses and continuity. This changed during the twentieth century. Garden Cities were the utopian response of Ebenezer Howard (my first planning guru) to the worst urban slums. Low density suburbs and exurban 'parks' were the commercial variants. Social neighbourhoods and diversity gave way to family privacy and car dependency. In pursuit of 'the American dream', while the population increased by 60%, urban areas increased sixfold. This is unsustainable.

Chapter 2: Throughout the last century, we also destroyed too much of the existing urban fabric through slum clearance, town centre renewal and freeways. Slum redevelopment was based on the dystopian vision of Le Corbusier (the next planning guru), with his high rise 'machines for living in'. Most of this destruction was unnecessary, and created alien megaliths which seldom worked. All relied on the bulldozer of compulsory purchase to create the utopias of 'Big Brother'. This also is unsustainable.

Chapter 3: Conserving buildings and neighbourhoods retains centuries of economic investment and social roots, links past, present and future (E Burke), minimizes damage 'to that already possessed' (JS Mill), and is probably the one planning approach that is popular. My third planning guru, Jane Jacobs, did not argue how cities should work, but observed how they actually work – with high densities, short streets, mixed uses and old buildings. Yet conservation is largely ignored by the *NPPF* (*National Planning Policy Framework*), except for legally protected Conservation Areas and Sites of Special Scientific Interest. Government even imposes 20% VAT on all building maintenance and adaptations, while subsidizing all new building and redevelopment with zero VAT. This is unsustainable and perverse.

My first principle of urban entropy is that too much new building and redevelopment wastes energy, materials, land and capital. Extending the lifespan of buildings is cheaper and releases urban energy for more productive uses.

Chapter 4: turning (in part 2) to the main forces causing urban decline, out-of-town retail sheds are turning towns inside out. Their anti-competitive behaviour gives us some of the lowest shop densities in Europe. Foodsheds replace open wholesale markets between farmers and shopkeepers with their closed system that exploits both small suppliers and customers, who are becoming private consumers. We should restore the Retail Census, make business rates consistent with town centre prime shops, reduce the biggest chains, revive local chambers and introduce town centre management.

Chapter 5: during the Industrial Revolution, jobs and wealth shifted from farm to factory to office. Local economies were 'anchored' by many small firms, specialist clusters and an occasional large family firm, the classic Adam Smith market. Since the last war and 1979, the growth of global 'mega-corps' and the de-regulation of business and finance has created 'hoovers' that extract skills, management and wealth from local economies. However efficient through lower 'transactional costs' and 'command management' (from Ronald Coase), they exploit David Ricardo's law of comparative advantage by exporting jobs to cheap labour nations for their corporate advantage. By contrast, our industrial anchors like the Potteries and Cambridge science park develop skills and retain most of their wealth in stronger local economies. Essentially, mega-corps behave like empires, clusters like city states. The size of mega-corps also breeds inefficiency with internal sabotage, poor risk control and 'externalities' that include environmental harm, tax evasion (ipE), corporate welfare and corruption. Co-ops and the small business sector generally offer ways of strengthening local economies through Jacobs' twin objectives of innovation and import replacement. Healthy local economies release entrepreneurial energy, my second principle of urban entropy.

Chapter 6: road traffic has never been so intrusive and polluting. Since 1901, rail freight and public transport greatly increased in every west European nation except Britain. In 1963, Beeching closed a third of the railways, while Buchanan endorsed massive urban roadbuilding. The RCEP report, "Transport and the Environment" (1994) recommended less road traffic, pollution and emissions, greater use of existing transport infrastructure and better quality of life. In 2012, the Royal Commission was disbanded and its report ignored in the disgraceful *NPPF*. While 75% of trips are under five miles and 25% under a mile, governments persist with the ludicrous HS2 and major highway schemes rather than electrify the railways, upgrade regional networks, improve local roads and create safe networks for pedestrians and cyclists who, until recently, were regarded solely as a 'road safety issue'. Urban entropy 3 suggests that social technology like sewers and trains improve cities, private technology like cars and 'social platforms' are severely disruptive.

Chapter 7: social roots are the basis for civilization. Whatever their words, deeds and artefacts, I suggest six inputs that are pre-requisites for civilization: a balance between *Liberté! Egalité! Fraternité!*, written records, the rule of law and better care of the young. The French slogan may be regarded as three aspects of freedom: free to enjoy ourselves, our families and hobbies, free (with rights) to access education, health, justice and welfare, and free from abuse, discrimination and exclusion. In dense, mixed neighbourhoods, fraternity (social behaviour or Smith's 'fellow feeling') develop. In gated communities, private schools, boardroom greed and rampant tax evasion, fraternity is undone by anti-social greed and gross inequality (from Wilkinson and Pickett). It even infects our language. Urban entropy 4 argues that money, serving both social functions and private independence, 'should be spread like manure' (Persian proverb) if we are to release everyone's energy.

In short, the book is full of antitheses. In physical terms, there is the antithesis between centrifugal suburban sprawl and centripetal urban intensification (chapters 1 and 3), and between alien megalithic monuments and small-scale vernacular buildings (chapter 2). The main economic and social antitheses (chapters 4-7) are the following: anti-social retail shed consumers or high street shopping customers; global meg-corp profiteers and market manipulators or local innovative clusters and social enterprises; private motoring and air travel or social transport, walking and cycling; and personal greed and boardroom tax evasion (ipE) or social wealth and welfare.

We now need to discuss three political antitheses. Chapter 8 contrasts local planning and central control, based on local, small-scale problem-solving rather than idealistic transformations. Chapter 9 defines sustainable development based primarily on conservation against the failure of the *NPPF*. And finally, chapter 10 distinguishes between central and local management of public services, showing how central government powers and spending have increased significantly since 1900. This should be reversed to restore local democracy, my seventh essential for civilized societies.

Part Three
Urban Democracy, Planning and Power

Chapter Eight: Planning Cities

This book is structured on triads. Part one reviewed the physical growth of cities through new building, redevelopment and conservation. Part two reviewed the current decline of local economies, social neighbourhoods and urban transport. Now, in part three, we discuss how town planning, sustainable development and local government could revive our cities.

Cities provide shelter, security and markets and thrive on density, diversity and democracy. Throughout the first century of planning, they have developed in a completely different way from all previous centuries. Density gave way to sprawl, diversity to ghettoes and local democracy to central control. If we are to restore urban texture, economic health and social roots in our cities, planning is essential. Or is it?

"Plan, v.t. To bother about the best method of accomplishing an accidental result." (Ambrose Bierce (1842-1914): *The Devil's Dictionary.*)

If bees can design and build their hives without beekeepers, do we need planners to design and build cities which for centuries managed without? The Royal Town Planning Institute thinks so. Its rather gnomic definition of planning is "the mediation of space, the creation of place." This clarifies how and why we plan. Mediating space means negotiating with developers, owners and residents from an approved 'local plan', in order to create places. Since about 1900, planning has been goal-oriented, development-led, future-focussed and idealistic. Most urban problems became 'opportunities' to create new places, with planners as artists, scientists or managers.

After a century of practice, however, we still lack a coherent theory of planning based on how cities actually work and few methods for tackling complex issues without bulldozers. So, while society accepts the roles of doctors, priests and prostitutes, a general suspicion surrounds planners. This lack of legitimacy may be temporary. After all, it wasn't long ago that 'quacks' fed leeches on bleeding patients. This chapter proposes a different approach that may be more acceptable: let planning focus on problem-solving and conservation through 'small-scale incrementalism' and minimum destruction.

It may be clear why we plan – to manage cities. Less clear is how. Is planning an art, a scientific process or part of the political process? This confusion is reflected in the various analogies and metaphors used to describe cities. Apart from my (unoriginal) analogy with beehives, the most frequent analogy is with the human body: our cells as buildings, lungs as parks, arterial roads, intestinal sewers and the *The Heart of Our Cities* by Victor Gruen (1965) being relocated in his first out-of-town shopping mall. (Some architects have difficulty with anatomy, it seems, or geography.) Other physical or natural analogies include the solar system, a modern factory, library, orchestra and hospital, trees and single cell organisms. More abstract metaphors include the soul (St Augustine), the tower of Babel, a semi-lattice structure (Kevin Lynch), Howard's magnets, Olsen's city as a work of art and various perpetual motion machines: a river of life and Le Corbusier's futurist "a city built for speed is built for success."

Planning as art

The earliest Town Planning Acts had three planning objectives: "Proper Sanitary Conditions, Amenity and Convenience". These meant clean water and drains, parks and buildings, and roads. Hence the early division of planning into architect planners who designed buildings and highway engineers who built roads and sewers.

Up to about 1950, architect visionaries were dominant despite Howard being an engineer. Planning was a new art, its canvas of town maps painted red, blue, brown and green for shops, factories, houses and parks. Patrick Abercrombie (1943) translated those three planning objectives as "Beauty, Health and Convenience." Note his order of priority. He found "the true vein of English Town development" in another architect, Raymond Unwin, designer of the first garden suburbs.

In France, Le Corbusier was tougher. "The Plan is the Generator" (*Vers une Architecture* 1923) is his most trenchant aphorism. Others include: "Without a plan, you have lack of order, and wilfulness... The great problems of to-morrow, dictated by collective necessities, put the question of "plan" in a new form [and] Modern life demands, and is waiting for, a new kind of plan, both for the house and for the city."

Yet cities have functioned and prospered for so many centuries without plans. Subjecting them to 'the great problems of tomorrow' puts designers (from Le Corbusier to Foster and Rogers etc) in charge through their credulous belief in technology and a better tomorrow. In refusing to conserve the past, as argued by Edmund Burke, John Stuart Mill and Karl Popper etc, surely it is 'starchitects' who are wilful, imposing their grand visions on us all.

- Le Corbusier (from page 53) proposed to rebuild central Paris with 60-storey tower blocks punctuating 15-storey slabs marching across parkland crisscrossed with urban highways, central railway and, on one roof, an airport.
- We had our own Corbusier in Robert Bruce who sought to redevelop central and inner Glasgow after the second world war, and succeeded in destroying all the Gorbals tenements.

- Frank Lloyd Wright went one stage further, ignoring the horizon altogether and designing a skyscraper city one mile high. This is not far removed from what is happening now in many Chinese cities.

As with the Futurists, "so little [of this mania was] thought through, so little felt" (page 71). Many twentieth century monuments will survive and be venerated. Sheffield's Park Hill, for example, is quite the equal of Bath's Royal Crescent. But future generations may notice that few of these monuments generate neighbourhoods ('creation of place') that animated the slums they replaced. Indoors they have clean water and services, but outside there is little economic activity and street life. They are less sustainable.

"One building standing alone in the countryside is experienced as a work of architecture, but bring half a dozen buildings together and an art other than architecture is made possible", which Gordon Cullen (1971) called "the art of relationship." From this art came design guides for new development, as pioneered by the Essex *Design Guide*, 1973. These attempts to improve estate design failed largely because they stuck to suburban densities, wasteful road designs and no mixed uses. Dressing up estates with a make-up of vernacular styles, building materials and roof heights is as fake as the streets are empty. The beauty of dense vernacular townscapes lies precisely in the centuries of small-scale changes by local builders and bodgers, mixed with vulgar commerce and civic dignity. Art can be involved in planning, but it is vestigial, shrunk to matters of street furniture and, however vital, tree planting.

With its emphasis on new towns and slum redevelopment, it is not surprising that early planning was largely an artistic enterprise, with *deus ex machina* status thrust upon architects with utopian visions. But Jane Jacobs was surely right when she said that, David Olsen's excellent book (1986) to the contrary, a city is not a work of art. The twentieth century did produce genuine forms of collective art in film and jazz, but their great films and records are complete works. Cities and neighbourhoods are always works in progress, the physical expression of our economic activities and social nature. There is no ideal form or finished state. Cities are constantly being adopted and adapted by all who live and work in them.

Planning as social science

In the early years, local planning in Britain was usually led by county surveyors and borough engineers, not generally renowned for their artistic temperament. Building sewers and bypasses focusses on practical sanitation and convenience rather than amenity. Post-war, however, planning adopted a more market-led scientific approach. Gradually, normative architect/planners ceded, first to engineers' 'predict and provide' computer modelling before adopting more generic 'systems planning'.

Computers (first introduced in the US) allowed engineers to design whole road networks by predicting future traffic patterns based on growth projections covering population, consumer spending, car ownership, trip length and frequency etc.

The designers' palette of physical models and detailed plans gave way to computer modelling based on statistics. Following highways, planning policy for shops, jobs, housing and schools all succumbed to modelling future scenarios.

Planning became a social science. Unlike physical scientists for whom facts tend to be either true or false, for social scientists facts give way to probabilities. There are few certainties in social behaviour, even when expressed in percentages. Predict and provide planning raises three dangers. First, the aura of scientific objectivity can be spurious. Models of human behaviour are based on a number of prior assumptions. These often reflect the modellers' own values and skew the results. (Hence the programmer's mantra of 'garbage in, garbage out'.) Most traffic models, for example, assumed that everyone wanted a car and would be granted free access to the roads.

Second, models can become self-fulfilling, being too closely aligned to 'market demand' and led by developers. If 80% of households (and rising) own a car and use foodsheds, while only 20% have no car (and falling) and use local shops, these trends largely determine the contents of any plan – more roads and foodsheds, fewer buses and local shops. Few councils willingly adopt policies that go against the majority. But (from a notice in a Nottingham headteacher's office):

> *What is popular*
> *is not always right.*
> *What is right*
> *is not always popular.*

New roads soon become congested and retail parks close local shops. Simply reinforcing current trends is hardly scientific. Predicting and providing for future demand replaced the ego of the designer and Big Brother's slum clearance with the 'rational' planner delivering the American Dream of suburban autopia. It also led to seriously unsustainable development. Dismissing objectors as NIMBYs is as risky as ignoring the few economists and journalists who predicted the bankers' crash well before 2008.

And third, whether skewed or self-fulfilling, scientific predictions can only be verified quantitatively. The quality of their outcomes and external costs cannot be measured with confidence. Had one or two cities listened to their NIMBYs earlier and stopped slum clearance, suburban sprawl, out-of-town shedscapes and urban freeways, we could have made useful comparisons. But, unlike medicine, town planning has no placebo and cities were denied any freedom to act differently as 'controls'. By projecting future needs, planners and engineers pre-determined what in previous centuries the open market and local bodies supplied, but only incrementally and retrospectively as demand became clear.

A systems approach to *Urban and Regional Planning* (McLoughlin 1969) introduced 'management science' to clarify the planning process. Cities are "the interaction of activities and connections," where planners can optimize individual behaviour patterns and group decisions by analysing costs and benefits for alternative urban strategies. Here, like any architect/planner, McLoughlin is playing at God, but he provides a useful guide to "the planning process as a series of steps in a cycle:

1. *The decision to adopt planning* and... what methods of planning to adopt...

2. *Goal formulation and the identification of objectives* for physical planning by appropriate agencies...

3. *Possible courses of action* are studied with the aid of models... These studies show how the system might behave as it changes through time under... a variety of... private actions and public activities and interventions.

4. *Evaluation* of these courses of action in order to select an operational course...

5. *Action* to implement the plan including both direct works and the continuous control of public and private proposals for change. The essence of such control is to study the impact on the system of proposed changes in order to see whether or not they would deflect the system from the course charted for it in the plan... As the process goes on it becomes clear that we must...

6. *Review* the plan and its control mechanisms from time to time, in minor ways at shorter intervals and in major ways at larger intervals. This is necessary because we are dealing with a probabilistic system, one in which changes cannot be foreseen with certainty..." (McLoughlin's italics).

The plan is still the generator but planning becomes an iterative process. This was radical. No longer was the process Abercrombie's 'survey, analysis, plan', or Buchanan's predict and provide from whence, once complete, they moved onto the next challenge. Now, planners had to review progress, repeat the process and rewrite the plans perhaps every ten years. This recognized the importance of feedback and continuity, at least in planning if not on the ground.

When the government sought to transform development control, its planning process had seven key stages (draft PPS on *Development Management*, 2009):

1. "A positive and proactive approach to place shaping
2. Putting planning policy into action
3. Front loading
4. A proportionate approach
5. Effective engagement
6. Proactive delivery
7. Monitoring and reviewing outcomes" (CLG in association with *Planning*).

With such headings, desire to read further dries up. Only the seventh element is clear and welcome. Monitoring and reviewing the impact of major development is obviously crucial. But it is also (all so) obvious. What all planning frameworks and government advice ignore is whether to adopt planning at all – McLoughlin's first stage. Do we need 'a positive and proactive approach to place shaping' if the place is already shaped and works well. Or, if the place is not ideal, could one or two small schemes improve it for a fraction of the cost and disruption?

London's roads illustrate both artistic and scientific approaches. Abercrombie's London plan (1944) proposed a spider's web of five orbital and nine radial roads in green wedges for the capital. In the 1960s, the new GLC produced a London Traffic

Survey, finding that drivers made twice as many trips as those without cars (averaging 1.87 or 0.93 trips/day). To accommodate this increasing traffic and reduce congestion, the GLC modified Abercrombie's spider's web, with four orbitals (including one in the green belt) and fourteen radials, all now urban motorways rather than express arterial roads. The Layfield Inquiry approved (with modifications) the new roads in 1973, before the whole scheme was dropped. Peter Hall's *Planning Disasters* (1992) includes this saga: "In this way, they [the relatively small number of objectors] won. The technical-professional planning process was simply overcome by the political planning process." His "Analysis of a Negative Disaster" suggests regret that the motorways were not built rather than (a double negative) approval for an early NIMBY triumph of local people changing planning policy.

In the end, both planning approaches are wrong-headed. Whether an idealistic and normative art, or a predictive and market-led science, both accord with Jeremy Bentham's (1748-1832) principle that government should seek "the greatest happiness of the greatest number." Planning may improve the homes of the poor or reflect the wants of the 'silent majority', but as schemes got bigger, so reactions became louder. Instead of seeking progress with minimum disruption and focussing on the more specific needs of minorities, both planning approaches became fascistic bulldozers.

Permit me a short digression. "Genius is 1% inspiration, 99% perspiration." (Thomas Edison) This applies equally to art and science. The last century saw the reversal of this creative spectrum. Since Marcel Duchamp put a urinal in an art gallery, we now venerate art that is 99% inspiration and 1% perspiration. An unmade bed took days to arrange, a wall of coloured dots was painted by someone else and a noble shark perhaps chose to rot in quiet dignity in its tank rather than remain endlessly gawped at under the cartoonist's clever caption. In science, it seems that early on, Sigmund Freud uncovered childhood sexual abuse in many of his patients. Rather than raise a scandal and take on reactionary Vienna (with at least 99% perspiration), he invented the concept of 'interpreting' dreams, projecting myths onto the subconscious involving the superego, Oedipus and penis envy etc.

The first century of planning has produced its own conceptualists who have been equally dogmatic and disruptive. From 'homes fit for heroes' and 'cities built for speed' to 'cities for constant change' and 'a presumption in favour of all development', the emphasis has been on inspiration and the grand scheme, largely ignoring what is there and how cities actually work. Our first urban naturalist, Jane Jacobs (from chapter 3) defined the essential features of successful cities as high density, old buildings, short streets and mixed uses. All four have been largely negated in the first century of formal planning.

Planning as legislation

Our third approach, suggested by *formal* planning, is the political process. Utopian and predictive planning schemes all required legal powers, and these were based on normative standards. From the outset, legislation had three major impacts:

- planned development replaced 'organic' growth,
- local planning, largely controlled by government, became more uniform, and
- governments (naturally tending to think big) encouraged or enforced much more ambitious development schemes.

The roots of planning lie in the great Public Health Acts dating back to 1848, and Housing Acts starting with the *Housing of the Working Classes Act 1890*. The following (from Desmond Heap 1982 and 1996) summarize the key planning acts.

Planning proper began with *The Housing, Town Planning, etc., Act 1909*. Local authority 'town planning schemes' to control new development and secure "proper sanitary conditions, amenity and convenience" shifted planning from building improvements to area planning. However, only the Local Government Board permitted a council to prepare a new scheme, and only Parliament could approve the scheme.

The Housing, Town Planning, etc., Act 1919 made town planning schemes obligatory for larger local authorities with final approval by the Local Government Board, (then under the Ministry of Health). From the outset, planning was defined, controlled and approved by government.

The Town and Country Planning Act 1932 consolidated four Acts on health, housing, town planning and local government, and now made planning comprehensive, covering new development, the existing built-up areas and surrounding countryside. Councils still needed permission to prepare a planning scheme, and approval before implementation.

The Town and Country Planning Act 1947 was a milestone. It consolidated local authority powers to undertake development themselves, reduced the number of planning authorities and strengthened their compulsory purchase powers. New planning principles were introduced, like 'positive planning' and flexible 'development plans' to replace the rigid planning schemes, and all 'development' was prohibited without prior consent.

The Town and Country Planning Act 1968 created the two tiers of 'Structure Plan' and 'Local Plan', and what is now the quasi-independent Planning Inspectorate. All planning law was then repealed and consolidated in *The Town and Country Planning Act 1971* – plus the *Town and Country Planning (Amendment) Act 1972*!

The Local Government Reorganization Act 1974 created the two-tier local government structure. 53 county councils (including six new metropolitan councils) would prepare structure plans, 369 district or borough councils the more specific local plans. The 10,200 parish councils, including many sizeable towns, were effectively disenfranchised (where many still refer to the *Local Government Disorganization Act*). Difficulties also emerged in separating overlapping functions in district and county.

A plethora of planning-related Acts followed, covering Conservation Areas and Listed Buildings, a development land tax (and its repeal), Stop Notices, Control of Office Development (and its Cessation), Minerals extraction and reinstatement of land, public Access to Information in local government, Planning Compensation,

The Local Government Act 1985, which abolished the GLC and the six metropolitan counties, and The Housing and Planning Act 1986 which introduced Simplified Planning Zones.

Finally, *The Planning Act 1990* was the third major consolidation Act (after 1947 and 1971). Here I gave up. Since 1910, there have been 36 Planning Acts and over 1,200 Statutory Instruments.

Table 32: Planning legislation: 1910-2010+

• 1910s	1
• 1920s	0
• 1930s	1
• 1940s	6
• 1950s	8
• 1960s	7
• 1970s	173
• 1980s	228
• 1990s	230
• 2000s	379
• 2010s	217

http://www.legislation.gov.uk/title/planning

Heap (1996) points out that planning was "a constantly evolving process... Town planning law never stops! Within days of the consolidating Act of 1971 receiving the Royal Assent on October 28, 1971, a short amending Bill was introduced into Parliament on November 3, 1971." He also quotes Lord Justice Harman from 1962. "Hard indeed are the paths of local authorities in striving to administer the town and country planning legislation of recent years. It is a sorry comment on the law and those who administer it that between the years 1947 and 1960 they had succeeded in so bedevilling the administration of the legislation that Parliament was compelled to come to the rescue and remove a great portion of it from the purview of the courts. Not for nothing was I offered a book yesterday called *Encyclopedia of Planning*. It is a subject which stinks in the noses of the public, and not without reason. Local Authorities, until they have been recently rescued, have had practically to employ conveyancing counsel to settle these notices which they serve in the interests of planning the countryside or the towns which they control. Instead of trying to make this thing simple, lawyers succeeded day by day in making it more difficult and less comprehensible until it has reached a stage where it is very much like the state of the land which this plaintiff has brought about by his operations – an eyesore, a wilderness and a scandal." (Britt vs Bucks CC [1964] Q.B. 77 @ 87)

Governments were aware of problems. The Planning Advisory Group (PAG), reporting in 1967 to the Minister of Housing and Local Government, identified three. "*First*, [the planning system] has become overloaded and subject to delays and cumbersome procedures. *Second*, there has been inadequate participation by the individual citizen in the planning process, and insufficient regard to his interests. *Third*, the system has been better as a negative control on undesirable development than as a positive stimulus to the creation of a good environment." Unlike Harman, PAG seems to identify local councils as the guilty party, not 'the legislative eyesore, wilderness and scandal'.

The first problem of overloading and delays has simply mushroomed, as table 33 shows. (Lest we forget, excessive statutory flux and overload affects all functions of local councils, including health care, education, the environment and public transport as well as planning.) Local plans have also become increasingly complex.

- The original town planning schemes became development plans in 1947, then two-tier structure and local plans after 1968.
- From 1998, structure plans had to conform to new regional economic and spatial strategies (RESs and RSSs) produced by the nine regional development agencies.
- From 2004, two-tier plans were replaced with local development frameworks (LDFs), which include a core strategy, a statement of community involvement and any mix of sustainability appraisals, an infrastructure delivery strategy, an annual monitoring report and a local development scheme with proposals map and site allocations plan, plus optional local area action plans, supporting technical appraisals, local development orders and simplified planning zones.
- And in 2014, a new lower tier of neighbourhood plans was introduced, to be drawn up by local people (usually with consultants), but to comply with the LDF and *NPPF*.

These plans remain subject to central control and approval, first through the Local Government Board, and from 1919 to a succession of different ministers. Once local people were involved, post 1971, plans were subject to public inquiries under Planning Inspectors and then, from 1998, to regional priorities. This loose mesh of government ministers, civil servants, regional development agencies and planning inspectors, with frequent recourse to lawyers and judges, creates long delays and usually puts national priorities above local diversity and property law above local plans.

With national priorities and programmes in constant flux, requiring new laws, statutory instruments and government guidance, it creates havoc in the planning system for all councils, inspectors, judges and even Lord Chief Justices. It puts local councils at a serious disadvantage to lawyers who, as Harman noted, are making law "more difficult and less comprehensible." This is 'the politics of change', which led the inimitable Chris Shepley (past president of the RTPI and former head of the Planning Inspectorate) to write that, "After a decade of constant change, we have now entered a period of genuine chaos." (*Planning* 6/5/2011) Yet the flood of bumf persists.

Leaving PAGs second problem of no public voice till later, the third problem was that planning is better at negative control than as a positive stimulus for good environments. This might be the subtext for twentieth century planning. Since 1979, development control has got much worse (or more in line with government ideology), while good environments are still not being created. The sameness of our suburbs and tower blocks, urban freeways and ring roads, shopping malls and retail parks is not because we lack creative planners. We will only reverse the prevailing zeitgeist of down-market quality in pursuit of maximum profits and minimum government spending with more negative development control officers, not more 'pro-active' and weaker.

The *National Planning Policy Framework* (*NPPF1*) sought to simplify the whole process. Launched in 2012 with some fanfare, over 1,000 pages of government planning advice were replaced by 59 pages, supported by a dozen short *National Policy Statements* covering energy, transport, water and waste management.

The revised *NPPF* (2018) summarizes the scope and functions of statutory planning, under 'plan-making' and 'decision-taking'. Plans must be 'succinct and up-to-date', look ahead at least 15 years, cover all strategic issues and provide the framework for non-strategic or neighbourhood plans. Strategic issues include all likely commercial development (providing housing, shops and jobs etc), all infrastructure requirements for transport, water, energy and waste, and all public investment in schools, health and culture. Councils must also conserve the natural, built and historic environment, and "address climate change mitigation and adaptation" – without defining what makes development sustainable

The problems with the 'plan-making' process are that comprehensive plans cannot be succinct and, with planning cut to the bone (along with all other council services), it is nigh impossible to keep them up-to-date. And without a current plan, major decisions will be removed from local control. Looking ahead 15 years largely means predict and provide planning, but predictions for housing based on local need must conform to government targets. Planning policies deemed unreasonable will be thrown out by planning inspectors.

Yet town planning only comes into sharp focus at local level. Formerly, planning departments could be divided into yes-men and no-men (and women). After many happy years in planning, this may slander some of my former colleagues, but consider the role of the creatives and controllers. 'Forward planners' (rather than backward planners?) create positive visions for urban growth and seek development to match. But every plan is subject to government approval, every council restricted by financial constraints and creativity hampered by the *ultra vires* rule. Occasionally a council breaks rank. In 2003 the London borough of Merton made all larger commercial developments generate at least 10% of their energy renewably on-site. Five years later, the 'Merton rule' became national policy. Other creative policies, to reduce traffic, lower speed limits, delegate planning decisions and protect community assets like pubs, post offices and village greens, have all been resisted or delayed by government, tied down in legal process or diluted to produce too little too late.

With an up-to-date plan, development controllers then find reasons to refuse (or improve) all planning applications. Now, the *NPPF* would have even 'development managers' 'approach decisions on proposed development in a positive and creative way.' This upends the purpose of planning control and ignores the PAG finding that 'the system has been better as a negative control on undesirable development than as a positive stimulus to the creation of a good environment.' Today, according to the RTPI, 80% of all planning applications, and a staggering 90% of major schemes, are approved. This must be wrong. Too many councils are almost certainly making too many wrong decisions largely because they must. Few believe that big is better.

Refusing a good major scheme is regrettable but eventually another, perhaps better, scheme will emerge. A bad scheme is destructive, costly and difficult to adapt. It also sets an awful precedent. The bizarre City of London skyscrapers only took off in response to Canary Wharf. Then, when Johnson was mayor, he approved 400 phallic icons in town centres, beside parks and anywhere by the riverside – despite electoral promises to refuse all new towers. Even Battersea power station, a true icon in the capital, will be largely eclipsed by towers quite alien to anything outside modern Chinese and Persian Gulf cities.

What most of us would regard as unnecessary and undesirable development, the *NPPF* insists is sustainable. Their gross scale, environmental intrusion, social disruption and carbon footprints are only matched by the benefits enjoyed by their developers, owners and landlords. And many private monuments in regeneration schemes depend on government subsidy and compulsory purchase (see below).

Refusing more small schemes and extensions from local firms and homeowners is perplexing. National Parks have a history of resisting small, self-build energy-efficient dwellings while allowing (or having to allow) large mineral extraction, roadstone and concrete batching plants and typical suburban housing estates that could be anywhere. In one National Park, Dai and Maria... had built a modest family house of timber on their smallholding. It was invisible from any road, unlike the bungalow estate outside their nearest town. Two years later, the building was discovered by a park officer and refused retrospective planning permission. The authority then refused permission to convert the adjacent roofless stone barn (as the walls had to be slightly raised for internal head room). Eventually, it was allowed on appeal. In another tourism pressure area, my wife bought a cottage in her birthplace to convert into an activity centre for small groups of schoolchildren. When asked about the local planning authority, the estate agent said "When you're dealing with **** district council, Mr Williams, you're down to a vest and pants job." (He was right. We were refused permission. Today, that district is part of the unitary county council which may be poetic justice.)

Refusing small developments and extensions stifles personal freedom and the growth of a local vernacular. Permitting large developments based on developer profits and designer egos, often facilitated by government funding and legal powers, is too deterministic and the antithesis of organic growth.

Since the impact of most development is only local, control should also be local, with arbitration or appeals limited to planning inspectors. Government only needs audit checks to guard against corruption. As a rule of thumb, we should allow most small schemes and refuse most large schemes as being unsustainable. And there are few larger than our current regeneration schemes.

The regeneration game

Regeneration, like civilization, is a big concept, pregnant with potential. It means either "to replace (a body part or tissue) by new growth", or "to change something radically and for the better" (*Penguin ED*). Crabs can regrow a lost leg, urban regeneration is radical change – rarely for the better. Holding local councils responsible for the failure to tackle local deprivation and responding belatedly to the PAG criticism that planning lacked positive stimulus, from 1969 central government developed 'regeneration programmes' under the generic Urban Programme.

Regeneration programmes included Urban Development Corporations, Estate Action and City Challenge programmes, then Single Regeneration Budgets, Action Zones, Neighbourhood Renewal Funds and New Deals for Communities before a modified slum clearance programme called Housing Market Renewal was revived in 2002. They shared three important features: a focus on the most deprived economies or neighbourhoods; central control managed by local partnerships rather than councils; and guaranteed funding from three to ten years, except Sure Start that was open-ended.

Problems emerged from the outset. Councils lost key local functions. Michael (helicopter) Heseltine based his regeneration programmes on American practice. According to one Boston (or Baltimore) official: "Regeneration needs

- politicians with long-term vision,
- developers with a social conscience, and
- officials with entrepreneurial skills."

This mild fascism meant that people were to be regenerated rather than involved. The early programmes focussed on commercial rather than economic development, as in the first City Challenge programmes and Urban Development Corporations in Liverpool and London Docklands. Each Board comprised local employers, developers, councillors and senior officers, with minimal government oversight to guard against 'misapplication of funds'. In at least one UDC, never properly audited, it seems that public contracts were simply shared out among Board members. Significantly, funding for later programmes all went through the relevant local authorities.

Funding the early programmes was also skewed; over half the UDC funding was spent in one of the wealthiest cities in the world.

Table 33 Urban Development Corporations, Grant in Aid (£m at 1981 prices)

•	Birmingham Heartlands	29.5
•	Black Country	439.9
•	Bristol	126.6
•	Central Manchester	116.5
•	Leeds	88.3
•	London Docklands	2,528.2
•	Merseyside	463.5
•	Plymouth	14.6
•	Teesside	407.3
•	Trafford Park	263.9
•	Tyne and Wear	390.6
Total		4,869.9

Source: Hansard

From the mid 1990s, 'bricks and mortar' schemes (mostly tinsheds and tarmac) switched to 'hearts and minds' programmes. The Single Regeneration Budget (SRB) targeted areas of serious multiple deprivation, as measured by unemployment, crime, school and health figures, housing and environmental conditions. This meant improving local services rather than local economies with a more comprehensive and collective approach. Boards were replaced by broader Local Strategic Partnerships (LSPs) representing schools, health, police and voluntary sectors, as well as council and large employers.

Each programme was tightly controlled by civil servants. They vetted all programme bids and required quarterly progress reports with financial statements, perhaps recognizing the stink, if not the facts, of local corruption in some earlier programmes. As with teachers and trains, it is odd that civil servants are given so much control with so little relevant experience.

From inception to approval, each programme accelerated alarmingly. Programme design was leisurely with background research, clear objectives and mechanisms that involved the Cabinet Office, relevant government departments and the Treasury, plus consultations. Once launched, each area had to set up its LSP to prepare a programme bid, usually within six weeks. This allowed local agencies and groups a few weeks to prepare their own project bids with clear targets, innovation, risk assessments and exit strategies. Finally, all bids had to be collated and approved by the LSP into its bid, often within 24 hours, before submission to the regional offices and Westminster for final approval or rejection.

Everything was top-heavy. Every local project officer reported to their local programme manager who reported to the LSP, which liaised with the regional government offices, who deferred to their departmental heads in Westminster and thence to the Treasury. Competent programme managers were crucial. Some took a few months getting to grips with the job and the last year looking for their next job. And a good manager leaving mid-term could cause serious disruption.

- Every project in every programme was target-driven. The SRB programme had about 70 targets to choose from, covering the following:
- jobs and training numbers, from jobs created to teachers placed in business (1L),
- new businesses included numbers advised (2D),
- number of homes built, improved, tenant-managed or brought back into use (3D),
- community safety, like youths attending crime prevention schemes (5D(ii)),
- physical improvements from new roads (6D(i)) to recycling schemes (6F),
- numbers using new health, sport and cultural facilities (7B (i-iii)),
- number of community groups, volunteers and capacity building initiatives (8F),
- total funding of programme, including private sector 'leverage' (9A(iii)), and
- number of new child-care places.

Every project had to report quarterly on the outputs achieved against their targets. Thus was regeneration measured. The following comments come from over 50 SRB- and NRF-funded groups that I met.

- Overstating outputs, prepared at short notice with little consultation, put the project at risk, creating stress. Understating them showed lack of ambition.
- 'Joined-up thinking' meant that every project within every programme had to conform to national objectives. Local priorities were secondary.
- While many programmes sought innovative projects with all the risks attached, most areas needed basic services for known demand, not 'rocket science'.
- Many local projects had to rely on 'community infrastructure organizations' (like CVSs) to liaise with the LSP. Like programme managers, some CVSs funded by the programme were not up to the job.
- Targets became 'output mania'. Quality outcomes were generally ignored, being unmeasurable. Projects involving young people, for example, often achieved real change in personal skills and confidence for some whose life experience had included drug abuse, early parenthood, family stress or homelessness.
- Training targets focussed on employability with qualifications that then required Ofsted inspections, with all the stress and formalities involved. Non-vocational courses for specific groups uncomfortable in formal courses, like single parents, disaffected youths and old people, were sidelined, despite positive personal and social outcomes.
- Programmes were generally inflexible. Falling short of quarterly milestones (or 'millstones') of progress put future funding in jeopardy. Asked how they coped with such stress, some groups and project managers, smiling, said that they

simply told lies. (This truth may well reflect what happens under most 'command management' regimes, whether mega-corps' or Stalin's 5-year plans.)

Value for money, measured as funding per output, also raised comment.

- Funding was skewed towards the various statutory agencies – councils, health authorities, colleges and the police – often "for doing little more than their day job." Community projects were the poor relations. Thus, in one of the safest districts in the country (in the east Midlands), the police took almost one third of the NRF budget for community safety.

- 'Capacity building' projects were encouraged. Yet, while a £25m SRB programme in east London earmarked £1m for community-led projects, it then commissioned a national opinion pollster to do an initial community survey, when a few local groups could have done the job probably better for a fifth of the price, gained skills and raised their local profiles.

- Small businesses, social enterprises, community groups and voluntary agencies find all government (and European) grant applications over-complex and time-consuming. One head, managing a school budget of £750,000, sought a £30,000 school transport grant but gave up when faced with the paperwork. Some simply employed a funding officer or consultant.

- And in the funding stream of all these programmes were civil servants to assess and monitor programmes, local managers and funding officers to co-ordinate bids and liaise between partners, and consultants to advise projects, programmes and partnerships. This significantly reduced local control and funding in the deprived areas. And funding was considerable.

From table 34 overleaf, we were spending an average of £1.5 billion a year on these regeneration programmes. This was about a third of the annual capital spend or 5% of revenue spending by all English councils. Yet outcomes were modest. Few community projects secured mainstream funding beyond the life of the various programmes. Sure Start, perhaps the most successful programme, gradually fell away with severe local council cuts (see chapter 10). Few areas were genuinely regenerated to become models for other areas. Most still languish or have been transformed by redevelopment. New offices, restaurants and flats improve local statistics but are of little benefit to existing residents, most of whom are forced to eke out their tough existence elsewhere.

Regeneration has shifted back to 'bricks and mortar' (now mostly concrete and glass) redevelopment. *Towards an Urban Renaissance* (Urban Task Force 1999) included positive policies for empty property, VAT, contaminated land, urban densities and a Renaissance Fund for local groups. However, the general emphasis was similar to earlier government programmes. The summary report included:

- town improvement zones, with spatial masterplans, urban design frameworks and public realm strategies;

- Urban Priority Areas (UPAs) "where regeneration can be undertaken by dedicated [development vehicles], assisted by streamlined planning decisions, easier land acquisition, tax incentives and additional resources";
- "speedier compulsory purchase orders," all funded and controlled by central government;
- a new PPS (planning policy statement) to define urban regeneration, with new powers over the UPAs allowing the secretary of state to "take action against authorities that fail to deliver planning permissions within a reasonable period," by overruling them, and finally, without any sense of irony or history,
- "A new Urban Policy Board [to] co-ordinate the implementation of urban policy at every level." This simply revives the Local Government Board of 1886 (see page 342 below).

Table 34: Regeneration programmes, 1977-2007

Generic Title Specific Programme	Cost (£bn)
Policy for Inner Cities 1977	
• Urban Programme 1969 – 91	£3
Action for Cities 1988	
• Estate Action 1985 – 97	£2.4
• Urban Development Corporations 1981/94	£5
• Housing Action Trusts 1991/04	£1
• City Challenge 1992/98	£1.2
• Single Regeneration Budget 1994/02	£5.7
• European Regional Development Fund 1994/06	£3.6
• Training and Enterprise Councils 1996/01	£6.1
Bringing Britain Together NSNR 1998	
• Sure Start 1999/06	£21
Towards an Urban Renaissance 1999	
• New Deal for Communities 1998	£2
• Education Action Zone 1998/03	£0.3
• Health Action Zone 1999/02	£0.3
Sustainable Communities Plan 2003	
• Rural Development Action 2001/08	£6.1
Strong and Prosperous Communities 2006	
• Neighbourhood Renewal Fund 2001/08	£2.8
• Housing Market Renewal Programme 2002/11	£2.2
Total	£44bn

2008 Source: Hansard

Triggers for regeneration have become increasingly bizarre. The Olympic park in east London and a new concert hall in Birmingham perhaps, but football stadiums, a high speed station at Ebbsfleet or, extraordinarily, a super casino in Blackpool suggest panic. And where £44bn was spent on regeneration over 30 years (table 34 above), in 2013, the top 100 regeneration schemes in Britain required total funds of almost £80 billion to be spread perhaps over ten years:

- schemes ranged from £122 million to £13.460 billion (the Nine Elms scheme discussed in chapter 9),
- eight of the top ten were in London costing £38.735 billion, and
- £25.5 billion of private and £17 billion of public funds had been committed (*Planning* with *Regeneration and Renewal* 9/4/2013).

After nearly 40 years, regeneration projects have produced:

- few politicians with the long-term vision needed to reduce their megalithic complexity and inhuman scale;
- few developers with a social conscience. Most minimize social housing and seek further reductions during construction; and
- few officials with entrepreneurial skills. The risks are borne by taxpayers, most of the profits go to developers, banks and investors.

If half of that £80bn is public funding, spread over ten years, local councils and community groups could surely achieve more tangible and permanent results, with a much greater variety of solutions and far fewer bulldozers leaching money out of the area for developers, landlords and consultants. Even increasing welfare benefits might work, but we don't know. The 'municipal gospel' was gradually stamped out by the Local Government Board, and Victorian Salvation Army hostels, Methodist 'missions' and non-Conformist 'settlements' have not been replaced by today's secular agents, except as food banks. As argued in chapter 2, physical solutions are often irrelevant (or counter-productive) to strategic problems of poverty, unemployment, petty crime and under-resourced schools and health facilities.

Let us leave grand regeneration schemes and turn to a specific planning problem.

'Increasing housing choice'

After more than a century of planning and four decades of an unregulated market, how have we arrived at a housing crisis for perhaps 20% of the population?

From 1890, councils were permitted to build houses for the working classes and since 1945 they were major housebuilders. Under both Harold Macmillan and Harold Wilson, housing was a numbers game, reaching 378,324 new houses in 1969, roughly 50/50 council (and housing association) homes for rent and private homes for sale. Housing, though not ideal, was not a problem.

From 1961, all council houses had to conform to Parker Morris 'egalitarian' space standards (page 228 above). Used to justify the last throes of slum clearance, they also produced uniformity and fewer homes. Typical standards were between

900 sq ft and 1,050 sq ft for six people, 720 to 800 sq ft for four people, and 310, 480 and 610 sq ft for one, two and three person flats. These normative standards normalized domestic life. With minimum sizes specified for kitchens and bedrooms, the large, all-purpose parlour disappeared, in which (forgive the stereotypes) 'our mum cooked and ironed, dad washed in't bath and read t'paper, son Joey mended t'bike while our lasses did th'homework'. From Parker Morris, family life became a little less sociable.

The Essex *Design Guide for Residential Areas* (1973) justified these norms. "New houses are built to last at least sixty years. During this time, higher incomes and changing life styles are likely to lead to families needing more space in the home. It is therefore important that new houses do not become obsolete, due to their size or plan form." If space were critical for family life, this would make obsolete most Tudor and Jacobean cottages with their pokey rooms, sloping floors, low ceilings, small doors and cramped stairways. Yet, after three or four centuries, they remain some of the most sought-after properties in the county.

Space standards ignored location. Those families in Cromac (page 56 above) clearly led cramped lives in 500 sq ft cottages, but enjoyed extended families, neighbourly streets, local shops, central location and cheap rents. Today, many single Japanese in Tokyo live in less than half the Parker Morris standard of 310 sq ft. Larger homes at lower densities in central locations would be unaffordable. Demolishing most of our remaining terraced housing under 'market renewal' was government vandalism.

Parker Morris standards were rescinded in 1980, although both English Partnerships (in 2008) and the Mayor of London (in 2011) have revived even more generous space standards for their public housing. Essentially, building bigger homes 'just in case' of future demand means building fewer homes 'just in time' for those who need them now. In a skewed housing market, this opportunity cost is borne, as ever, by those at the bottom of the housing ladder. Like congestion, high density terraces reflect high land values where people are happy with modest homes in return for urban life.

While social housing accounted for almost 30% of the total stock, private renting was largely controlled and homelessness was not a problem. *The Housing Act 1980* transformed this market. Council housebuilding stopped and every council tenant had the 'right to buy' their home.

Table 35: Great Britain housing tenure (%age), 1984–2012

Tenure	1984	2001	2012
Owner occupied	60.6	69.8	64.0
Private rented	9.5	10.2	17.9
Local authority	27.4	13.3	7.8
Housing association	2.4	6.7	10.1
	99.9	100.0	99.8

Source: ONS, *Annual Abstract*

40 years later, social housing is less than 18%, the gap largely filled by private landlords and the homeless. Selling nearly three quarters of our council houses, to halve social housing and double private rented properties to the same 17.9%, has all-too-predictably made housing increasingly expensive. Market rents, replacing fair rents, enrich landlords at the expense of tenants. 'Affordable rents' are now set at 80% of commercial rents rather than by housing association rents, while austerity lowered the poverty threshold for receiving state benefits. Neo-conomists fail to see that deregulating markets creates 'asymmetries' between landlords and tenants, as between employers and workers.

Nor did the government save money. Capital savings were simply replaced by revenue spending. "In 1975 more than 80% of public expenditure on housing went on supply-side capital funding (building homes and their upkeep), with rent support and rebates low. By 2000, things had gone into reverse with, as the [*Together at Home* IPPR] report states, "85% of spending being routed through demand-side revenue funding in the form of housing benefit". Today 40% to 50% of the annual £23bn cost of housing benefit goes to private landlords, many of whom have taken advantage of buy-to-let schemes and used the shortage of social housing to drive up rents... Millions cannot hope to buy because prices are too high, supply is limited as builders see little demand, and banks are reluctant to lend. So people are forced into an overheated rented sector." (Toby Helm, *The Observer* 31/3/13)

The ideology of a property-owning democracy is not achievable. Some people can't afford to buy and others prefer to rent. Home ownership peaked at 73.3% in 2008, but is now returning to 1979 levels. Norway (82.8%), Spain, Portugal and Greece have significantly higher levels, the Netherlands, France and Denmark are comparable, while Austria (57.3%), Germany (53.3%) and Switzerland (44.0%) provide more social housing (Wikipedia 2015). Our unregulated housing market creates serious stress for young people and the lower paid.

"The interest of the landlord is always opposed to the interests of every other class in the community." (David Ricardo, 1817) In this market, it is in the interests of all volume housebuilders, banks and landlords to retain a housing scarcity. The more unscrupulous have invented another fiddle, the builder selling the ground freehold to a 'landlord' before selling the houses. These homeowners now have to pay a ground rent that, doubling every five to ten years, soon makes their homes unsaleable. So serious was this swindle that the government has actually stopped it – except for those already stuck with it: either stuck where they are or force to sell at a depressed price to landlords who then simply pass the ground rents onto tenants.

Building lots more houses would lead to lower house prices, eventually. But over 40 years, despite increasing demand, housebuilders have not increased their supply to replace the loss of council housebuilding. In a civilized society, this would be viewed as a 'market failure', but who to blame?

- Local councils approve planning applications for 200,000 to 250,000 new houses every year, yet only about 190,000 are actually built, see table 36 below. Through the Local Government Association (LGA), many councils claim that housebuilders are not 'building' homes but land banks with planning permission.
- The government vets every core strategy to ensure there is sufficient land for new housing to meet demand. Those councils without an approved plan will have housing applications approved by the minister. There is therefore no shortage of housing land.
- Housebuilders, through their Home Builders Federation, complain of planning delays and unreasonable conditions. Yet their underperformance against planning permissions seems to support the LGA. Housebuilders and their banks also have a conflict of interest. Building more houses would increase turnover but lower house prices. Keeping low their house completions maintains high prices and profits. They also make substantial donations to whichever party is in power. Now government offers first time buyers significant financial help onto the housing ladder, costing taxpayers some £4 billion pa. This subsidy largely goes to increase house prices and housebuilders' profits. As with Enron's Matrix programme, political donations can reap significant rewards.

In this search for scapegoats rather than solutions, governments have left it to the volume housebuilders and their banks to 'make good' the serious reduction of affordable homes. *NPPF2* section 5 (paras 59-79) "Delivering a sufficient supply of homes" at least improves on the earlier version "Delivering a wide choice of high quality homes" (the mantra of 'wider choice' having moved to sustainable transport). It starts well: to provide sufficient land where it is needed, meet the needs of "groups with specific housing requirements" and develop "land with permission... without unnecessary delay." The text then undoes the intentions with two 10% rules.

First, it only expects 10% of housing land to be brownfield sites, compared with an earlier government target of 60% (see below). New housing "can often be best achieved ['sometimes' in *NPPF1*] through... larger scale development, such as new settlements or extensions to existing villages and towns." Green field development suits the volume housebuilders but is unsustainable. Belatedly, it now requires local councils to monitor whether sites with permission are actually being developed or simply land-banked, but with no powers to withdraw permissions left unbuilt. It is silent on housing density and intensification. It is silent on the potential of vacant houses except in rural areas. It is restrictive on infill and windfall sites, which must "provide a reliable source of supply" and not include residential gardens. In its silence on the need to conserve existing homes and bring vacant properties back into use, while subsidizing new green field housing with zero VAT, infrastructure subsidies and the Help to Buy scheme, the *NPPF* contradicts basic sustainable principles.

Second, it only expects "at least 10% of the homes" on all larger sites to be affordable (and none expected on small sites). This also is much lower than previously required, and the affordable homes can be provided off-site where "an appropriate financial contribution [can be] robustly justified." This is highly contentious. It ignores the common practice of developers who negotiate minimum levels for approval and then, during construction, renegotiate to reduce that level. This often succeeds in Conservative boroughs happy to reduce typical Labour voters in their area. And in mixed tenure schemes, it is silent on the practice of separate access for social tenants and private residents. Hence two new terms in our planning lexicon: 'class cleansing' in schemes where tenants are removed from wealthy areas, and 'poor doors' for tenants in mixed tenure schemes.

An early example of moving affordable housing off-site occurred in central London. Designed by Rogers Stirk Harbour + Partners, the scheme included two towers for luxury flats and a third for affordable flats. During construction, the developers sought permission to change the affordable block to commercial offices in return for several £millions. They argued that, such were the construction costs, a mortgage for an affordable flat would cost more than £75,000 a year – affordable only for a couple of primary headteachers or similar. Incredibly, the Labour council approved the change. (Ironically, some of the luxury flat owners (who don't like net curtains) now object to being overlooked by visitors to the new Tate Modern extension cafe.) Separating owners and tenants is now common practice. We don't know how many of mayor Johnson's 400 tower blocks have benefited from this cynical policy. Whatever the figure (regard 400 as a Johnson variable), it increases profits from higher house prices and it bamboozles debt-laden councils unused to £multi-million payments with no strings attached. But in segregating the wealthy and *hoi polloi*, it denies 'a strong, healthy and just society' from *NPPF1*.

Whatever the target for affordable homes and where they are sited, the *NPPF* then ignores how new houses are actually used. Affordable homes are used as homes, but many private houses for sale are used as second homes, holiday lets, airbnb, time shares or simply vacant investments. It is also silent on the common practice of providing ground floor car parking in urban housing blocks instead of homes.

Overall, *NPPF2* is a charter for the volume housebuilders, and ignores the difference between market demand and social need. Consider the two extremes. In England, households living in temporary accommodation (in B&B hotels, hostels, women's refuges, social and private sector accommodation) rose from 37,900 in 1989 to over 100,000 in 2005, falling to 61,930 in 2014 (House of Commons *Briefing Paper* no 02110, 17/8/2015). It is now about 150,000. Mortgage repossessions are a factor. In 2005, following a sustained housing boom, there were 14,500 repossessions; in 2009, 48,900 when that boom went bust. Temporary housing and excessive rents create poverty and stress, rent defaults, mental and marital breakdowns, inadequate social care, homelessness and street begging, and affect up to one quarter of our children.

At the other end, "a wide choice of high quality homes" includes this development. "Set around six lakes in 260ha of stunning scenery, [it] comprises 160 timber and glass luxury homes perched on the banks of former gravel pits and supported by concierge housekeeping. Advertised as being only 90 minutes from London by car... the homes start at £775,000 and rise to £2.2 million." (*Planning* 4/7/2008) Marketed as second homes (would any choose to live there?), the whole concept is unsustainable from designer's first doodle to residents' drive time. Yet even today, such schemes can be approved if they include, say, energy efficient homes and electric chargers.

In an unregulated housing market, architects, developers, landlords and bankers prefer profits of 20% to 50% building mansions and comfortable estates, rather than 5% to 10% building affordable homes for councils, housing associations and co-ops. Yet investing in social housing would pay for itself by reducing housing benefits and temporary accommodation, and ensure that everyone is housed. Second homes for commuters around some gravel pits in the Cotswolds are just one legacy of right wing ideology which wilfully ignores the difference between choice and need.

Is there a housing shortage?

The media is uncertain. 'We need to have more homes' (*The Observer* 31/3/13) is the usual headline, but sometimes 'Do we really need to build more houses?' appears (*The Guardian* 15/2/14).

Table 36: Great Britain population and dwellings (000's), 1984–2012

	1984	2012	Av increase pa	% increase
Population	54,909	61,881	49.0	12.70%
Dwellings	21,654	27,008	191.2	24.73%

Source: ONS, *Annual Abstract*

The annual population increase of 249,000 only needs 108,260 rather than 191,200 new homes, based on the average household size of 2.3. Even if the Census underestimates the population by 5%, we can still safely assume that the annual supply of new homes exceeds new households.

Yet the housing crisis is clearly worsening for two main reasons. First, many houses are built in the wrong place. "Public investment in affordable 'social' housing must... also prioritise the areas where there is a proven need for more housing. This may mean diverting resources away from some areas of the North and Midlands with surplus stock." (Urban Task Force 1999) And second, as stated above, housing supply includes second homes, holiday lets, time shares and empty investments, so reducing homes for those in need. Despite enough houses for everyone, there is a severe shortage for many. To address this market failure, I suggest three planning strategies:

- conserve the urban fabric by restoring all vacant houses,
- intensify towns and cities by developing infill sites, and
- tax those houses not used as primary homes.

Shelter for all – i) vacant houses

Conserving old buildings is the Cinderella of planning. One can understand why volume housebuilders dismiss the potential of vacant houses but the inaction of successive governments is inexplicable. The problem is getting worse.

- In 2007, 663,000 houses were vacant in England (2.9% of the total), of which 290,000 had been vacant for more than six months.
- Four years later, 750,000 houses were vacant, almost half for more than six months (*Planning* 7/12/2007 and 7/10/2011).

Vacant houses can provide decent homes cheaply, release capital, revive local builders and regenerate neighbourhoods. Many large houses, under-occupied by empty nesters, divorcees and pensioners could provide and extra flat or two, introduce new neighbours and even carers for some pensioners. There are also some innovative council schemes.

- The Living Over The Shops (LOTS) initiative from the 1980s has had modest impact to date. Ipswich council was a pioneer, offering shop owners 75% grants towards the conversion of upper floors into habitable flats. A typical scheme in 1986 created four flats for a total cost of £45,000, generating rents of £5,000 pa. This was a healthy annual return of 11%, or 45% for the owner.
- Kent had 8,000 long-term empty properties. The county, with the 12 districts, "ring-fenced £6 million to provide loans of up to £25,000 for renovations, [which] attracted an additional £8 million from private developers." By 2011, when the No Use Empty project won a Regeneration Award for partnership working, 1,677 empty homes had been restored (www.regen.net 7/10/2011).

By contrast, the government's HMR (Housing Market Renewal) programme spent £2.2 billion building 4,000 homes while demolishing 16,000. Had this money been a revolving loan fund for a national No Use Empty scheme, it could have restored well over 500,000 properties.

In many former industrial towns, vacant houses can exceed 5% of the total stock with whole streets boarded up, even as new suburbs are being built. Vacant homes require proper council resources to bring them back into use, offering unemployed people building apprenticeships while actually restoring the houses over their heads. These 'homesteading' schemes have been tried in various cities and are good value. Meanwhile the government imposes 20% VAT on all such conversions but zero VAT on new housebuilding. (Forgive the repetition.)

Unusually, despite strong demand, Kensington in central London has the second highest vacancy rate in England and most of Johnson's vanity towers will suffer similarly. Here, investors buy houses in a rising market to yield capital gains of around 10%, fuelling both bubble and greed. Leasehold tenants and agency fees would reduce those profits. Keeping them empty raises scarcity value, house prices and private rents, while business custom in local shops, pubs and restaurants falls. (This speculation mirrors the fish market in Japan, where one bank froze all the tuna it could buy, speculating that when the species is over-fished to the point of extinction, their tuna would become priceless. Short-term speculative profit invariably reduces long-term husbandry of both wildlife and city life as we know it.)

The *NPPF* ignores this issue. If councils were empowered to curb speculators, they might impose a punitive council tax after a period of grace, compulsorily purchase the property at below market price since the owner could not find tenants or even serve a compulsory occupation order to house those on its waiting list.

Despite the unfairness of compulsory purchase discussed in part 1, its roots are more positive. "Rome in 1420 [was] 'so dilapidated and deserted that it had hardly any resemblance to a city... Everything possible was done to encourage private individuals to build new houses in new quarters of the town, or to rebuild or improve in the existing town. From 1480 owners of derelict houses had to sell to anyone who wanted to rebuild on their site, and owner-occupiers wanting to rebuild and enlarge their houses were allowed to make a compulsory purchase of adjoining properties if they were not owner-occupied." (Girouard 1985) Desperate measures but necessary to curb speculators who buy cheap or derelict property, let others improve their properties, wait for prices to rise and then sell to reap the capital (social) value that others have created. Punitive taxes or occupation orders on vacant properties in areas of high demand may be the only way to deal with these cuckoos.

ii) Infills and windfalls

Vacant sites and buildings, like black holes, suck economic and social life out of their surroundings. Restoring 750,000 vacant houses and converting under-occupied houses and vacant upper floors to produce 500,000 flats should meet most housing needs. We may still need new houses (from table 36 above), but fewer of them.

In 2006, the government expected councils to build 60% of all new housing on brown field sites (*PPS 3: Housing*). This raised eyebrows. One planning consultant thought that no town south of a line from the Bristol Channel to the Wash had any significant brownfield land. An academic thought that three or four million new homes could be built in London Docklands alone, at densities found in Camden or Islington.

In a joint study by the Civic Trust Regeneration Unit and the Civic Trust for Wales (1995), a small Welsh market town discussed three options for town growth in the first of three community meetings:

- no growth kept the town and its environs much as it was, in part because of an inadequate sewage treatment plant. Yet this option saw the potential for modest internal growth by converting vacant upper floors and some under-occupied houses into flats;
- organic growth allowed new housing for local people and new workers employed by local firms expanding or new firms moving in; while
- commercial growth allowed developers to build houses in response to market demand, for outside visitors and retirees as well as locals.

By far the most popular option was for organic growth, confirmed by a subsequent household survey (with a 20% response): 8% supporting no physical growth, 65% for organic growth and 27% for commercial growth. In my experience, this preference is general. One commented that: "Whether it's new build or refurbishment, we want greater intensity of use." However professional the planners, local people live in the area and understand planning basics. 'Experts' call this NIMBYism.

The *NPPF* is coy about windfall sites, only requiring 10% of housing on them, and "there should be compelling evidence that they will provide a reliable source of supply... having regard to the strategic housing land availability assessment, historic windfall delivery rates and expected future trends... [but] resist inappropriate development of residential gardens."

Could we contain all new housebuilding within existing urban boundaries? This would intensify neighbourhoods, employ local builders, strengthen local economies and conserve green fields. The Urban Task Force estimated their potential as follows.

Table 37: Supply of previously developed land and buildings, 1996-2021

Type of land	Total area (ha)	Housing area	No of homes
Existing supply of:			
• Derelict land	28,800	5,600	164,000
• Vacant land	16,200	5,300	150,000
• Vacant buildings	na	na	247,000
Projected additional supply of:			
• All sources	na	na	1,526,000
Total	**45,000**	**10,900**	**2,087,000**

Source: Urban Task Force

These estimates are valuable but raise serious issues.

- 2 million new homes over 25 years (80,000 pa) is only 42% rather than 60% of the 191,000 actually built.
- There are wide regional variations. Brown fields are much more common in the north and midlands where housing demand is lower.
- Derelict and vacant land only include sites over 0.25 hectares (0.6 of an acre), with an allowance made for smaller sites assessed by each local authority.
- Only 20% of derelict land and 33% of vacant land is considered suitable for housing. The rest are either seriously contaminated, retained for other uses or developed at a very slow rate.
- Those sites that are developed provide only 150,000 homes on 5,300 hectares. Housing about 350,000 people at less than 30 people/acre (70/ha) is suburban density, and contradicts not only Jane Jacobs but also the report itself.
- The potential from vacant buildings is only 20% of the total potential of vacant and under-used buildings and upper floors suggested earlier.

We should also distinguish between large and small windfall sites. Redundant industrial sites and estates, like slum clearance areas, involve a huddle of architects, developers, planners, politicians and civil servants planning for mixed use schemes, viability and deliverability through special purpose vehicles, with compulsory purchase to circumvent those who cannot see the vision. Yet, having already demolished most of our industrial heritage, the pressure is actually to reduce any further loss of employment sites to housing (as Harvey-Jones noted, page 133 above).

By contrast, small urban sites, although more valuable than farmland, are sidelined as mere windfalls, left to rot slowly in their area. This is odd. A small windfall site (like a derelict building, back garden or SLOIP ('space left over in planning')) will involve a local builder or self-builder, a few neighbours, a local planning officer and perhaps a ward councillor. Being unseen but always in the pipeline, windfall sites have real potential and could fuel the organic process of urban growth. Perhaps they are undervalued because they can't be planned.

- The specialist Pocket Living developer has built over 200 micro-flats in central London with support from the Greater London authority. These flats are at least 80% below market prices and, for council support, the buyers have to have joint incomes less than £66,000 (*The Observer* 13/10/13). The Mayor of London is investing £25 million to help create 1,000 homes for first time buyers. Pocket Living may not be Parker Morris but these flats sell. Let future generations decide whether they also like them.
- To house the homeless, some councils have converted ship containers into small homes, grouped together on small urban sites. This might be thought regressive, but a floating hotel in one of London's docks is constructed largely of those same containers. Properly-funded councils, hospitals and universities could build high quality hostels for the young, students and nurses as well as the homeless. When private equity investors provide such flats in converted office blocks, they are usually of poor quality and overpriced.

Self-builders also use windfalls. "When the Office of Fair Trading recommendations were published in September, Whitehall discovered that self-build is the largest sector in UK housing supply, accounting for around 16,000 homes a year." (*Planning* 12/12/2008) They are also remarkable value for money.

- A few self-builders completed 12 two- and three-bedroom homes outside a Cornish village in 14 months. Each cost £78,000 or £84,000, less than half the cost of a new semi or bungalow.
- The modest but perfectly built home of Dai and Maria... cost them £6,500.
- In a field outside Glastonbury, 16 igloo-shaped 'benders' built of hazel twig frames covered and insulated with two or three layers of tarpaulin cost as little as £300. The young residents seemed content with their homes. One was proud to be saving taxpayers the housing benefits to which he was entitled. Another saw it as a creative period in her life, however temporary, while working for a local council.

Yet, despite their ecological value, self-builders meet hostility from most planning authorities. It took Tony Wrench and friends ten years to get permission for a low-impact settlement in Pembrokeshire Coast national park, and ten years before he felt secure in his timber, straw and turf roundhouse (*Planning* 14/11/2008). So most urban self-build homes are required to merge into their surroundings. This reinforces an earlier point that development control is too negative on small developments, particularly if they stand out visually. Yet at the mega-scale, 'daring' and 'original' towers from 'starchitects' are all too often received with great enthusiasm, despite their unsustainable use of materials and energy.

The supply of local housing, a primary function of cities, is surely best left to local councils. Although the frequent butt of both government and housebuilders, councils have three strengths; local knowledge of housing need, local providers and urban capacity. The national Census and Annual Abstracts are priceless, but they are fallible. Local councils can correct local population figures through their Registrars, school rolls, council tax payers, electoral rolls and housing waiting lists etc. Not all councils would ignore their local builders, housing associations and co-ops so pointedly, some would refuse the most egregious housing schemes and most would act more vigorously to provide shelter for the young, marginalized and homeless. Some might even build council houses again.

Of course there would be teething problems. Some councils will thrive, others will need to revive the requisite skills, and a few might 'cheat', relying on neighbouring councils to make good their own shortfalls. But such problems could be resolved with joint working arrangements and through the Planning Inspectorate. The role of government would then focus on three essentials: to audit council progress on housing waiting lists and homelessness and share best practice; advise on likely numbers of immigrants, with safeguards for specific minorities like travellers, asylum seekers and temporary migrant workers; and fund all local housing authorities properly.

iii) Market demand or housing need

The housing market is bipolar. To the poor, a decent home that they can afford is a luxury. To the comfortable, it is both home and an investment for their children. For the 'filthy rich', 'home' is an item of their spending on the continuum between space, time and luxury. Flitting between country estate, town house, company flat, hotel suite and island retreat in their luxury yachts and private jets, employing chauffeurs, butlers, chefs, personal assistants, nannies, gardeners and domestic servants, so that the sophisticates can enjoy their culture, caviar and premier cru, or the libidinous their casinos, cocaine and courtesans. Buying property as investments merely feeds billionaire greed. Of course this is bile, but it's anger with the 'intensely relaxed' response of senior politicians rather then envy.

We build too many new houses to increase choice for those who can afford them, and too few homes for those who need them. This is feast for housebuilders and private landlords, famine for social landlords and tenants. Despite any Conservative reputation for financial probity, it is also very inefficient with public money. Instead of building council houses as a public asset, we are now paying rent to private landlords. The HMR programme wasted £2.2 billion (from table 34 above), that might instead have renovated 500,000 vacant homes. More infamously, George Osborne's bedroom tax led some housing associations to demolish 'oversized' family homes for which they now had no tenants, and build smaller replacements.

Now government is directly subsidizing private housing. The annual £4 billion to support first time buyers plus a £2.3 billion housing infrastructure fund for new estate roads and the zero VAT subsidy clearly benefits the volume housebuilders above all others. And in the massive £80 billion regeneration programme above, only 10% of the homes need be 'affordable' at the higher rents set at 80% of market rents.

General taxation is discussed in chapter 10. Here we focus on housing taxes to address the specific problems of offshore ownership, second homes, unscrupulous landlords, office conversions, social ownership and Osborne's bedroom tax. First, properties bought, managed and sold 'offshore' should all be taxed as comparable properties owned in this country. Where property deeds are kept is irrelevant. The capital value and rental income is generated here. Concealed ownership to avoid property taxes would be countered by punitive council taxes, compulsory purchase or legal proceedings.

ii) 5.2 million UK residents own a second home (ONS), particularly visible in all coastal districts and national parks. Until April 2013, second home owners were only charged half the council tax, even some residents in 1 Hyde Park. Now it is merely discretionary. In a popular Devon district, "more than ten per cent of homes are registered as second homes, [pushing house prices] up to 16 times the average annual income... the most severe house-price-to-wage ratio in the country outside central London." (*Planning* 22/8/2008) (Second homes can even distort local elections, their owners casting their votes in the more marginal constituency of their homes – or even voting in both.) Rural Devon's resident population of roughly 750,000 live in 310,000 houses and flats. If only 5% are second homes with an average council tax bill of £1,000, doubling their council tax would raise over £15 million, a significant revenue for six rural districts. Nationally, such a council tax surcharge could raise well over £5 billion. Some second home owners might have to sell, thereby easing local house prices, but surely most would happily pay to ease local housing problems.

iii) The enforced rise in private renting since 1980 has attracted many unscrupulous landlords. In many HMR areas, cheap houses were bought by agents (for some reason, solicitors from Sevenoaks and Tunbridge Wells were often mentioned). These were then converted into HMOs (houses in multiple occupancy), all rooms let to young single people on housing benefit as separate bedrooms, with shared kitchen, dining room and bathroom. This assured income, paid direct to the landlords, provided annual returns often above 50%. As with privatization and private equity, maximum profits are extracted with minimum investment in proper refurbishment, repair and maintenance. For too long, private rents, like rail fares, have outstripped all cost of living indexes and inflation. Only local rent tribunals under council control can resolve disputes fairly between market rents and local wages.

iv) Today, many new homes don't need planning permission. "Since 2015, 30,575 housing units have been converted from offices to flats in England without going through the full planning system, with a 'potential loss' of 7,644 affordable homes." (*The Planner* June 2018) This ratio of 25% affordable homes in large schemes is now 10%. The Centre Point office block in London (page 332 below), having survived an early takeover by the Centrepoint homeless charity, has now been converted into 82 private flats, only half of which were sold in 2018. The rest were withdrawn from sale until house prices rise again. If affordable housing is indeed a government priority, the loss of local jobs could be mitigated if those offices could only be converted and managed by local councils, housing associations or co-ops.

v) Social forms of home ownership only charge affordable rents and are more democratic. "Unlike the UK with 0.6% of housing within the cooperative and mutual sector, in Sweden it's 18%, 15% in Norway, 8% in Austria, 6% in Germany and 4% in Ireland." (*New Start* August 2009) It would have been better to transfer council housing to housing associations, co-ops and tenant management organizations (TMOs) than sell them to tenants who usually sold on to landlords. TMOs manage their council estates by agreement with the relevant council. (Unfortunately, not all TMOs are managed by the tenants themselves as became clear after the Grenfell Tower disaster.)

Now, universities are privatizing student accommodation. "According to student housing charity Unipol, student rents rose 25% between 2010 and 2013 as universities sold off their own low-rent stock and private companies built luxury accommodation, while the National Union of Students has described the cost of housing as being at an absolute crisis point." (Emma Lunn, *The Observer* 6/9/2015) Hospitals have also sold most of their student nurse accommodation with much the same result. However, the Sheffield Student Housing Co-operative, set up by three students, leased a five-bedroom house from the Phone Co-op and all five residents manage the property and agree the rents. Small, viable and ignored by government.

vi) The infamous bedroom tax, or 'under-occupancy penalty', is only collected from those on housing benefit who enjoy one or more bedrooms than required. This wretchedly stingy mansion tax on the poor, introduced by Chancellor George Osborne in 2012, actually increased the housing crisis, hitting disabled couples and older tenants whose children had left home especially hard. At the same time, while inflicting austerity on us all, Osborne reduced the tax on income above £150,000 from 50 to 45 pence. Originally, the welfare state meant taxing the rich sufficiently to ensure that the poor were at least housed. Today's Robin Hood is the Sheriff of Nottingham.

A new focus for planning

Cities, like maths, music and sex, are *sui generis*, understood only on their own terms. However much they differ, cities are a basic fact of human life. They combine 'Place, Work, Folk' (Patrick Geddes) and provide shelter, security and markets (Fernand Braudel), typically in dense environments of short streets, old buildings and mixed uses (Jane Jacobs). Whether 'organic', where streets reflect the local topography of rivers, contours and coastlines, or 'planted' to a rigorous grid, all cities centred around key civic buildings and market place.

The roots of planning lie in the serious public health problems that emerged during the massive urban growth of the early Industrial Revolution – overcrowding in bad housing and raw sewage polluting water supplies. These were largely resolved by the Victorians. The first century of *formal* planning grew around the more nebulous concepts of sanitation, amenity and convenience, from which we have tested various approaches. *Utopian planning* gave us vision-led garden suburbs and new towns, and *market-led* suburban estates (many now 'jerry built'). These increased the urban footprint about sixfold, reducing both farmland and social behaviour. *Normative planning* demolished about 60% of our urban fabric deemed slums, and replaced them with council estates, another form of ghetto. Car ownership introduced us to *predict and provide planning*, which left a destructive trail of urban freeways and bypasses. Since 1979, *market-led* (*laissez-faire*) planning replaced the utopian and normative approaches, but it was skewed. *Supply-side planning* of exurban parks and shedscapes ceded control to landowners and retail chains; *development-led planning* underpins regeneration programmes that are destroying most of those slum clearance walk-ups and tower blocks. Will these new monuments suffer the same fate?

These planning approaches all share the same general focus – ambitious, development-led, driven by greed or ego and forward-looking. In a word, 'proactive'. While this 'politics of change' sought 'the creation of place', there was a simultaneous decline in local markets, neighbourhood security and adequate shelter.

The alternative, based on the politics of continuity, might be called reactive planning. Political life (and planning) should be a social contract between past, present and future generations (Edmund Burke), allowing social progress with minimal disruption (John Stuart Mill) through small-scale incrementalism (Karl Popper). The planner as local GP should focus on today's problems, 'make the best use of existing infrastructure' (RCEP, page 191-2 above), and adapt buildings, protect markets and improve services. Adapt the past, improve the present and let the future look after itself. One graffito put it more succinctly: "Live in the past, 'cos the future's fucked".

After a century of transformative planning, let us jettison all ideological baggage. Classic economic theory that market forces of supply and demand will provide for everyone's needs doesn't work with unregulated markets where basic social needs are secondary to profits. Markets don't always know best. Liberal sentiments about improving living conditions for all, based on notional future standards, risk needless destruction through compulsory purchase that undermines local democracy. And we must unbuckle the legal straightjacket of planning law from 1909, when councils needed permission to prepare town schemes, to the current *NPPF* that controls all major planning decisions and grants approval for major developments where councils lack a current plan.

Returning to first principles, reactive planning is essentially pragmatic. First, we must react to current ills by addressing their causes rather than symptoms. This takes us back to public health. Had we reduced family poverty rather than housing squalor, slums might have improved from within as tenants could afford better housing and landlords improve properties. Schools might provide healthy meals as they used to. People should walk and cycle more (and live longer) by reducing road traffic and pollution. And full employment improves local economies and personal health.

Second, we should only build what is needed now 'just in time', rather than 'just in case' future generations demand bigger and newer. On what we leave, let them decide between old and new, monumental and vernacular. It is right to conserve what we can and develop through organic piecemeal growth, rather than build large schemes that contradict urban form and honest market principles. Conservation is the one planning approach that is widely popular – people like old buildings, historic areas, dense neighbourhoods and green belts.

Above all, pragmatic planning must be local. Addressing current problems, conserving the built fabric and minimizing our impact on future generations can best be planned locally. National control of local planning (and other public services) fails in much the same way that Stalin's five year plans failed. If governments can't hand out European grants to farmers quickly or welfare benefits to the disabled humanely, manage its own property portfolio without using tax evaders (ipE) or provide sufficient personnel and kit for the armed services at reasonable cost, then let planning be devolved to local councils. However politically fudged and contrary local decisions may sometimes be, it is better to restrict large egos to small theatres than let them loose on the national stage.

Finally, local planning can decide what issues need to be addressed, either singly or as a combined plan for urban health. In effect, every planning authority needs its own strategy for sustainable development. The *NPPF* is inadequate. The new focus of planning would cover the 'nested hierarchy' that begins with each house, street, neighbourhood and town centre, economic cluster, the town and hinterland, up to the large city and sub-region. This is the subject of the next chapter. It only remains to say that, over this hierarchy, the influence of central government is significant at city and county level, but becomes negligible with streets and buildings. And the more local we get, the more important it is to involve local people.

No people, no plans

Planning is the political process that seeks to balance liberty, equality and fraternity in our built environment. Yet up to about 1970, all planning was controlled by central government and managed by local councils. Patrick Abercrombie defined the plan process as 'survey, analysis, plan', and professionals firmly controlled this ladder of information, knowledge and wisdom.

- Survey, based on Census, local statistics, projections and site visits, provided essential but only partial data. Planners largely ignored the views and expertise of local residents, workers, shopkeepers, the young, old and most minorities.
- Analysis was the planners' own black box where architects' utopian designs or engineers' computer programmes could be set free. Yet there should be no mystique. Analysis is little more than defining key issues, identifying policy options with cost estimates and justifying preferred options.

- From this, the formal plan became an inflexible blueprint that was long-winded and full of jargon. The quasi-legal circumlocutions and pseudo-professional jargon usually obscured the contents and excluded even those directly affected.

This exclusion highlighted the weakness of local democracy. With every slum clearance, shopping mall and urban freeway, objectors became ever-more vociferous. The problem of inadequate participation was recognized by PAG in 1967 (page 275 above). The subsequent Skeffington report *People and Planning* (1969) had its main recommendations included in the *Town and Country Planning Act 1971*. Now, people were to be involved in the plan process, at least during the draft report stage when it was 'on deposit'. Unsurprisingly, at this stage, most draft policies were fairly fixed. Antagonism between planners and the planned remained.

Also in 1969, the American Sherry Arnstein published her ladder of citizen participation, see opposite. Where Skeffington gave the professional's perspective, Arnstein reversed the telescope to provide a citizen's viewpoint. Her ladder of overlapping rungs helps to explain why antagonism is common. Most people resent being patronized on the lower rungs and treated like mushrooms, although most would also feel uncomfortable on the upper rungs with all the meetings and voluntary work involved. They would like to be one or two rungs higher than their local councils would like them. Also, as we rise up the political hierarchy from parish to government, so ordinary people are pushed lower down the ladder. As power tends to corrupt, so manipulation is the default mode of central government, curtesy of their spin doctors and sections of the media. And at least in the UK, I would include a new bottom rung of her ladder: 'Compulsion' for all those slum clearances, shopping redevelopments and urban freeways.

"All professions are conspiracies against the laity." (GB Shaw) Planning, like most professions, came slowly to the idea of working with ordinary people. Lawyers, journalists and the police may be held in lower public esteem but most professionals tend to the aloofness of 'faceless' bureaucrats. Doctors and teachers perhaps learned more quickly because they work every day with those they serve. Planners spend too much time with colleagues, councillors, developers, architects and owners, working under increasingly authoritarian government targets. They have little time for the public. Planning is primarily about people and their problems rather than visionary plans and developers' profits. Rather than 'mediation of space, creation of place', planning becomes the 'mediation of power between social need and corporate greed'.

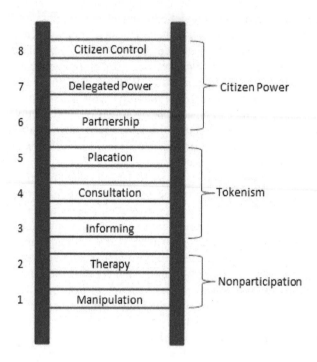

People should inform all new development. Development controls, introduced in 1909 and extended in 1932 to include all development, did not involve the public until 1971. Two new problems emerged. First, *The Local Government Act 1972* in England and Wales replaced 58 counties, 83 county boroughs and 1,249 urban and rural parish councils with 53 new counties (including 6 new metropolitan counties) and 369 new districts. This reduced the power of all parishes and pushed development control into larger more remote councils.

Second, where PAG saw development control as preventing *bad* development, the public were now seen as NIMBYs (not in my back yard) objecting to *all* development. This is a dangerous response to a basic market force.

- Where people's homes, businesses and neighbourhoods are directly affected by any redevelopment, it is dishonest to override their views on the omelette principle of destruction for the greater good. Had compensation reflected full market value, relocation costs and a generous allowance for disturbance to lives and livelihoods, objections would have been reduced.

- It is also natural to object to new houses on the fields beyond their back gardens, however selfish (or hypocritical in the case of Nicholas Ridley, see page 28 above). The *NPPF*, encouraging large-scale green field suburbia while refusing back garden intensification, is surely meddling in what are clearly local issues.

- And objectors not directly affected by new development are an essential aspect of local democracy. Their arguments frequently unearthed the use of inaccurate data, flawed assumptions, biased technical assessments, spurious national priorities and fictional cost projections. These have affected far too many major public investments, from slum clearance and new bypasses to PFI projects, the scrapped NHS national IT project and the current HS2. Public investment in local development must be open to public scrutiny – and local control. Anything less is undemocratic.

Involving people in planning still puzzles many professionals. In ten years to 2008, government departments produced 43 documents on the subject. This extract gives their flavour. "In the Statement of Community Involvement [an essential of Local Development Frameworks] authorities should set out their main principles for community involvement, including:

- Access to information. Documents should be available in a variety of formats, to encourage the widest possible readership. This is likely to include paper and electronic versions of key documents, and should include languages other than English where appropriate.
- The opportunity to contribute ideas. Community groups and the wider public should have the opportunity to put forward their own ideas and feel confident that there is a process for considering and responding to their concerns.
- The opportunity to take an active part in developing proposals and options. Where appropriate, there should be opportunities for people to actively engage with planning professionals.
- The opportunity to be consulted and make representations on formal proposals. This is a statutory requirement as set out in Regulations and represents the minimum in terms of community involvement.
- The opportunity to get feedback and be informed about progress and outcomes. Keeping local communities and stakeholders informed will foster interest in planning issues. In time, this will enable authorities to benefit from local knowledge and experience which will in turn result in better planning outcomes.

"It must be demonstrated to all sections of the community that the process of community involvement is legitimate and timely with outcomes in the public interest. Processes should be simple to follow, and delivered in a fair, transparent and efficient manner. This will require authorities to identify the limits to community involvement as well as the forms it will take." (ODPM 2007)

This approach lies somewhere between therapy and consulting on Arnstein's ladder of participation. Access to information should by now be a right under Freedom of Information, however often government and councils deny FoI requests. 'Key documents' can swamp people under a forest of paper. Accurate summaries are overlooked, as are local surveys and community meetings, which can be as important as key statistics and national policies. Local people's views can only influence the process. The focus of most statutory plans is on development needs over the next 15 years. Failing schools, street crime, inadequate health services, traffic pollution and other more immediate issues need plans based precisely on 'local knowledge and experience'.

The whole process is controlled. People are given opportunities to contribute ideas, to be consulted, to get feedback and to work with planners *when appropriate*. Local ownership is not mentioned. The sting is in the over-defensive final sentence, requiring "authorities to identify the limits to community involvement".

Consultations should form the basis of plans, not vice versa. This brings us to "the process of community involvement". Traditional public meetings are seldom successful. Typically, people in rows face a raised table from where the chair introduces the team who explain their proposals before inviting comments and questions. That allows perhaps 5% of the audience to represent all those present. If an early critical question elicits a defensive response from officers, the meeting usually descends into a 'them and us' situation, often ending with a call for a vote to gauge local opinion. With so few questions, meaningful discussion of the issues and options is impossible. This may produce good theatre, like eighteenth century hustings perhaps, but it is counter-productive.

The website www.communityplanning.net lists 53 techniques for involving people in planning. These include activity weeks, briefing workshops, community profiling, design fests, elevation montages, feasibility funds, future search conference, gaming, ideas competitions, interactive displays, mapping, mobile units, models, neighbourhood planning offices, open house events, photo surveys, planning weekends, reconnaissance trips, simulations, task forces, user groups and video soapboxes. Apart from the faintly militaristic sound of some, most rely on structured events that still tend to manipulate the planning process and patronize those involved.

In general, community meetings, group workshops and personal interviews are sufficient. Community meetings must be informal with people sitting around tables rather than in rows. After outlining the agenda, a short presentation illustrates the issues and options which are then discussed in groups at each table. Reports back from each group are summarized on flip charts or similar to clarify areas of dispute and agreement, before saying what happens next and thanking all participants. Informality is key, preferring images to text, avoiding jargon, knowing something of the area but acknowledging their expertise, and offering refreshments on arrival or during group discussions. If those group discussions are noisy with banter when reporting back, if people stick around afterwards, talking among themselves, holding the officers back or joining them in the nearest pub afterwards – then the meeting has been successful.

Communities should be engaged throughout plan preparation. A local strategy should involve three sectors: the general community, minorities and professionals:

- community meetings in perhaps three stages: a) to agree the main issues to be addressed like housing, jobs, transport and environment, b) to prioritize (adding and rejecting) 20 to 30 draft recommendations, and c), with a public exhibition, to approve and modify the overall strategy and discuss next steps;

- smaller meetings for specific minority groups like young parents, local schools and clubs, the unemployed, old people, the disabled and, for market towns, local villages and farmers; and
- professional workshops and personal interviews with the 'local mafia' (including officers and councillors, local editors, chambers and community leaders) to discuss their views, data sources, technical issues, policy options, funding sources and who would implement and monitor the plan.

The process for single issues can be simplified. For example, to 'rationalize' five primary schools in an inner-city area, Tellus 42 met the following in each school: the head teacher, the staff (both teaching and ancillary staff), the school council (with or without a teacher present), the school governors and two meetings for parents – one after school and one in the evening. We also interviewed key council officers and local agencies, and held an open community meeting in the area for all who might be interested, including former pupils. At the outset, the council officers preferred one large (three form entry) school to replace the five, but willingly accepted the strong local preference for three small schools. The outcome was that, during the statutory process for closing and re-opening the three preferred schools, there were no public objections.

Local expertise can also inform plans. For a Civic Trust strategy for Frome in Somerset, the local civic society surveyed the historic town centre for a modest fee. This survey of all 828 buildings identified vacant shops and under-used upper floors, eyesores, those of townscape value (with more buildings pre-1700 than post-1900) and six clusters of buildings at risk. School pupils can complete resident or visitor attitude surveys, and should complete safety audits of all routes to school and town centre.

Local experts can often replace external consultants. Local chambers can monitor town centre health with regular pedestrian counts, turnover trends and marketing campaigns, while local estate agents can often undertake town centre commercial audits more cheaply, with more local nous and no back agenda from major developers. All external consultants bring risks. Some under-price first contracts in the hope of 'growing the contract' with repeat fees. This makes them liable to place too much emphasis on the views of those who commissioned them (as with the four accountants and government). Another risk is the conflict of interest when national consultants find and promote major regeneration opportunities with the potential for huge subsequent fees. And all large consultancies suffer repeat fatigue, as with Ofsted inspections mentioned earlier (page 238).

The black box of planning, analysis, contains perhaps the kernel of early planning failure. Normative and idealistic planning focussed on physical condition with a heavy bias in favour of the big and the new. Market planning simply provided what the models predicted but it too was big and new. There was scant analysis of viable alternatives in conservation. For example, in the 1990s, a Hampshire district employed the Civic Trust to prepare a strategy for its town centre, and three national consultancies (in planning, transport and management) to prepare a sub-regional strategy. During a one-day conference with officers, one consultant identified two central development sites that would attract 'low-end' retailers such as Aldi and Lidl. His analysis reflected the town's gentle decline and the loss of a national department store five years previously. It ignored an alternative of improving the existing town centre – making it cleaner, refurbishing vacant buildings, rescuing the street market from a multi-storey car park and marketing it to attract more shoppers, reverse its decline and even, perhaps, persuade the department store to return. Any consultant can identify and reinforce existing trends. Analysis should go deeper.

Plans in plain English

After survey and analysis, we come to the written plan. Unfortunately, as in most professions, planning verbiage is endemic. The US has word creep. Gruen (1965) utilized clusterization for cramming, compartmentalization for zoning, scatterization for sprawl, transportation, accessibility, public transportation media and accessory pedestrian transportation for public transport, access, lifts and escalators. The UK prefers the longwinded. In development control, "Detrimental to the local visual amenity" means out of place, too big or plain ugly, while "Prejudicial to the quiet enjoyment of the local residential amenity" means too much noise or traffic.

Our statutory plans are also riddled with pomposity. "WHERE THE LOCAL PLANNING AUTHORITY CONSIDERS THAT A LOCAL NEED EXISTS IN A PARTICULAR VILLAGE LISTED IN POLICY 1 THEN IT MAY EXCEPTIONALLY PERMIT HOUSING NOT COMPATIBLE WITH NORMAL STRUCTURE AND LOCAL PLAN POLICIES BUT COMPATIBLE WITH STRUCTURE PLAN POLICY H14A BEING ON A SITE OUTSIDE BUT ADJOINING THE DEVELOPMENT ENVELOPE OF THE VILLAGE IF THE PROPOSED SCHEME WILL CLEARLY MEET THE LOCAL NEED. SUCH SCHEMES WILL NOT NORMALLY BE PERMITTED IN OTHER VILLAGES/HAMLETS, ON SITES SEPARATED FROM THE VILLAGE OR ON ISOLATED SITES IN THE COUNTRYSIDE. SUCH SCHEMES WILL BE SUBJECT TO A PLANNING OBLIGATION WHICH WILL ESTABLISH PRIORITIES FOR THE MARKETING OF THE DWELLINGS TO ENSURE LOCAL NEEDS ARE THE FIRST PRIORITY, AND WILL ENSURE THE ONGOING AVAILABILITY OF THE DWELLINGS TO MEET LOCAL NEED. SCHEMES WHICH OFFER A DISCOUNTED INITIAL PRICE ONLY WILL NOT BE ACCEPTED UNDER THIS POLICY. NO SCHEME WILL BE CONSIDERED UNLESS SUPPORTED BY A LOCAL NEEDS SURVEY." Only barristers relish fighting their way through this thicket from the 1990s – it's where their fees lie. In essence this policy says that new housing will only be permitted in those villages listed in Policy 1 when there is a clear local need, the houses continue to meet local need beyond their initial sale, and they are built within or adjoining the village boundary. In all other villages and rural sites, new housing will not be allowed.

In *Plain Words* (1948), Gowers advised official writers to 'Be short, be simple, be human'. In any text, as in any town, legibility is crucial. Readers, like pedestrians, should be able to find their way round with ease and confidence, without being cowed by capital letters – a pet hate of the Plain English Campaign. Key documents are still written for barristers rather than residents, testing the resilience of the committed and deterring the rest of us.

According to GR Elton (1967), the three keys to the historian's craft are 'Facts, Analysis and Narrative'. This differs little from Abercrombie's Survey, Analysis, Plan. "The discovery of truth requires not only... acquaintance with the available evidence and scholarly assessment of it – but also imaginative reconstruction and interpretation. Evidence is the surviving deposit of an historical event; in order to rediscover the event, the historian must read not only with the analytical eye of the investigator but also with the comprehensive eye of the story-teller."

Historians rely largely on written records and have to allow for their partial and patchy nature. Much remains hidden and unrecorded, supporting the truism that most history is written by the victors. Planners should mine past and present records but they also have a host of living witnesses for accurate description and analysis of today's conditions and problems. The plan process might now read thus:

1. Profile, describing a town or subject (such as traffic congestion or urban growth) in all its complexity;
2. Options, identifying and comparing alternatives for tackling them with impact assessments, costs and preferences, and
3. Plan, the draft writing it all down for amendments before the final Plan with summary.

This revives Edmund Burke's social contract between the living, the dead and the unborn. And living people are usually the best judges of how to balance that contract. The following illustrates a good plan. I was privileged to work with a voluntary design group in a market town near the large suburb called Milton Keynes. *Buckingham: Vision and Design Statement* (2000) was based on an audit of every street, noting all design features that make Buckingham special and listing all potential windfall sites suggested by open land, vacant sites and un(der)used buildings.

Three points stand out. First, the whole town was involved by the design group: the local society, town council, traders' association, business and camera clubs, heritage trust, parish church and the local schools. More than 60 people completed the street audit, photo competitions and quizzes were supported by the local newspaper, stalls were taken at summer shows and fairs, the group made presentations to other town groups and clubs, an art competition on the Spirit of Buckingham was held for the schools, and several hundred people participated in two open workshops.

Second, the final *Vision and Design Statement* is of the highest quality, being simple, short and human. It is easy to read, has attractive maps, photos and line drawings and includes many quotes from locals, all within 18 pages.

Third, the *Statement* was both design guide and urban capacity study (or 'strategic housing land availability assessment' in the *NPPF*). 96 open sites were found, including cemetery and allotments, covering about 20 hectares (48 acres). In a closer look at 24 sites, 18 could have been developed to provide over 300 houses. If this 25% sample was typical, the potential of all 96 sites might have exceeded 1,000 new homes (allowing 100/ha on central sites and 50/ha in the suburbs). At the same time, the draft local plan then 'on deposit' allocated two large green fields off the new bypass for 450 new houses, plus a smaller (unspecified) number allowed for windfall sites in the town. With some enthusiasm, I suggested that Buckingham's green fields were safe for at least two generations. The design group listened politely and as politely ignored my assessment, deciding that only four hectares might be developed to provide about half the council's new housing. (Such lessons are important: while external consultants are paid to advise, local people are usually better judges of what can be achieved.)

And so it proved. At a subsequent meeting, the relevant planning officer said that the survey did not affect the housing requirement. Windfall sites had already been accounted for in the draft plan, though this seemed to be an unquantified guess. I suspect this would be a typical planning response. Yet, in meeting several local firms, one substantial central business confirmed, confidentially, that it was planning to move within five years. Such events illustrate the potential of windfall sites. When redeveloped for housing with some workshops, it could have saved at least half of one of those green fields, and intensified the town centre. Windfall sites can be substantial and they are sustainable.

Before we turn to that subject, however, let me summarize the three distinct models of planning and link them back to part 1.

- Architects gave us prescriptive planning, imposing their suburban visions on new towns, and their megalithic destruction of urban neighbourhoods. These combine designer ego with developer greed.
- Computer scientists gave us predictive planning that imposed monolithic shopping malls, urban freeways and exurbia that, with modest demand, were mostly supply-led.
- Planning legislation and government control has imposed a normative planning system that is uniform throughout the land. Too many major planning decisions end up with planning inspectors, city mayors, government ministers or high court judges. Local planning authorities are largely a contradiction in terms.

Exurban shedscapes and urban megaliths are not portents of an urban renaissance, but a blighting remnant of mid-twentieth century fascism, being big, overbearing and bulldozed through. All three models are development-led. Few are viable, none are sustainable and few are worth sustaining.

Chapter Nine: Sustainable Cities

Part 1 argued that cities, housing socially organized populations, are innate to humans. Over the last century, however, we transformed their physical texture. Gradual change through small scale incrementalism gave way to the sprawl, tall and brutal. Homogenized suburbs slipped anchor drifting into shedscapes, skyscrapers created ever-more bizarre erections and urban renewal created alien megaliths.

Part 2 discussed the need for vibrant centres, healthy economies, social transport and stable neighbourhoods, allowing cities to revive local economies and social roots. Again, these anchors have all too often been swept aside by the hoovering oligopolies of foodsheds, mega-corps, oil industry and volume housebuilders, driven solely by profit. Rarely before has so much been owed by so many and owned by so few.

Chapter 8 argued that, the scope of planning being largely local, its practical focus should be to conserve the built fabric, sort out current problems and minimize our impact on future generations. Now we return to the physical fabric of cities and discuss what sustainable development means.

Sustainable development defined

Sustainability is another big word, pregnant with promise but slippery as a new-born babe. The *Shorter OED* (2007) gives nine definitions for "sustain":
"1. Support … (a cause or course of action).
"2. Keep (a person, the mind, spirit, etc.) from failing or giving way.
"3. Cause to continue in a certain state;
"4. Maintain or keep going continuously (an action or process);
"5. Support life in;
"6. Provide for the upkeep of (an institution, estate, etc).
"7. Endure without failing or giving way;
"8. Undergo or experience (something);
"9. Support, bear the weight of, esp. for a long period."

Key words in all (except 8) are support, keep, continue, maintain, upkeep and endure. All imply conservation.

As a political concept, it emerged in the 1960s with 'sustainable economic growth'. This sought to break free of the 'stop-go' or 'boom-bust' cycles and sustain economic growth over decades, but the emphasis was on economic growth, not sustainable economies in terms of jobs, waste and pollution. By contrast, the 1970s introduced 'sustainable fishing quotas' which sought to sustain the fish, the jobs and the food supply. Unfortunately, poor management of quotas shows how short-term economic gain too often outweighs long-term sustainability.

With inevitable word creep, 'sustainable development' emerged in the 1980s. Stephen Wheeler (Le Gates and Stout 2005) provides four definitions.

- The most common, from the Brundtland Commission in 1987, defines it as "development that meets the needs of the present without compromising the ability of future generations to meet their own needs."
- From the World Conservation Union in 1991, it is "improving the quality of human life while living within the carrying capacity of supporting ecosystems."
- For David Pearce, "Sustainability requires at least a constant stock of natural capital, construed as the set of all environmental assets", while
- Wheeler's own definition is "development that improves the long-term health of human and ecological systems."

While Wheeler's is the simplest and clearest, they all raise questions and conflicts. Who will represent the future to achieve intergenerational equity? What is natural capital, how do we measure environmental carrying capacity and balance it against short-term profits?

NPPF1 (*National Planning Policy Framework*, 2012) uses the Brundtland definition, but adds five 'guiding principles' from "The UK Sustainable Development Strategy *Securing the Future*, [namely]: living within the planet's environmental limits; ensuring a strong, healthy and just society; achieving a sustainable economy; promoting good governance; and using sound science responsibly." To these, it added three dimensions:

- economic, building a strong, responsive and competitive economy,
- social, supporting strong, vibrant and healthy communities, and
- environmental, to contribute to protecting and enhancing our natural, built and historic environment.

In the introduction, "Sustainable development is about change for the better, and not only in our built environment. [It is also] about positive growth – making economic, environmental and social progress for this and future generations... Our lives, and the places in which we live them, can be better, but they will certainly be worse if things stagnate." There is a Panglossian fervour to this developers' charter and building for the future. Not building is stagnant.

NPPF2 omits the five guiding principles and upgrades the three dimensions to 'overarching objectives'. These are now seriously skewed in favour of developers. We build strong economies, and all development can be argued to strengthen economies. We only support social development and 'contribute to protecting' the environment.

Without the five 'guiding principles' and the general "presumption in favour of sustainable development", social investment and environmental protection become secondary and more difficult to secure.

Taken as a whole, *NPPF2* is incoherent, being "1 not clearly intelligible, inarticulate [and] 2 lacking in logical connection." (*Penguin ED*) It is inarticulate or silent on the need to:

- conserve the existing urban fabric, not just Conservation Areas,
- conserve farming, which is not even one of the five purposes of Green Belts,
- halt or reduce the wholesale destruction involved in urban regeneration. (It is, of course, silent on the need to remove the VAT subsidy which encourages this wanton destruction of urban fabric and green fields),
- increase housing densities and reduce parking standards,
- refuse all schemes with 'gated communities', social segregation and privatized public space, and
- reduce road traffic. It backtracks on previous weak policies with one reference to reducing carbon emissions, and the (inadequate) definition of 'pollution' in *NPPF1* is omitted from the nine-page Glossary.

The framework also fails to make some fairly crucial 'logical connections':

- the presumption in favour of 'sustainable development' without defining it is a challenge. It is not even balanced by a presumption against development in protected areas of outstanding natural beauty (AONBs) and Conservation Areas. Ominously, reference to sites covered by the EU Birds or Habitats Directives (that enjoy a presumption against development) are omitted from *NPPF2*,
- large green field development is preferred over urban intensification and windfall sites, with no reference to urban sprawl, loss of countryside and increased road traffic,
- it does not distinguish between local anchors and national hoovers, whatever their impact on local jobs and competition,
- it supports street markets without referring to foodsheds and their impact on local food chains, farms, abattoirs and wholesale markets,
- it is wholly inadequate on housing need, reducing targets for affordable homes while ignoring second homes, holiday lets and vacant investments, and
- the public are largely absent. Yet the new neighbourhood plans, though only dealing with non-strategic matters, are still expected to conform to the *NPPF*. Its reach is total, almost totalitarian.

Perhaps this incoherence derives from its title. The *NPPF* provides a national planning policy framework for local strategic planning but excludes "specific policies for nationally significant infrastructure projects" for which the *Planning Act 2008* and national policy statements apply. Current national transport schemes for new roads and HS2 largely disregard at least four of the five guiding principles for sustainable development, while the third Heathrow runway ignores all five: global environmental limits, healthy and just society, good governance and sound science, while sustaining an unsustainable economy.

NPPF2 reads more as a developers' charter than a sustainable framework. With every weasel phrase, so the idea of sustainable development fades like the Cheshire cat's grin. Of course the authors understood the key principles, but they got lost in the editing. Perhaps junior civil servants drafted a reasonable framework, but as it passed up the ladder, senior civil servants (working alongside advisers seconded from 'key agencies' like the housebuilders, foodsheds, road lobby and management consultants) produced the final draft for ministerial approval. Senior civil servants have a distaste for idealistic policies, while government ministers are prone to ideological rather than logical thought. The problem is that so many involved take highly paid jobs with those same key agencies. Since 2010 (*Private Eye* 1407, 11/12/2015) there were 276 applications from former ministers and 487 from top civil servants to move from government to the private sector. None were considered unsuitable by Parliament's advisory committee on business appointments.

Perhaps few governments practice what they preach. Yet the *NPPF* sermon is woefully inept or simply devious. It would be better to let local councils determine what is and is not sustainable development. Many would demonstrate greater respect for the past, relevant action for today's citizens and cautious concern for future generations. With the five guiding principles of the UK strategy for sustainable development, cities need three 'overarching objectives' for planning; namely conservation, intensification and pragmatism.

a) Sustainable development that focusses only on today and tomorrow ignores the huge potential of the past. Our urban heritage is not just those precious areas of architectural and historic value as the *NPPF* would have it. It is the built fabric of all our towns and cities that is the real heritage. The advantage of conserving all old buildings is that they provide an enormous store of accommodation that is efficient, cheap, adaptable and comforting. Increasing their lifespan reduces the waste of demolition and landfill, building materials, transport and energy, construction and capital. It also retains the familiar and the quirky as the setting for economic health, social vitality and stable neighbourhoods.

b) Intensification complements conservation of the urban fabric with new small-scale infill developments. Some NIMBYs might not like it next door, but it promotes BANANAs ('build absolutely nothing near anything') into the more reasonable BANNANAs 'build absolutely nothing not absolutely necessary anywhere'. This is a reasonable prophylactic principle. In any growing society, some new houses, workspace, facilities and bits of infrastructure are essential, quite apart from those old buildings that are worn out or burn down. Small infills intensify their surroundings, and avoid the empty utopia of suburbs and the dystopian megaliths of battery farms.

c) Pragmatism is rooted in the present, solving current needs. Norman Foster (*Utopia*, BBC 4, 2017) said we should "believe in the future". Given the poor record of large twentieth century urban projects, we should not seek to satisfy future needs or impress future critics. Like GPs, local planners should address specific ills of today. That means sufficient buildings and services to ensure that everyone is safe, housed, employed and able to lead a full life. Let the future look after itself. We must improve the present with minimum disruption.

Sustainable development conserves farmland, buildings, energy, fuel, materials and money, intensifies cities by increasing density and diversity, and revives social neighbourhoods, local economies and councils. Sustainable cities are compact, efficient and independent.

Sustainable development conserves and intensifies cities, meets the needs of all citizens and protects future generations against known hazards of today.

If "I think, therefore I am" (Descartes, 1596-1650), perhaps only humans can think, assess, monitor, reflect and modify in order to progress. However, "I build, therefore I am" is the ideology of today's suburban housebuilders and urban redevelopers. From Ebenezer Howard and Le Corbusier to Lord Rogers and the *NPPF*, assertive ideology has replaced reflective policy, change has displaced continuity and short-term profits have overridden embedded efficiency.

Let us now discuss what sustainable development might mean in Sheldrake's 'nested hierarchy' of subregion, city, neighbourhood, street and building. Within this hierarchy, different economic and social forces apply. Another analogy from physics might clarify the point.

- At the macro scale, gravitation explains the dance of our solar system. So citywide, the urban forces are largely economic, including the physical infrastructure. The larger the city, the stronger its economic pull over the region.
- At the micro scale, sub-atomic particles are held together by electromagnetic forces. Gravity is negligible. So at street level, it is largely social forces that bind families, friends, neighbours and colleagues together, at home, school and work, in shops, cafes, pubs and streets.

The following is a national framework for sustainable development. The eight sections cover all 13 chapters of *NPPF2*, but arranged in the hierarchy from subregion to buildings. Each section suggests national strategic, legal and tax objectives (discussed more fully in the final chapter) and local policy options for sustainable growth.

Revised *National Planning Policy Framework*

1   Land use, or town and country planning.
(replacing *NPPF* chapters 11, 13 and 15 – to make effective use of land, protect Green Belts and conserve the natural environment.)

The overriding objective should be to conserve all open land, farmland and Green Belt, with a general presumption against green field development. Centrifugal investment in unsustainable sprawl and exurbs should be replaced with centripetal forces that intensify cities as compact settlements, expanding inwards and upwards in dense clusters around local centres. Conserving countryside and intensifying cities are mutually reinforcing. Both reduce flood risk, road traffic and carbon emissions. Using permeable tarmac minor streets and surface car parks, and installing green roofs on larger buildings and soakaways for new homes would all help, together with urban tree planting and countryside management in the uplands.

Protecting open countryside and productive farmland against all but essential development would reduce food imports and strengthen rural economies and village life. It would also allow all natural habitats to be managed to restore biodiversity.

To encourage this shift away from unnecessary development (apart from VAT reform) there should be much stronger legal protection for existing AONBs and SSSIs and, longer-term, extending natural habitats and woodlands.

At local level, let us first distribute all farming subsidies, whether European or national, through local councils. The ministry of what was agriculture, fisheries and food (MAFF) is incompetent. It was fined £647 million from 2005-14, and another £230m in 2015-16 for failing to pay EU subsidies to 80,000 English farmers on time (*Private Eye* 1452, 8/9/2017). With funds, local rural strategies could address some of the serious challenges faced by local farmers and natural habitats. For example:

- food security is ignored in the *NPPF*,
- power between farmers and foodsheds is unbalanced,
- global food chains have replaced local markets and seasonal variety,
- most farm subsidies, whether the land is farmed or left fallow, reward wealthy landowners rather than low paid farmers. This contradicts the original purpose of the 'common agricultural policy' to protect small farms and rural jobs,
- agro-business is largely unregulated. Prairie farms and crop monocultures have poisoned natural habitats with fertilizers and pesticides (visible in the twin tracks) and uprooted trees and hedges (audible in the silence of the birds);
- the dramatic loss of small abattoirs, caused by excessive veterinary charges by government, means that profits of the few large abattoirs are offset by increased stress among livestock and longer journeys to and from abattoirs,
- similarly, since the Milk Marketing Board was closed in 2003, dairy farming has spiralled into decline with no national action, and
- while genetically modified (GM) crops are a national issue, super dairies and battery farms might be more forcefully controlled by competent councils.

It could be worse. In China, when Chairman Mao once asked why farm crops had not met their five-year target, he was told that too many chaffinches were eating the corn. "Get rid of the chaffinches." Five years later, Mao asked the same question. With no chaffinches, plagues of insects were eating the crops. "Get rid of the insects." Five years later, crop targets were missed, this time because fruit crops failed. Bees are also insects. Today in south China, small teams handpick pollen from the earlier flowering fruit trees and sell it to farmers back north to hand pollinate their trees.

This is either a positive increase in GDP with new jobs for pollen gatherers and pollinators, or an external cost of agrochemicals. Take your pick.

Farming needs to be re-integrated in the local economic and social fabric. Local councils, chambers and NFUs should produce local strategies a) to agree how best to distribute farm subsidies that support sustainable farming, and b) to develop local food chains. Food produced and sold locally reduces food miles, transport, refrigeration and packaging costs, air pollution and imports, retains food quality, local jobs and social traditions, increases food security, reduces the grip of the foodsheds and is popular. It also commands higher prices. This makes small-scale mixed farming more viable, with higher land values and better use of green belts.

Local policy options are many and varied. Councils might:

- restrict subsidies to small farms, tenant farmers, young farmers or shepherds in marginal uplands, or to support mixed farms or those at risk like dairy herds, or continue to subsidize wealthy farmers and landowners. And when landowners simply increase rents when tenants receive subsidies, perhaps some councils would extend rent tribunals (as for housing tenants) in order to ensure that the working farmers are fairly rewarded for their labour;
- encourage more organic farming with income support during the changeover period. We may have led Europe in improving the care of livestock, but organic farming is modest. Early this century, Austria sought to double its organic farming from about 25% of existing farms. We sought to triple ours – from 0.5% of farmland;
- revive smallscale food production in cities with urban farms, smallholdings, market gardens and orchards, allotments, parks and gardens;
- develop local marketing boards and farm co-ops to strengthen local farmers in negotiations with foodsheds, and secure local abattoirs and wholesale markets;
- develop local food chains from farms to shops and restaurants, support new food manufacturers and brewers using local produce; and
- return food waste to piggeries, subject to local public health officials.

Farming should be encouraged in Green Belts, which at present are valued more for their scenic value, leisure pursuits, dirty trades, shedscapes and development potential. And to reduce urban sprawl, cities should develop 'green wedges' along existing green chains and corridors like railways, rivers and canals, parks and cemeteries, gardens and allotments, school grounds and sports fields (see 4 below).

With strategic vision and adequate funds, it should also be possible to increase biodiversity beyond protected habitats, with more organic farms, small ecology parks, more hedgerows, wildlife corridors and native copses.

2   Traffic reduction

(Replacing *NPPF* chapters 9 and 10 – promoting sustainable transport and high quality communications.)

The strategic transport objective must be to reduce road and air traffic, their poisonous emissions and the number and length of trips. These can be achieved through improved social transport services, increased urban densities and diversity and safer walking and cycling networks. Government can help in two ways. First, it should rationalize all transport taxes to discourage the most polluting modes of transport. These might include new fuel and noise taxes on all aircraft, a new tax on all larger car parks, removing the 'escalator' on rail fares and re-applying the fuel escalator so that more drivers return to trains. The fuel escalator could be made 'tax neutral' with a comparable tax cut for the average household.

Second, it should match its transport investments with comparable regional spending. HS2 will be a reckless waste if the regional networks are not upgraded. The successful French TGV network masks the dramatic decline of its regional networks. Essentially, this means re-establishing PTAs (passenger transport authorities) to co-ordinate, implement and manage regional transport services.

The many strategic options (from chapter 6) include transferring heavy road freight to rail and more rail links to ports, quarries and large industrial estates, reviving the use of canals, opening transhipment depots to transfer goods from HGVs to local LGVs, improving regional rail networks, with better integration and through-ticketing between national, regional and local services, and comprehensive networks for safe walking and cycling, including links to surrounding villages.

All this and more could be covered by the PTAs. The striking success of the Merseyside PTA should be repeated in all metropolitan and rural regions like East Anglia, north Wales and the south west. Integrated regional networks and major transport hubs would also become the focus for urban intensification.

At neighbourhood level (Buchanan's 'environmental cells'), all traffic should be calmed with pedestrian priority streets throughout, and reduced through car sharing and less parking. In urban neighbourhoods where 40% of households do not own cars (ONS 2006), councils should start to introduce traffic-free streets.

It is not mere nostalgia for those times when hundreds of workers walked and cycled to work (as seen for example in *I'm All Right, Jack* and Pathe Newsreel clips). It remains the norm in the Netherlands. "The Holland development [in Bremen] will cover 2.6 hectares and supply 250 homes. There will be just 30 parking spaces instead of the 200 normally required in such a development and these will be used for car sharing and car pooling schemes. A quarter of the total land area will be released for other uses because of the parking space savings." (*Transport Retort*, issue 17/4 1994) One wonders whether, 20 years on, such development would be permitted here under the *NPPF*, with density at almost 100 homes/ha (40/acre) and parking of only one space for eight homes. These space savings result in better buildings, safer streets, less pollution and, for anyone who has visited the Vaubun neighbourhood in Freiburg, the noise of children playing outside with relaxed parental supervision.

Safe streets are a priority. Every week during term time, between 3pm and 4pm, one or two children are killed and about 40 seriously injured walking or cycling home from school. (The figures rise in the winter months.) The killing of innocents can be stopped with slower driving and far more pedestrian crossings to create pedestrian networks that are safe and comprehensive.

3   Economic development, anchors vs hoovers
(Replacing chapter 6 – building a strong, competitive economy.)

To strengthen city economies, the two objectives should be to reduce imports through SMEs (small and medium sized enterprises) and to support innovation through the growth of clusters.

To support SMEs and clusters, government should first reform all corporate taxes as set out in chapter 10. It should tax turnover rather than profits, remove all artificial tax allowances and all tax relief on borrowings (except those essential for production and internal growth). It should also strengthen anti-competitive agencies and make membership of chambers of trade and industry obligatory. These would then work in partnerships with local councils, colleges and other agencies as required.

Strong economies based on SMEs are vital. Once Victorians understood how raw sewage contaminated water supplies, clean water supplies and sewers were installed fairly quickly because cities were engines of economic growth and social vitality. No longer. Today's councils are unable (or reluctant) to reduce traffic and its toxic emissions that are killing citizens as surely as contaminated water.

As argued in chapter 5, cities with healthy SME sectors are more resilient during recessions, more flexible in expansionary times and occasionally create specialist clusters. All our cities, however, pale beside Prato in northern Italy. With a population of 189,000, the city has 7,194 firms in the textile sector alone, employing 34,746 in 2014 (www.ui.prato.it.). If Prato has 9,000 SMEs in total, that is 476 for every 10,000 residents compared with London's 418.

SMEs reflect the health of local economies. From table 38 opposite, of the 64 largest UK cities (Small Business Factbook 2014), eight of the top ten are in the south east, 19 of the bottom 20 reflect the decline in our industrial regions. The top ten have fewer manufacturing SMEs than average, and more in knowledge, information and business systems. This is reversed in the bottom ten and reflects government indifference to the manufacturing sector generally.

Local policies to revive urban economies include the following:

- prefer local anchors and clusters of SMEs to a few mega-corps, focussing on internal growth rather than inward investment,
- consider work as a basic right, both economically and socially, with open-ended education to develop everyone's potential, college training to develop skills and SME research links with universities,
- encourage more social enterprises as the third arm in all economies,
- develop local supply chains, partly through local purchasing by public agencies,
- support small firms in every neighbourhood, survey older buildings at risk that could provide affordable business premises, and
- develop the local financial infrastructure through local and regional banks.

Table 38: SMEs per 10,000 urban population, 2013

City by rank	SMEs/10k	City	SMEs/10k
Top 20:		Bottom 20:	
1 London	418.4	45 Wakefield	215.7
2 Reading	364.6	46 Coventry	211.2
3 Brighton	360.8	47 Derby	209.5
4 Aldershot	359.8	48 Wigan	208.3
5 Milton Keynes	349.2	49 Sheffield	207.0
6 Aberdeen	348.0	50 Luton	205.1
7 Crawley	318.3	51 Swansea	204.3
8 Southend	307.1	52 Barnsley	202.6
9 Cambridge	305.5	53 Stoke	199.1
10 Bristol	301.5	54 Birkenhead	198.3
11 Bournemouth	298.9	55 Newport	196.8
12 Warrington	293.3	56 Doncaster	196.1
13 Preston	292.2	57 Mansfield	192.8
14 Edinburgh	291.6	58 Newcastle	187.7
15 Norwich	287.3	59 Middlesbrough	183.7
16 Northampton	280.1	60 Liverpool	180.3
17 York	280.0	61 Hull	175.5
18 Manchester	273.1	62 Dundee	173.9
19 Blackpool	271.2	63 Plymouth	172.5
20 Worthing	270.6	64 Sunderland	150.2

Source: Centre for Cities, 2014

4   Urban intensification ('town cramming')
(Replacing chapters 16 and 17 – conserving the historic environment, and reducing the use of minerals.)

The strategic objective, in tandem with land use (1 above), is to restore towns and cities as compact diverse settlements by conserving the existing built fabric and intensifying it through small scale extensions and infill developments to minimize the waste of minerals.

Government will support a general presumption against major redevelopment schemes in all urban areas, protect the settings of Conservation Areas and Listed Buildings, recycle more building materials, minerals and aggregates, and impose a reinstatement tax on all quarries and open cast mines for when they cease operations.

As should be clear by now, conserving old buildings to increase their lifespan over centuries saves materials, energy and money wasted on needless demolition and redevelopment every 50 or 60 years. Having survived 50 years, most buildings should last for centuries, providing cheap premises, strengthening local economies, releasing capital for other purposes and retaining a 'sense of place' and continuity. Yet wanton destruction continues due to the perverse VAT:

- Victorian multi-storey factories and warehouses, often terraced, were expensive to build, but energy efficient, of long life, with low maintenance and small land take. Most have been demolished and replaced by cheap single-storey sheds;

- in Bristol, a Victorian school was improved with new electronically-controlled double-glazed windows to maximize solar gain and natural ventilation, and reduce heat loss, boiler output and fuel bills. The total investment was recouped in less than five years. Yet Victorian schools are increasingly rare, demolished as part of ruinous PFI schemes and replaced with inferior buildings;

- most walk-ups, better built than most Georgian terraces, have gone within 80 years mostly through regeneration schemes. In 1982/3, in England and Wales we demolished 17,074 homes, in 2001/2 (the last year figures were collected), 25,300 homes in England alone (ONS); and

- substantial commercial offices are being demolished after 50 years and, in Docklands, a few buildings within a decade. This is unsustainable.

The public money invested in the HMR and Regeneration programmes, about $40bn, could have restored most of the 750,000 vacant homes, with over £50,000 a property, with training for many thousands of young people. All urban neighbourhoods should be treated as Conservation Areas in their solidity and as shanties in their vernacular adaptability. Destroying them is foolish, dangerous and unsustainable.

Intensification ('cramming') suggests overcrowded buildings and overloaded services. In reality, it refills existing schools and surgeries, revives local shops and pubs and makes more efficient use of buses, sewers and energy. Sometimes, a facility may need to be extended or rebuilt, but most people walk to these buildings and keep fit. New suburbs all require new facilities to which most will drive.

Old cities were usually constrained by outer gated walls to protect against armies and marauders. Ebenezer Howard retained this constraint, fixing the size of Letchworth at 30,000 people (as in Thomas More's *Utopia*). Around this garden city, he proposed smaller satellite towns, all separated by working countryside and connected by public transport. (This town-country pattern resembled the German geographer Walter Christaller's regional urban network of administrative capital, with manufacturing cities and market towns surrounded by farmland and villages.)

In our largest cities, perhaps the suburban centres could be restored as independent satellite towns separated by green chains, as Abercrombie proposed in his plan for London (1943): to "form a continuous park system... of green wedges and parkways, linking the centre of London with the Green Belt, where the aim should be to preserve a broad area of unspoilt country with easy access for London's inhabitants." Bristol retains a green chain of park, woodland, allotments, riding stables and an urban farm from the north east of the city to within a mile of the centre. Typically, this wedge also contains Bristol's motorway link to the M4. Most large cities and conurbations have this potential. Over time, cities might even revive some intensive farming. When the Huguenots settled in Hackney, they set up market gardens, smallholdings, orchards and wildlife in backland sites. In inner Detroit, small scale farming is one of the few thriving 'cottage' industries, but the city lacks the funds to invest in the rundown centres, so intensification will struggle to get started.

Policy options for urban intensification include:

- refusing all green field development,
- treating all neighbourhoods as informal conservation areas,
- focussing most new building around district centres, transport routes and rail stations, with improved social transport to connect the revived centres,
- raising urban densities, local convenience and land values, and
- reducing the built-up area by creating green wedges with existing parks and cemeteries etc, with some small-scale farming within city boundaries.

5   Housing need before choice
(Replacing chapter 5 – "delivering a sufficient supply of homes.")

Every local authority should ensure that every citizen is comfortably housed, working with local developers and builders, social and private landlords, local co-ops, TMAs (tenant management associations) and self builders. This will include restoring vacant houses, converting under-used buildings and vacant upper floors, extending and infilling existing houses and maximizing the potential of windfall sites for social housing and self-build homes.

Government will grant local councils flexibility to tackle problems associated with houses not used as primary homes. Options will include increasing the council tax on all second homes, treating holiday lets and airbnbs as businesses to be taxed and controlled like hotels, and requisition homes kept vacant as investments. Additionally, councils might bring the conversion of offices back under planning control, and set up local rent tribunals so that private rents reflect local wages more fairly and reduce total Housing Benefits.

In addition to the above, local councils might consider the following policies:

- in their survey of old buildings, to identify those particularly suitable for affordable housing with or without workspace,
- intensify local areas by building new homes on windfall and backland sites, increasing local densities and strengthening local economies,
- diversify the supply of affordable housing through social landlords, housing co-ops, TMOs and self-build, and
- by conserving urban neighbourhoods, encourage stability and continuity for residents across generations.

Like most urban issues, housing is primarily a local issue for local management, with the role of central government reduced to that of funder and auditor. Chapter 8 suggested how local councils could renovate vacant homes and, through a second home tax, provide affordable housing.

We should also bring the conversion of offices to housing back under planning control. Centre Point, designed by Colonel Seifert and opened in 1967, was kept vacant for several years while its owner Harry Hyam sought a single 'blue chip' office tenant to increase the property value. A homeless charity (already named Centrepoint) gained much publicity by occupying the building for two days in January 1974 before being evicted. Largely forgotten is how the 33-storey block (greatly in excess of plot ratio standards at the time) was negotiated with the London County Council. In return for extra floors, 'planning gain' was a large gyratory around the tower, greatly increasing traffic at the busy crossroad of Oxford Street and Tottenham Court Road.

50 years later, the gyratory is being adapted more for pedestrians than cars, and the office block has been converted to expensive private flats. Half have been withdrawn from sale because offers were too low. We learn from one mistake, it seems, only to commit another. With control over such conversions restored, the local council might have approved the conversion on condition that it only provided social housing.

However, here we need to discuss the potential for intensification in neighbourhoods. On the way to our allotment, we pass a small site between housing terraces and a railway station with a small pottery in a disused railway building. This site had two garage courtyards separated by a small all-purpose sports pitch with some mature trees. While children were often playing in the cage, we never saw anyone using the garages. Today, six three storey houses have been built on part of the site, but as three pairs of semis rather than a terrace of seven homes. Fully two-thirds of the front gardens are paved for parking, increasing flood risk and reducing biodiversity – even while street parking bays remain visible in front of their gardens. Worst is that it was the popular cage that was first redeveloped. Only five or six years later were the garages redeveloped, but again solely for housing. No small workshop or two on the site adjacent to the pottery to diversify the local area.

6   Town centres

(Replacing *NPPF* chapter 7 – ensuring the vitality of town centres.)

Every town centre is a unique social neighbourhood and vital cluster in the local economy. However, it also sits in a retail hierarchy of regional, town and district centres, down to local shopping parades. This hierarchy needs to be intensified so that every centre functions as an economic and social hub, however modest.

There is a correlation between urban density and shop numbers, as shown in table 39 overleaf. This correlation combines the insights of Jane Jacobs and Adam Smith. High density supports the diversity of more shops more widely dispersed throughout the town, attracting more customers on foot and improving their health. More shops also means more independent shopkeepers providing more choice and competition on service and price.

Table 39: UK urban and shop densities, 2004

Town/City	Population	Shops	Shops/1,000
The most dense:-			
Brighton and Hove	206.6	3,941	19.1
Luton	185.5	1,666	9.0
Southampton	234.2	2,348	10.0
Blackpool	142.3	2,810	19.8
Sunderland	177.7	2,644	14.9
London	7,172.0	na	na
Bradford	293,7	6,038	20.6
Southend	160.3	2,685	16.8
Oxford	143.0	1,496	10.5
Coventry	303.5	2,762	9.1
The least dense:-			
Ipswich	138.7	1,391	10.0
Norwich	174.0	1,925	11.1
Rotherham	117.3	2,216	18.9
Peterborough	136.3	1,383	10.1
Poole	144.8	1,287	8.9
Telford	138.2	1,206	8.7
Crawley	100.5	595	5.9
Milton Keynes	184.5	1,522	8.3
Bolton	139.4	3,041	21.8
Sutton Coldfield	105.5	na	na

Source: ONS and Valuation Office Agency, 2004

These figures ignore size of shops and vacancy rates. The cities (from table 8, page 80) also include some anomalies like the 'car towns' of Coventry, Luton and Oxford, and former industrial towns Bolton and Rotherham. If we exclude these outliers, compact towns support 15-20 shops, suburban towns 8-10/1,000 people. Figures for inner and outer London are 21.1 and 11.2 shops/1,000 respectively.

Two cities above have a working population of about 70,000 people. Blackpool supports 2,810 shops and at least 1,500 more entrepreneurs than Poole with only 1,287 shops. While SMEs create economic wealth, shops also create social bonds between shopkeepers and customers. Today, however, shops are also falling victim to the same 'gravitational' economic forces of globalization.

Government should reform the Uniform Business Rates based on turnover rather than rental value, so that the Rates for shops and sheds are more uniform, evaluate a tax on car parking, refuse all further retail sheds and, as with economic development (3 above), empower local chambers of trade.

Apart from increasing density, council policy options include:

- improving town centre management in partnership with chambers,
- supporting street markets, local suppliers and wholesale markets,
- converting vacant upper floors over shops, and
- developing under-used car parks to diversify the centres and address local commercial, civic and social needs.

7   Neighbourhoods – the wonderful immensity of streets
(Replacing chapter 8 – promoting healthy and safe communities.)

The strategic objective must be to diversify every neighbourhood physically, economically and socially. One way to achieve this is to give neighbourhood plans more autonomy from more general planning frameworks.

Neighbourhoods are where we experience daily city life. Higher densities support more commercial outlets and social activities, increasing local prosperity and land values. This tends to raise densities and diversity further, a rare example of a virtuous positive feedback loop which worked over centuries until the rise of zones and suburbs. And of Jane Jacobs' four criteria for urban life – high density, short streets, old buildings and mixed uses – in neighbourhoods, diversity may be the most important. It produces attractive townscapes, small businesses prosper and residents find life convenient and convivial.

Suburbs are mostly quiet, single-use single-class ghettoes. Social stratification was first studied by the University of Chicago school of sociology from the 1920s. Ernest W Burgess (LeGates and Stout 2003) divided a typical city into five concentric zones: city centre, the zone in transition (for immigrants and underworlds), the zone for working men, the residential zone and the commuters' zone. Today, our cities have a centre, inner areas for regeneration, outer suburbs, exurbia and the long-distance commuter belt.

As inner area families settled and their children moved up the social ladder, so some moved out one or two rings. While a steady influx of migrants exceeded the exodus to the outer rings, cities prospered, pushing up land prices, building heights and urban densities in inner areas. During the last century, however, inner city populations declined, at least in Britain and the US, the exodus fuelled by slum clearance and reinforced by race and class discrimination. In US cities, the influx of black Americans from the rural south was exceeded by the exodus of white working and middle classes. Fewer and poorer residents drastically reduced city revenues for public services and investment, an extreme example being Detroit. In Britain, this flight from inner cities, encouraged by the new town programme, left poor inner city neighbourhoods at densities too low to revive local economies. This downward spiral culminated in empty tower blocks and boarded-up terraces.

There are two types of neighbourhood: those where developers won't go, and those where you can't keep them out. Zoning affects them both. In popular neighbourhoods, following the relocation of 'non-conforming uses' by planning, the developers now redevelop all remaining non-residential sites with minimal risk due to the stressed housing market and rising house prices. In my neighbourhood, in 30 years, several small warehouses, cinemas, historic factories and large mill, office block, chapel and at least three schools have all been converted or redeveloped for housing. None were retained and converted to provide attractive and affordable business units and perhaps a community facility or two. The herd instinct for short-term capital gains and rental streams are at the expense of long-term sustainable economic health. Jacobs saw that mixing primary functions of commerce, employment, civic buildings and housing increased customers, opening hours, turnover and rents for secondary shops, sandwich bars, cafes and pubs, making the buildings more efficient. Segregating workers, shoppers, residents and visitors means that the few local shops and cafes in each zone only trade in short periods, like desert cacti. Contrary to the racists, we must replicate successful ethnic ghettoes that have retained dense neighbourhoods with social and economic diversity.

The increasing lack of local diversity may also reflect the undue emphasis we place on visual appearance. We can all regret the loss of regional variation of texture, style and materials. Black granite in Aberdeen, red sandstone in Carlisle, millstone grit in the Pennines, oolitic limestone in the Cotswolds, knapped flintwork in Norfolk, timber frames in Kent, Portland stone in Dorset (and the City), the humble brick in Essex and yellow London stocks etc all gave regional variety. The twentieth century has replaced this with residential brick and render, concrete, steel and glass for commerce, sheet metal and breeze blocks for sheds.

The great architectural historians, including Pevsner, Clifton Taylor, Mumford and Hoskins, tended to focus on the monumental, emphasizing the nobility and scale of such examples found in Bath (the Circus and Crescent by the elder and younger Woods), Edinburgh New Town (by Craig), Hastings (St Leonard's Warrior Square by the Burtons, father and son), Newcastle city centre (by Grainger and Dobson), London's Regents Park and Street (by John Nash) and its many Georgian squares.

By contrast, modest vernacular neighbourhoods were sniffily patronized. Two critics used the same aerial photo of Preston terraced streets, which was "far from the worst example of the palaeotechnic disrespect for life" according to Mumford (1966); "neither good enough to promote happiness nor bad enough to produce hopelessness" for Hoskins (1970). Yet these dense Victorian terraced neighbourhoods provided urban life on their doorstep: shops and pubs round the corner, mills and factories, churches, schools and the town centre a short walk away, with buses and trams for trips further afield. The handsome dignity found in Bath, Edinburgh and London's Berkeley Square cannot mask their dullness. Urban life is offstage, round the corner in the busy narrow streets. Most cities have such contrasts between the sublime and the earthy, the empty film set and the noisy street theatre.

Samuel Johnson saw this: "Sir, if you wish to have a just notion of the magnitude of this city, you must not be satisfied with seeing its great streets and squares, but must survey the innumerable little lanes and courts. It is not in the showy evolutions of buildings, but in the multiplicity of human habitations which are crowded together, that the wonderful immensity of London consists." (Boswell 1951) Booth's London maps showed the wealthy living in streets near those housing the 'Lowest class. Vicious, semi-criminal'. Most cities were the same.

Street life is vital. In one of his BBC wildlife programmes, David Attenborough said that in every flock or shoal, each bird or fish is in constant communication with its seven nearest neighbours. Something similar happens in terraced streets. In front or back gardens, on the way to work, shops, pubs and school, streets provide neighbourly security and the backdrop for friendly chat, children's play and local support. Terraced streets are one of the few positive images of cities, ingrained in our collective folklore about street life, class solidarity, extended families and friendly neighbours. How else explain the enduring popularity of *Coronation Street* and *Eastenders*?

In 1900, perhaps 90% lived in terraces and flats. By 2001, through slum clearance, housing renewal, freeways and regeneration schemes, only 26% lived in terraces (ONS 2004). Although in desirable locations, terraced houses remain the most expensive housing per sq. ft. of floor space, we still demolish terraces in stressed neighbourhoods that could, with modest funds, provide so many affordable homes. In the suburbs, 32% live in semis and 23% in bungalows, where pedestrians have been replaced by rat runners and parked cars. The rest (18%) live in flats and maisonettes, increasingly in regeneration schemes where lanes and courts have made way for the 'showy evolutions' of the megaliths, icons replacing acorns.

We have lost 'the wonderful immensity of streets'. Suburbs don't have streets. They have avenues and drives.

The Urban Task Force (1999) stressed the need for higher densities through good urban design, which it then neglected to define. (There is a pattern here. I'm not so modest.) Why the committee, chaired by a famous architect with eminent planners and consultants, should duck this issue suggests a lack of nerve or verve. Defining key urban design principles might have provided some useful guidelines for the *NPPF*. Instead, it referred the task back to government, calling for "a national urban design framework, disseminating key design principles," and "dedicated Planning Policy guidance etc." So here is that urban design framework. And let us first talk of urban form and texture rather than urban design. Urban designers should feel the physicality of streets and neighbourhoods before meddling with what was, before the era of planning, rather simple.

Apart from the development of small infill sites, like that described above under housing need, there are three other ways we can intensify our neighbourhoods – through suburbs, terraces and shanties. Eight million of England's 23 million homes are semi-detached (ONS 2006), many occupied by old couples whose families have long since moved out. Converting 10% of them over twenty years into two one- and two-bedroom flats would yield about 40,000 new homes a year, doubling the number of windfall gains in table 37 above (page 291). With rear extensions and redeveloping or building over the garages could add another 10,000 homes a year.

This would increase local densities and existing residents' pensions and even prolong their independent living. This would open a long-term market for local builders, and could increase the social housing stock for housing associations and councils.

Figure 5: Urban intensification

Existing 3-storey shopping parades and station, showing 12 semis redeveloped for 3- and 4-storey blocks of flats, with 3- and 2-storey terraced workshops and cottages

Except in back gardens, new infill buildings should be at least the same height or one or two floors higher than adjoining buildings. This seldom happens. Most bomb-sites were rebuilt with two-storey infills even when next to three- and four-storey terraces. And in Liverpool, when Derek Hatton was council leader, apparently all new housing was restricted to two storeys even when redeveloping substantial inner areas. The subsequent loss of scale, people and businesses reduced once-thriving neighbourhoods to quiet suburbs. Bungalows should be consigned to the history bin.

Figure 5 opposite offers a more ambitious scheme for intensification around a small suburban centre and two side streets. Based on the typical suburban plot of 20 by 120 feet (Howard's plots in Letchworth were 20 by 130 feet), six adjacent semis and the six they back onto in the next street produce more than half an acre (120 by 240 feet, 36 by 72 metres). This could provide 30 new flats on three or four floors fronting the two streets, with a dozen two-storey cottages, studio workshops or small offices off the new lane linking the two streets. Even eight adjacent semis could provide as many as 24 new homes, all with small private or communal gardens. Mixing private owners with private and social landlords would diversify neighbourhoods, enliven quiet streets, revive local shops and benefit local schools and surgeries, with the greatest impact near town centres, railway stations, local shopping parades and along busy transport routes. Our twentieth century suburban vernacular should be intensified gradually rather than mothballed. Over time, local land values would rise and demand grow.

Terraced streets were the 'building blocks' of our urban fabric. Any visual tedium was relieved by differences in width and length, trees, front elevations and gardens, and all the variations since the first terraces from the early fourteenth century (Platt 1976).

- My first house was a standard two-up, two-down terrace with kitchen and bathroom extension in the back yard. The 'show house' in Liverpool's Granby Street GIA in the 1960s, the terraces were demolished some 40 years later under the Housing Market Renewal programme despite their solid construction.
- A few back-to-back terraces remain in Leeds with one converted terrace off Duke Street in Liverpool. Most fell foul of Building Regulations for lacking through-ventilation. With today's technology, single-aspect homes can house specific transient groups like students, some singles and couples, tourists and residents of cardboard cities.
- My next house was in a more substantial terrace on four floors, including semi-basement ('lower ground floor' to estate agents) and attic bedroom. Built in the 1840s for larger families with a servant or two, some have now been divided into two maisonettes.
- Edinburgh has some four-storey terraces divided into two maisonettes, the lower with garden fronting one street, the upper with garden fronting the next street. Similarly, on the steep hillsides of Hebden Bridge, in some four-storey terraces, the lower floors access the lower street, the upper the higher street.

- Glasgow's Gorbals tenement blocks on three or four floors had common stairwells to six or eight flats with a small communal garden at the back. Virtually all have been demolished despite Ian Nairn's pleas for their retention.
- London's grand terraces originally had mews stables to their back gardens. These have long since been converted into cottages despite not meeting Parker Morris standards. (One planner thought that they should become garages.)
- Largely unsung has been the loss of back courtyards, where Syd Garrett played "marlies and tip cat, and 'op, skip an' jump in that courtyard in old Ladywood".
- The six ancient terraces in East Looe, however (also from chapter 2), have survived. Without gardens or yards, the front steps have potted plants with front doors opposite, the back doors opposite back doors distinguished by dustbins.

Well-designed terraces achieve high densities, enclose secure streets and are very adaptable with roof space, basement and back extension. They are also very efficient. Just as hexagonal honeycomb makes the most efficient use of beeswax, space and heat, so terraced houses and flats, typically one room wide and two rooms deep, maximize internal floor space and daylight to site area, their party walls reducing building materials and heat loss. Compared with a bungalow of 1,200 sq ft, a mid-terrace four-storey home with the same floor space has

- a quarter of the ground footprint, which increases densities and social behaviour over garden fences and in the street,
- less than half the external surface area, reducing both building materials and heat loss,
- ditto two party walls, while terraced flats are even more efficient with three or four party walls.

Terraces are solid and sustainable. Yet vexatious government policy seems bent on their destruction. Terraced streets can create safe environments where neighbours develop social roots and some interest in strangers passing through. In the analogy between city and human anatomy, pedestrians are the lifeblood between arterial roads and capillary streets with safety in numbers. In general, suburbs protect privacy, terraced streets promote society. Popular streets are also safe. Street criminals, like tax evaders, are opportunistic and value their privacy and assess the risks before they commit or go elsewhere: is the victim alone or the house easily entered, is the area visible from other houses, is anyone looking if the victim protests or retaliates, could residents hear and would they phone the police or come out themselves, and finally, would the perpetrator still have time to commit the crime and escape? Eyes and feet on the street are deterrents.

Physical determinists (also known as architects) believe that safe neighbourhoods can be created by design. Oscar Newman's *Defensible Space: Crime Prevention Through Urban Design* (1972) introduced concepts of territoriality and natural surveillance in urban areas. In a typical residential street, between private control indoors and public access to the street, residents largely control the semi-private space in back gardens even when shared and overlooked by immediate neighbours. Front gardens are semi-public space over which residents only have informal control.

Design features for success include the following.

- Streets should be dense, short and open-ended, convenient for local shops and social facilities. Cul-de-sacs preclude strangers' short cuts and increase the length of residents' trips.
- Traffic must be calmed to encourage more pedestrians, social activity and playspace, with parking space for car pools rather than private cars.
- Terraces should front each other to maximize eyes on the street and avoid blank gables, ill-lit alleys and blind corners where petty crime can happen.
- Similarly, rear gardens should back onto rear gardens of the next street. Back allies or 'jiggers' for rear access should be secure at each end.
- Terraces all facing south (and rear gardens of the next terrace) and Radburn layouts (with cars in back lanes and pedestrians in front streets) should both be avoided.
- Street width should be between 30 to 65 feet (10 to 20 metres), allowing for mature trees between two- to five-storey terraces to create a sense of enclosure. Two-storey town centres, as in Plymouth, waste valuable urban space.
- Building plots should be narrow. In two late Victorian road improvements in London, the Strand retains most of its narrow frontages, giving visual, social and economic variety along its length. About half of Victoria Street consists of two dull office blocks that are dead frontage, adding nothing to pavement life.
- Privacy in terraces requires solid party walls, while some mix of house types by size and tenure is desirable.

Not all terraced neighbourhoods are safe. Local gangs, fostering drugs, bigotry and/or racism, guard their 'territory' on insularity and menace. Strangers feel unsafe, neighbours are cowed and, in extreme, residents can be afraid to look out of their windows in case they are seen by the little criminals. However, this social breakdown can fester in suburbs as in terraces. In the long run, these deep-rooted failures of social cohesion require, not redevelopment, but concerted action through youth workers, drug teams, the police and others, plus a more varied mix of residents and housing tenure. This was the norm in cities before the twentieth century. Mixing residents and house tenure may be social engineering, but it would enliven those we have engineered in the last century, including sink estates, ghettoes and no-go areas, peripheral estates, executive enclaves, dormitory settlements, commuter villages, tourism pressure areas, a sea of middle class suburbia and now gated communities. Without diversity, class isolation and individualism will prevail over social tolerance and fraternity.

Gated communities, usually in high-rise slabs and tower blocks, offer the security of private space and social exclusion. Here, developers maximize profits, councils reduce public highways and the police are replaced by private security firms, to be included in the landlords excessive rents and service charges. Locking residents in and society (and social tenants) out, contradicts urban life. And they are not new.

"The green squares [in Georgian London] were quiet and calm, away from the traffic of the main streets. The approaches from the great arteries like Euston Road and Oxford Street were closed by gates, and people who had no business in Bloomsbury were not admitted to the quarter. The grocer could not even send his errand-boy across to Bedford Square, he had to bring the goods himself in order to get in. This lasted until 1893 when an Act of Parliament was passed enjoining that the gates should be abolished." (Rasmussen 1960) Ironically, the twentieth century exacted its own revenge. Many of these handsome Bloomsbury squares with central gardens are used as large roundabouts for fast-moving traffic.

There is now a worrying trend to privatize public streets. New 'public' spaces in grand commercial developments are privately owned – as in London's Cabot Square, Broadgate centre and St Paul's office development – controlled by security guards and liable to be closed at the whim of the owners. Even pavements are not immune. A wheelchair-bound friend and partner, collecting for an MS charity, were moved off their local shopping centre forecourt (in Ilford) because that part of the pavement was private land.

The Georgian snobbery of those within, causing inconvenience and anger for those without, is being revived. Gated communities are neither social nor civil. Heaven may operate pearly gates to exclude sinners and infidels, but civilized cities are not celestial suburbs. They thrive on diversity and tolerance.

Early slum clearance usually led to four and five storey blocks of flats. These walk-ups replaced the social streets with balcony access but, despite the first tenants' pleasure and pride on moving into fine new flats, their history is not a happy one. Most have been demolished within 80 years. Social problems on the street were replaced by council problems and escalating costs of maintaining common areas, repairing lifts, replacing windows, cleaning stairwells and controlling anti-social behaviour. Relations between councils and tenants soured. In Liverpool, two tower blocks were known by housing officers as 'the piggeries', managed from the local housing office known as 'the fortress'.

Yet the Karl Marx Hof walk-ups in Vienna remain pristine and they retain shops and community facilities on the ground floor. Germany manages its larger rented housing far better, because most is owned by housing associations, co-ops and trade unions rather than local councils. Residents are more involved in management decisions and protected against landlord exploitation. Here, the Guinness and Peabody housing trusts owe much of their enduring success to their charitable status.

Finally, Olsen (1986) notes that "[T]he archbishop of Vienna finds nothing compromising in there being a Pizzaland on the ground floor of his palace: his dignity does not depend on such external circumstances. By living in the Stephansplatz he has the most desirable address possible." By contrast, Lambeth Palace (our archbishop of Canterbury's second home), with its substantial gardens, is mostly concealed behind blank walls like a gated community that turns its back on urban life.

Intensified neighbourhoods can be illustrated with two extreme examples. An informal settlement is the polite term for what are more widely known as shanty towns, townships and squatter camps. Local terms include *kampung* (an Indonesian village) *las barriadas* or *pueblos jóvenes* in Peru, *favelas* in Brazil and *villa miserias* in Argentina (Girardet 1996). Remarkably, most of them perform Braudel's three urban functions of shelter, security and trade.

Shelter may be in shacks of recycled timber, corrugated iron, old windows and other scrap materials that serve to keep the house up and the weather out. Despite the poverty, these homes are habitable. The most serious problem is the lack of basic services, notably clean water and sewers. Were councils to provide pipes and sewers at modest cost, these neighbourhoods would be acceptable.

The lack of security in most shanties foments the rise of rival drug gangs, with sporadic violence with police over law enforcement. Yet crime levels differ little from other poor neighbourhoods. Given security of tenure, however, crime levels fall. In Diadema, an industrial city in Brazil, the favela residents were given land-tenure rights "to stay on their properties for 90 years, encouraging them to maintain their homes and invest in the neighbourhoods. Residents helped to widen and pave streets, install clean-water and sanitation systems. Today... the annual homicide rate, a standard measure of civic order and public health, has dropped to 14.3/100,000 from its high of 140 during the 1990s." (Michael Kimmelman, *The New York Times* 30/10/11) This compares with a national murder rate of 23/100,000 in 2004.

Shanties sustain many small firms. A *Raconteur* supplement (*The Times*, 25/6/11) reported that in Dharavi in Mumbai, with between 700,000 and 1 million residents, "the area has more than 5,000 informal businesses, according to a report by the Harvard Business School", including snack shops, restaurants, tailors, bakeries, welders, barbers, potters and pepper grinders. With less than 100 SMEs/10,000, Dharavi is well below our bottom cities in table 38 above. But with secure tenure and safer streets, its firms could become legitimate, access bank loans, improve work conditions, expand and proliferate.

Kevin McCloud, after living a few days in Dharavi (*Slumming It*, Channel 4 2010) said that, once acclimatized, he found the narrow alleys safe, the houses reasonably comfortable and a thriving recycling industry in their midst. What was unacceptable to all was the lack of drains and sewers, the main slow-flowing ditch stinking as any open would. Proper sanitation would have transformed Dharavi and its residents' lives.

We prefer urban surgery to self-build neighbourhoods. Consider the Nine Elms project, from chapter 8:

- it will cost a predicted £13.46 billion, with less than £2 billion required from public funds, the lowest public input of the top 100 regeneration projects. But was it needed at all in central London?
- the 482 acre site (195 hectares) includes Battersea power station, New Covent Garden, Nine Elms and Vauxhall. The mixed scheme includes 16,000 homes at a density of perhaps 75 people/acre (180/hectare), mostly in tower blocks;

- the final number of affordable homes is unclear, but it will probably be less than the number of parking spaces;
- in scale, it resembles London Docklands. Perhaps it will avoid the latter's dreary street scene, crowded by tower blocks with few local shops, firms and pubs, with public (privately owned) open spaces underused, few pedestrians and intrusive traffic.
- Had it been planned in Paris, with terraced boulevards up to eight floors, it would have achieved Parisian densities well over 100 people/acre) and retained the dramatic impact of Battersea power station. As proposed, this icon will become an ambitious Lego structure largely concealed by glass towers.

Most of these regeneration projects could have achieved better results through conservation with modest infill developments and intensification. This would have minimized disruption, construction costs and energy consumption, and retained the social and economic roots of each neighbourhood.

Back in Mumbai, the city fathers and a major developer saw the opportunity. Rehouse the Dharavi residents in multi-storey blocks of flats and redevelop the area with a multi-trillion rupee scheme of expensive offices, executive housing and exclusive hotels. Major urban surgery with global professionals would significantly increase the national GDP. Basic infrastructure improvements would be a modest local tax burden – perhaps costing less than the architect's fees for the monumental scheme. Given leases, sewers and legitimate businesses, shanty towns could be models of sustainable development. The threat is that bulldozers will regenerate the area and the tower blocks for the displaced residents, meanly proportioned and less homely than the shacks, would quickly become real slums.

If, as Adam Smith said, most wealth is created through division of Labour rather than from Land or Capital, it is perverse that an expensive group of professionals and developers with almost unlimited capital and technical resources can't provide better environments than the poor themselves. Smith thought that landowners and capitalists did not know what was in their own best interests. John Maynard Keynes thought that they were not ignorant but sick – billionaires disease perhaps.

Dharavi and Nine Elms offer stark contrasts between informal vernacular and planned monumental neighbourhoods. Here are Howard's two magnets, either shanty or megalith:

- either entirely self-built, or need a small army of designers, advisers, developers, contractors, planners, bankers, investors, officials, ministers and 'special purpose vehicles' with management fees to match;
- very cheap and subsidy-free, or hugely expensive and usually subsidized;
- based on informal agreements, or on compulsory purchase;
- essentially risk-free, or passing most of the risks onto the public sector;
- constant low-key maintenance and improvement, or high maintenance costs and occasional costly 'upgrades';
- frugal recycling, or profligate with new, expensive materials;

- social wealth that is profit-free, or private profits extracted from the area;
- dense despite its low profile, or of modest density despite its overbearing scale;
- resilient, flexible and adaptable to changing conditions, or inflexible and almost indestructible;
- minimum use of energy, or maximum consumption for construction, heating, cooling, lighting and air conditioning;
- residents and firms have some control over their environment, or they have little or nothing invested in their environment;
- largely traffic-free, or not, despite major social transport services; and
- one creates an intensely urban environment with minimum entropy, the other creates an ambiguous environment with maximum entropy.

What they share is that both are ghettoes. Both support economic diversity but suffer a lack of social diversity, their citizens being either very poor or very wealthy. It will be interesting to observe Nine Elms when it loses its sheen, rents decline, the less wealthy move in, perhaps with a social landlord or housing co-op converting one or two blocks with affordable flats. But when the first shanty town, given secure tenure and sanitation, gentrifies as a few students and young couples, small families and even some young professionals move in, then we might see how our medieval towns grew, progressing from paupers' hovels, workers' cottages and cheap workshops to more solid and commodious neighbourhoods.

Reviving Patrick Geddes, in shanty towns the essential need for residents is to provide clean water and proper sewers. The essential improvement for residents is security of tenure so they can upgrade their homes.

Shanties are more sustainable than megaliths. Their very density offers some protection against large-scale redevelopments. Perhaps neighbourhoods are simply too big to be rebuilt successfully. Only renovations and windfall sites can improve neighbourhoods and retain the social roots found in streets. We might also give neighbourhoods more control over all modest local developments.

8 Good design. Aesthetics or efficiency.
(Replacing chapters 12 and 14 – achieving well-designed places, and meeting the challenge of climate change, flooding and coastal change.)

Buildings, the last element in my sustainable strategy for cities, consume as much as half of our nation's energy while releasing the energy of their occupiers. The strategic objective is therefore to reduce the former and increase the latter. Essentially, we need to increase the energy efficiency of every building – during its construction and throughout its lifespan. New buildings must reduce the energy 'embedded' in its construction energy, materials, aggregates and transport. And we must reduce energy consumption during the lifespan of every building, retrofitting existing buildings with more efficient insulation and energy controls.

New buildings may be more energy-efficient than existing, but this argument for redevelopment is spurious. My terraced house, built in the 1840s on three floors plus attic, costs about £2,000 a year in electricity and gas.

- Rebuilding it to be energy neutral would cost at least £150,000. This gives a payback period (capital cost divided by annual savings) of 75 years, or perhaps 100 years if we include the energy embedded in the demolition, transport, new materials and construction of the new building.
- However, spending £20,000 on our existing home, insulating external surfaces and draft proofing doors and windows, could have reduced our energy bills to less than £500 a year, a payback period of 12 years – increasing the payback for a new building to over three centuries. This would release capital for essential construction. Which is more sustainable?

Despite energy efficiency targets for new development, many homes built by the volume housebuilders will be short-lived. In six months, Persimmon, the second biggest housebuilder, sold 7,584 homes at an average price of £216,914 and making more than £67,000 gross profit (32%) on each home. In a stable industry, this is profiteering, which the government subsidizes with zero VAT and the £4bn Help to Buy scheme. Yet former boss Jeff Fairburn "qualified" for a bonus of £110 million, scaled back to £85 million before he was forced to quit. Such huge executive rewards, despite its deserved reputation for shoddy buildings, suggests that the jerry builders are back.

Shoddy construction also infects many PFI (private finance initiative) buildings. Most new schools, libraries, hospitals and prisons have been built under contracts by developer consortiums, who build, manage and maintain them for up to 30 years before handing them back to their public owners. (Only then, curiously, do the capital assets appear in the public sector balance sheets. This creative accounting by successive chancellors was done to 'reduce' capital public spending, despite the ruinous revenue costs of each PFI contract.) The assumption (that everyone knew to be false) was that PFI buildings cost less than local authority buildings, despite inflated bank charges, construction costs and management fees. Predictably, most PFI buildings are cheap designs, shoddily built and with minimum services and equipment, but full of revenue-generating vending machines and annual service charges that might include £75 to change a light bulb which staff are by contract forbidden to do. When Carillion went bust, its incomplete Royal hospital in Liverpool was found to have serious faults, including floors that had to be reinforced. Yet, so profitable are the management fees, maintenance costs, service charges and profits extracted from the public purse, that most PFI contracts are at least part-owned by the banks, alongside their train leasing companies.

The scandal of the PFI is that there is no scandal. Politicians seem relaxed, the media indifferent and everyone else resigned to the rise of these corporate landlords whose collective grip on so many public sector contracts is impossible to loosen except by buying them out, also at huge cost. Hoovers indeed.

At the other extreme are the corporate monuments that embed and consume excessive energy. With our rash of city skyscrapers, money is no object. If a typical house costs about up to £200 psf (and the Persimmon houses above might cost about £160 psf), then serviced offices could be built for perhaps £150 psf (with their simpler construction, services, fixtures and fittings). Compare that with the cost of London's most phallic icons (from Wikipedia):

- the Cheesegrater on 48 floors, opened in 2014 and cost an estimated £286 million for 908,730 sq ft, or £315 psf;
- the Shard (2012) had a contract cost of £435 million for 1.2 million sq ft, or over £360 psf;
- the Gherkin (2003) on 41 floors, cost £228.6 million (including over £90 million for the land) for 516,100 sq ft, or £443 psf; while
- One Canada Square in Docklands (1991, (perhaps starting the 'sky rush' in the City) cost £624 million for 1.2 million sq ft on 42 floors, or £520 psf.

These hoovers distort local economies. They inflate land values so that every owner expects the same 'development value' for their sites. They also inflate office rents and consequently all fees charged by the business occupants. Both reinforce the herd instinct of developers and the 'egos' of the mega-corps. Smaller buildings would encourage them to split their operations into manageable units. 'Back offices' don't need prime locations. Moving them to suburban centres or other cities would benefit those local economies while reducing central costs to increase profits or reduce fees.

Apart from hoovering social wealth, skyscrapers consume huge amounts of energy. Construction, the opposite of jerry building, is time-consuming and complex, requiring huge volumes of concrete and steel, half of it underground, huge quantities of expensive glass and other materials, and the new technology of cranes.

Expensive buildings should be relatively cheap to run. Not these. Laying a skyscraper on its side and dividing it into separate plots would be much more efficient.

- A six- to eight-storey terrace would need perhaps a quarter of the concrete and steel for the foundations and frames, reduce embedded energy and increase floor space by perhaps 10%.
- The terrace would need less heating with shared party walls and less external surface area. A skyscraper also sets up a chimney effect that cools its nearest streets and, however marginally, increases the heating costs of its neighbours.
- Traditional masonry walls with high thermal capacity greatly reduce heating costs. Glass towers have difficulty controlling solar gain and heat loss throughout the year.
- Traditional windows light and ventilate most rooms. Dark glass reduces solar gain but also natural light, so lights have to be left on. Closed environments also require air-conditioning although the Gherkin incorporates ventilating flues which reduce energy costs but also usable floor space.
- Fewer lifts in low buildings release floor space, save energy and let more staff use the stairs. One Canada Square has 37 lifts and still requires fire-proof stairwells which are seldom used.

No longer is it enough for architects and engineers to satisfy the requirements of owners and occupiers. Their buildings must also reduce their energy consumption, harmful emissions and waste of materials. Apparently, the Shard, with its combined heat and power plant and double skin of glass, uses 30% less energy, and the Gherkin uses 50% less energy – than comparable buildings. I suspect, however, that in their technological grandeur, skyscrapers are more like Concorde, a public folly from the 1960s that was also shrouded in secrecy to hide its ever-escalating costs, before inflicting its excessive noise and fuel emissions on the public at large. We need honest comparisons between these towers and the most energy-efficient buildings.

The difference between fashionable glitz and functional efficiency can be seen in Leicester. The older engineering block of Leicester university, designed by James Stirling, became an instant icon of modern architecture, despite a fairly consistent history of building faults, maintenance problems and high energy costs. The newer Leicester de Mountford university engineering block, by Short and Ford, is a well-insulated building that is naturally ventilated and widely unknown. No energy-efficient building has achieved iconic status. Today's private icons may point the way forward for their innovation, testing new structures, materials, technologies, layouts and controlled environments. Or, future critics may well see them as meretricious examples of post-modern eclecticism, and value instead the many handsome but modest low energy buildings. This is nothing new. Ancient windmills that ground corn and drained wetlands are venerated now that they are safely mothballed. Today's windmills generating energy still arouse fierce resistance.

"Aesthetic control is likely to take precedence over energy control." (Max Hutchinson, president of the RIBA, 1989-91).

Max was right. While energy efficiency should be the prime objective, the appearance of new buildings is also important. Here the collective problem, reflected in the *NPPF*, is that "great weight should be given to outstanding or innovative designs which promote high levels of sustainability, or help raise the standard of design more generally in an area, so long as they fit in with the overall form and layout of their surroundings." Skyscrapers sport innovative design, but they are not sustainable and they signally fail that last injunction.

No-one knows what good design means. The following generalizations and assertions outline the problem. Throughout the twentieth century, there have been two significant shifts in the nature of our buildings, affecting both the vernacular and the monumental. In the SIC (standard industrial classification, table 13), construction sits between manufacturing and the service sector.

- If "A house is a machine for living in" (Le Corbusier), vernacular buildings, whether factory-made, built on-site or self-built, are in the manufacturing sector. Every neighbourhood has a mix of vernacular buildings. But step inside a home or workshop, and you enter private space where the emphasis is on basic functions and comfort.
- By contrast, a public monument is firmly in the service sector. Walk inside a cathedral, library or railway station and you enter public arenas. These public assets increase the balance sheet of social wealth.

The urban vernacular of our modest terraced streets, local shops and workshops, with modest monuments housing local libraries and schools, have mostly been redeveloped for monumental housing developments. After Corbusier's *Unité d'Habitation*, our own Byker Wall, Park Hill and Roehampton estates may be uplifting and as memorable as the Georgian crescents and squares. But most of the walk-ups, slabs and tower blocks have themselves been demolished, while the surrounding suburbs retain the pristine uniform of the semi-detached villa. They have not yet gained that vernacular 'lived-in feel' that comes with myriad small changes and extensions. Figure 5 above suggested how we might 'break the ice'.

The second shift, particularly since 1979, has been from public to private monuments. This accelerated through the growth of mega-corps, banks (following the 'big bang') and large developers, the growth of PFI hospitals and schools, and of major regeneration schemes being developed by public/private consortia. This has led to increasingly sublime private monuments and increasingly mean public monuments.

"Small is beautiful; Big is sublime." (Jonathan Meades, *Bunkers, Brutalism and Bloodymindedness*, BBC 2014)

All monuments aspire to the sublime. Cathedrals, libraries and railway stations loom large in the glory of our cities. Monuments, ancient and modern, are capable of "producing an overwhelming sense of awe, reverence or high emotion, by reason of great beauty, vastness, or grandeur," the fifth definition of sublime in the *Shorter OED*. Perhaps feelings of reverence or high emotion arise because we feel they belong to us all.

Private monuments are not felt the same way, being "Dignified or lofty in bearing; aloof; haughty, proud," the first *Shorter OED* definition. By nature they are fascistic. The City of London icons differ little from Mussolini's haughty neo-Roman EUR (the *Esposizione Universale Romana*), or Stalin's overbearing government offices from Disneyland. These monuments, increasingly inhuman in scale, exude state power or corporate status that belittles all citizens. In Prague, you can see all three, albeit more modest in scale: fascist pre-war state buildings, communist post-war concrete blocks and, post 1989, the sunglass blocks of global banks.

My favourite modern monument is the British Library. A generous public courtyard and modest entrance doors open into a dramatic internal space, expanding beyond reception to its priceless collection of rare books, with cloakroom and shop to one side, stamp collection and cafe behind and access to the many reading rooms beyond. The whole is friendly, dignified and uplifting. By contrast, Will Alsop's modest Peckham library manages to be overbearing, its rather splendid library held aloft on some skew-angled stilts and a narrow two-storey glazed block of small offices, lifts and stairwell. This increases external wall surfaces for no obvious reason, and forces users into one of two lifts or the pokiest metal staircase I have found in any public building. Carnegie libraries with books on the ground floor are convenient, efficient and adorn their street settings.

The contrast between public and private monuments can be seen in Paris and London. The conceit of Richard Rogers and Renzo Piano in the Pompidou centre was to turn the building inside out. Putting the structural frame, service ducts, lifts and stairs on the outside freed up the internal floor space. Outside, the struts, ducts and cables have to be well insulated and sealed where they rupture the walls, while pigeons and peeling paint have inevitably made their mark. Despite this, the Pompidou is a popular icon, partly for the escalators that carry people up the front elevation, overlooking a generous public space for social theatre.

The same structural idea was used for the Lloyds building in London by Rogers and Partners. Its one dramatic feature, the large atrium from ground floor to roof, has escalators giving this volume form and movement. Unfortunately, it is seldom open to public viewing. And, as with the Pompidou, the exterior steel framework of struts, services and lifts presents an aggressive moat aspect to St Mary Axe, one of the most dispiriting pedestrian walks in the City: from the Gherkin on its bleak concrete plinth, the Cheesegrater rising from a green garden, the Lloyds building reflected in the blank glass block opposite, to the Walkie-Talkie on Fenchurch Street. Some regard their cheeky monikers as public affection. Indifference or contempt are as likely.

Public monuments are one way of redressing the imbalance between private and social wealth, offering some return for the 'earned' income of Labour. Private monuments are not social assets. They reflect the 'unearned' wealth of Land and Capital, from the handsome Georgian country houses of the landed gentry, the noble Victorian mills and factories of the manufacturers to the inscrutable towers of the bankers. This shift in wealth reflects the shift from farm and factory to finance house, from chapter 5. Most private skyscrapers, in pursuit of aesthetic impact and corporate status, lack the ground floor shops, kiosks, cafes and other public uses that support street life. Their ground floor is usually a large corporate lobby: walk into any tower block and not feel intimidated by their sheer scale and opulence. Public intimidation is the corollary of command management.

The sublime aloofness of private monuments is by design. A building has two distinct aspects: crudely, its form reflects how it works inside, style is how it looks outside. What this usually means is that, throughout history, in the design of most buildings 'Form follows function' while style follows fashion.

Now, again over-simplifying, in many modern monuments, both public and private, function is made to follow form, putting users at the mercy of designers. And increasingly, that form is dictated by stylistic fashion, whether post-modern, hi-tec, neo-futurist, structural expressionist or sculpturalist. Those that become icons are as aloof as *Mona Lisa*'s smile, as overbearing as Klimt's *Kiss* or evoking Munch's *Scream* from many users and onlookers. Consider some modern icons.

The Faber building in Ipswich is an aloof triumph of style, where form follows fashion, except that here, Norman Foster largely established the style. Its blank undulating wall of windowless black glass defines the whole site and reflects the buildings opposite, its one positive street feature. The annual energy cost psf may be three to five times more than for traditional buildings, let alone energy-neutral buildings. Yet earlier uses of glass, as for example in the pre-war *Daily Express* buildings (by engineer Owen Williams) and Liverpool's Oriel Chambers of 1864 (by Peter Ellis) show that original designs can enliven the street scene while keeping energy costs similar to their adjoining buildings.

The 'Walkie-Talkie' building, by Rafael Viñoly, was awarded the Carbuncle Cup as the worst building of 2015, largely due to its ungainly shape that expands with height. Yet here was a building where 'form follows finance' (Rowan Moore 2012). In skyscrapers, rents on upper floors are up to 50% higher than on the bottom half. On 35 floors (plus the modest 'planning gain' of a public roof garden), the building provides 668,926 sq ft and was bought by Hong Kong investors for £1.3 billion. This values each square foot at an astonishing £1,943. As with most towers, it creates wind tunnels and heat chimneys. What was novel was that the reflected solar glare from the building's concave profile also melted shopfront mats and car paintwork at street level (repeating the problem with a similar design by the same architect in Los Angeles). One other fact quietly ignored is that the Walkie-Talkie replaced a perfectly serviceable 1960s office block of 25 floors. Some hope that it will not last as long, but that would merely compound such wanton destruction.

Occasionally, 'form *is* the function'. Apart from any building by Zaha Hadid, Frank Gehry's Guggenheim museum in Bilbao is a triumph of style over content, outshining anything on display inside and the Jeff Koons poodle outside. Although this iconic sculpture (not the poodle) attracts many visitors, it is a poor relation to the city's handsome, efficient and much cheaper *Museo de Bellas Artes de Bilbao*.

Perhaps the most flagrant monument is the Shard of Renzo Piano. This "spire-like sculpture" is the tallest building in the UK, towering 96 floors over London Bridge, but only 72 are habitable. It has several dubious sustainable features.

- One critic described it as our first 'vertical village', but exclusive flats, restaurants and hotels do not make a village and lifts, the antithesis of social streets, actually inhibit conversation.
- In the gents to one restaurant reviewed by a food critic, men urinate against the inner glass wall. This triumph of the elite over *hoi polloi* is only outdone by the behaviour of Robert Maxwell who, waiting for his helicopter, would sometimes urinate off the roof of the *Daily Mirror* building onto the street below.
- Like the Cheesegrater and the Walkie-Talkie, the Shard also demolished a solid 24 storey office block that was only built in 1975. Metaphorically, these are replaced by the empty 24 floors at the top of the building.
- No solar panels were allowed to compromise the Shard's 56,000 sq m of glazed purity. Had energy trumped aesthetics, the building might have installed a modest 15,000 sq m of solar panels to supply 1,500 homes with electricity.

- The development also includes a second plain glass block of 'only' 18 storeys which presents three blank walls on the ground floor to a busy bus/rail interchange concourse.
- Evan Davis (*Made in Britain*, BBC 2013) saw the Shard as part of our export drive. Would that we could export such towers to places like Baku and Abu Dhabi where they belong.

Most private monuments are unsustainable in their excessive consumption of energy and materials during construction, and of energy during occupation. They have serious social impacts and cannot be said to "fit in with the overall form and layout of their surroundings" as required by *NPPF2*. And they distort local economies in favour of developer and landlord Capital, whose interests, to repeat David Ricardo, are "always opposed to the interests of every other class in the community."

In summary, the politics of change must give way to continuity. We should treasure our modest vernacular buildings rather than sweeping them away, curb the worst excesses of private monuments, prioritize energy conservation and once again, like the Victorians, spend generously on important public monuments. Cherishing our heritage and addressing today's real problems would improve the heritage we leave for future generations. And to achieve these improvements, we need to reform democracy and revive the Victorians' 'municipal gospel', the subject of my final chapter.

Chapter Ten: Urban Democracy

C ities affect all our lives. According to GG Simpson, "the human species has properties unique to itself among all forms of life... Man's intellectual, social, and spiritual natures are altogether exceptional among animals in degree, but they arose by organic evolution. They usher in a new phase of evolution..." (See Dawkins 2008)

This is "the social, moral and intellectual attainments of a society" definition of civilization, from the opening of chapter 7. If civilization, both civic and civil, is what makes the human species unique, then we might call Simpson's organic evolution 'the political process'. And civilization only progresses (or evolves) when senior politicians like Joseph Chamberlain and Clement Attlee emerge on the stage.

Social breakdown and climate change do not suggest evolutionary progress in human development. The problem is that, during the first century of planning, we have largely ignored the five principles of sustainable development quoted in *NPPF1*:

- suburbs, monuments, traffic and flying stress the planet's environmental limits;
- agrochemicals, drugs and pollution challenge sound science;
- sustainable local economies are undone by global market manipulation;
- poverty, surveillance and tax evasion undermine strong, healthy and just societies;
- and below, this chapter argues that side-lining local authorities negates good governance and democracy.

The political spectrum

Most English dictionaries, including Chambers, Penguin and the Oxford, define politics as "the art or science of government". Collins has "the art *and* science of government." However, in chapter 8, I argued that planning, being neither art nor science, is a branch of politics. JK Galbraith cuts through the fog. "Politics is not the art of the possible. It consists in choosing between the disastrous and the unpalatable." This is wise. In planning, we've gone further, approving developments that are both disastrous and unpalatable, largely as the result of centralized control.

Politics has two basic dimensions, as hinted in previous chapters. The first is between Left and Right. One is called 'the profligate party' – the reverse compliment is 'the nasty party'. But while each might find the other 'unpalatable', it is how government is delivered that borders on the 'disastrous'. This second dimension is the division of powers between state and councils: being one of the most centralized nations in western Europe, we have reduced local government to an oxymoron. This is political regression.

Throughout history, government is usually seen as a duopoly between state and individual, societies comprising an elite governing *hoi polloi*. Hobbes thought we were savages who needed government to control us. For Rousseau, we were noble savages who entered a social contract with government to ensure fairness for all. Machiavelli showed how a cynical tyrant could maintain his grip over people, while Mandeville suggested that clever rulers could exploit our vices for everyone's benefit. Cities only appear twice in JS McClelland's fascinating *History of Western Political Thought* (1996): first as the Greek city-states which replaced a national authority and, second, as the setting for crowds and their tendency to mob rule and riots against their rulers.

"For Hegel [1770-1831], there are only really three great world-historical epochs: the world of the ancient despotisms, the world of the classical city-states, and the modern period which is Christian Europe leading to what he will call Constitutional Monarchy." (McClelland) I would suggest three rather different forms of government.

1. The lawless anarchy of the Dark Ages, in which marauding tribes were a perpetual threat to defenceless farms and villages, left no records and few artefacts.

2. The central tyranny of empires. Neil Ferguson (2007) justifies our British Empire. Despite its birth in naked piracy, expansion through the superiority of the machine gun over the spear and its suppression of all revolts, he summarizes the gains thus: "What the British Empire proved is that empire is a form of international government that can work – and not just for the benefit of the ruling power. It sought to globalize not just an economic but a legal and ultimately a political system too." This is right wing history written by the 'victors'. Local histories are ignored. As power corrupts, so all empires are based on the 'superiority' of race, creed and rapacious greed.

3. The tripartite hierarchy of state, city and individual. The ancient Greek city-states recognized the need for national government, if only when threatened by a common enemy. The Renaissance city-states in Italy never found this common purpose.

Most of Europe during the last millennium has worked this tripartite system. In England, the *Magna Carta* sought to balance the rights and responsibilities of the state (then vested in the divine right of kings) and the individual in the name of the barons. John cunningly insisted that if he was to recognise their rights, then they should give similar rights to their yeomen, scribes and villeins. With these duties between king, barons and society, the *Magna Carta* laid the foundations for both local government and human rights.

Towns developed independence through charters. In return for annual fees, town charters from the crown, bishops or barons granted freedom from existing tolls, rights to collect tolls, fees and rents, and powers to maintain the liberty of their citizens, imprison criminals and provide for the poor and orphans etc. Their wealth grew as merchants, manufacturers and guildsmen developed trade, skills, products and services. Councils elected burghers (or citizens) and employed clerks to keep records for their shire, borough, town or parish. Thus many French burgers migrated to the new towns in northern Spain. Many Spanish burghers later migrated to the new towns in southern Spain after the Moors were expelled. Similarly, many Germans migrated to new towns in eastern Europe, while English burghers migrated to new towns in the Celtic nations. Following the Norman Conquest, the town charter of Breteuil in Normandy was used for Hereford, then for Rhuddlan in Wales in 1086 and finally in Drogheda in Ireland in 1169 (Bartlett 1993). With schools, colleges, hospitals and almshouses founded by local monasteries, landowners and merchants, towns and cities became largely self governing. However rudimentary the democracy, towns provided powerful shields between state and citizens.

Local government peaked during the Victorian era. After Chinn's review of slum clearance (chapter 2), let us return to Birmingham with Asa Briggs' excellent *Victorian Cities* (1968). Until about 1870, the local Tory 'economic group' resisted all local government investment. Once the Whig 'extravagant group' was in control, with Joseph Chamberlain as mayor from 1873-76, Birmingham was transformed:

- its central library, 1866, came 16 years after the *Free Libraries Act*,
- its School Board was set up the same year as Forster's *Education Act 1870*,
- a major sewage scheme was begun in 1871,
- its medical officer of health was appointed in 1872, 30 years after Liverpool appointed the first,
- the three private gas companies, bought in 1873 and '74, became the Birmingham municipal gas board,
- 93 acres of central Birmingham (including some real slums) were 'Improved', creating a new Corporation Street,
- the private water company was bought in 1876 (over House of Lords objections to its compulsory purchase) and,
- after Chamberlain had become an MP, the Council House was opened in 1879, the Art Gallery in 1885, the latter built on the municipal gas profits with the motto over its entrance, "By the gains of industry we promote art".

Birmingham now led the emerging 'municipal gospel'. Chamberlain justified buying the gas and water companies thus: ""When the purchase of the Water Works comes before you, it will be a question concerning the health of the town; the acquisition of the Gas Works concerns the profits of the town, and its financial resources. Both are matters of 'absolute public necessity'." The two other reasons for 'municipalizing' gas were more general. All monopolies in any way sustained by the State should be in the hands of the elected representatives of the people, to whom their profits should of right go. Municipalization would increase the power and influence of the local council, which should be encouraged to become a real local parliament, supreme in its own sphere of jurisdiction." (Briggs 1968)

Independent boroughs controlled all local public services. The Contents of Fairlie's *Municipal Administration* (1900, covering Europe and the US), show the range of council activities in Victorian times:

- Public health and safety covers police administration, fire brigade, health departments [including food safety and isolation hospitals], building departments and economic regulation;
- Charities and provident institutions include poor relief [social welfare], pawnshops and savings banks [like today's credit unions];
- Education covers schools [initially under separate school boards], libraries and museums; and
- Municipal improvements cover a); streets, bridges, sewers, scavenging [refuse collection], baths and parks, and b); waterworks, public lighting, [gas], urban transportation, docks, markets, cemeteries and municipal ownership.

These were substantial responsibilities. Manchester then had 16 main committees, Leeds 15 with 40 subcommittees. And, from table 40 below, councils' total spending exceeded government spending, except during wartime. The undermining of local government can be traced back to three dates: 1871, 1945 and 1979.

In 1871, with local council powers at their height, the Local Government Board was set up. According to Sir Robert Ensor (*OEH* 1988), "it is difficult to over-estimate what the country lost through having its local authorities down to 1914 placed under a central department constantly on the alert to hinder them and rarely, if ever, to help. The much greater progress made by Prussia between 1870 and 1914 on many sides of local government administration was associated with an almost opposite relation between centre and circumference." When Chamberlain stepped down as mayor and "became a Cabinet Minister in 1880, he wrote that unless he could secure for the nation the same social improvements which he had already secured in Birmingham 'it will have been a sorry exchange to give up the Town Council for the Cabinet'." (Briggs) History confirms that it was a sorry exchange.

Following 1945, many municipal services were nationalized:

- the NHS transferred (and greatly expanded) all existing private and municipal hospitals, GP, dental and nursing services to regional hospital boards and local health authorities, all under the Minister of Health. Local councils were left with social services and community protection (child protection, care of the old and food safety);
- municipal and private electricity and water companies were all transferred to regional bodies (like the London Electricity Board and Thames Water Authority), again under central government control;
- gas, like the railways and airways, were nationalized as British; while later
- the police and probation services were effectively removed from council control by successive amalgamations so that, by the mid 1990s, there were only 37 quasi-autonomous police authorities under Home Office control.

Here, the fault lay not in the *principle* of public services, but in their management by unelected regional authorities, national boards and government departments. This disenfranchised local councils and local democratic control ceased.

Finally, from 1979, most remaining council services were privatized along with the nationalized industries:

- all refuse collection was subjected to 'compulsory competitive tender', allowing private firms to scavenge on public funds;
- many services like housing management, road maintenance and council payrolls were outsourced, usually resulting in inferior services and often costing more;
- most municipal bus companies had to be sold off, leading to higher fares and fewer services;
- while state schools were increasingly micro-managed, new multi academy 'trust' schools were directly (more generously) funded and managed by government, with executive salaries out of all proportion to state schools; and
- council housebuilding ceased and all existing council houses had to be offered to existing tenants. Today, a third of them are owned by private landlords who charge full commercial rents, exploiting an unregulated housing market.

Councils are no longer 'supreme in their own sphere of jurisdiction'. When Margaret Thatcher called for the return of Victorian values, she over-shot her target, reviving a neo-Georgian era of private privilege, naked profiteering and political indifference to poverty and public squalor. We have replaced public services with commercial contracts, quality control with performance targets, value for money with private profits and democratic control with commercial confidentiality. Local government is now an arm of central administration, with local councils removed from meaningful democratic control – even in planning. We need to revive the Victorians' 'municipal gospel'.

Urban entropy 5: the first tier of democracy is local

During elections in the 1960s, the Tory Quentin Hogg (later Lord Hailsham) warned us that "A vote for Labour is a vote for elective dictatorship." This puzzled many who thought we were living in a period of consensus politics. Only after 1979 did we experience 'elective dictatorship' under the conviction politics of Thatcher, with her strident 'There is no alternative' (Tina) and "Is he one of us?" Blair followed with his insistence on 'Joined up thinking' and the perpetual 'politics of change'. (This last inanity, aimless and dangerous, conjures up the image of an oil tanker, its engine of compulsory purchase on full steam pushing through heavy seas without rudder or anchor.)

"Ideologues, people who had seized, or been seized by, an idea… tended to lack an appreciation of the full script." (Didion 1994) The problem with nationalization was not the ideology of free access to key services like education and health, but its implementation through central government and regional boards which inevitably reduced local democracy. Privatization, the ideology since 1979, is faulty in both principle and practice. It derives from economist/philosopher Friedrich von Hayek (1899-1992) who argued, post-war, that all socialist governments and command economies restricted freedoms and created inefficiencies. We should let private enterprise supply the demand for both public and private goods and services because they know what consumers want. They are more efficient because the profit motive generates higher rewards, making them more innovative and risk-taking. That, crudely, is the ideology of the 'free market' (see for example Sloman 2006).

These assertions raise more questions than answers. Capitalist freedom and socialist equality are not mutually exclusive. Civilized societies manage mixed economies to protect personal freedoms while ensuring that everyone has access to basic rights such as education, healthcare, water, energy, public transport, libraries and parks. Two private industries that understand this private/social duality are street markets and public houses.

The concept of a 'free market' also raises problems. Chapter 5 showed how reducing government regulation (as 'socialist and self-defeating') has created a 'free (or closed) market' in which mega-corps impose command management while manipulating their specific markets. Thus, a dozen US mega-corps control the junk food market between two million farmers and 275 million consumers. From page 151 above, every day, an average 200,000 consumers suffer food poisoning, with 900 hospital admissions and 14 deaths. Junk food is a major cause. "[A] simple explanation for why eating a hamburger can now make you seriously ill: There is shit in the meat." (Schlosser) These mega-corps (with high rewards) may be efficient but they are unsustainable long-term. They cut costs and put profit above health and safety, thus transferring serious risks onto staff and customers.

Finally, the 'law of supply and demand' actually differs between private and public sectors. In the private sector, demand is subject to what economists call the theory of 'marginal utility'. Many people love their first burger of the day, but by the third, even junkies start to feel sick. His first car may be essential, but the third merely displays status. This law of diminishing returns is the only curb on consumerism. The conspicuous consumption of the wealthy in yachts, jets, bling and mansions merely confirms their sick addiction to money. Private suppliers, profit-driven, want to increase demand beyond what we need, whether through addiction, fashion, marketing or built-in obsolescence. Increasing turnover and profits creates a few more jobs and personal choice. Social costs can include fat children, terminal disease, congested roads, poisoned rivers, polluted air, excessive noise, needless waste, depleted resources and excessive carbon footprints.

Where the private sector is profit-driven, the public sector is cost-controlled. Public demand is based on rights rather than desires, need rather than greed. We all need shelter, food, clothes, water, warmth and a school, GP and bus stop nearby. Demand for most public services is inelastic. We all hope to keep out of hospital and prison, and public suppliers also want to reduce demand for most services, including hospital beds, prison cells and energy. The two exceptions are social transport, which we only increase to reduce road traffic, and education. This is the only positively elastic public demand in the wider Greek sense – not just schools, colleges and universities, but parks, sports grounds, gyms, swimming pools, libraries and evening classes. This suggests a new law of increasing returns ('utility') when, after the fifth or fifty fifth lesson, we suddenly experience our own 'Eureka' moment. Junk food is mildly addictive, good education sets you free.

The other neo-con argument is that public services are inefficient. Back in 1900, Fairlie (from Michigan university) saw through this. "The difficulties and limitations of comparison of private with municipal undertakings are numerous. In the first place, undertakings which are municipalized... have, in addition to the purely business side (profit and loss), an important social aspect; and municipal control means in almost every case a greater degree of attention paid to these social aspects, such as better facilities to the consuming public and better compensation to the employees. This amelioration of social conditions cannot be balanced in figures against diminished profits." Birmingham demonstrated these social benefits in the 1870s. Within five years, the new Gas Committee extended and modernized plant, greatly improved working conditions for all staff and twice *lowered* gas prices (Briggs). Privatizers ignore 'the full script'.

Let us focus on the NHS to summarize the difference between public and private control. The NHS accounts for less than 8% of GDP, compared with 11% in France and perhaps 20% in the US. Serious bed and staff shortages, extreme levels of stress and high staff turnover (made worse by Brexit) and inadequate resources ensure that it struggles to meet demand for acute treatments, youth and mental services, social care and for all emergencies and epidemics. Yet the service remains incredibly efficient, suggesting that improving patients' lives is a more effective motivator than high salaries.

The inefficiencies affecting the whole NHS service are its mismanagement by successive ministers (imposing, for example, 'internal markets' so 7% of the budget is now outsourced, or trying to impose a seven-day week on all hospitals with no extra staff or resources), the chronic underfunding and frequent use of management consultants that wastes £billions and the sheer scale of the business. Yet private health services are also inefficient. When two Australian dentists travelled across the continent arranging dental appointments in every town, over 70% of those private dentists recommended unnecessary treatments. In UK private hospitals, about 30% of hysterectomies are unnecessary. The NHS does not have the resources for such waste, nor the ethical vacuum. Cost control, rather than profit, means it has to focus on clear needs. The NHS is more efficient with staff and resources because it needs money to operate, not needs to operate to make money. Which sector would you trust with 10% of GDP?

Yet ideologues persist with privatizing various services to save money. Consider an NHS service that costs £100 million pa.

- To justify outsourcing, the NHS will want some saving, say £5 million.

- Management costs will often double from say £2 million, and with fees for head office support and consultants, this will cost at least another £5 million.
- Set aside (government-approved) profit margins of 8%, which are distributed to shareholders. Already, the outsourced service has £16 million less to spend on the actual service.
- The less scrupulous then seek to raise prices where possible (as with buses and trains) over and above the profit margins. All seek to cut costs. Employing fewer staff on less pay demotivates them, but can raise profit margins well above 15%.

So, the outsourced service will actually cost about £75 million instead of £100 million. (On page 172, the sorry tale of the Langwith GP surgery was discussed.) Some may find this example hypothetical, which is the point. While the NHS is awash with hard data and statistical analysis of all inputs and outcomes, private health services are subject to far less rigorous analysis. It is nigh impossible to see the outsourced contracts under freedom of information and their financial accounts are strictly private. This is uncivilized and breeds inefficiency. Open markets rely on hard information.

Most privatized services – the probation service, GP surgeries, court translation service, the forensic science and transport research laboratories, prisons and most academy trusts and care homes etc – while profitable, provide inferior service. Patients, passengers, pensioners, pupils, students, probationers, prisoners, trainees, the unemployed, disabled and housebound suffer, frontline staff are underpaid, stressed and demotivated and profits are extracted, often while increasing corporate debt. Some outsourcers even lie and increase profits simply by adding ghost trainees, probationers or unemployed. This doesn't bar the fraudsters from other public contracts. Some have a conflict of interest. Privatized prisons not only put profit above the welfare of prisoners and wardens who work in very stressful conditions. They also skimp on rehabilitation services which increase costs but reduce numbers of prisoners re-offending. However desirable to society, fewer prisoners are not in their corporate interests. The US government, which started this craze, has now brought all privatized prisons (15%) back under public control.

Both nationalization and privatization reduced local control and local spending on local public services. All ideologies increase political entropy and stunt 'man's intellectual, social, and spiritual natures' – creating what is called a 'democratic deficit':

- In 1989/90, only 44% of council seats were contested in England's 8,159 parish councils. An average parish income of £17,032 (or £123.2m in total) may explain why. Increase their average income tenfold, and local citizens would take them more seriously. Lest we forget, town and village parish councils represent 30% of the English population, with about half (seven million people) living in 660 towns with an average population of 10,600 (Aston Business School 1992).

- For district, borough and county council elections, turnouts barely reach 40%, the lowest in western Europe where most nations achieve over 70%. In our most deprived city wards with the most urgent needs, turnouts are often below 20%.
- Apathy now infects general elections. The average turnout in the four elections of the 1950s was 80.5%. In the first three elections since 2000, turnout averaged 62.0%. (Parliamentary Research Services, House of Commons library.)

Involving people in any social contract between government and the governed is the essence of democracy. Restoring control of many public services to cities, towns and villages under Chamberlain's gospel of 'municipalization' is how political energy can be released and the social contract developed.

For completeness, Newton's third law of motion states that "If one body exerts a force on another, there is an equal and opposite force, called a reaction, exerted on the first body by the second." Something similar happens in politics. For every action, there is a reaction – but it is not equal. A healthy democracy seeks to minimize or reduce negative reactions by leaving local decisions to local councils, businesses and citizens. As Lord Balfour put it: "The foundation of a democracy is a people so fundamentally at one that they can be safely left to bicker." Perhaps this is what makes the Dutch 'pathologically happy'. It is certainly preferable to the 'urban renaissance' of the Urban Task Force (1999), promoting world-leading regenerators constantly building absurdly grand schemes with speedy local decisions and stronger compulsory purchase powers, all joined up by a central Urban Policy Board. Why not just recall the Local Government Board and have done with it?

Central government – i) foreign affairs

The three broad functions of all governments cover foreign affairs, domestic policy and finance. All three affect towns and cities to some degree.

The Foreign Office functions to prevent war and promote trade. Empires go one step further, using war to expand trade. Both provoke migration refugees escaping the horrors of war, economic migrants bringing trade with them. None are scroungers.

One impact of war is refugees. From 1975 to 1995, about two million Vietnamese people fled the war zone and its aftermath, caused by the obduracy of the French and then the US fighting a war both knew early on was unwinnable. The war in Syria is another human catastrophe for refugees. Asylum seekers emerge from domestic tyrannies. Who wouldn't try to escape the risk of imprisonment without trial, torture, rape, 'defenestrations' and 'disappearances'?

However, rather than impose sanctions on various despots and tyrants, we sell arms either to those 'on our side', or to those seeking to overthrow those 'on their side'. "Who's providing the arms to Africa? We are. The Western countries. Africa is awash with arms, and they're still selling millions of dollars every year." (N Davies

2009) Our collusion is justified as 'trade'. Refugees are merely 'collateral damage' in these humanitarian voids. The real scroungers are our arms manufacturers. Not only does UK Export Finance (UKEF) offer them cheap finance, it also underwrites the risks involved with the contracts. This negates a core principle of capitalism – that company owners bear both risk and profit. UKEF even supports arms sales that are known to involve bribery and corruption (eg *Private Eye* 1370 and 1445). Since the arms trade invariably produces refugees and asylum seekers, perhaps we should impose a refugee tax on the arms traders.

With external trade comes the migration of skills, ideas, money, technology and people, or 'economic migrants'. Throughout the nineteenth century, we welcomed them, however poor and downtrodden. Successive post-war governments encouraged Commonwealth migrants to help run our health service, schools and public transport. And throughout our membership of the EU we welcomed a whole host of Europeans, mostly young, many highly skilled and all enriching our economy and culture. Each year our farms and fishing fleets employ about 90,000 east Europeans to pick the crops and work the boats.

Jane Jacobs argued that the wealth of nations increases through trade between comparable states (see page 154). Between poor nations, trade would develop as they gradually replaced imports from the rich nations. This would release them from the global yoke of unfair trade agreements imposed by the rich nations. For example, under NAFTA (the North American free trade agreement), many American workers lost their factory jobs to Mexicans while Mexican farmers lost their livelihoods, perversely, to heavily-subsidized US farmers. This increased Mexican migrants to the US. Trade between unequal partners is seldom equitable.

The beauty of the EU is that Europe has successfully created a trading block that is based on fair trade in goods and services, the freedom of movement of capital and people and, sometimes overlooked, the avoidance of war. Of course, as with all governments, there are problems, as with VAT on foreign company purchases not applied uniformly, the bureaucratic stress on 'harmonization' so only large apples can be sold as 'Grade 1', the uneven impact of the Euro, largely to the detriment of weaker peripheral economies, and the lack of transparency that affects its annual accounts, which have not been 'approved' for about 20 years. These problems can be solved, and are fairly modest compared with the incompetence of most of our own government departments, from the Treasury and Home Office down to MAFF and the MoD.

The disastrous European Referendum of 2016 forced us to participate in an internal dispute between the racist and liberal wings of the Conservative party. Pro-Europeans failed to provide any positive vision. The EU ideal encapsulates the best of European history where trade, skills and ideas were developed by artists and artisans, scientists and inventors, pilgrims and diplomats moving across borders and surmounting language barriers to adapt and fertilize the great eras of European civilization: the Romanesque and Gothic, the Renaissance and Reformation, Baroque and the Enlightenment, the age of Reason, the Romantics and Revolutionaries.

Europe has evolved through this constant shuffling of people, ideas, language and customs. Casting our nation adrift from perhaps the most civilized trading block in the world makes no sense economically, socially or politically. We lose the cover of important employment and environmental Directives, lose access to the European Court of Justice and joint research programmes and lose protection, however limited, against some of the biggest global monopolies.

The actual referendum was poisoned by the bankers' crash and Osborne's austerity that cut welfare benefits and taxed many social tenants while reducing taxes for the wealthy. With unclear (probably unlawful) sources of funding, the shady Brexit campaigns fuelled the racist xenophobia of little Englanders standing in front of a poster of asylum seekers, the unprincipled lies and dismissal of experts by opportunistic politicians in pursuit of their careers, and newspaper editors like the rancid migrant from a north London suburb who headlined three senior judges as 'enemies of the people' when they explained what national sovereignty actually meant in the EU/referendum case before them. So, we are now forced to increase trade with those states with fewer employment, political and environmental safeguards like China, Saudi Arabia and the US.

And, as with the *Aliens Act 1905*, we shall try once again to exclude all immigrants except the highly skilled and wealthy, despite shortages in most sectors of the economy. Yet, as shown in table 31 (page 257), UK immigration has been consistently lower than those in mainland Europe. Most refugees happily fill the more menial jobs in exchange for the freedom to settle and raise their own families. Alarmingly, the 'hostile environment' operated by our racist government affects not only foreign nationals but also many British citizens who happen to be of different race or creed. It is both inefficient and uncivilized. Leaving the EU is an act of self-harm, forcing us to poach doctors and teachers from poorer nations, and rely on our own mercenaries (in the guise of bankers, mega-corp directors and merchants of death) to maintain our way of life.

Central government – ii) domestic policy

Within our borders, government sets policy frameworks covering all areas of public life at three broad levels: international agreements, national welfare and market regulation.

International agreements cover human rights, world health standards, trade agreements, shipping, climate change and environmental protection etc. Depending on their status, these are reflected in our national policy. Since 1979, however, governments have chipped away in particular at human rights and climate change through the racist 'hostile environment' policy, unlimited detention of asylum seekers, reliance on food banks and most of our transport strategy.

National welfare has also suffered. We have retained universal access to health care and education, and introduced the minimum wage. But privatized water, energy and public transport services are less affordable and all welfare benefits have been cut in real terms. With national policy frameworks like the *NPPF*, there is also a change of emphasis. While government often treats international policy as advisory, its own national policies are mandatory on all councils. Government laws define exactly what local councils must do. All other council action is *ultra vires* ('outside its powers') and therefore unlawful. In general, local diversity through local initiative and local solutions for local problems are prohibited.

During the 1960s, when seven planning acts and statutory instruments were passed, Lord Justice Harman thought that the planning system 'stinks in the noses of the public'. In the 2010s, an average of 38 planning acts and statutory instruments were passed *each year* (table 32). This bumf leaves all councils struggling to interpret and implement planning law with its frequent shifts, contradictions and repeals. The results are long delays, high costs and often arbitrary outcomes when a developer take a local decision either to Court for judicial review or to a friendly government minister.

Legal hyper-inflation is a systems failure of government and affects all public services. It is also unnecessary. All 600 bits of planning law since 2000 should be consolidated into one Act, revised perhaps every 15 to 20 years. This would simplify matters and allow some flexibility (or anarchy) in local interpretation to suit both Hereford and Hartlepool. In planning, as in all walks of life, there is no one size that fits all. The consolidated *Planning Act* would set out general principles, national imperatives and local enabling powers which might be extended through perhaps 200 local bye-laws.

By contrast, market regulation since 1979 has been characterized by a 'light touch' (leading to the bankers' crash), 'a bonfire of red tape' (indirectly leading to fatal fires well before the Grenfell tower tragedy) and 'free markets' (that absolve various mega-corps and their bankers, accountants and solicitors from market abuse, gross incompetence and conflicts of interest). The Competition Commission and Office of Fair Trading has been largely indifferent to the unregulated growth of a 'big four' in most sectors, notably accountancy, banking, builders, foodsheds and the media.

A modest tax proposal

"It is the creation of worth, not wealth, that's important. One will follow the other." (John Garnett, former director of the Industrial Society.)

In addition to setting national policy, government also delivers public services and invests in major projects, both directly and through local councils. Over the last century, this spending has shifted from local to central government. Before discussing that shift, however, we look at taxation, the third major function of government.

Essentially, we tax people (reducing their 'marginal' liberties) to improve public health (basic equality) and increase social wealth (and fraternity). To Victorian public libraries, sanitation and universal education, we have added national insurance, state pensions and welfare benefits for those in need, introduced the NHS and legal aid, redistributed income through graduated taxes and the minimum wage, and invested in public monuments and social transport infrastructure. This is social progress. Since 1979, however, governments have been complacent about commercial regulation and complicit in a needlessly complex tax system. This has created unjustified levels of inequality and the re-emergence of begging, homelessness and slavery.

Taxes indicate the strength of a democracy on the principle of 'no tax without representation', a rallying cry of the American war of independence. Our democracy is weak, giving billionaires and mega-corps unrivalled representation despite their rampant tax evasion (ipE). All political donations above personal annual membership fees, all hospitality for officials, all secondments to government departments and all subsequent jobs for key civil servants and ministers should be banned. To our lexicon of euphemisms like free trade, public schools, corporate responsibility, shareholder loyalty, offshore trusts and self regulation, we must add tax avoidance which is usually plain fraud.

Taxes cover income and inheritance, purchases, capital gains, corporate profits, commercial properties, various duties and the council tax. At present most favour private profit over social benefits. In a healthy and just society (*NPPF1*), taxes should distinguish between absolute need and personal choice; between the right to shelter, security and jobs, and the desire for second homes, private jets and unearned income.

"Capitalism can't work if private rewards are unrelated to social returns." (Stiglitz 2010) Rather than address specific malfunctions highlighted in previous chapters, the following tax reforms are designed to release the energy locked up in my five principles of urban entropy (UE 1-5). In general, they focus on

- simplifying all taxes, making them fairer between earned and unearned income,
- supporting internal corporate growth rather than external acquisitions, and
- taxing harmful external costs rather than added value.

UE 1: cities function best in a steady state system (page 90)

The more we conserve existing buildings and infrastructure, the less we need to build and redevelop. This releases energy for other activities. Yet, all building maintenance and extensions attract 20% VAT (except for Listed Buildings), while all new development and redevelopment is zero rated.

This is perverse. Sweden offers tax breaks on repairs to things like bicycles and washing machines, so we should zero-rate building conservation (and repair shops), while charging full VAT on new buildings that consume excessive materials, energy, labour and land.

Furthermore, workers pay income tax while producing goods and services, and then pay VAT when buying those same goods and services. This seems to be a double tax. Instead of a general purchase tax, we should reform VAT so as 'to curb excessive demand', much as we charge duties on fuel (but not jet fuel), alcohol and tobacco. A new VRT (value reduced tax) might cover luxury goods, fashion and cosmetics, wasteful packaging, advertising, junk food, sugar drinks, street drugs and environmental polluters.

UE 2: cities create efficient markets (page 172)

Only government can ensure a fair market open to a healthy small business sector. Apart from their market domination, most mega-corps choose not to pay their taxes. According to HMRC, in 2011/2, lost tax revenues totalled £40 billion of unpaid VAT, income tax, national insurance and corporation tax, which could rise to £47 billion in 2014/5. This is well over 10% of total government income. Many, including the *Ethical Consumer* (issue 149), believe these figures are gross underestimates.

The example of Vodafone illustrates the problem. Dave Hartnett, then a Permanent Secretary for Tax at HMRC, met key Vodafone directors and their accountant from Deloitte to settle a disputed £6 billion tax bill. Without any of his senior tax and legal colleagues, Hartnett negotiated a tax settlement of £1 billion plus £0.25 billion deferred interest-free. Some months later, *Private Eye* found in Vodafone's latest set of accounts an extraordinary item of £3 billion brought forward. Vodafone would not confirm whether this was money set aside against a final tax bill settlement. If it was, while HMRC sought £6 billion and Vodafone had set aside £4 billion, Hartnett settled for less than £1.25 billion.

The government encourages tax evasion. "In 2010, the coalition's then tax minister David Gauke, unveiled a corporate tax 'roadmap' that included a new tax break encouraging multinationals to divert profits into tax haven subsidiary companies. It had been drawn up by a "working group" that included the most infamous offshore profit-shifter, Vodafone. Rather than facing a full corporate tax bill under laws brought in by the 1980s Tory government, the diverted profits would henceforth be taxed at a third (later reduced to a quarter) of the headline rate." (*Private Eye* 1456, 3/11/2017)

Our government is corrupt, not through naked bribes in brown envelopes for key officers but a general corruption of 'decay, putrefaction' of the body politic (*Shorter OED*), and the 'impairment of integrity, virtue or moral principle' (*Penguin ED*). Apart from perverse tax treatment of mega-corps compared with plumbers, government corruption includes 'political donations', the discredited honours system and the 'revolving doors' syndrome, in which senior ministers and civil servants oversee legislation before taking up lucrative jobs with firms that gained from those same laws. This conflict of interest negates the ideal of an impartial civil service. (Hartnett is now with those same accountants Deloitte.)

This preferential (or deferential) treatment of mega-corps is anti-competitive, and we have to make good the tax shortfalls or accept lower welfare benefits and less public services. Tax evasion (ipE) is also big business. In 2012/3, PwC, Deloitte, EY and KPMG together earned £1,853 million for their 'tax planning' services (*Private Eye* 1349). If these fees represent 10% of the total monies involved, it means that up to £18 billion should be added to those Treasury estimates of £40bn in tax evasion. (In the same year, the oligopolistic accountants also 'earned' £489 million 'advising' government on such disasters as PFI and HS2.) Meanwhile plumbers guilty of tax evasion are sent to prison.

Before 1965, corporation tax was based not on profits but on turnover. A corporate income tax (as for individuals) would be consistent and easier to collect. It would nullify most creative (and false) accounting, making irrelevant all artificial payments, fees and loans between subsidiary companies, head office and tax havens.

We also need a bonfire, not of red tape but of tax allowances. Most are unnecessary or counter-productive perks, fostering tax evasion (ipE) through false accounts, finance vehicles and legal obfuscation. There are about 1,000 allowances of which perhaps 50 are useful:

- allowances for research have not reversed the long-term decline of R&D spending,
- allowances on debt have fuelled anti-competitive mergers and acquisitions,
- when private equity firms convert equity into debt, taxable profits become subsidized bank charges, which debt they often increase to unsustainable levels with excessive dividends, while
- those claiming the allowance for their chauffeurs should be treated the same as disabled people claiming their mobility allowances.

The only allowances against corporate income tax would be the direct costs of staff (who already pay income tax) and the costs of internal expansion. All other expenses, including outsourced labour, bought-in services, subcontracts and interest repayments, would be after tax. Like personal income tax, it should also be graduated. For example, turnover up to £50,000 might be tax-free, rising to 10% above £100m and higher still above £1bn. This would control oligopolies more effectively than any Monopolies Commission.

UE 3: technology can seriously disrupt cities (page 221)

Technology is not neutral. Socially, it can be beneficial or disruptive. Drains and trains facilitate social wellbeing, domestic appliances release us from drudgery. However, the private benefits from cars, machinery and e-technology should be taxed to offset their serious social costs.

The fuel duty on cars (a form of VRT) should be put back on the 'escalator' that John Major introduced, supplemented by a parking tax, to reduce traffic, pollution and roadkill. And the escalator on rail fares should be dropped.

Computer-aided machines and robots all attract tax relief. "Right now, the human worker who does, say, $50,000 worth of work in a factory, that income is taxed and you get income tax, social security tax, all those things. If a robot comes in to do the same thing, you'd think that we'd tax the robot at a similar level." (Bill Gates, 2017) Work is a basic activity of life. Machines that make workers redundant should be taxed on their earnings.

There are two possible tax revenues from the tech-cos, apart from the proposed turnover tax. We could tax them on their free use of the web, gifted by Tim Berners-Lee, Linus Torvald and all those who maintain the web free of glitches (in much the same way as we levy mobile phone companies on their use of the public airwaves). More importantly, we should tax all tech-cos on their advertising revenues that accrue from their invasion of our private data.

UE 4: money primarily serves a social function (page 262)
The Persian proverb, that money is best spread like manure, is ignored. Being one of the most unequal among the wealthy nations, poverty is rife and acute. To redistribute money (and its energy) more fairly and efficiently, we must first stop all offshore tax evasion (ipE). Apparently, oligarchs are not taxed on income from their offshore wealth funds if they call the transfers 'bank loans'.

Second, all personal income, earned and unearned, should be treated the same. Income from rents, bonuses and dividends, one-off capital gains, pension lump sums, share options, 'golden hello' and contract termination payments should all be treated as income and taxed as such.

And third, we need to graduate income tax bands to set a fair ratio between minimum wage and boardroom pay, based empirically on hours worked, efficiency and skills required. (However crude these ratios, I take confidence from the lexicographer Eric Partridge who, when unable to find a word's derivation, said it was better to make one up than to admit 'etymology unknown.')

- The maximum ratio for hours worked is 2:1, assuming a 35-hour working week. Few people can work more than 70 hours a week. Nor should they.
- Whatever the task and however motivated – waiting tables, driving buses, preparing accounts or performing surgery – few are more than twice as efficient as their colleagues. With speed comes carelessness, mistakes or danger. Putting aside the misogyny that pays women (and immigrants) at least 20% less than males doing the same work, let us set a maximum efficiency ratio also of 2:1.
- Traditionally, there are five work categories: unskilled, semi-skilled and skilled blue collar jobs, clerical and professional/managerial white collar jobs. Since most manual and office skills overlap in complexity, we can reshuffle them into five categories: unskilled, semi-skilled requiring basic skills, skilled requiring specific training, supervisory roles, and highly skilled with serious risk attached, as with test pilots, brain surgeons and judges. This suggests a ratio of 5:1.

Combining these ratios arithmetically (2 + 2 + 5), we arrive at a relative wage ratio of say 10:1 within any company, which suggests a top 'reasonable' wage of £125,000 a year, though ratios would be less in smaller firms and social enterprises. These ratios (including all emoluments) should be published in annual accounts to inform economists and investors, staff and ethical customers. According to Wilkinson and Pickett, wage differentials are about 16 to 1 in Japanese businesses, about 31 to 1 in ours. This reflects Japan's much lower levels of inequality and may partly explain its reputation for efficiency. The ratio would also suggest income levels at which to increase tax rates to discourage excessive differentials.

Combining the ratios geometrically (2 x 2 x 5) provides an absolute wage differential of 20:1. Thus, at £250,000, income tax rates should start to rise punitively, perhaps reaching 90% on income beyond £2m. This would curb naked greed, if only by shareholders querying why their companies are paying so much to HMRC. The extraordinary wages of casino bankers and private equity managers are offensive, and stink when they still employ outsourced contract cleaners on less than a living wage. (One senior manager failed to notice that, for nearly two years, her PA was robbing her personal account of several hundred thousand pounds. It is unfortunate that the PA chose to spend the money among family and friends. Had she given it to charities, the jury at her trial might have had difficulty agreeing a just verdict.)

While few business leaders would survive one week teaching an average class of nine-year olds, many competent teachers would comfortably last a term as CEO, simply by listening to staff, customers and suppliers as well as directors. Punitive tax rates at the top would also promote 'enlightened self-interest' – directors raising minimum wages so they could raise their own. The two are linked.

UE 5: the first tier of democracy is local (page 343)

As stated earlier, since 1871, local government has been undermined, particularly following nationalization and privatization. This is also reflected in reduced local government spending (see below). If we are to revive local councils' responsibilities, they will need more devolved powers, more freedom from *ultra vires* and more funding to release the energy of local decisions and innovation. To this end, the council tax must be reformed and cover *all* property and land taxes.

Currently, council income is very roughly about 25% direct from the council tax based on house values, up to 25% from the UBR (uniform business rate) based on commercial property values, and about half from government grants for education, social care and other local services.

The UBR, based on some notional historic value of each commercial property, needs to be rescued from government incompetence (as discussed in chapter 4). The notional values are unfairly low for foodsheds and usually too high in marginal shopping areas, often equalling or exceeding rents. Basing the UBR on annual turnover, as with the proposed corporate income tax, would give all businesses, not just shops, a fairer, more rational overhead with some protection for both tenants and landlords against volatile markets.

The council tax, apparently the most difficult tax to evade, also needs updating. House prices, from 1991, are graded in eight bands (under £40,000 in Band A to over £320,000 in Band H), against which each council sets a rate. These bands are of historic interest only, with the lowest gap between rich and poor. "[S]omeone who lives in a £multimillion mansion will only pay 3 times more than someone in a bedsit which falls into Band A" (Wikipedia). And since all (!) houses in central London are in Band H, this allows those councils to set some of the lowest tax rates in the country. Thus residents of 1 Hyde Park (with 86 flats costing up to £40 million, developed by the Candy brothers and designed by Rogers Stirk Harbour) pay less council tax than Band H residents elsewhere in the UK, even without the second home council tax relief some claim. Low council tax rates do not indicate efficiency.

"Both Kensington and Chelsea, and Westminster councils, which contain most of the alpha territory, have announced plans to place homeless people in accommodation in outer London and beyond because they can no longer afford to house them." (David Batty, *The Observer* 24/1/16) Worse, some even loan money to cash-strapped councils at slightly higher rates of interest than the public sector borrowing rate set by Treasury. We should insist that those central London boroughs perform their statutory duties by raising their council taxes. Keeping them artificially low is a form of gerrymandering, removing Labour voters and creating wealthy slums.

The council tax should serve as a wealth or mansion tax which would greatly increase local council income. Bands should be realistic, rising from £125,000, £250,000, £500,000, £750,000, £1m, £2.5m, up to and finally, in Band H, above £5m. And the tax from Band H should be ten rather than three times the rate for Band B. The only caveat is that the tax collected from the higher bands should be redistributed more fairly to all councils to avoid the wealthy London boroughs (and the rotten borough known as the City of London) becoming fabulously wealthy and reducing their council taxes even lower.

Additional sources of council revenues might include the following:

- the Stamp Duty on every property purchase currently rises from 0% on houses less than £125,000 up to 7% on house purchases above £2 million. These should coincide with the council tax bands, and the Duties redistributed fairly to councils, as proposed for the council tax;
- councils should be allowed to raise an additional tax on second homes and vacant properties through local bye-laws as they think fair; and
- Osborne's infamous bedroom tax should only apply to mansions with more than five or six bedrooms with or without private cinemas and swimming pools. If the wealthy can afford their own pool, they can help subsidize public baths.

From chapter 7, insular elites are unfairly perpetuated through inherited wealth in offshore trusts. When the 6th Duke of Westminster died in 2016, his estate, valued at about £9 billion, was inherited by his son via an offshore family trust. This evaded (ipE) a tax bill of some £3 billion – roughly equal to the yearly total of inheritance tax. Such trusts, like mega-corps, should be broken up. In addition, rather than tax the whole estate at probate as at present (or not in the case above), we might introduce a graduated tax on the inheritors. Allow £50,000 tax free, rising to perhaps 50% above £20m. This would present the wealthy with an unpleasant dilemma: either break up their trusts or pay higher taxes. Both would benefit society.

Land offers a third potential source of council funding. In 2016/7, research showed that landowners received £13 billion tax-free when they sold their land for development (*The Planner* September 2018). Developing farmland increases its value on average well over 200-fold. Since 1945, all attempts to tax such 'land betterment' have been repealed. In Germany, local councils identify and then buy the land needed for urban growth, before inviting tenders from developers. This retains the increased land values for the councils and society generally rather than the lucky landowners.

Finally, property taxes must apply to all properties. Yet, for about 18% of our land and perhaps 10% of properties in expensive areas, the Land Registry has no ownership details. The legal owners of every field and every building should be registered and subject to the same taxes as their neighbours. And to be seen to be fair, every council must have access to the Land Registry and even, as in France, provide local registries open to public inspection without charge.

In summary, against the five principles of sustainability, the tax reforms above would release much energy in towns and cities against my five principles of urban entropy:

- fair VAT and fuel escalators, using science responsibly, would conserve green fields, intensify cities and reduce pollution;
- a value reduced tax (VRT) would husband the planet's resources, reducing energy and material waste;
- fairer corporate taxes would support SMEs, clusters and healthy economies;
- fairer income and property taxes would reduce inequality and create healthy and just societies; and
- empowered local authorities would revive local democracy and good governance.

Government, central or local

Throughout the last century, control of public services and tax spending has shifted from local to central government, reinforcing the trend for 'elective dictatorships'. The case for stronger local councils has both negative and positive aspects. Conservative 'economic' governments generally support low taxes and public spending in pursuit of individual freedom. Liberal and Labour 'extravagant' governments tend to raise taxes and public spending in pursuit of social improvement. Whether nasty or profligate, however, since 1979 most governments have managed to be both, reducing the tax burden on corporate and personal wealth while wasting substantial amounts of money on unsustainable capital investments and corporate welfare.

Stronger councils could achieve much better value for money because they are in direct contact with the staff delivering the local services and with those people affected. And by their very diversity, councils will try different approaches. Some might outsource all their services to the likes of Capita, Serco and Virgin, some would keep them in-house, while others might deliver some services in partnership with local chambers and social enterprises. Then we could assess what works and what doesn't.

Table 40 shows that public spending from local to central government and this is not sustainable:

- before World War I, local and central government spending was about equal,
- between the wars, local government spending was significantly higher, being 57% of the total current government spending from 1925-35,
- since World War II, local spending peaked at 41.5% of the total in 1973,
- since 2000, it has reduced to below 30%, and now
- with austerity from 2008 it has dropped to nearer 20%.

Table 40: Total current government expenditure by source, 1900-95 (£bn 1997 prices)

Year	Current expenditure local govt	central govt	% local/ central	Total govt expenditure*	% local/ total
1900	3,541	7,382	48.0	13,505	26.2
1905	4,926	4,748	103.7	12,464	39.5
1910	5,342	5,001	106.8	13,526	39.5
1915	4,680	41,457	11.3	51,037	9.2
1920	4,629	6,064	76.3	24,648	18.8
1925	6,979	5,744	121.5	30,077	23.2
1930	9,063	6,203	146.1	36,700	24.7
1935	10,453	7,973	131.1	41.011	25.5
1940	11,787	76,301	15.4	103,379	11.4
1945	10,212	88,839	11.5	129,145	7.9
1950	10,775	28,135	38.3	73,480	14.7
1955	12,191	33,489	36.4	78,880	15.5
1960	16,432	36,230	45.4	93,901	17.5
1965	22,227	40,692	54.6	114,177	19.5
1970	30,235	46,189	65.5	139,460	21.7
1975	44,233	62,378	70.9	191,476	23.1
1980	44,649	70,654	63.2	218,757	20.4
1985	46,497	78,823	59.0	247,845	18.8
1990	53,490	87,565	61.1	251,338	21.3
1995	55,821	102,173	54.6	302,207	18.5

Source: Halsey and Webb

(*Total government spending also includes subsidies and grants (not to local councils), rising from £0.7 to £73.3bn, National Insurance, rising from £0.4 bn to £43.6 bn, and debt interest, from £1.9 to £27.3bn.)

In broad terms, since the bankers' crash, local government spending has fallen from £135.0bn in 2008/9 to £89.8bn in 2017/8, much less than half of which is now funded by government grants. I believe we should aim to restore parity between central and local current spending, and identify those public services that could be better delivered locally. Increasing local council tax income (above) will only partly achieve this. Could we raise council spending to about £300bn? Let us look at the main government spending departments in turn.

Table 41: Government current spending on key services, 2008/9

Department	Central gov't	Local councils
Education	36,725	52,293
National health	110,435	-
Welfare benefits	173,476	-
Social services	1,200	25,548
Housing	17,734	20,740
Transport	23,000*	6,709
Defence	38,579	-
Total (incl misc)	563,711	135,038

Source: ONS, *Annual Abstract*

(*Transport figure are for 2009/10 and include both current and capital expenditure.)

In education in 1990/1, only 17% of the £26.7bn budget was central government spending on universities, vocational training and pre-school education. In 2008/9, it rose to 42% through the new schools funded directly by government. Whatever the financial abuses within these multi-academy trusts, at least 80% of education funding should return to education authorities. Let some test the idea of private academies if they wish but return all primary and secondary education to local control.

The NHS is fully funded by central government, personal social services 95% by local government. If 40% of the combined budget (£137.2bn) were managed locally, the social care of children at risk, the elderly, community nursing and care homes could be integrated with all primary healthcare services including GP surgeries, dentists, cottage hospitals and even preventive medicine.

10% to 20% of welfare benefits must be delegated. Withholding essential benefits from disabled people through government indifference and corporate profiteering is shameful. Whether under council control or managed in partnership with local GPs and social enterprises, few would be as incompetent or inhuman.

Housing is primarily a local issue since all councils are duty-bound to ensure that all residents are suitably housed. Yet most council spending is on housing benefits while government funds major regeneration projects with little notable success. With local control, some would start housebuilding again, others would support social housing, self-builders and even local builders.

Under transport, since 80% of all road trips are local, much more spending on roads should go to local councils. Similarly, most Inter-City services are profitable, so their surpluses should go to strategic councils and PTAs to improve regional railways.

While defence is rightly government-controlled (however incompetently), other spending includes about £30bn on industry, agriculture and employment. Few councils would be as inefficient as the government at handing out farm subsidies and £30bn on industry and employment could be better spent through local chambers and councils.

Finally, the National Lottery (£0.85bn) is a quango with a large advertising budget, regional offices and bureaucratic application systems. Run by local councils (instead of the department for communities and local government) the Lottery might support more locally relevant and successful schemes. This would avoid many of the big vanity projects that should be government or privately funded.

While all councils would initially struggle with enlarged roles and budgets, they managed in the past. The more dangerous risk is in not restoring those powers. This will only increase general apathy and the 'democratic deficit' mentioned earlier.

Consider the democratic energy that could be released with electricity, a public service that has been municipalized, nationalized and privatized. In 1947, the *Electricity Act* of the Attlee government nationalized all 551 electricity companies. 360 were local authority undertakings from Aberystwyth to Kettering, St Pancras and York councils, 191 were private companies from Woking to Ormskirk and the Clyde Valley. These were replaced with 15 regional electricity boards (REBs) as follows:

- North of Scotland Hydro-electric Board and REBs for South East and South West Scotland; and
- REBs for the North East, North West, Yorkshire, Merseyside and North Wales, South Wales, the Midlands, East Midlands, Eastern, London, the South East, Southern and the South West.
- In addition, electricity generation and the national grid came under the British Electricity Authority, which became the Central Electricity Generating Board (CEGB) in 1957.

In 1989, the REBs were privatized. A year later the CEGB was broken up and sold as Powergen, National Power and the National Grid Company. Today, 90% of our homes are supplied by six major electricity companies: SSE (the only British company), EDF (French), E.ON UK and RWE npower (both German), Scottish Power (Spanish) and UK Power Networks (owned by three far east holding companies). Most were undersold. In 1990, SWEB was sold for £300 million. Five years later, it attracted an offer of £1 billion from an American company (*The Observer* 16/7/95).

Despite the regulator Ofgen, profiteering is a problem. In 1999, journalist Gregory Palast found that "Scottish Power earned 29 per cent on equity last year." When Scottish Power sought to buy the American utility, Pacificorp, to achieve similar 'efficiencies', it learned that the state of Oregon banned the export of cheap power and set a legal limit of 10% (later reduced to 9%) on that rate of return. Excess profits were to be reinvested in lower prices. In Palast's words (*The Observer* 7/2/1999), "Americans believe the public has an 'equity interest' in utility properties, despite nominal ownership by stockholders. Therefore, local communities and states retain the final authority over sales, pricing and profits. This is an unashamed rejection of far right free-market tenets." The Americans, happy to promote free-market capitalism abroad, actually regulated capitalism in their own backyard, until they unregulated energy prices and unleashed Enron in California (page 149). Meanwhile our electricity companies can be bought for say £2 billion, have annual profits of over £400 million extracted as dividends rather than invested in plant, staff and lower prices, and sold five years later for the same £2 billion.

Adam Smith saw that returns of 20% in a stable business "lead inevitably to ruin". Shareholders and directors gain at our expense, with high electricity prices, high subsidies for nuclear power stations and excessive charges to cover energy short-falls in winter with polluting diesel generators.

- The new Hinckley Point nuclear power station finally agreed in 2018 between our government and EDF would produce 3,200 MW (megawatts) at a cost of £24.5 billion to cover construction and finance charges. The agreed sale price for the electricity is about £95/MW. (Nobody knows the nuclear decommissioning costs, not even the French, nor how many noughts to add to current best estimates. This heritage is a poisoned chalice for future generations, and negates all criteria for sustainable development.

- The 'world's largest' offshore wind farm off the Yorkshire coast will cost £6 billion and deliver up to 1,800 MW at less than £50/MW (*The Planner* Sept 2016). This is more realistic as the technology is largely established, and while the supply obviously fluctuates, decommissioning costs are modest. (The Swansea Bay tidal lagoon scheme actually sought £148/MW from the government before it was quietly dropped.)

Returning electricity supply and generation to local councils, small companies and local consortia would be difficult at present, as the market is rigged in favour of a few national or mega-corp generators. But there were no major problems with supply, incompetence or profiteering when there were 551 electricity suppliers.

In 2008/9, 418 councils in the UK spent £135 billion on all its services, about 9% of GDP. Sharing just half the upfront cost of the Hinckley nuclear plant (£12.25bn) would increase council spending by nearly 10%. If this were invested in local electricity supply and demand, the following would happen.

Some would increase supply with small wind turbines and solar panels on public buildings and social housing, with grants for homeowners to do likewise. Others would invest in more reliable sources like ground pumps, heat exchange units, tidal and river turbines, wave generation and other low carbon systems. These would be cheaper/MW than nuclear generation with minimal risk.

Other councils would try and reduce demand, installing and grant-aiding building insulation, draught exclusion and temperature control systems. Some might even develop 'smart meters' to allow each household the basic essential of say three kW a day at cost, raising the price for the next three units and say trebling it for each subsequent kW. This would address both 'fuel poverty' and profligacy.

We would still need a National Grid to equalize between areas with surplus energy and areas in deficit. And we would still need a national generator like the CEGB to maintain supply and cope with winter peaks. But after 40 years of 15 nationalized electricity boards and 30 years of six private suppliers, 500 local suppliers, independent or in consortia, could reduce demand and produce electricity more efficiently and cheaply, with more innovation and less harm and danger than at present. Instead of lagging behind most of Europe, the UK might catch up with greater energy efficiency, or emerge under Chamberlain's 'municipal gospel' in the vanguard of the renewables market to combat climate change.

The will is there. With the current climate crisis, many councils are already switching to renewable energy, insulating buildings, planting trees and reducing road emissions. But councils need more money. Again Germany shows the potential. Munich city council now generates about half of the city's electricity, while Freiburg is known as an eco-city for its cycling and recycling, low energy buildings, less road traffic and lower carbon footprints than other cities.

How might delegation work? Public services would be devolved logically through the three tier hierarchy of local parish, strategic council and national state.

- Town councils and most villages could manage their local nursery and primary schools, even keeping 'uneconomic' schools open with modest local taxes to supplement council pupil budgets. City and county councils would retain overall responsibility for primary and secondary education, local colleges and adult education, with back-up support for teachers and mentors, special needs, languages, music, libraries and residential centres. This would leave government responsible for universities, curriculums and audit functions.
- Most parishes could manage their GP and dental surgeries. Cities and counties could manage general hospitals as well as preventive medicine, social services and care homes, leaving government with strategic health policy, university teaching hospitals, drug safety and audit functions.
- Planning could also be devolved: parishes responsible for all local housing and minor development, cities and counties responsible for strategic housing and development, with the Planning Inspectorate as backstop. Government should refer all national developments to the Infrastructure Planning Commission and provide a clear legal framework.
- The police should be brought back under democratic control, with more police stations and magistrates courts retained and managed by strategic councils.

National agencies would be needed only for such serious issues as organized crime and corporate fraud.

- Parishes could undertake modest highway duties like road maintenance and cycle networks as well as car parking. Strategic councils and regional PTAs would manage urban and regional public transport networks and local highway investment, leaving government responsible for trunk road and Inter-City rail networks, with clear objectives to reduce road traffic and pollution.

This only indicates the potential of devolution. Local councils should be empowered to make their own choices between the disastrous and the unpalatable, their own solutions replacing central government *diktat*. Despite initial 'teething' problems sorting out tensions within the tiers, benefits could be substantial. All towns and villages would become more resilient, retaining more local post offices, shops, pubs and police stations, reducing local traffic with school buses and community transport and, longer term, stemming rural emigration.

Cities and counties would have more control of public service costs, staff and quality. Council officers would work closer with local schools, hospitals, housing groups and transport providers, unlike civil servants with "their present corporate structure, independence, and aloofness." (Namier 1965) Strategic plans could focus on investment needs rather than land use patterns, councils choosing between the two options: permit large commercial developments with library or swimming pool 'tacked on as planning gain', or build those public assets and restrict commercial development to known demand within the existing urban scale.

Central government would become smaller (to satisfy neo-conomists) with clear responsibilities and more focussed strategic and audit functions. Had Margaret Thatcher become mayor of Birmingham instead of prime minister, her privatized refuse, education and transport services would have provided useful comparisons with other cities in terms of costs, staff pay, safety, service quality and value for money. In comparing the different approaches, governments could then identify those to be emulated, those discarded, and how struggling councils might be helped or mentored rather than penalized for failing targets.

Controlling more public services locally would also benefit society at large:

- the public regulators – CQC, Ofcom, Ofsted, Ofgen, ORR and Ofwat etc – would be reduced to the overall audit function. For local management, they would be replaced by public scrutiny in council chambers and the local press;
- private monopolies would return to public monopolies, so any eight and nine figure annual profits would be reinvested rather than extracted as dividends. Thames Water, for example, has increased company debt to unsustainable levels even while extracting huge dividends. Public regulators are unable to prevent such behaviour. Had they been given the necessary powers, that would have severely reduced the sale price when first privatized;
- local councils would become more innovative and more collaborative, working with local chambers, banks and neighbouring councils, with wider consortia

like PTAs, ILEA (inner London education authority) and CLASP (a school building consortium); and

- staff and customers would benefit from improved services.

Citizen power

The other benefit of devolving powers and funds is that residents, businesses and the local media would take more interest in local politics – the first essential of citizen power. After government and councils, we arrive at what citizens – and you, dear reader – might perform, personally, socially and nationally.

Personally, we all need to reduce our carbon footprints. Most measures of personal CO_2 production cover key aspects of life: food, travel, domestic comfort, non-essential spending and our use of public services. The UK carbon footprint in 2004 averaged 9.2 tonnes per person (Heritage 2004). My carbon footprint was about three tonnes. Now I may be unusually tightfisted, but I enjoy levels of personal comfort, freedom and convenience that are little different to the rest of my friends.

- The average allowed for food is 840 kgs CO_2 pa. This increases for those regularly eating ready-meals, lots of flesh and out-of-season fruit and veg. It reduces for vegetarians and vegans, those buying local, organic and non-packaged fruit and veg, and those with allotments.
- I travel perhaps 4,000 miles a year by bus and train (at 0.1 kgsCO_2/mile). I have no car (producing 2.8 kgs/litre of petrol) and I don't fly (at 150 kgs per hour flying).
- At home, our seven solar panels produce nearly as much electricity as we use (at 1.0 kgs/kWhr), and in winter our gas Aga (at 1.8 kgs/cubic metre) provides sufficient hot water and 'central heating'.
- Our non-essential spending (producing 60 kgs/£100) is modest.

There is nothing exceptional in this. Those on benefits ('benefit scroungers' to the media moguls) will have lower carbon footprints – because they are often hungry and cold, make few trips and have no disposable income. It is the mindless wealthy who are the scroungers: scrounging off the poor by paying minimal wages, scrounging off us all through tax evasion, scrounging 'allowances' and bail-outs off the state and scrounging off future generations by polluting the planet and wasting its resources.

Reducing your carbon footprint may be mildly irritating. But using local facilities more often supports local economies while giving social pleasure. If your lifestyle depends largely on cars, foodsheds and 'brands', try a gentle detox. Leave the car at home two days a week, use local butchers, greengrocers, delicatessens and markets, independent cafes and pubs, and reduce non-essential spending. Within three months, you should have graduated from simple recognition to welcome customer, saved money and become a little fitter. Also, for at least six months, avoid consumer brands and ignore national adverts. In all this diversity, you may discover better products, cheaper food, friendly shopkeepers, stallholders and cafe/bar staff, and enjoy the social banter as customer, whether observer or participant.

Restoring local government may also attract more citizens to take an active part in local affairs and, like worker bees, ensure that the hive and highways are clean and maintained, the young, the sick and the old are properly cared for, the dead suitably disposed and the peace kept.

Yet, with the vertical hierarchy from government to council and citizen, the risk of elective dictatorship remains. The great will remain in control over the good, as history's great emperors, generals, politicians and villains dominated friendly, honest citizens. Both Henry Fielding (in *Jonathan Wild*) and Lord Acton (page 140) saw through the powerful. The good still do all the work while today's villains (including media moguls, captains of industry, senior politicians, top bankers and mafia oligarchs) still control all the money. Only the Supreme Court can curb the government, and only on points of law.

We need to convert the hierarchy of government over council and citizen into a virtuous circle. For this, I suggest a reformed House of Lords based on a new citizen's assembly. This new House would sit for three sessions a year as at present, coinciding with the Commons. However:

- each session would be held in a different city, rotating between the four UK capitals and say 12 regional cities;
- 100 (or 150?) new lords and ladies, sitting for each session, would be selected from that region as juries are selected;
- each temporary lord and lady would have a daily allowance of say £250, four days a week, 10 to 5, with sick leave, travel expenses (excluding cars obviously) and hotel expenses for those beyond commuter distance; and
- the new House would be served by a modest civil service of advisors, recorders and administrators.

For the new lords and ladies, unlike the existing, this would be a full-time job during the session. Its specific powers might include the following:

1. approve draft Acts of Parliament from the Commons, suggest amendments or veto the Act for a term or a parliament, as with the existing House;
2. the new House might even have the primary role in approving and vetoing bye-laws in order to free up the Commons;
3. wrest from the government the duties of the National Audit office so that there is some independent overview of all government spending;
4. also wrest from the government responsibility for all Public Inquiries into natural, corporate and government disasters;
5. be responsible for MP's pay and conditions;
6. have a small budget to commission original research; and
7. be responsible for a newly formed independent Press Council to ensure that the media are responsible and accountable.

The first two duties above might be considered too onerous for mere commoners, but that is the point. Lord Harman on the stink of planning legislation (see page 274) was only repeating a more general point. "Political language... is designed to make lies sound truthful and murder respectable, and to give the appearance of solidity to pure wind." (George Orwell, *Politics and the English Language*) If national laws that affect us all can't be grasped by commoners, then they are not 'fit for purpose'. Every draft Act, accurately summarized in a few pages with key points highlighted, would be presented to the new House by two advisors, for and against, and the following discussion chaired by an independent legal expert and experienced arbitrator. We might even allow each session of the new House to recommend one substantive piece of new legislation, such as an Act to protect all whistleblowers.

Duties 3 and 4 are both onerous but crucial to effective government. At present, too much government incompetence is simply glossed over. The National Audit office should report to the new House on such subjects as the NHS IT disaster, almost any major defence contract, corporate tax evasion, the PFI scandal and the shameful treatment of disabled people. Only an independent House could shine a light on such poor government, order prompt inquiries and identify those responsible. Having to wait years before a public inquiry is wrong for victims, as with bloody Sunday, the Marchioness, Herald of Free Enterprise and Hillsborough disasters (as well as several fires that preceded Grenfell Tower). Justice delayed is all-too-often justice denied. And having to report to commoners rather than government ministers might stiffen the resolve of some judges, allowing them to resist pressure from various powerful agencies to obfuscate and water down their findings.

Making commoners responsible for MP salaries and terms of employment (5) could ensure that they focus on what they were elected to do. The new House might insist that being an MP is a full-time job, so barring second jobs in chambers, boardrooms or elsewhere. Equally, it might not allow any MP to 'declare an interest' before speaking in any debate where that interest is due to financial or other personal rewards. For example, many MPs are housing landlords. Whether they should be allowed to speak or even vote in relevant debates needs to be agreed. A more strategic new House might decide that all political parties should be funded solely from two sources; individual party members (with a limit on fees) and modest state funding related to their share of the last vote. This would make all corporate and private 'donations', hospitality and sponsorships unlawful.

The sixth duty might adopt Sheldrake's suggestion (2012) that 1% of all government research funding (currently about £4.6bn) should be reserved for research suggested by the public, "from membership organisations like the National Trust, the British Beekeepers' Association, the National Society of Allotment and Leisure Gardeners, Oxfam, the Consumers' Association, the Women's Institute, as well as local authorities and trade unions" rather than allocated "according to agendas set by committees of establishment scientists, corporate executives and government bureaucrats."

Finally, and perhaps most controversially, the new House should be the body that oversees and protects a healthy, competitive and responsible media, upon which all democracies depend. The House, acting directly or through a permanent agency that reports to it, would cover all sections of the media.

- The BBC, a major asset in our social 'balance sheet', is too often subject to unmerited government interference by senior politicians who feel they have been unfairly reported. Power over BBC funding and the governing body should pass from vengeful politicians to the new House.
- Similar conflicts arise when the government approves who is 'fit and proper' to own our national newspapers and sets policy on cross media ownership. Markets do not function efficiently when tied up with PR spin, commercial confidentiality, political donations and perverse taxation. An independent media engaged in investigative journalism is vital. It is this dereliction of duty, rather than web news pages, that explains the collapse in newspaper circulations. The Barclays, Murdochs and Rothermeres are focussed on maximizing profits by cutting costs rather than increasing readers by exposing scandals and tax evasions of which they themselves have inside knowledge.
- Most local newspapers also need to be rescued from the dozen or so owners that have, all-too-often, closed local offices, outsourced sub-editing and even centralized the journalists to Cardiff or elsewhere. In their focus on advertising, local news is subservient and journalists restricted to the web for their stories. These oligopolies should be broken up with owners restricted to a maximum of five titles that serve the same sub-region to allow for some local economies of scale.

This arrangement would replace or reform the existing Press Complaints Committee, which is a self-regulating body. If this model works and the new House can ensure an independent media and adjudicate fairly on complaints, it might be extended to other self-regulating bodies like those for solicitors and accountants.

It is surely time that councils and citizens were freed from unnecessary, undesirable and unsustainable curbs on local decision-making. If government is indeed a social contract between Parliament, local councils and citizens, only as powers are passed down to the appropriate local level will civilization emerge, from universities to nurseries, hospitals to care workers, InterCity to cycleways, the Old Bailey to local cop shop.

The way ahead

This is an ambitious programme for urban revival and democratic reform. What might set it in motion? The obvious trigger is central government, but it is also the major obstacle. No elected government willingly reduces its own powers when our binary system has delivered almost continuous power to either left or right. Without proportional representation, the diversity of the country is largely ignored. Green, centrist and other minority voices are unheard in 'the mother of all parliaments'.

Yet occasionally, major reform has occurred through strong leaders with social agendas. From 1911, Lloyd George introduced the concept of the welfare state through National Insurance for ill-health and unemployment, state pensions for all and rent tribunals. Post 1945, Clement Attlee nationalized water, energy and the British Railways, and set up the NHS and legal aid. Both programmes required strong leaders blessed with intellectual rigour, social understanding and the felt need for fair play.

Since 1979, Thatcher ideology has had a largely negative impact on social life: burgeoning personal and corporate wealth but reduced manufacturing jobs, skills and welfare benefits, widespread poverty, food banks, begging and homelessness. After 40 years, the ideology of neo-conservatism and privatization is exhausted.

In part 1, I used Hinduism to illustrate the forces behind urban growth of creation, destruction and preservation. Let me now introduce another 'religion' to clarify the essence of government: one that is rational and responsible (head and heart) but without the faith (or soul). Humanism, as I understand it, seeks to avoid all dogmas and respect all forms of life. Such a government should be:

- transparent. Secrecy breeds lies and corruption. Only through open government can we make progress,
- fair in how it distributes social wealth (largely through taxes) to reduce gross inequality. It is inhumane to deprive substantial minorities the freedom to enjoy the essentials of life, and
- sustainable or responsible in its use of science, with less pollution, more recycling, protecting all wildlife and expanding natural habitats.

While hard data is one of the fundamentals of civilization, we have become one of the most centralized (and secretive) governments in Europe. We need to revive the retail and employment Censuses providing data on premises, staff and turnover to improve economic strategies and planning decisions. Corporate annual accounts should reveal relevant details on production conditions, external costs, carbon emissions and wage differentials. This might curb some boardroom greed through sheer embarrassment. More importantly, we could assess whether 'fair traders' are more efficient than the 'profiteers', as Robert Owen first showed. And all public service contracts must be opened up to public scrutiny. Today, so many contracts conceal 'cost creep', inefficiency, poor service and occasional fraud. In some quarters of Europe, we are referred to as 'Treasure Island'. Perhaps Europe will be better off without us. Such inefficiencies reinforce the importance of investigative journalism. The Barclays, Murdoch and Rothermere are unfit owners of such a crucial institution.

It is odd to ask any government to be fair or even-handed in its dealings with rich and poor, big and small, safe and dangerous, clean and polluting etc. Can we at least unify VAT on all construction, discourage green field development rather than small-scale intensification and stop subsidizing urban regeneration with compulsory purchase? Could we tax foodsheds and mega-corps consistently with town centre shops and local employers based solely on national turnover? Should tax allowances not be treated as grudgingly and meanly as welfare benefits, and earned and unearned income taxed equally? If rail fares must be escalated annually, why not petrol let alone aircraft? For those who think it essential to tax the poor on any 'surplus' bedrooms, by what logic is this mansion tax not imposed on us all? And while plumbers are jailed for tax evasion, why are none of the 'filthy rich' in prison? These inconsistencies reverse Hammurabi's legal code (page 235) under which wealthy Babylonians were punished *more* harshly than commoners for serious crimes.

And finally, a government needs a 'green strategy'. I have avoided that label as it tends to divide us between committed activists and deniers. Yet all the policies in this book – on planning and development, on health, education and housing, poverty, pollution and food security, justice, freedom and equity etc – also happen to be green in accordance with the five principles of sustainability (quoted in *NPPF1*). We need lower carbon emissions, a just society, healthy local economies, sound science and, as discussed here, good governance. To repeat the quote from page 282

> *What is popular*
> *is not always right.*
> *What is right*
> *is not always popular.*

Both major parties are in this bind. In a weak democracy like ours, a few media outlets strongly influence policy, politicians know that unpalatable decisions lose votes and so make too many disastrous decisions. A wise government might see a way out of this conundrum. Adopt and adapt the general framework above and let local councils develop their own specific policies. For this, the government need only rescind the *ultra vires* rule and allow councils to spend say 10% of their budget beyond their legal duties. This would release local innovation.

Even without such freedom, might a few strong councils band together to agree a basic carbon reduction strategy (to reduce traffic and refuse all new foodsheds and tower blocks etc). This would require co-ordination, support from such agencies as the Local Government Association and the RTPI, and use of existing law such as the *Climate Change Act 2008* and the sustainable principles in *NPPF1*. It would also require public consultations to overcome the right or popular conflict. These would include at least schools, community groups, minorities, the business community and voluntary sector, tenant associations, groups deemed 'hard to reach', councillors, officers, political wards and the local press so that everyone is involved. Consultations are the first step in making local government more transparent, as well as providing a solid base for policies to improve schools, public health, housing supply and social transport etc. A strongly-approved green strategy would also stiffen the resolve of a caucus of councils when, inevitably, a foodshed or developer appealed any refusals. This would force legislators to clarify priorities as between statutory plans that define sustainable land use as against private property rights.

Fair policies might only permit affordable new housing schemes, at least until the homeless were decently housed and waiting lists reduced. Some might also set up rent tribunals and tax second homes. Schools might be assessed on 'real' performance rather than the current academic focus that excludes perhaps 30% of all pupils. And some, learning from Chamberlain, might replace the profiteering and poor service in most private equity care homes and private bus monopolies with council undertakings or social enterprises through compulsory purchase.

Green policies might, at least temporarily, refuse all green field development, urban redevelopments, new foodsheds and 'hoovers', and intensify neighbourhoods. Local economies might focus on small businesses, including local farms and builders, specialist clusters, full employment, local production and local purchasing. And road traffic and pollution must be replaced with healthy forms of social transport.

Even parishes, with the approval of villagers, could implement various sustainable policies to improve village life, preferably with others under a supportive city or county council. They should define their vital 'community assets' (or social hubs) like GP surgeries, village schools, post offices and pubs, and retain those threatened with closure. They might also refuse all developments outside their boundaries and calm all through-traffic with more safe pedestrian crossings to improve village life.

Such freedom and diversity would rebut the inertia and incompetence of central government. The danger is that, after a century of de-urbanization and four decades of neo-conservatism, our social behaviour has been stunted by free market individualism. Perhaps only through local action can we begin to set our nation on a fairer more sustainable path, and reduce carbon emissions more quickly and effectively. And perhaps it is only local councils that can restore a fair balance between liberty, equality and fraternity, revive our social nature and rebuild civilization.

In short – Think local. Act local.

Afterword on Covid-19

From these turbulent times, with Brexit and Trump preceding the coronavirus crisis, a short review of the pandemic and how it affects cities might be useful. What will be 'the new normal'? This afterword discusses the impact of Covid-19 and how it reinforces or contradicts key arguments in *Civilizing Cities*. We look first at the risks of infection and our political response, second at the dangers of infection as it affects different sectors of society, third at the wider social and economic impacts of Covid-19, and finally the way ahead. Running through the whole is the importance of public health that takes us back to the roots of planning in the *Public Health Act 1848*, and the first *Housing, Town Planning, etc. Act 1909*, requiring local councils to secure "proper sanitary conditions, amenity and convenience."

(On a personal note, my uncle John Pemberton, who with an Indian and an American doctor set up the International Epidemiological Association, would have given this paper some scientific rigour. All I can suggest are the likely variables of the pandemic that affect urban life. And rather than reference every source, the following are the main sources from March to September 2020: BBC 1 (*Coronavirus: A Horizon Special*, May 2020), BBC 2 (*The Forgotten Frontline*, 30/7/20), Channel 4 (*The Country that Beat the Virus: What Can Britain Learn?* 14/5/2020), *The Observer, Private Eye* and the website www worldometers.info (12/8/2020).)

A: The political response to Covid-19

The risk of being infected depends initially on our political response, which may follow the minimal, reactive or preventive models. Doing nothing is designed to let the virus spread to develop 'herd immunity', as in Sweden. The reactive model responds with lockdowns as the virus spreads and death tolls rise as in most of Europe. Prevention means investing in a clear strategy for dealing with any new virus with border controls, test and tracking contacts (T&T) and isolating those infected, as in South Korea.

The reactive model differs from my "reactive planning based on the *politics of continuity*" from chapter 8 (page 297). There, reactive planning should be pragmatic as opposed to pro-active and idealistic, seeking "progress with minimal disruption"

(JS Mill) through "small-scale incrementalism" (K Popper). And it is eminently pragmatic to learn from experience and develop *preventive* plans in order to cope better with future plagues, minimize social and economic shocks and maintain some continuity.

The scale of the Covid-19 plague can be seen in my final table.

Table 42: World statistics on Covid-19; 12/8/2020

Nation	Cases	Deaths	Cases/ 1M pop	Deaths/ 1M pop	Tests/ 1M pop
1 US	8,829,951	230,085	26,684	694	399,708
3 Brazil	5,381,224	156,926	26,260	737	102,799
4 Russia	1,513,877	26,050	10,372	178	392,588
5 Spain	1,110,372	34,752	23,746	743	331,544
6 France	1,086,597	34,645	16,634	530	224,090
11 UK	854,010	44,745	12,850	660	458,213
14 Italy	504,509	37,210	8,700	618	242,482
17 Germany	429,181	10,111	5,166	121	243,003
26 Belgium	305,409	10,737	26,316	925	389,956
27 N'lands	281,052	7,019	16,986	411	169,238
41 Portugal	116,109	2,297	11,650	227	309,898
43 Sweden	110,594	5,933	10,929	586	205,031
47 Switz'land	103,653	2,083	11,949	240	199,022
49 Japan	95,835	1,706	764	14	20,368
54 China	85,790	4,634	60	3	111,163
68 Austria	80,811	979	8,956	109	231,457
65 Ireland	56,108	1,882	11,323	380	310,431
79 Denmark	39,411	700	6,960	121	846,025
84 Greece	29,992	564	2,958	55	160,103
86 Australia	27,513	905	1,075	35	332,330
89 S Korea	25,836	457	504	9	49,649
94 Norway	17,749	279	3,283	51	281,253
99 Finland	14,848	353	2,678	64	253,102
161 N Zealand	1,935	25	387	5	213,339

Source: www:worldometers.info

Hard accurate data is a fundamental of civilization (chapter 7). It clarifies the nature of viruses and suggests strategies to prevent or moderate future plagues. Some of the figures above may appear 'unrealistic'. For example, China's figures show how a powerful tyranny can control an epidemic (or information). In the UK, there were 46,706 deaths reported on 12/8/20, yet 2,000 fewer two months later. A more accurate measure compares the total number of deaths with the average in previous years. Thus, in the UK, when Covid-19 deaths stood at 35,000, there were 52,000 more deaths than the average in the previous five years. This is higher per million than most other countries. Perhaps an international agency like the WHO (world health organization) should have the right to check national data during global plagues.

South Korea was prepared for any pandemic and reacted promptly to Covid-19. In a population of 50 million, there were only 457 deaths by late October. T&T, however, raises a serious social issue. It seems that South Koreans are content to cede their privacy to government health agencies by being 'tracked' on their phone GPSs and self-isolating if infected to prevent Covid spreading. In thus protecting society, economic and social life is allowed to carry on, albeit at lower levels than normal. Only in one South Korean city was there a lockdown when local infections rose, showing a healthy flexibility between central and local government.

The UK tried all three responses. Being one of the slowest in Europe to react, our initial response (hoping that it wouldn't interfere with international trade) was, like Sweden, to let the virus take its course 'to develop herd immunity'. When Italy showed how serious it was and Covid-19 took hold here, unlike Sweden, our relaxed response changed to a panicky lockdown. "Stay at home. Protect the NHS. Save lives." This delay of up to six weeks cost lives.

Some cardiac, cancer and other patients died prematurely when their treatments were delayed. While some would have died later in the year, many under 50 died prematurely because they 'stayed at home' and ignored symptoms of varying seriousness, either to 'protect the NHS' or to avoid getting infected in hospital.

Having imposed lockdown later than most of Europe, we then relaxed it too soon. 'Stay at home' became 'Stay alert'. This was confusing and controversial. While infections in London and the south east had reduced (the R rate then below 1 and falling), Scotland, Wales, Northern Ireland and many regions and cities, affected later by the virus, still had rising infection rates. Unsurprisingly, the nations did not feel ready to relax and stuck with the lockdown.

And for too long, we ignored WHO key advice for all pandemics: 'test, test and test'. The repetition was not just for the hard of hearing. Only through testing can we track the spread of infection, understand how Covid-19 behaves and protect key workers and vulnerable groups. Slow to introduce testing, six months on the system remains inadequate compared to most other nations in table 42, being over-reliant on remote test sites and three large laboratories.

As well as bad timing, our government response was inept. First, public information was centrally controlled and badly managed. Minutes of all SAGE meetings (scientists' advisory group on emergencies) were confidential – the default mode for politicians but not scientists. And while Dominic Cummings attended their meetings, SAGE lacked any public health experts. So an 'alternative' Sage was set up by other scientists to provide and investigate alternatives. Most nations were more open. Sweden did not 'do nothing'. It developed an effective T&T system and advised everyone how to reduce risk with social distancing, masks and working at home if possible. So it avoided the full economic impact of lockdown and kept death rates lower than here. 'Successful' nations treated their citizens as adults. Our government treated the national crisis more as an election campaign, while rigorously excluding all press photographers from Downing Street.

Given the resources and responsibilities outlined in chapter 10, local councils could assemble data about infections and deaths from local sources more quickly and accurately than the ONS data filtered through central government, the NHSx and private contractors. And develop their own T&T systems. Leading European nations relied heavily on local councils, health officers and GPs.

A second failure was in the delivery of essential equipment and support.

- PPE (personal protective equipment) was both late and insufficient, even for hospitals and care homes. (One 'election' trick was to count 1 million pairs of gloves as 2 million items of PPE.) And when the EU ordered ventilators and PPE for all member states, we opted out while first denying that we had been included.

- Schools were promised laptops for pupils without so that they could participate in the web-based learning. Few were delivered. And free school meals through the holidays were only agreed after a footballer's intervention.

- Against expert advice, exams were cancelled and pupil grades assessed by computer algorithms. This reliance on technology echoes the problem of COBA 'objective analyses' (pages 188-90) with their built-in bias. The exam algorithms were even found to favour private school pupils.

- The government set up a £300 million fund to pay 75% of the private tuition fees of pupils when they returned to school, but schools had to find the other 25%. Why were schools not given that budget direct?

- Unlike most nations, our government took a curiously 'macho' attitude to the wearing of masks, which only became mandatory in July. As in the US, this suggests that as a nation we place more emphasis on individual liberty than social fraternity (from chapter 7). It was reinforced by almost constant advice to avoid buses and trains. This encouraged train operators to reduce services, while increasing road traffic, congestion and pollution.

More serious still, the delivery of an effective test and trace system was late, poorly co-ordinated, grossly ineffective, expensive and even now, eight months on, inadequate. The national testing system was delivered by Deloitte, accountants whom few would associate with public health services. Test sites were all in large exurban car parks. Central sites accessible to all had to wait until August. Test targets were missed even when numbers 'booked' were added to the actual tests, and booking a test often resulted in round trips of over 200 miles. These results were often subject to long delays, perhaps due to over-reliance on the three large testing labs. This meant that tracking by local health teams was often futile, especially when the data omitted postcodes. Local hospital, university and research institute labs were sidelined.

Typically, the national tracking was given to Serco (despite dubious links to government and being fined for 'fraud' on two public contracts) and the US call centre firm Sitel. In the first 12 weeks to the end of August, these two trackers 'earned' £192m. (For the whole year, that would become £720m.) Yet 75% of the tracking, including *all* the 'complex' cases, was done by local health teams, for which councils have received £300m. Even if this is just to the end of August, it is still excellent value for money. If it is for the whole year, just how efficient must local councils be to sever this government from its ideology (and party donors)?

Overseeing this privatized system was Public Health England, a body set up under Cameron against professional advice at the time. And, as with Beeching from ICI being brought in to 'modernize' our railways (page 186) and BP's Lord Browne defining the 'business' case for universities (page 240), Dido Harding (a Conservative peer with experience in Woolworths, Tesco and Talk Talk) was brought in to oversee public health. Gove's dismissal of 'experts' during the referendum is official policy.

After information, equipment and T&T, a fourth fault line was the inability to define priorities. Of course we were woefully ill-prepared for any health emergency. 'Stay at home. Protect the NHS. Save lives' was essential to protect the NHS and its hospitals after 40 years of chronic staff stress and vacancies, long-term underfunding (partly reversed by the New Labour government 'interregnums') and several ill-conceived management 'transformations'. Other nations were better prepared. They may have been as relaxed as us beforehand, but most of them had more hospital staff and beds pro rata and so could cope with the plague more effectively. The army provided the 'Nightingale hospitals' on time, but bed shortages led to dangerous decisions, like releasing recovering hospital patients (without testing whether they were still infected) into care homes, many private equity-owned, that were 'suffering' serious cash flow problems. A Covid-19 inquiry might investigate whether these two facts were related.

And finally, in care homes our response was shameful. I should stress that only 15% of care homes are owned by private equity. Many small privately-run care homes do fantastic jobs but staff and residents were left unprotected and untested. Even now. The high death rates were not highlighted early on, but even when they could no longer be concealed, there was no urgency to prioritize them along with hospitals. According to a *Private Eye* correspondent, 125 deaths were recorded in 15 private care homes in Ealing. There were no infected residents in 17 council-run care homes in his Danish town with their protective gear and regular testing. He wondered if ownership might be relevant. The one government policy that got through was that visits by relatives were stopped. (Yet Dominic Cummings' drive to his parents's estate in Durham even while he and his wife were infected, suggests that, with 'no such thing as society', Thatcher's successors accept no social responsibilities.)

B: The health risks of Covid-19

From the political variables in controlling the risk of infection, we now look at social and cultural variables that affect the risks of infection and mortality. Perhaps among these tentative variables covering age, poverty, ethnicity, health and density there lurks a 'sociability index' that is relevant to cities.

All respiratory viruses target old people. Apparently the average age of our Covid victims is over 80 years. Yet between Spain and the UK (from table 42), with similar numbers of cases, our death toll was significantly higher. Perhaps in Spain more old people remained in the community among their extended families. This was less safe than being 'isolated' in well-managed care homes as in Denmark, but safer than living in UK care homes without PPE or tests. The differences between Spain and Portugal or Belgium and the Netherlands relate to political rather than social factors.

Poverty, a second factor, reduces personal health with overcrowding and poor diets. On the other hand, the relative immunity of the wealthy may simply be a symptom of their sickness (JM Keynes, page 158): spacious mansions, but little or no social life. Inevitably, sections of the media will blame the poor for spreading the virus, ignoring the choice that faces most of them – go to work or go hungry.

Ethnic minorities are also more vulnerable. This reflects greater poverty pro rata than among the ethnic majority and their greater exposure to the virus since, again pro rata, more of them are frontline staff in hospitals and care homes, also on low wages. (While every minister went out of their way to praise NHS staff on every available occasion, none of them offered an apology for voting down a bill in 2017 to increase nurses' wages – some even cheering when the vote was declared.) With no policy on frontline staff wages, this clarifies the different meanings of risk: for the poor it affects life and limb, but mere status for the wealthy (page 251). Poverty and frontline exposure may not fully explain the higher death rates. Living with constant covert discrimination and occasional outbreaks of naked racism may also affect the immunity (or simple will to live) for many British citizens.

Those with underlying health conditions are also vulnerable. It seems that our sedentary lifestyles (affecting 66% of the population, page 220) and our culture of junk food put us more at risk than the Japanese and South Koreans with their fresh fish and vegetable diets, or the Swedes who are healthier and fitter.

The socio-geographic variable of population density is more complex. In low density nations, as in Scandinavia, Australia and New Zealand, it may be easier to control the spread of the virus. The poor record of the US and Brazil (with equally low population densities below 100 people/sq mile) may simply reflect headstrong leaders who were slow to understand or unwilling to accept the political risks.

Within Europe, it is in cities that differences begin to emerge. For example, as between north and south, might Mediterranean towns and cities have retained more sociable behaviour with their extended families and cafe culture, bars and markets, siestas and evening promenades. When loved ones become infected, might friends and relatives feel the need to visit and comfort them despite any lockdown rules? This would spread the risk but be hard to control.

Also, within the Mediterranean cities and dense neighbourhoods, might citizens with millennia of urban life have developed stronger immune systems that improve their resistance to infection and/or their ability to survive? By contrast, in the UK, our cooler climate and suburban lifestyles, weekly shops and less street life might slow down the spread of any virus, but weaken our collective resistance to infection.

Between neighbourhoods there are clear differences between rich and poor. From chapter 7, wealth buys time, luxury and, crucially, space. Poverty enforces poor housing and overcrowding. The danger here is that the plague will allow politicians and developers to use overcrowding as an excuse for redevelopment (see section D below) just as we justified the needless slum clearances of the last century (chapter 2). It ignores the cultural differences in which urban societies accept cramped family life, either temporarily as families grow up or in return for living in lively neighbourhoods with all social facilities where it is the social norm, as discussed in chapter 3.

The notion of a 'sociability index' is mere speculation. Here, as elsewhere, we need far more detailed regional and local data, showing the differences between town and country, urbs and suburb, rich and poor neighbourhood. If every city and county council collected this data from their hospitals, care homes and coroners, they could manage more effective local T&T programmes, even isolating a few streets as has happened in various city neighbourhoods to control local infections, and (largely forgotten) providing support for those isolated who have no other means of income.

Finally, we need to promote a better understanding of 'risk'. T&T should be targeted at those most at risk – in care homes and hospitals, local surgeries and all those delivering public services in transport and 'hospitality' sectors etc. The aim must be to avoid future lockdowns for its known and unknown impacts:

- local economies will take many years to recover and fulfil their essential social functions,
- the mental stress and ill-health, particularly on the young, may be more serious and longer lasting than anyone at present realizes, while
- with the disruption to our hospitals, the 'excess' deaths due to other untreated conditions are killing citizens much younger than the Covid victims.

We need the best of the South Korean and German approaches.

C: Economic and social impacts of Covid-19

The lockdown has given us a foretaste of the structural problems highlighted in chapters 4 to 7 on town centres, globalization, traffic and social decline.

With most shops shut, **shopping** has become increasingly globalized. During the lockdown, we were encouraged to limit our essential shopping to one trip a week. The Amazon monopoly increased its market share significantly, foodsheds increased home deliveries and cash was further replaced by credit card. Furthermore, one shopping trip a week was impossible for all without a car, nor could we indulge in panic buying. So we continued shopping three to five times a week at our local shops and markets to support our traders as they continued to support us. Yet in March, Tesco received £585m in rates relief. In April, it paid shareholder dividends of £635m. This is difficult to justify when all food shops were still trading. We will need to compare the support given to the 20 major retailers with that given to our local shops and markets, cafes, pubs and restaurants during the lockdown. Until we curb the retail oligopolies, street markets and local shops will continue to decline, along with the social custom of shopping.

The **economic impact** of the lockdown will be the closure of many businesses and a recession, probably lasting many years. While government financial support far exceeded the bank bailouts of 2008, it is less than in many European nations. As with the cliché in crime fiction, we must 'follow the money' and be able to monitor exactly who has received financial support. For that, every company (public and private) must include such support in their annual accounts, alongside their political donations:

- as with Tesco above, we need to compare the support given to large firms with that given to the small business sector. We should focus support on the small business sector and specialist clusters rather than repeat 2008 in which we bailed out the banks while leaving small firms to sink or swim.
- many firms received 'furlough' money for their temporarily unemployed staff, (including one firm run by the Tory party treasurer), when some of those staff continued working from home. This was probably a fairly common problem;
- private equity firms, like care homes, may receive government money because they employ many people. For those with unsustainable levels of debt based on excessive annual dividends, this would be indefensible; and
- when the crisis fades, some mega-corps will sue countries that imposed lockdowns for their loss of profits. All future international trade agreements must cease to protect foreign firms and investors under their 'investor state dispute settlement' clauses. Mega-corps should accept those risks alongside the profits, and use their reserves to survive the crisis.

We must also avoid the 'austerity' that followed the bankers' crash. Government debt should be reduced through sustainable economic growth. (And we need a more sustainable measure than GDP that increases with every gallon of petrol bought and every road crash that generates work for the emergency services.)

Unfortunately, on **transport and the environment**, the auspices are not good. During the lockdown, road traffic reduced by as much as two thirds while cycling increased by about 70%. In every urban street, we could hear just how noisy the birds were (even though they were singing more quietly). Road pollution was much reduced though diesel particulates remained at dangerous levels. But (from chapter 6), lower traffic volumes also increases traffic speeds, making them more dangerous for cyclists and pedestrians. Grounded planes also transformed the lives of those who live under busy flight paths, although with fewer flights, each plane seemed far more intrusive. And during most of the lockdown, we were advised to avoid public transport.

Now their proposed spending takes us back to "1963 and all that" (page 186):

- The chancellor has earmarked £27bn for major road schemes. Of this sum, £5.5bn was actually earmarked for carbon reduction measures and a further £10bn was reshuffled from other spending programmes.
- The ludicrous HS2 scheme persists despite the fact that, even on its own cost benefit analysis, it will never 'pay its way', and
- the government's continued support for a third Heathrow runway is inexplicable, it having being dismissed by the courts on environmental grounds and 'opposed' by Johnson.

The opportunities for rail electrification to phase out diesel trains, improve local public transport and reclaim the streets for cycling and walking are ignored. These would create more jobs, clean the air, make us fitter and healthier and reduce the 40,000 premature deaths every year caused by road pollution. Instead, as we emerge from lockdown, the return of road congestion is likely to be heralded as a sign of economic recovery.

There is also malice in this perversity. When lockdown began, the rail franchises were quickly protected with government funding except the local Merseyrail franchise (page 210). City transport networks had to wait until early May for support, while Transport for London will only receive support when it agrees to increase fares.

The **social impact** of Covid-19 is the most difficult to determine, on young and old alike. All we know is that whatever the impact, it will be the poor, unemployed, marginalized (and other 'scroungers' – see page 364) who suffer. We have little idea how this will affect the young (my sixth key for civilization), but much will depend on their background. A term not at nursery and reception will affect all pupils with their first experience of 'organized social life'. The impact on comfortable households will generally be marginal, but for children who need school meals, don't speak English, live in one-room 'temporary accommodation' or in abusive households, the impact could be traumatic, making them realize how 'marginalized' their lives are. Other 'rites of passage', moving to secondary school and university, were also affected.

The lockdown encourages the use of web-based learning, further discriminating against the poor. And now many universities see it as a very 'cost-effective' way to reduce the number of lecturers. Stiglitz (2010) notes that the best US universities are 'not-for-profit' enterprises. Universities lose their intrinsic value when they are managed as businesses, with students as customers and knowledge as a commodity (page 240). And there remains the large disparity between university students and the rest of school leavers entering a dysfunctional jobs market in the so-called 'gig economy', with low skills, minimal training, zero hour contracts on minimum wages and no benefits. Many will find the jobs market as closed as the housing market. For those still with jobs, many will be encouraged to continue working from home. This denies the social nature of work, reinforcing 'command management' at the expense of collaborative work, problem solving, innovation and humour in the workplace.

There is also a serious discrepancy in the housing market. During lockdown, Stamp Duties were cut by £3.8bn. This was no help to first time buyers, who already 'enjoy' exemption. It only benefited private landlords and existing home owners, fuelling both house prices and demand for second homes. Perhaps all MPs should now disclose how many homes they own, including properties for rent.

Isolation, unemployment, family stress, housing insecurity and the basic lack of regular social chat and humour have also led to serious, but largely concealed, levels of mental stress when our mental health services are already seriously under-funded. Johnson's promise of 'shiny new hospitals' ignores this strategic issue.

Meanwhile, the government remains hopelessly compromised over immigrants. The Home Office will not reunite a few hundred asylum-seeking children with their families here. 4,000 refugees a year arriving by small boats is apparently a serious threat. And foreign health workers in hospitals and surgeries, including those who helped Johnson to survive the virus, were still expected to pay an annual fee for NHS treatment until, 'after careful consideration', the policy was dropped. That such meanness needs any consideration confirms this government's institutional racism. Meanwhile, since 2015, Germany has accommodated 1.7 million refugees, 10,000 of whom learned the language sufficiently to gain entrance to a university.

We are not all in this together. This government's treatment of immigrants (apart from the wealthy), disable people and children living in poverty is truly shocking. In chapter 6 (page 224) I suggested that, on current trends, we could be entering a new Dark Age. If we allow the lockdown to define 'the new normal', more local shops and street markets will cede to the foodshed and Amazon monopolies delivering to your doorstep, more work will be domesticated (like medieval cottage industries controlled by the capitalist merchants), town centre office blocks will be converted to unfit flats, public transport will spiral into decline, cash will largely disappear and all major spectator events will be owned by a few TV billionaires. Street life would be a few cafes, restaurants and pubs for some stroppy youths and the homeless. Social life would disappear and civilization collapse.

D: Emerging from Covid-19

If the first rule of government is to use any emergency to push through unpopular measures, that might explain the virulent Chinese crackdown on all their minorities. My more modest example is how Heathrow airport was pushed through under WWII emergency powers (page 210), avoiding scrutiny by experts. Now the government proposes to 'simplify' all planning controls.

Meanwhile, the disastrous Brexit has continued unabated with little or no challenge. Throughout this plague, trade in essentials like food and medicines has continued throughout Europe without hindrance. Yet while lockdowns have seriously affected all firms in the 'hospitality' sector, Brexit will seriously destabilize our farming, manufacturing and financial sectors. The new agriculture bill would allow the cheap (and heavily subsidized) food imports from the US and China. This will raise the profit margins of our foodsheds (by not passing all the lower prices onto consumers, see page 107), but force our farmers to follow suit with lower safeguards for our health, animal welfare and the environment – or stop farming. This is insane.

To heap an abrupt exit with no negotiated deal onto an economy already in recession may be an act of Churchillian proportion, but he would have seen the folly of leaving the most civilized trading block simply to appease 'the enemy within', being the right wing of the Tory party. The irony is that, once we are established outside the tyranny of Brussels, we will find ourselves back in an empire but, with more than a hint of poetic justice, our proud nation will be subservient either to the democratic ideals of China or the business acumen of the US. It is impossible to talk sensibly about this impending disaster without resort to Laurence Sterne's blank page and ▮▮▮▮▮▮▮▮▮▮▮. It requires the satire of Swift, the nous of Burke and the grasp of Galbraith.

At home, the 'new normal' might well be used to justify more green field sprawl and destructive 'regeneration' schemes (from chapters 1 and 2). Suburbs may slow down the spread of any virus and support Patrick Geddes' invalid generalization that "the essential improvement of family life is more space." However, urban sprawl denies eight centuries of successful city life based on density and diversity, and would be futile simply to mitigate future plagues. Nor do suburbs grow more fruit and vegetables. In the 1960s, it was thought that all suburban lawns would cover Surrey county. Today, suburban gardens tend to be 'low maintenance' with tarmac in front for parking and decking and paving in the back. If we were serious about increasing food security, we would provide more allotments to meet existing demand, to use urban land more efficiently, reduce road traffic, conserve farmland and retain an important social activity.

On regeneration, one can imagine architects and developers discussing new design features to allow physical distancing, 'safer' densities, wider aisles and queue trails, which *might* help reduce the spread of any new virus. The core argument of chapter 2, however, was that the wanton destruction of dense neighbourhoods (or 'slums'), and then the estates that replaced them, was itself a major plague displaying symptoms of credulous utopianism, wilful ideology and naked self-interest. We need politicians with the right vaccine that gives them on a clear understanding of social neighbourhoods, value for money and public probity. As slums were the result of chronic poverty rather than cheap buildings, so this plague is caused, not by urban life and its buildings but by the viruses of Covid-19, our destruction of natural ecologies and global travel. Bulldozers and jerry builders are irrelevant.

Instead, to prepare for any future virus, we need a strategic approach:

- first we need to invest in public health with an effective test and trace system nationally that tests all incoming air and sea passengers (visitors and returning citizens`), with hotel/hostel accommodation for all those testing positive;
- second we must invest in local public health and primary healthcare services so that they are prepared not only to test and trace all those infected, but ensure that those isolated are secure and given proper support to meet all requirements;
- third, all councils must draw up their own public health strategies managed by every local council. Public health is not about illness but how to reduce disease and promote health. That includes not just diet and fitness, but also full employment, proper housing, less pollution and poverty, better social support and mental wellbeing.

This requires serious funding, a challenge for any leader. Unfortunately, Johnson's expertise for serious government is limited (largely based on shallow rhetoric, half truths, naked lies and 'spaffing public money up the wall'), Gove dismisses experts and Cummings believes he is the expert. Looking at the whole cabinet, one can see that, after 40 years, the Conservative party is bankrupt, bereft of ideas outside the ideology of 'free market' capitalism, privatization and deregulation and in hoc to an unsavoury mix of mega-corps and billionaires. Huge pockets of unearned private wealth shielded in tax havens now 'stink in the nose of the public' (page 274) and have impoverished the social wealth of all our public services. The auspices for the 'new normal' are not good.

Rather than leave on a sour note, however, let me suggest a silver lining. Occasionally, governments of social reform emerge, led by prime ministers with 'intellectual rigour, social understanding and a strong sense of fair play'. The text above cites Lloyd George with his National Insurance and rent tribunals, and Clement Attlee for British Rail and the NHS etc. We need such a government now. Covid-19 offers a platform on which to develop, not just better healthcare, but also healthier lifestyles, less pollution, greener environments, more local production of food, goods and services, less poverty and, above all, more local democracy.

Local democracy is the core of chapter 10. And here, the auspices are a little more positive. Our inadequate response to the plague has shown that rejecting local council expertise and experience in public health in favour of national profit-driven amateurs is dangerous. Now that the three smaller nations have displayed degrees of independence within the 'united kingdom' (an issue that Brexit brazenly ignores), some larger councils are also showing signs of resurgence. In Greater Manchester, for example, all the council leaders and sitting MPs (Labour and Tory) agreed that the government's central control of Covid-19 was woefully inept. They all felt better able to tackle the problems locally more quickly and effectively, and wanted the money and powers to do so. This confirms one underlying message of this book: that diversity is vital not just in city neighbourhoods and economies as Jane Jacobs saw, but also in politics. Without more devolution, local authorities are an oxymoron – and undemocratic.

The roots of local councils lie in improving public health by addressing specific health problems. This formed the basis of planning as defined in chapter 8. With the decline of local government over the last century ('the first era of planning'), the NHS has become overloaded with serious diseases and emergencies, many of which are preventable. This emphasis on treating illness rather than promoting 'wellness' is inefficient and dangerous. We need to move from palliative to preventive medicine.

And preventive medicine starts with council public health teams, to which all primary healthcare services should be added to local councils. (See for example page 172 on two village surgeries.) Given the resources, most councils would have integrated local surgeries, care homes and cottage hospitals, as well as investing in PPE, testing equipment and local laboratories in anticipation of epidemics. But as stated above, public health is not just about illness and epidemics. Local medical officers of health and public health teams, working with colleagues in economic development, education, environmental health, housing, planning and transport etc, could develop various health strategies for the following:

- full employment strategy with Churchill's local wage boards to ensure fair pay, plus training and adult activities for those out of work;
- providing healthy school meals (as legally required before 1974) to reduce obesity, diabetes and pressure on local hospitals;
- housing the homeless and those in 'temporary accommodation', with local rent tribunals and other measures to tackle profiteering landlords;
- ensuring welfare benefits are sufficient to close down local food banks (another Thatcher legacy); and
- reducing road traffic and pollution with better social transport and safe pedestrian and cycle networks to promote fitness and health.

No longer should local councils be sidelined. This requires two things. First we must ditch the ideology of privatization. And second, we need half a dozen new Joseph Chamberlains, supported by the Local Government Association to promote the ability of councils to deliver more local services, share best practice and co-ordinate joint working on regional education, health and transport initiatives. If some councils were prepared to ignore government directions during this plague, then some might be emboldened to implement other national policies in ways they think more appropriate to their areas. There is strength in numbers, even if it is just a dozen councils refusing all new tower blocks. As stated in chapter 10, the use of existing law such as the *Climate Change Act 2008* and the sustainable principles quoted in *NPPF* (1st edition) should be sufficient justification. And as to the efficiency of local councils, let me repeat Fairlie's quote (page 345) from his survey of European and US councils in 1900: comparing "private with municipal undertakings... municipal control means in almost every case a greater degree of attention paid to social aspects, such as better facilities to the consuming public and better compensation to the employees."

My final point is this. Throughout this book, I have hesitated to stress its 'green' credentials. While all the strategies and policies are undoubtedly 'sustainable',

I have stressed that they are driven, first and foremost, by the need to be fair or at least consistent between rich and poor, big and small, that some regulation is essential to maintain fair (efficient and open) markets, that the negative costs of waste and pollution should be reflected in GDP statistics, and that we need to modify our own behaviour. This, dear reader, may be thought naive rather than sustainable. Yet it is vital that we replace our car trips, mouse clicks and self-service blips with walks, customer smiles and the occasional joke.

Too often, the global crisis is described in terms of climate change, which stems from human greed and the 'external costs' of carbon emissions, ocean pollution, deforestation, destruction of natural habitats and extinction of species. In truth, to all species on earth, we humans are the plague – climate change being the most serious outcome of our behaviour. As with civilization, we have to change our inputs. And the level at which we can make the most effective impact is in our towns and cities.

Think local. Act local.

Bibliography

A friend once told me that academics gauge the virility of their colleagues by the length of their bibliographies. This is not much help to the busy student. The following shortlist provides the foundation for urban studies. The bibliography follows.

- On general planning and social issues, Fernand Braudel, Peter Hall, Jane Jacobs, Lewis Mumford, David Olsen, and Wilkinson & Pickett
- On economics, Galbraith, Sloman, Smith and Stiglitz
- For statistics, the ONS *Annual Abstracts*, Mitchell's *European Statistics* and *Jane's Urban Transport Systems* are invaluable.
- On politics and history, LeGates and Stout, McClelland and, for current events, Wikipedia, *The Observer* and the indispensable *Private Eye*.

AA: *Illustrated Road Book of England and Wales*; AA, 1965. *Road Atlas Britain*: AA, 2013

Abercrombie, P : *Town and Country Planning*; OUP, 1943. *County of London Plan 1943*; Macmillan and Co, 1944

Ackroyd, P: *London: The Biography*; Vintage, 2001

Lord Acton: *Lectures on Modern History*; Fontana, 1960

An APPEN Report: *The Bhopal Tragedy – One Year After*; Sahabat Alam Malaysia, 1985

The Architecture Foundation: *Living in the City – An Urban Renaissance*; 2000

Arnstein, S R: *A Ladder of Citizen Participation in the USA*; Journal of the American Institute of Planners, July 1969

Arvill, R: *Man and Environment*; Penguin, 1973

Aston Business School: *Town and Parish Councils in England: A Survey*; Dept of the Environment, 1992

Ayto, J: *Dictionary of Word Origins*; Columbia, 1994

Bailey, P: *An English Madam*; Fontana, 1983 (p 103)

Banham, R: Los Angeles: *The Architecture of Four Ecologies*; Pelican, 1973

Barker, F & Jackson, P: *The History of London in Maps*; Barrie and Jenkins, 1990

Barnes-Svarney, P (ed): *The New York Public Library Science Desk Reference*; Macmillan, 1995

Bartlett, R: *The Making of Europe*; Penguin, 1993

Bell, C & R: *City fathers: The Early History of Town Planning in Britain*; Pelican, 1972

Benevolo, L: *The origins of modern town planning*; Routledge & Kegan Paul, 1967

Beresford, M: *New Towns of the Medieval Ages*; Lutterworth, 1967

Bierce, A: *The Enlarged Devil's Dictionary*; Penguin, 1971

Bingham, T: *The Rule of Law*; Allen Lane, 2010

Bower, T: *Branson*; Fourth Estate, 2001

Boston, R: *Beer and Skittles*; Collins, 1976

Boswell, J: *The Life of Dr Johnson*; Dent, 1951

Braudel, F: *The Mediterranean and the Mediterranean World in the Age of Philip II*; Fontana, 1975. *Civilization and Capitalism: 15th-18th Century; vols 1-3; The Structures of Everyday Life, The Wheels of Commerce,* and *The Perspective of the World*; Collins, 1981, '82 and '84

Briggs, A: *Victorian Cities*; Pelican, 1968

Briscoe, S: *Britain in Numbers*: The Essential Statistics; Politico's, 2005

de Brunhoff, J: *Babar the King*; Methuen, 1953

Buchanan, C et al: *Traffic in Towns*; HMSO, 1963

Burgess, A: *Urgent Copy*; Penguin, 1973

Burke, E: *Reflections on the Revolution in France*; Pelican, 1968.

Bury, J P T (ed): *The New Cambridge Modern History*; CUP, 1960, vol X, 1830-70; including Pevsner, N: *Art and Architecture* and
Thomson, D: *The United Kingdom and Its World-wide Interests.*

Bushel, C (ed): *Jane's Urban Transport Systems*; Jane's Information Group

Byrne, T: *Local Government in Britain*; Penguin, 1994

Cathcart, B: *The Case of Stephen Lawrence*; Viking, 1999

Centre for Cities: *Small Business Factbook*; 2014

Challoner, J: *1001 Inventions that Changed the World*; Quintessence, 2009

Child Poverty Action Group: *National Welfare Benefits Handbook*; CPAG, 1993

Chinn, C: *Homes for People; 100 Years of Council Housing in Birmingham*; Birmingham, 1989

Chomsky, N: *Hegemony or Survival*; Penguin, 2004

Cipolla, C M (ed): *The Fontana Economic History of Europe vol 3*; Fontana, 1973

Clark, P (ed): *The Early Modern Town: A Reader*; Longman, 1976 – including
Everitt, A: *The Market Towns*
Hoskins, W G: *The Elizabethan merchants of Exeter*

Clements, S: *Municipal Year Book*; Newman Books, 1996

Connors, R J (ed): *Warren Buffett on Business; Principles from the Sage of Omaha*; Wiley, 2010

Cooper, A: *World Issues: Fair Trade*; Aladdin/Watts, 2005

Le Corbusier, J: *Towards a New Architecture*; Architectural Press, 1946. *La Ville Radieuse*; Boulogne, 1935

Cowe, R (ed): *The Guardian Guide to the UK's Top Companies*; Fourth Estate, 1993

Crosby, T: *How to play the environment game*; Penguin and Arts Council of Great Britain, 1973

Cruver, B: *Enron, Anatomy of Greed*; Arrow Books, 2003

Cullen, G: *The Concise Townscape*; Architectural Press, 1971

Davies, N: *Flat Earth News*; Vintage, 2009

Davis, E: *Public Spending*; Penguin, 1998

Dawkins R : *The Selfish Gene*; OUP, 2006. (ed) *The Oxford Book of Modern Science Writing*; OUP, 2008

Dept for Communities and Local Government: *National Planning Policy Framework*; March 2012 and July 2018

Dept of the Environment: *Planning Policy Guidance: Town Centres and Retail Development*; HMSO, 1996. *Planning Policy Guidance: Transport*; HMSO, and *Planning Policy Statement: Housing*; HMSO, 2006

Dept for Transport: *Transport Statistics*; HMSO, 2008

Didion, J: *The White Album*; Penguin, 1981. *Miami*; Flamingo, 1994. *A Book of Common Prayer*; Fourth Estate, 2011

Dyos, H J & Wolff, M: *The Victorian City, vol 1*; Routledge & Kegan Paul, 1973

Ecotec: *Reducing Transport Emissions Through Planning*; HMSO, 1993

Elton, G R: *The Practice of History*; Fontana, 1967

Ensor, Sr R: *England 1870 – 1914*; Oxford History of England (vol 14), Clarendon, 1988

Essex County Council: *A Design Guide for Residential Areas*; Essex CC, 1973

Euromonitor: *European Marketing Data and Statistics 2004*; Euromonitor, 2003

Evenson, N: *Le Corbusier: The Machine and the Grand Design*; Studio Vista, undated

Fairlie, J A: *Municipal Administration*; Macmillan, 1901

Ferguson, N: *Empire*; Penguin, 2007

Financial Times: *World Desk Reference 2004*; Dorling Kindersley, 2004

Fishwick, D: *Bank of Dave*; Virgin Books, 2012

Galbraith JK: *The Galbraith Reader* (ed Gambit); Andre Deutsch, 1979

Geddes, P: *Cities in Evolution*; Williams and Norgate, 1915

Gilbert, M: *British History Atlas*; Weidenfeld and Nicolson, 1968

Girardet, H: *The Gaia Atlas of Cities: New Directions of Sustainable Urban Living*; Gaia Books, 1996

Girouard, M: *Cities and People: A Social and Architectural History*; Yale UP, 1985

Goodall, C: *how to live a low-carbon life*; Earthscan, 2007

Goss, J: *Braun and Hogenberg's The City Maps of Europe*; Studio Editions, 1991

Gower Davies, J: *The Evangelistic Bureaucrat*; Tavistock Publications, 1972

Gowers, Sir E: *Plain Words*; HMSO, 1948

Grogan, P: *Grogan's Companion to Drink*; Virgin Books, 2010

Gruen, V: *The Heart of Our Cities*; Thames and Hudson, 1965

Hall, P: *The World Cities*; Weidenfeld and Nicolson, 1966. *Great Planning Disasters*; Pelican, 1980. *Urban And Regional Planning*; Routledge, 3rd ed, 1992

Halsey, A H and Webb, J: *Twentieth-Century British Social Trends*; Macmillan, 2000

Hammond, Dr P and Mosley, M: *Trust Me (I'm a Doctor)*; Metro Books, 1999

Harrison, P: *Inside the Inner City*; Penguin, 1983

Harvey-Jones, J: *Trouble Shooter 2*; BBC Books, 1992

Heap, Sir D: *An Outline of Planning Law*; Sweet and Maxwell, 1982 & 1996

Hibbert, C: *Cities and Civilizations*; Weidenfeld and Nicolson, 1986

Hinsley, F H (ed): *The New Cambridge Modern History*; CUP, 1962, vol XI.
    Pevsner, N: *Art and Architecture – Material Progress and World-Wide
    Problems*: 1870-98.
Hobhouse, H: *Lost London*; Macmillan, 1976
Hobson, D: *The National Wealth - Who Gets What in Britain*; HarperCollins, 1999
Honderich, T (ed): *The Oxford Companion to Philosophy*; OUP, 1995
Hoskins, W G: *The Making of the English Landscape*; Pelican, 1970
Howard, E: *Garden Cities of Tomorrow*; Sonnenschein, 1898
Inwood, S: *A History of London*; Macmillan, 2000
Jacobs, J: *The Death and Life of Great American Cities*; Pelican, 1961. *Cities and the
    Wealth of Nations*; Random House, 1984
Jencks, C: *Le Corbusier and the Tragic View of Architecture*; Allen Lane, 1973
Kapuszinski, R: *The Other*; Verso, 2008
Keeble, L: *Principles and Practice of Town and Country Planning*; Estates Gazette,
    1964
Levitt, S D & Dubner, S J: *Freakonomics*; Penguin, 2006
LeGates, R T and Stout, F (eds): *The City Reader*; Routledge, 2003, including
    Burgess, EW: *The Growth of the City*, 1925
    Wheeler, S: *Planning Sustainable and Livable Cities*
Lipsey, G: *Positive Economics* (4th edition); Weidenfeld and Nicolson, 1975
City of Liverpool: *Development Plan*; 1958
Mandeville, B: *The Fable of the Bees*; Pelican, 1970
Manning, A and Dawkins, M S: *An Introduction to Animal Behaviour*; CUP, 1998
de Mare, E: *Victorian London Revealed*; Penguin, 2001
McBain, E: *Jack and the Beanstalk*; Hamish Hamilton, 1984
McClelland, J S: *A History of Western Political Thought*; Routledge, 1996
McLoughlin, J B: *Urban and Regional Planning*; Faber and Faber, 1969
Mill, J S`; *Utilitarianism – Liberty - Representative Government*; Dent, 1960
Mitchell, B R: *European Historical Statistics 1750 – 2000*; Macmillan, 2005
Moore, R: *Why We Build*; Picador, 2012
John Moores University: *Livable Towns and Cities*; 1994
Morgan, N: *Vanished Dwellings: Early Industrial Housing in Preston*; private
    publication, 1988
Mosley, W: *Black Betty*; Serpent's Tail, 1994
Mumford, L: *The City in History*; Pelican, 1966
Munby, L M: *The Hertfordshire Landscape*; Hodder and Stoughton, 1977
Nader, R (ed): *The Consumer and Corporate Accountability*; Harcourt Brace
    Jovanovich, 1973
Nairn, I: *Outrage*; Architectural Press, 1955
Nairn, I and Pevsner, N: *The Buildings of England: Sussex*; Penguin, 1965
Namier, Sir L: *The Structure of Politics at the Accession of George III*; Macmillan,
    1965
Olsen, D J: *The City as a Work of Art*; Yale, 1986

ODPM: *Planning – Creating Local Development Frameworks*; HMSO, 2004

OECD: *PISA 2012 Results in Focus*; OECD, 2013

ONS (Office for National Statistics): *Annual Abstract of Statistics*; TSO, annual. *Social Trends*: TSO, 2004

O'Rourke, P J: *Eat the Rich*; Atlantic Monthly Press, 1998. *On The Wealth of Nations*; Atlantic Books, 2007

Ordnance Survey: *Historical Map and Guide: Roman Britain*; 2001

Parker, M: *Map Addict*; Collins, 2009 (p 240-3)

Parker Morris, Sir: *Homes for Today and Tomorrow*; HMSO, 1961

Pevsner, N: *An Outline of European Architecture*; Pelican, 1943

Platt, C: *The English Medieval Town*; Secker and Warburg, 1976

Poole, A L: *Domesday Book to Magna Carta, 1087 – 1216*; OUP, 1988

Popper, K: *The Open Society and Its Enemies; vol 2 Hegel & Marx*; Routledge, 1966. *Unended Quest, An Intellectual Autobiography*; Flamingo, 1986

Powicke, Sir M: *The Thirteenth Century, 1216 – 1307*; OUP, 1988

Rasmussen, S E: *London; The Unique City*; Pelican, 1960

Reed, M: *The Georgian Triumph 1700 – 1830*; Routledge & Kegan Paul, 1983

Rhind, D & Hudson, R: *Land Use*; Methuen, 1980

Royal Commission on Environmental Pollution: *Transport and the Environment*; HMSO, 1994

Rugman, A: *The End of Globalization*; Random House, 2000

Sandars, N K (ed): *The Epic of Gilgamesh*; Penguin Classics, 1964

Sassoon, J: *Ancient Laws and Modern Problems*; Intellect Books, 2005

Schlosser, E: *Fast Food Nation*; Penguin, 2002

Sheldrake, R: *The Science Delusion*; Coronet, 2012

Shepherd, R: *Enoch Powell – A Biography*; Hutchinson, 1996

Simms, A: *Tescopoly*; Constable, 2007

Skeffington Committee: *People and Planning*; HMSO, 1969

Slater, J (devised): *Company REFS*; Capital Ideas, August 2010

Sloman, J: *Economics* (6th edition); FT Prentice Hall, 2006

Smith, A (Skinner A ed): *The Wealth of Nations*; Pelican, 1970

Sprouse, M (ed): *Sabotage in the American Workplace*; Pressure Drop Press, 1992

Stiglitz, J: *Freefall*; Penguin, 2010. *Globalization and Its Discontents*; Penguin, 2002

Taket, A et al (eds): *Practising Social Inclusion*; Routledge, 2014

Tellus 42: *Killing Two Birds with New Homes*; Friends of the Earth, 1998

Terkel, S: *Working*; Wildwood House, 1975

Toussaint-Samat, M: *History of Food*; Blackwell, 1992 (Eng trans)

Roger Tym and Partners: *The Merry Hill Impact Study*; HMSO, 1993

Urban Task Force: *Towards an Urban Renaissance, Executive Summary*; UTF, 1999

Vonnegut, K: *Bluebeard*; Jonathan Cape, 1988

Ward, C: *Utopia*; Penguin, 1974

Washburn, K and Thornton, J: *Dumbing Down*; Norton, 1997 – including Rifkind, C: *America's Fantasy Urbanism*

Weinstock, M and Woodgate, S: *Living in the City: An urban renaissance*; The
    Architecture Foundation, 2000
Wiener, M J: *English Culture and the Decline of the Industrial Spirit*, 1850 – 1980;
    CUP, 1981
Wilkinson, R & Pickett, K: *The Spirit Level*; Penguin, 2010
Zamyatin, E: *We*; Raduga Publishers, 1999
Zuboff, S: *The Age of Surveillance Capitalism*; Hachette Book Group, 2019

Index

Lightning Source UK Ltd.
Milton Keynes UK
UKHW020156301220
375763UK00004B/96